CORPORATE CRIME AND VIOLENCE

CORPORATE CRIME AND VIOLENCE

Big Business Power and the Abuse of the Public Trust

Russell Mokhiber

Sierra Club Books • San Francisco

The Sierra Club, founded in 1892 by John Muir, has devoted itself to the study and protection of the earth's scenic and ecological resources—mountains, wetlands, woodlands, wild shores and rivers, deserts and plains. The publishing program of the Sierra Club offers books to the public as a nonprofit educational service in the hope that they may enlarge the public's understanding of the Club's basic concerns. The point of view expressed in each book, however, does not necessarily represent that of the Club. The Sierra Club has some sixty chapters coast to coast, in Canada, Hawaii, and Alaska. For information about how you may participate in its programs to preserve wilderness and the quality of life, please address inquiries to Sierra Club, 730 Polk Street, San Francisco, CA 94109.

Library of Congress Cataloging-in-Publication Data
Mokhiber, Russell, 1954–
    Corporate crime and violence.

    Includes index.
      1. Corporations—United States—Corrupt practices—
Case studies. 2. Commercial crimes—United States—
Case studies. I. Title.
HV6769.M65 1988   364.1'68'0973   87–4730
ISBN 0-87156-723-7

Jacket design by Paul Bacon
Book design by Lorrie Fink
Printed in the United States of America
10 9 8 7 6 5 4 3 2 1

Table of Contents

PART ONE
Overview

1
Corporate Crime and Violence

Name a crime.

Outside of the context of this book, many would respond "burglary" or "robbery" or "murder." Few would respond "monopoly" or "knowingly marketing unsafe pharmaceuticals" or "dumping of toxic wastes."

Name an act of violence.

Similarly, many would respond with examples of violent street crimes, such as assault. Few would respond with examples of violent corporate crime, such as the marketing of a dangerous automobile or the pollution of a community's water supply.

People respond this way despite a near universal consensus that all corporate crime and violence combined, both detected and undetected, prosecuted and not prosecuted, is more pervasive and more damaging than all street crime. The electrical price fixing conspiracy of the early 1960s alone cost American consumers $2 billion, more than all the burglaries in America in one year. According to the Federal Bureau of Investigation, there were 19,000 victims of street murder and manslaughter in 1985. Compare that one-year total with the numbers of victims of corporate crime and violence in the United States today:

- One hundred and thirty Americans die every day in automobile crashes. Many of those deaths are either caused by vehicle defects or preventable by available vehicle crashworthiness designs.
- Almost 800 Americans die every day from cigarette-induced disease.
- Over the next 30 years, 240,000 people—8,000 per year, one every hour—will die from asbestos-related cancer.

• The Dalkon Shield intrauterine device seriously injured tens of thousands of women who used it.
• An estimated 85,000 American cotton textile workers suffer breathing impairments due to cotton dust (brown lung) disease.
• 100,000 miners have been killed and 265,000 disabled due to coal dust (black lung) disease.
• One million infants worldwide died in 1986 because they were bottle-fed instead of breast-fed.
• In 1984, 2,000 to 5,000 persons were killed and 200,000 injured, 30,000 to 40,000 of them seriously, after a Union Carbide affiliate's factory in Bhopal, India, released a deadly gas over the town.[1]

This book is about the human consequences of our failure to curb the excesses of corporate power. It profiles 36 of the more egregious cases of corporate crime and violence. Its focus is not the conventionally discussed white-collar crimes such as embezzlement, tax evasion, and fraud—although it does profile serious crimes against the marketplace (Oil) and a serious case of bribery (Lockheed). The primary focus is on acts of corporate violence—against women (Dalkon Shield), against children (Thalidomide), against the environment (Reserve Mining), against workers (DBCP), against consumers (Oraflex, DES), and against veterans (Agent Orange). A number of these acts of violence have resulted in successful criminal prosecutions of the corporations, the executives, or both (Three Mile Island, MER 29, Oraflex, Selacryn, among others). The three dozen profiles raise two important questions:

Why is it that despite the high numbers of victims, when people think of crime, they think of burglary before they think of monopoly (if they think of monopoly at all), of assault before they think of the marketing of harmful pharmaceuticals, of street crime before they think of corporate crime? And what can be done to curb corporate crime and violence?

Why Do People Think of Street Crime Before They Think of Corporate Crime?

Many corporate executives assume that preventable violence is a cost of doing business, a cost that we as a society must accept as the price of living in an industrial America. With advertising campaigns aimed at molding public opinion and policy, some corporations have covered their violent behavior with a veneer of misinformation and distortion in an attempt to make acceptable what in any other context would be morally repugnant. A case in point is the advertisement run by Monsanto on the heels of many chemical disasters during the late 1970s with the theme "Without Chemicals, Life Itself Would Be Impossible."[2]

Furthermore, in the United States, corporate lawbreakers double as corporate lawmakers. Corporate America has saturated the legislatures with dollars in order to promote laws making legal or non-criminal what by any common standard of justice would be considered illegal and criminal, and to obstruct legislation that would outlaw the violent activity. For example, the tobacco and automobile industries have, over the years, blocked attempts to ban or curb the marketing of tobacco, and to require that automobiles be manufactured with life-saving passive restraints.

When public pressure does produce legislation curbing corporate excesses, corporations then lobby, often successfully, to weaken the constraint. When Congress passed the auto safety law, for example, auto industry lobbyists on Capitol Hill defeated an effort to add criminal sanctions to the bill for knowing or willful violations.

The result is a legal system biased in favor of the corporate violator and against its victims. Because the higher standards of proof in criminal trials are more difficult to meet, and because of finely tuned corporate methods of delay and obfuscation most federal prosecutions of corporations seek civil, not criminal, sanctions; few serious acts of corporate violence are criminally prosecuted. Moreover, most of the penalties that are imposed in civil cases are mere slap-on-the-wrist settlements known as consent decrees.

Even when the criminal prosecution of a corporation is successful, the imposed sanctions are rarely effective. When, for example, General Motors was convicted in 1949 of conspiracy to destroy the nation's mass transit systems, surely one of the more egregious corporate crimes in U.S. economic history, the judge fined the company $5,000.

There are many corporate wrongdoers allowed to go free and many street criminals punished harshly for minor violations. Not one corporate executive went to jail, nor was any corporation criminally convicted for the marketing of thalidomide, a drug that caused severe birth defects in 8,000 babies during the early 1960s, but Wallace Richard Stewart of Kentucky was sentenced in July 1983 to ten years in prison for stealing a pizza.[3] No Ford Motor Company executive went to jail for marketing the Pinto automobile, with its deadly fuel tank, nor was the company convicted of criminal charges (although in one case it was indicted, tried, and found not guilty of reckless homicide). Not one Hooker Chemical executive went to jail, nor was Hooker charged with a criminal offense, after the company exposed its workers and Love Canal neighbors to toxics, but under a Texas habitual offenders statute William Rummel was given life in prison for stealing a total of $229.11 over a period of nine years.[4]

"Crime is a sociopolitical artifact, not a natural phenomenon," Herbert L. Packer wrote in 1968 in *The Limits of the Criminal Sanction*. "We can have as much or as little crime as we please, depending on what we choose to count as criminal."[5] By setting up a system of civil fines, consent decrees, recalls, and other noncriminal controls on corporations, we have chosen to have very little corporate "crime," in Professor Packer's sense of the word, and by so choosing, we have insulated the corporation from the effective sanctions and stigma of the criminal process. In addition, we have sent the outnumbered and underfunded police who investigate corporate crime—euphemistically known as regulators—up against some of the most powerful lawbreakers in society without access to meaningful sanctions.

In light of the failure of the federal regulatory apparatus to control corporate wrongdoing, in recent years local and state prosecutions of violent corporate activity have been initiated under criminal laws designed to control individual criminal behavior—in particular state homicide statutes.[6] An unsuccessful criminal prosecution was brought in 1979 by a Republican prosecutor in Indiana against the Ford Motor Company for reckless homicide in connection with the fiery deaths of three teenage girls who were riding in a Ford Pinto when it was rear-ended. A successful murder prosecution of three executives of a small chemical firm, Film Recovery Systems, Inc., was brought in 1985 by a prosecutor in Cook County, Illinois, in connection with the job-related death of an employee from cyanide poisoning. And similar cases are being brought by state and local prosecutors around the country.

But although the Cook County prosecutor was able to gain

an impressive murder conviction against executives of the small chemical company in Illinois, the Indiana prosecutor was unable to prevail over the resources of the Ford Motor Company, a powerful multinational automobile maker. There is little question that the imbalance of legal resources between the prosecutor and Ford in that case played a major role in the outcome. State and local prosecutorial resources have never been a match for offending multinational giants such as tobacco companies, A. H. Robins (Dalkon Shield), or Manville (asbestos). Corporate crime is clearly a national problem that calls for a national response.

Sidestepping the Criminal Justice System

Professor Christopher Stone, of the University of Southern California Law School, has observed that up until the nineteenth century, the law was paying increasing attention to the individual, and less to the group. During this period, according to Stone, laws, rules, and concepts were being developed to deal with what motivated, what steered, and what was "possible, just and appropriate in the case of individual human beings."[7] Corporations did not move to center stage until late in the nineteenth century, and when they did, the criminal law, developed to bring justice to individuals, was not equipped to answer the question: what motivated, what steered, and what was possible, just, and appropriate in the case of corporations?

At the turn of the century, as corporations became increasingly wealthy and powerful, legislatures moved to protect the public from corporate abuses. In 1890, Congress passed the Sherman Antitrust Act, which forbade monopolizing or attempting to monopolize trade and made illegal "every contract, combination . . . or conspiracy in restraint of trade." The act was aimed at busting the corporate monopoly makers that were threatening the competitive economic system. Violation of the act was a criminal offense, punishable by a fine not exceeding $5,000 or by imprisonment up to a year, or both.[8]

But the Sherman Act and a host of subsequent laws aimed at controlling corporate wrongdoing were different in one crucial respect from the criminal laws that governed the noncorporate citizenry. In a radical departure from the historical development of criminal law, legislatures gave prosecutors of corporate crime the option of seeking a *civil injunction* to enforce a law with *criminal sanctions.*

Rather than charging the corporation with a criminal violation and then prosecuting the case in open court before a jury of citizens who would determine guilt or innocence, prosecutors choose instead, in the overwhelming number of cases, to go to civil court and seek to enjoin the corporation from further violations of law. Today, this civil injunction against crime has become the option of choice for federal "regulators."

By relying on the civil injunction, federal police avoid branding the defendant corporation with the symbols of crime, thus crippling the intended punitive and deterrent effects of the criminal sanction. "The violations of these laws are crimes," commented Edwin Sutherland, who formulated this concept of corporate crime, in his ground-breaking 1949 book *White-Collar Crime*, " . . . but they are treated as though they were not crimes, with the effect and probably the intention of eliminating the stigma of crime."[9]

A second radical departure — or "clever invention," to use a Sutherland phrase — from the traditional criminal procedure came in the guise of the abovementioned consent decree. A consent decree is essentially a compromise between two parties in a civil suit, the exact terms of which are fixed by negotiation between the parties and formalized by the signature of a judge.[10]

Thus while the civil injunction against crime removed the corporate defendant from the criminal sphere, the consent decree provided further insulation by moving the legal process from the open courtroom to behind closed doors. Although the defendant corporation invariably emerged from behind those closed doors consenting to an injunction against further violations of the law, it did so without admitting or denying the allegations.

Most federal cases brought against corporations are settled in this manner. The "neither admit nor deny" clause is understandably relished by corporate defendants because it precludes the use of the decree as an admission of guilt in subsequent court proceedings, be they civil or criminal. In many cases, this clause is worth millions of dollars to corporations; without it, private plaintiffs could use the decree as evidence of law violation in private damage actions. Corporate defendants cite numerous other reasons for agreeing to consent decrees (prompt resolution of the case to avoid expensive and protracted litigation, and opportunity to negotiate the language of the consent decree and of the allegations of the complaint), but the "neither admit nor deny" clause is itself the primary motivation for a defendant to settle a case. Once the consent is signed, the public perception is that the corporate defendant is not a lawbreaker, not a criminal, not a crook. The defendant is merely "enjoined."

Sutherland proffered three reasons for this "differential implementation of the law as it applied to large corporations." Most important was the status of businessmen in the United States. According to Sutherland,

> Those who are responsible for the system of criminal justice are afraid to antagonize businessmen; among other consequences, such antagonism may result in a reduction in contributions to the campaign funds needed to win the next election. . . . Probably much more important than fear, however, is the cultural homogeneity of legislators, judges, and administrators with businessmen. Legislators admire and respect businessmen and cannot conceive of them as criminals; businessmen do not conform to the popular stereotype of "the criminal." The legislators are confident that these respectable gentlemen will conform to the law as a result of very mild pressures. The most powerful group in medieval society secured relative immunity by "benefit of clergy" and now our most powerful group secures immunity by "benefit of business," or more generally, "high social status."[11]

Secondly, Sutherland recognized a shift away from implementation of penal sanctions in general, with the shift occurring "more rapidly in the area of white collar crimes than of other crimes."[12] And finally, Sutherland believed that the more gentle treatment of corporate criminals was due in part to "the relatively unorganized resentment of the public toward white collar crimes." This, he explained, was because the violations of laws by businessmen are "complex and their effects diffused," and because

> [T]he public agencies of communication do not express the organized moral sentiments of the community as to white collar crimes, in part because the crimes are complicated

and not easily presented as news, but probably in the greater part because these agencies of communication are owned or controlled by businessmen and because these agencies are themselves involved in the violations of many of these laws.

This two-track prosecutorial setup—a criminal system for individuals and a civil system for corporations—works to undermine the effectiveness of the criminal justice system. Individuals convicted by the criminal justice system must carry not only the burden of the penal sanction, but also the stigma of crime. The corporation is relieved of both. When a corporation signs a consent decree, little public shame attaches because the corporation "neither admits nor denies" violating the law. In arguing for the elimination of the criminal prosecution provisions of the Sherman Antitrust Act, Wendell Berge, who in 1940 was an assistant to the head of the antitrust division of the Department of Justice, made the point:

> While civil penalties may be as severe in their financial effects as criminal penalties, they do not involve the stigma that attends indictment and conviction. Most of the defendants in antitrust cases are not criminals in the usual sense. There is no inherent reason why antitrust enforcement requires branding them as such.[13]

Defining Corporate Crime: The Eyes of the Beholder

When a chemical company dumps deadly mercury into a lake and no law prohibits such dumping, has a crime been committed? Or when the company dumps toxic wastes into the lake, in apparent violation of federal law, but the police look the other way, has a crime been committed? Or if instead, the cops cite the toxic dumper, run to civil court and obtain an injunction against further dumping, has a crime been committed?

The answers to these questions vary with the definition of crime, and the definition of crime varies with the person putting forth the definition. Some argue that an act is criminal only if a criminal court has officially determined that the person or entity accused of violating the law has committed a crime.[14] Few harmful corporate illegalities or other wrongdoings fit this narrow legal definition of crime.

Were the stakes in human terms not so high, this debate over the definition of crime could be relegated to the stacks of law libraries and written off as another less than meaningful academic squabble. The word *crime*, however, carries with it explosive connotations. The corporate justice system has developed so as to shield the corporation from those connotations and the stigma of the criminal process. This shapes the public perception of the nature of the harm inflicted by corporate misconduct. The result is that in referring to corporate transgressions we speak of civil wrong, not criminal wrong; of consents, not convictions; of suits, not indictments; of "neither admit nor deny," not guilt or innocence.

Many corporate misdeeds that fall outside the narrow definition of crime as "conviction" qualify as crimes in a more fundamental sense of the word in that they contain the essential characteristic of crime as defined by Sutherland: that is, "behavior which is prohibited by the State as an injury to the State and against which the State may react, at least as a last resort, with punishment."[15]

U.S. law, for example, prohibits the discharge of toxic pollutants in significant amounts and provides for imposition of a fine on the polluter. Thus when a company dumps wastes into a lake, and the legal authority, be it criminal, civil, or administrative, makes a determination that the act violates the law, then the company's act of dumping would, according to Sutherland's standard, constitute a crime. Under the Sutherland definition, the act is a crime even if the legal authority refuses to punish the company for the unlawful act. "An unlawful act is not defined as criminal by the fact that it is punished, but by the fact that it is punishable," Sutherland argued.[16]

Two modern corporate criminologists, Marshall Clinard and Peter Yeager, join Sutherland in rejecting the narrow legal definition of crime as only those acts officially determined crimes by the criminal courts. They explain that

> This definition applies well to burglary and robbery; corporate crimes, however, cannot be defined and studied in such a limited manner. Our criminal laws represent only a part of a larger body of law; there are in addition administrative and civil laws. Although these laws are not applicable to the ordinary criminal offender, they are for the most part the manner in which corporate violations are handled. Violations of these civil and administrative laws

are also subject to punishment by the political state. From the research point of view, then, corporate crime includes any act punished by the state, regardless of whether it is punished under administrative, civil, or criminal law.[17]

While rejecting the narrow legalistic view, they also reject Sutherland's broader view that an "unlawful act is not defined as criminal by the fact that it is punished, but by the fact that it is punishable." Clinard and Yeager define corporate crime as "any act committed by corporations that is punished by the state, regardless of whether it is punished under administrative, civil, or criminal law." The Sutherland definition would include all successful actions brought against a corporation by private litigants under the antitrust laws, for example, while Clinard and Yeager restrict their definition to those successful actions brought by the state.

Even the Sutherland definition, which is broader than Clinard and Yeager's, withholds the criminal label from untold numbers of corporate wrongs that are "socially harmful." It excludes all those acts that are not prohibited by the state because of undue influence by the wrongdoers on the lawmaking process. The automobile corporations, for example, for ten years have pressured Washington in an effort to defeat legislation that would have prohibited autos from being sold in this country without passive restraints. As a result of this pressure, the corporations are now allowed to build unnecessarily dangerous automobiles — clearly socially harmful activity that should be considered, by any measure, "an injury against the state."

Despite the circumscribed nature of the Sutherland and Clinard definitions, both have come under heated criticism for what some of their academic colleagues regarded and regard as an expansive view of white collar and corporate crime. In the summer of 1947, sociologist Paul W. Tappan, in an article entitled "Who Is the Criminal," submitted that only convicted persons should be called "criminals." Sutherland argued back that common criminals such as murderers and burglars need not be captured or convicted to be reasonably regarded as criminals and that the same logic should apply to corporations who violated the law, regardless of the procedural options, if any, the government chose to apply against them.[18]

The debate over definition continues today, with the Sutherland supporters, led by a group of Australian corporate criminologists, arguing that "to exclude civil violations from a consideration of corporate crime is an arbitrary obfuscation because of the frequent provision in the law for both civil and criminal prosecution of the same corporate conduct."[19] The anti-Sutherland school has chastised Sutherland for what one such critic, Leonard Orland, a professor at the University of Connecticut, called "generalizations which are at war with fundamental principles of law as well as common sense."[20] Orland charges that Clinard's *Illegal Corporate Behavior* is "a more fundamentally flawed work than Sutherland's *White-Collar Crime,*" that the publication of Clinard's work under government auspices "creates the risk that this misleading study will be utilized to support the argument that corporate crime is widespread," and that "the Clinard study asserts that corporate crime is prevalent by pointing to a large number of incidents that have nothing to do with criminal law and even less to do with crime."[21]

Others who have looked at the problem of corporate crime have adhered closely to the narrow legalistic definition, or have set their own hybrid standard. *Fortune* magazine, in a December 1980 article titled "How Lawless Are Big Companies," surveyed those cases brought by the state that "resulted either in conviction on criminal charges or in consent decrees (or similar administrative settlements) in which the companies neither affirm nor deny past transgressions but agree not to commit them in the future."[22] *U.S. News & World Report,* in a September 1982 cover story titled "Corporate Crime, The Untold Story," surveyed records of the Justice Department, the Securities and Exchange Commission (SEC), and the courts and "counted only criminal convictions and civil actions involving serious misbehaviour"—actions that resulted in civil penalties (or settlements) in excess of $50,000.[23] And the *Harvard Law Review* decided to block out the vast majority of corporate wrongs by limiting its 1979 analysis of corporate crime to the narrow definition of crime; that is, only those wrongful acts sanctioned by the criminal courts.[24]

Clinard lists the following as examples of corporate crime: restraints of trade (price fixing and monopoly), financial manipulations, misrepresentation in advertising, the issuance of fraudulent securities, falsified income tax returns, unsafe work conditions, the manufacture of unsafe foods and drugs, illegal rebates and foreign payoffs, unfair labor practices, illegal political contributions, discriminatory employment practices, and environmental pollution.

As "types of corporate ethical violations, all of which are closely linked to corporate crime," Clinard lists misrepresentation in advertising, deceptive packaging, the lack of social responsibility in television programs, and particularly commercials, the sale of harmful and unsafe products, the sale of virtually worthless products, restricting development and built-in obsolescence, polluting the environment, kickbacks and payoffs, unethical competitive practices, personal gain for management, unethical treatment of workers, and the victimization of local communities by corporations.

Clinard also lists the following as "types of corporate ethical violations, all of which are closely linked to corporate crime": false inventory values (tax evasion); unfair labor practices involving union rights, minimum wage regulations, specific working conditions, and overtime; violations of safety regulations related to occupational safety and health; the fixing of prices to stabilize them on the market and to eliminate competition; food and drug law violations; air and water pollution that violates government standards; violations of regulations established to conserve energy; submission of false information for the sale of securities; false advertising; and illegal rebates.[25]

The Costs of Corporate Crime

The total cost of corporate crime has never been estimated, despite the need for accurate figures. The problem involved in quantifying the costs of corporate crime turns on the philosophical and political question discussed above: what is corporate crime? Any definition, however imperfect, raises another question: who are the victims of the crime? Once the victims are identified, the costs of the injuries must be measured.

The costs of corporate crime will fluctuate wildly with only the slightest modification of any number of variables. Take, for example, the definition of crime. As of this writing, it is legal for automobile companies to market their products without passive restraints, restraints that would save thousands of lives and injuries every year. Legislation that would make it a crime to market autos without passive restraints has been thwarted by the auto industry for over a decade. If not for the industry's considerable efforts to defeat this legislation, it would be a crime today to market such automobiles. Under all the definitions of crime discussed above, thousands of persons who are killed or injured after crashing through the metal and glass of their automobiles are not victims of auto industry crime. Why? Because there is no law to prohibit the manufacture of autos without passive restraints. Why? Because the auto industry pressured the federal government to defeat this legislation.

Sometimes, even with well-defined crimes, the extent of the victimization and the costs thereof will be literally impossible to measure. A chemical company dumps toxic wastes illegally into a river that provides drinking water for local residents. How are the effects of this crime to be measured? How many cancers will these toxics cause twenty years from now? Were the cancers caused from drinking the water, or from smoking cigarettes, or breathing polluted air?

Despite these analytical problems, efforts are underway to map out the academic terrain in search of a workable formula to determine the costs of corporate crime. Clinard estimates that the total cost of corporate crime runs into the billions of dollars, and supplies the following as indices of that cost:

- The Judiciary Subcommittee on Antitrust and Monopoly estimates that faulty goods, monopolistic practices, and similar law violations annually cost consumers between $174 billion and $231 billion.
- A Department of Justice estimate put the loss to the taxpayers from reported and unreported violations of federal regulations of corporations at $10 billion to $20 billion each year.
- The losses resulting from the conspiracy of the largest plumbing manufacturing corporations totaled about $100 million.
- During the 1970s Lockheed Corporation admitted to illegal payments of more than $220 million, primarily in concealed foreign payments.[26]

In addition to causing financial harm, environmental degradation, and physical harm, corporate crime also results in damage to the moral climate of society—or, as Sutherland puts it, "the great social costs of the erosion of the moral base of our society." In a paper titled "The Consequences of White-Collar Crime," Robert F. Meier and James F. Short, Jr. report that

because of the high social standing of white-collar offenders, some observers have maintained that these violations create cynicism and foster the attitude that "if others are doing it, I will too." . . . More fundamentally, it is held that white-collar crime threatens the [trust] that is basic to community life, e.g., between citizens and government officials, professionals and their clients, businessmen and their customers, employers and employees, and even more broadly, among members and between members and nonmembers of the collectivity.[27]

It may prove difficult to measure the direct costs of chemical crime, auto crime, oil crime, and other corporate crimes to consumers, employees, neighbors, citizens, and society as a whole, but the evidence points to a problem of a magnitude that dwarfs the costs associated with much more highly publicized street crime. Clinard points out that the electrical equipment pricing conspiracy cost $2 billion, a figure much larger than the total loss from the approximately three million burglaries a year in the United States. He compares this $2 billion corporate crime to the following street crime:

- The largest robbery ever to take place in the United States involved the 1978 theft of $5.4 million from Lufthansa airport warehouse in New York City. Previously, the famous Brinks armored car robbery of approximately $2 million in Boston had been the largest robbery loss. These highly publicized robbery cases are atypical; the typical robbery involves the armed theft of about $250, while a typical burglary is about $350 and a typical larceny about $125.
- The largest welfare fraud ever committed by a single person in the United States totaled about $240,000. It involved a woman in the Los Angeles area in 1978; she had used eight different names to collect money for 70 dependent children.[28]

Finally, indications are that violent corporate crime is taking staggering tolls. Approximately 28,000 deaths and 130,000 serious injuries each year are caused by dangerous products.[29] And in the workplace, the toll is even greater: 5.5 million on-the-job injuries, with hospital treatment for 3.3 million; at least 100,000 worker deaths each year from exposure to deadly chemicals and other safety hazards; and 390,000 new cases of occupational disease. Of the 38 million workers in manufacturing industries, 1.7 million are exposed to a potential carcinogen each year. Workplace carcinogens are believed to cause an estimated 23 to 38 percent of all deaths resulting from cancer each year.[30]

But these are only vague indications of the enormity of the problem. The absence of research in this area leaves us guessing as to the true cost of corporate crime.

How Prevalent is Corporate Crime?

In 1939, Edwin Sutherland, who was then a sociologist at the University of Indiana, delivered a paper titled "The White-Collar Criminal" before the 34th annual meeting of the American Sociological Society. Sutherland's presentation "altered the study of crime throughout the world in fundamental ways by focusing attention upon a form of lawbreaking that had previously been ignored by criminological scholars," wrote two present-day criminologists, Gilbert Geis and Colin Goff, in their introduction to the revised edition of Sutherland's masterpiece, *White-Collar Crime*.

Sutherland rejected the criminological theories of his day, which laid the blame for illegal behavior on poverty, lack of education, disruptions in family homes, and personal pathologies. He hypothesized that wealth, education, solid family homes, and strong minds did not necessarily deter individuals from violating the law. And for ten years following his path-breaking 1939 presentation, he studied the most powerful white-collar bastion, the corporate world. The result was a massive study, published in 1949 by Dryden Press, titled simply *White-Collar Crime*.

Sutherland studied the criminal records of 70 of the 200 largest nonfinancial U.S. corporations. Specifically, he looked at violations of laws governing restraints of trade; misrepresentation in advertising; infringement of patents, trademarks, and copyrights; unfair labor practices; rebates; financial fraud and violations of trust; violations of war regulations; and some miscellaneous offenses.

What Sutherland found supported his thesis: the 70 companies, commandered mainly by men from America's upper classes, had committed a total of 980 violations, for an average of 14 per company. Each of the 70 companies had at least one violation against it, with Armour & Company and Swift and Company topping the list with 50 violations each. General Motors ranked third with 40, with Sears Roebuck and Montgomery Ward tied for fourth with 39 each.[31]

Sutherland's work represented the first systematic study of corporate crime. He found that his evidence did not "justify a conclusion that the upper class is more criminal or less criminal than the lower class, for the evidence is not sufficiently precise to justify comparisons and common standards and definitions are not available." But he did conclude that his sample of corporations "violated laws with great frequency."[32]

The *Harvard Law Review* lauded *White-Collar Crime* as a "deadly exposé of a way of life which society complacently accepts,"[33] but for three decades scholars, prosecutors, and legislators continued this complacent acceptance. Not until 1979, 30 years after *White-Collar Crime* was published, did anyone attempt a systematic in-depth follow-up study. Sponsored by the U.S. Department of Justice, Marshall Clinard and Peter C. Yeager rushed in to fill the gap in corporate criminological research since Sutherland's death. Today their *Illegal Corporate Behavior*, together with *White-Collar Crime*, are the cornerstones for future sociological research and study in corporate criminology.

Sutherland had studied the life histories of 70 corporations (average age: 45 years), but Clinard and Yeager focused on a much larger sample: the nation's 582 largest publicly owned corporations. They limited their scope, however, to a time span of just two years, 1975 and 1976. There were other differences between the two studies. Sutherland focused on a narrow field of law violations, but Clinard and Yeager covered a broad spectrum of legal actions brought by 24 federal police agencies. Clinard and Yeager had access to a much broader data base from which to retrieve information and a computer to make that retrieval more efficient. Finally, as mentioned above, their definitions of corporate crime differed slightly. Sutherland, for example, counted as crime cases brought and won by private plaintiffs in antitrust actions, but Clinard and Yeager limited their study to cases successfully brought by the state.

Despite the differences, *Illegal Corporate Behavior* confirmed Sutherland's principal finding: corporations violate the law with great frequency. The 582 corporations surveyed by Clinard and Yeager racked up a total of 1,554 crimes, with at least one sanction imposed against 371 corporations (63.7 percent of the sample). And although 40 percent of the sample had *no* actions initiated against them, a mere 38 parent manufacturing corporations out of a total of 477—less than 10 percent—had *ten* or more actions instituted against them. These 38 recidivist corporations accounted for 740, or 48.2 percent, of all sanctions imposed against all the parent manufacturing firms surveyed.[34]

And Clinard and Yeager hypothesized that despite their advanced survey techniques, they didn't catch all cases brought by the police against corporations. "In this study undoubtedly there has been an undercount of administrative actions," they wrote. "What is being presented here, then, are minimal figures of government actions against corporations; the undercount may be as high as one-fourth to one-third."[35]

In the wake of the Clinard and Yeager study, business-oriented magazines began to ripple forth with their own short-term searches for corporate criminal behavior. In 1980, *Fortune* magazine surveyed 1,043 large companies that had appeared on its lists of the 800 largest industrial and nonindustrial corporations from 1970 through 1980. A total of 117, or 11 percent, of the corporations surveyed met *Fortune's* definition of law violation (conviction on criminal charges or consent decrees for five offenses: bribery, criminal fraud, illegal political contributions, tax evasion, and criminal antitrust). The *Fortune* survey found a number of companies, including Ashland and Gulf Oil, to be repeat offenders. In answering the question posed in the title of their article, "How Lawless Are Big Companies?" *Fortune* answered by concluding that a "surprising" and "startling" number of them had been involved in "blatant illegalities." Echoing both Sutherland and Clinard, *Fortune* declined to rule out an undercount, saying that "it is axiomatic that there was more crime than was exposed in public proceedings."[36]

Almost two years after the *Fortune* story, *U.S. News & World Report* conducted a survey of America's 500 largest corporations and found that "115 have been convicted in the last decade of at least one major crime or have paid civil penalties for serious misbehavior." (*U.S. News* defined "serious misbehavior" as criminal convictions, or civil penalties or settlements in excess of $50,000). In addition, the magazine found:

- Justice Department announcements of actions against corporations over the last decade show that of the nation's 500 largest

firms, 12.2 percent were convicted of or did not contest at least one criminal offense, and an additional 10.8 percent were penalized for serious noncriminal offenses.
- Reports filed with the SEC by the nation's 25 biggest corporations show that seven of the firms have been convicted of or have not contested at least one crime since 1976, and seven more have been forced into settlements of major noncriminal charges—a total of 56 percent linked to some form of serious misbehavior.
- During the decade from 1971 through 1980, at least 2,690 corporations of all sizes were convicted of federal criminal offenses, according to the Administrative Office of the U.S. Courts.[37]

U.S. News, like *Fortune,* was "surprised" by these findings, even though *U.S. News* was aware of and quoted from Clinard's damning two-year-old exposé.

Criminals in the Usual Sense: Laying the Groundwork for Decriminalization of Corporate Law

"Most criminals in antitrust cases are not criminals in the usual sense." That statement, quoted above, of Wendell Berge, who was assistant to the head of the Justice Department's Antitrust Division in 1940, epitomizes the view of a group of academics, including the likes of Richard Posner, and Sanford Kadish, and politicians, such as Ronald Reagan, who believe that criminal sanctions should not be applied to corporate wrongdoing, or should be applied only as a last resort.[38] Many in this camp are adherents to the view that a corporate polluter is not a criminal in the sense that an individual burglar is a criminal, that a corporate price fixer is not a criminal in the sense that an individual robber is a criminal, and that a white-collar criminal is not a criminal in the sense that a street criminal is a criminal.

Ronald Reagan was, before he became governor of California and then president of the United States, a public relations adviser to the General Electric Corporation. In 1961, after a number of GE executives were sent to jail for price fixing, Reagan wrote a letter to the *Los Angeles Times* arguing that GE operated according to the highest principles: "higher I might add than some elements of government which are so bent on destroying business."

Again, in 1973, after the Watergate break-in, Reagan disputed the criminality of those who broke into the Democratic headquarters in Washington because they "are not criminals at heart." Recognizing that the break-in was "illegal," he nonetheless argued that *criminal* was too harsh a term to be applied to those involved in the Watergate episode. "I think the tragedy of this," Reagan said, "is that men who are not criminals at heart and certainly not engaged in criminal activities committed a criminal or illegal act and must bear the consequences. . . . These are men whose lives are very much changed by this. I doubt if any of them would even intentionally double park."[39]

Whether the Watergate conspirators would intentionally double park we'll leave to Mr. Reagan's conjecture. What's important is the clear belief of the laissez faire forces generally that the laws governing corporations have been overcriminalized, that such overcriminalization of corporate law is the ultimate victory for those seeking to "impose" government "regulation" on business, and that such control is antithetical to the American free market.

The academic who argues for decriminalization is not as direct as Mr. Reagan in asserting that white-collar criminals are not "criminals at heart"—or, as in the case of Mr. Berge, in arguing that price fixers are not "criminals in the usual sense." Instead, the academics present a utilitarian argument for decriminalization that goes something like this:

Because of the heavy reliance on civil remedies and the complementary disuse of the criminal remedies, the criminal law governing corporations is in such an underdeveloped state that corporate criminal sanctions should be effectively scrapped in favor of exclusive reliance on civil monetary penalties, supplemented by equitable remedies such as injunctions and consent decrees. Furthermore, the only significant goal of corporate criminal law is deterrence, and deterrence can be adequately attained through civil monetary penalties and other civil sanctions without reliance on criminal sanctions.

Thus, this school advocates the effective crippling of corporate criminal law, the moral equivalent of throwing the baby out with the bathwater. Brent Fisse, a noted Australian legal scholar, has powerfully argued against such abolition and for a reconstruction of the corporate criminal law to control socially harmful corporate behavior. Fisse notes that "modern corporate criminal law owes its origin and design more to crude borrowings from individual criminal and civil law than to any coherent assessment of the objectives of corporate criminal law and of how those objectives might be attained."[40]

Embarking on such an assessment, a growing number of legal scholars have joined Fisse in reacting strongly against those who would prefer to condemn corporate criminal law to windowdressing in perpetuity. The academic dispute intensified when the *Harvard Law Review*, one of the most respected law journals, published a commentary by its editors in 1979 titled "Developments in the Law—Corporate Crime," which came down on the side of decriminalization by advocating a civil-fine model to control corporate wrongdoing. The Harvard commentary rested on the proposition that although deterrence, rehabilitation, and incapacitation are the traditional aims of the criminal law as applied to individuals, deterrence is the only aim that is important in the realm of the corporate criminal law. From this proposition, the Harvard commentary suggested that since successful deterrence of corporate crime requires the threat of substantial monetary penalties, "one must wonder whether the same or a higher level of deterrence could be better achieved through civil [as opposed to criminal] penalties."[41]

That suggestion takes insufficient account of the deterrent value resulting from the stigma of criminal conviction and punishment. Herbert Packer argued that "there is very little evidence to suggest that the stigma of criminality means anything very substantial in the life of the corporation. John Doe has friends and neighbors; a corporation has none. And the argument that the fact of criminal conviction may have an adverse effect on a corporation's economic position seems fanciful."[42] Millions of dollars spent since then on corporate image advertising by large multinationals argue against Packer's view. A recent study of the effects of adverse publicity on 17 corporations found the loss of corporate prestige was a significant concern of executives in 15 of the cases.[43]

The laissez faire school focuses on the financial motives of corporate executives, ignores other well-documented motivations. A strictly monetary scheme to control corporate wrongdoing addresses the corporation's drive for profits, not a corporate executive's urge for power, nor his or her desire for prestige, creative urge, need to identify with the group, desire for security, urge for adventure, or desire to serve others.[44] As Fisse has noted, "deterring unwanted corporate behavior may require sanctions which, unlike monetary exactions, would be unconstitutional if characterized as civil. Preventive orders and formal publicity orders would be needed to inflict loss of corporate power and prestige directly."[45]

How Can the Corporation "Know" Without a Mind?

Mens rea is a legal term used to identify the mental element in crime. If a harmful act is an accident, it is not a crime. The harmful act must be intended, the actor must possess the requisite *mens rea* for the act to be a crime. There is no crime without a mind at fault. Or, as Justice Holmes once said, "even a dog distinguishes between being stumbled over and being kicked."

The laissez faire school picks up on the issue of corporate *mens rea* to argue that corporate crime is a difficult proposition because, as the Harvard commentary put it, *mens rea* "has no meaning when applied to a corporate defendant, since an organization possesses no mental state."[46] The criminal law has overcome this problem in a variety of ways.

Some prosecutors might invoke that theory of managerial *mens rea*, a theory that attributes to a corporation the mental state of policy-making officials. The Harvard commentary argues that this is the most difficult to prove since liability rests solely on the conduct of top corporate officials. "Consequently, liability can be evaded whenever illegal activity occurs without the authorization or reckless toleration of top officials," according to the Harvard commentary.[47]

A second theory, composite *mens rea*, rests on the proposition that the collective knowledge of all employees is attributable to the corporation. This is easier to prove than managerial *mens rea*, but has come under scholarly attack because, as Fisse has charged, "composite *mens rea* is a mechanical concept of mental state that fails to reflect true corporate fault; discrete items of information within an organization do not add up to a corporate *mens rea* unless there is an organizational *mens rea* in failing to heed them."

Finally, strategic *mens rea* is *mens rea* manifested by a corporation through its express or implied policies. This is the only one of the three that comes close to the idea of a corporate mental state, but as Fisse points out, "requiring the prosecution to establish a criminal corporate policy at or before the time that the *actus reus* [guilty act or deed of crime] of an offense is committed would make corporate *mens rea* extremely difficult to prove. Corporations almost never endorse criminal behavior by express policy."[48]

Neither managerial, nor composite, nor strategic *mens rea* is true corporate *mens rea*, which leaves laissez faire forces with the argument that corporations cannot commit crimes. But Fisse, following his belief that corporate criminal law should be reconstructed, has put forth a theory of reactive corporate fault, that is, fault not merely at the time of the *actus reus* of the offense, which as we have seen is difficult to prove for a corporation, but fault based on the "performance of the corporate defendant in reaction to the occurrence of the *actus reus* of the offense."[49]

Fisse gives as a descriptive example the Kepone controversy, where he argues it is not clear that the *corporation* intentionally or recklessly committed illegal acts of pollution. "A few middle managers may have possessed *mens rea*, but, as we have seen, managerial *mens rea* alone does not indicate genuinely corporate blameworthiness," Fisse writes.

If, however, after proof that the corporation did in fact pollute the James River, a judge ordered a compliance report and the corporation provided an unsatisfactory report, then this would display strategic *mens rea*, and corporate blameworthiness. "In other words," Fisse concludes, "if society looks to a corporate defendant to generate a reactive prevention and cure strategy, then an unsatisfactory response would tend to indicate a noncompliant corporate policy and hence arouse attitudes of resentment and blame toward the corporation."[50]

Just because the criminal law has rarely worked in controlling socially harmful corporate behavior does not mean it should not be given the chance to work. Fisse's scholarship represents a new wave of academic scrutiny that will help inform and shape public policy. In contrast, the laissez faire position reflects a failure of will to control corporate activities that by all indications have inflicted more damage by far upon the human community than the crimes committed by human beings roaming the streets. The rebuilding process must focus not only on the areas of evidence, liability, and procedure, but also, and most important, on the area of sanctioning. Once a corporation is found to be criminal, or to have violated the law, the appropriate sanction may prove to be the key to controlling unwanted behavior.

Sanctions Against the Individual White-Collar Criminal

If a corporation engages in socially undesirable behavior, the odds are that neither the corporation nor its executives will ever face a sentencing judge. In some cases, the law will not prohibit the corporation's antisocial behavior, as when auto manufacturers knowingly market dangerously constructed or designed vehicles. If such behavior is covered, law enforcement officials may be looking the other way, as with many Reagan administration "regulators." If laws cover such behavior and law enforcement agencies are conscientious about their enforcement responsibilities, corporation-induced political pressures may force a cut of monetary or political support to hamper those agencies.

If an unlucky corporation makes it to the sanctioning stage, the chances are that the corporation and its executives will be treated with kid gloves, especially when compared with individual street criminals.

Street criminals, mostly poor and black, get long prison terms for minor property crimes, yet corporate and white-collar criminals, in the words of Braithwaite, "can fix prices, defraud consumers of millions, and kill and maim workers with impunity, without prison."[51] When General Electric was convicted of price fixing in the early 1960s, the company was fined $437,000. As Lee Loevinger, former chief of the Justice Department's Antitrust Division, put it, the fine was no more severe than "a three-dollar ticket for overtime parking for a man with a $15,000 a year income."[52]

In 1978, the Olin Corporation was convicted of false filings to conceal illegal shipments of arms to South Africa. The company was fined $40,000 and no Olin executive went to jail.[53] In July 1984, Elizabeth McAllister, a peace activist, was sentenced to three years in jail for participating in an antinuclear demonstration at an upstate New York U.S. Air Force Base.[54]

The Clinard corporate crime study found that serious violations by corporations generally receive minor sanctions, with only administrative penalties given in approximately two-thirds of the cases identified as serious violations.[55] The Clinard study also found that 16 executives of 582 companies studied were sentenced to a total of 594 days of actual imprisonment. Three hundred and sixty of those days were accounted for by two officers who received six months each in the same case.[56]

Professor Stone alleges that jailings do not guarantee significant changes in corporate direction since "the very nature of bureaucracy is to make the individual dispensable."[57] But prison sentences for corporate executives are an efficient deterrent mechanism, in terms of both specific deterrence (against the convicted individual) and general deterrence (against those other executives observing the proceedings), available to sentencing judges. Jail sentences in the electrical equipment conspiracy cases had both specific and general deterrent effects. Clarence Burke, a former GE general manager, told a congressional committee after the convictions, "I would starve before I'd do it again." A second GE manager told a senator, "the way my family and myself have been suffering, if I see a competitor on one side of the street, I will walk on the other side, sir."

Gordon Spivack, former assistant chief in charge of field operations for the Justice Department's Antitrust Division, discussing the general deterrent effect of the electrical price fixing prison sanctions, believed that "similar sentences in a few cases each decade would almost completely cleanse our economy of the cancer of collusive price fixing, and the mere threat of such sentences is itself the strongest available deterrent to such activity."[58]

However, there appears to be a general belief among judges that white-collar criminals, no matter what the crime, don't deserve prison. This despite the fact that judges believe in the deterrent effect of imprisonment and have no confidence that fines or other nonincarcerative sanctions would be as effective.[59] One federal judge is quoted as saying that he would not "penalize a businessman trying to make a living when there are felons out on the street."[60] A second judge is of the opinion that "all people don't need to be sent to prison. For white-collar criminals, the mere fact of prosecution, pleading guilty—the psychological trauma of that is punishment enough. They've received the full benefit of punishment."[61]

In one of the few empirical studies of sentencing judges' attitudes toward white-collar criminals, Yale Law School's research program on white-collar crime found that although judges take a serious view of white-collar crime, several factors lead them to find what the authors of the study call "a non-incarcerative disposition," that is, judges don't like to throw white-collar criminals in jail.[62] The authors attribute judges' reluctance to imprison white-collar criminals partly to their belief that such defendants are "more sensitive to the impact of the prison environment than are non-white-collar defendants." One judge put it this way:

I think the first sentence to a prison term for a person who up to now has lived and has surrounded himself with a family, that lives in terms of great respectability and community respect and so on, whether one likes to say this or not I think a term of imprisonment for such a person is probably a harsher, more painful sanction than it is for someone who grows up somewhere where people are always in and out of prison. There may be something racist about saying that, but I am saying what I think is true or perhaps needs to be laid out on the table and faced.[63]

The Yale study also found judges wanting to avoid eliminating the contribution to community and family that white-collar offenders make in the normal course of their lives. One judge described this feeling in the following manner:

Usually the defendant is one who looks as though he can resume his place, if indeed not just continue on his place, in society, as a valuable and contributing member of society. Almost always he is a husband and a father. Almost always he has children who are in the process of becoming what we like to think children ought to be—well brought up, well educated, nurtured, cared for—usually he is a member of the kinds of civic organizations in the community who value his services and derive value from his services . . . . As a result you are up against this more difficult problem in degree in the so called white-collar criminals as to whether you are not going to inflict a hurt on society by putting such person in a prison and making him cease to be a good father and a good husband and a good worker in the community.[64]

Finally, the judges felt that white-collar defendants' ability to make restitution to their victims militated against the argument for prison sentences. The judges also felt that community service orders were better suited to white-collar prisoners than was prison.[65]

If judges are not throwing convicted corporate executives in jail, then how are they punishing them? With fines and community service orders whose deterrent effect is questionable. The Clinard study found that the average fine levied against individual officers was $18,250, a pittance compared with the large salaries and bonuses granted corporate executives. In addition to inadequacy, other factors mitigate the effectiveness of the fine as a sanction against criminal activity. First, many corporations indemnify an executive who is found to be acting for the benefit of the corporation if he had no reasonable cause to believe that what he was doing was criminal. Secondly, in some states, notably Delaware, a corporation can take out insurance against fines levied against its executives.[66] One federal judge complained that "one jail sentence is worth 100 consent decrees and that fines are meaningless because the defendant in the end is always reimbursed by the proceeds of his wrongdoing or by his company down the line."[67]

Community service orders, which have grown in popularity over the years, can be seen as a mechanism by which judges try to "do something" to fill the void created by the widespread reluctance to throw white-collar criminals in jail. The most notable of the recent community service orders was U.S. District Court Judge Charles Renfrew's order in the paper label price fixing case. Five individual defendants convicted of price fixing were fined between $5,000 and $15,000 apiece and were put on probation. As a condition of their probation, each was ordered to "make an oral presentation before twelve civic or other groups about the circumstances of his case and his participation therein . . ." Robert Herbst has labeled Renfrew's sentence "a joke . . . no deterrent threat at all."[68]

In other cases, convicted white-collar criminals have been ordered to:

- give speeches about their violations to business and civic groups;
- work in programs designed to aid the poor;
- help former street criminals participate in community groups and secure job pledges for them from business concerns;
- work 40 hours a week in a drug treatment center for five months and eight hours a week for one additional year;
- work 25 hours a week for five months and 10 hours a week for an additional year in an agricultural school that he had founded;
- make a community service film. The film, about the dangers of PCP, so impressed the judges that he reduced the conviction to a misdemeanor.[69]

There is little evidence that these community service orders have any deterrent effect, either against the individual convicted criminal or generally against those observing the sanctioning process. Judges imposing these sentences further undermine the nation's system of justice. "To keep coming up with alternative sentences," charged Thomas Cahill, former Chief Assistant U.S. Attorney, "in the public's image makes it look like it's a technical violation. It's not. . . . It's a crime and should be treated as a crime."[70] Second, if community service orders are going to be used to displace prison sentences, they should be used to displace prison sentences across the board, for street as well as for corporate criminals. The current system of jail for street thugs and speeches for corporate thugs creates an inequality of justice that undermines respect for the law.

Sanctions Against the Corporation

The *Harvard Law Review* commentary on corporate crime rejected retribution as a goal of corporate criminal sanctions, and focused on deterrence as the sole goal. It concluded that corporations cannot be punished in a stigmatic manner; that if stronger deterrents are needed, they should come in the form of heavier fines; and that since criminal fines have no advantage over civil fines, they should come in the form of heavier civil fines.[71]

But the overwhelming evidence from scholars, prosecutors, and judges is that fines, often small and well below authorized ceilings, do not deter corporate crime. Criminologist John Braithwaite has called them "license fees to break the law."[72] Fines in the typical antitrust case rarely reach the authorized ceiling. W. Breit and K. Elzinger, in a study of antitrust violations between 1967 and 1970, found that the Justice Department recommended imposing the maximum fine in less than one-third of the cases where it obtained convictions.[73] Braithwaite, in a recent study of law enforcement in the mine safety area, found that about 90 percent of the mine operators stated that civil penalties assessed or paid did not affect their production or safety activities. "Penalty dollar amounts were not considered of sufficient magnitude to warrant avoidance of future penalties and improvements in safety procedure," he observed. Operators contemptuously classified the fines as a "cost of doing business" or as a royalty paid to the government to continue in business. Producers who were fined saw no connection between penalties and safety.[74]

Christopher Stone's study of laws governing corporations, *Where* the Law Ends, came to similar conclusions. "The overall picture," according to Stone, "is that our strategies aimed to control corporations by threatening their profits are a very limited way of bringing about the internal changes that are necessary if the policies behind the law are to be effectuated."[75] The trouble with using fines to control corporate crime, according to Clinard, is that the amount paid is more than offset by the financial gain from the offense. In his study of more than 500 major U.S. corporations, Clinard found that four-fifths of the penalties levied against corporations were $5,000 or less, 11.6 percent were between $5,000 and $50,000, 3.7 percent were between $50,000 and $1,000,000, and 0.9 percent were over $1,000,000.

A major criticism of using fines to control corporate crime has been described by New York University Law School Professor John C. Coffee, Jr. and others as "the deterrence trap." The corporation contemplating the commitment of a crime will be deterred only if the expected punishment cost of the illegal activity exceeds the expected gain. Coffee gives the following example: If the expected gain were $1 million and the risk of arrest were 25 percent, then the penalty would have to be $4 million in order to make the expected punishment cost equal to the expected gain.[76] Coffee observes that "the maximum meaningful fine that can be levied against any corporate offender is necessarily bound by its wealth." For example,

> if a corporation having $10 million of wealth were faced with an opportunity to gain $1 million through some criminal act or omission, such conduct could not logically be deterred by monetary penalties directed at the corporation if the risk of apprehension were below 10%. That is, if the likelihood of apprehension were 8%, the necessary penalty would have to be $12.5 million (i.e., $1 million times 12.5, the reciprocal of 8%). Yet such a fine exceeds the corporation's ability to pay. In short, our ability to deter the corporation may be confounded by our inability to set an adequate punishment cost which does not exceed the corporation's resources.[77]

Since corporate crimes are easy to conceal and all indications are that rates of apprehension are exceedingly low, most major corporations will not be deterred by the types of fines that federal sentencing officials currently are imposing.

A second practical objection to using fines to control corporate crime is that the costs of any given corporate crime and the corresponding retributive fine may be far larger than the amount a corporation is able to pay. This "retribution trap" is a barrier to effective control of corporate crime. Braithwaite makes the point by asking:

> [C]an we imagine any penalty short of revoking the corporation's right to sell drugs which would be commensurate to the harm caused by the fraud and deceit of a thalidomide disaster? Given what we know about how disapproving the community feels toward corporate crime, there may be many situations where the deserved monetary or other punishments bankrupt the company. The community then cuts its nose to spite its face.[78]

In addition, threatening the corporation as a monolithic "black box" ignores the possible role of individual motivations in directing corporate actions. Stone and others have observed that there may be a fundamental lack of congruence between the aims of the individual and the aims of the firm. A corporate executive may engage in criminal activity to further his own ends, not necessarily those of the firm. Coffee gives the hypothetical example of an executive vice president who is a candidate for promotion to president and may be willing to run risks that are counterproductive to the firm as a whole because he is eager to make a record profit for his division or to hide an error of judgment. In such situation a fine aimed at the corporation won't deter the perpetrator and will probably fail in controlling illegal conduct. Thus when a criminal sanctioning system aims at the "black box" of the corporation instead of the individual decision makers within the black box, it may prove irrelevant to certain kinds of misconduct. Coffee argues that

> the most shocking safety and environmental violations are almost exclusively the product of decisions at lower managerial levels. . . . The directive from the top of the organization is to increase profits by fifteen percent but the means

are left to the managerial discretion of the middle manager who is in operational control of the division. . . . The results of such a structure are predictable: when pressure is intensified, illegal or irresponsible means become attractive to a desperate middle manager who has no recourse against a stern but myopic notion of accountability that looks only to the bottom line of the income statement.[79]

Thus in firms where there is a strong "bottom line" ethic, one that loosens legal, moral, and ethical constraints, fines against the organization will fail to have the deterrent effect upon which the entire structure of fines is premised.

Even when fined, criminals tend not to pay. From 1977 to 1983 the federal government collected only about 55 percent of all criminal fines imposed. Since 1968, the dollar volume of criminal fines has increased by a factor of twelve; at the same time, collection rates have fallen from around 80 percent to less than 40 percent.[80] At the end of fiscal year 1982, the amount of delinquent debt owed to the federal government was a staggering $38 billion. This failure to pay fines has the effect of severely undercutting the deterrent and punitive effects of the sanction. As Senator Charles Percy stated in opening Senate hearings in 1983 on the subject, "the collection of criminal fines goes beyond mere fiscal responsibility. Five of every six fines are levied on criminals who do *not* go to prison. Half of the time, they are not even on probation. Therefore, in many cases, when these fines are not paid, these criminals go unpunished. It is as simple as that."[81]

Braithwaite, in his study of coal mine safety enforcement, found that at the time of the Buffalo Creek waste tip disaster, in which over 125 people lost their lives, the operator had been assessed fines exceeding $1.5 million, "not a cent of which was paid." In another case, a coal company had been assessed fines totaling $76,330 for 379 violations, 178 of them for electrical or trolley wire standards. Less than half of the amount had been paid at the time of a coal disaster at the company's Blacksville mine, in which a fire triggered by a trolley wire ignition caused the death of nine men.[82]

The failure of fines as deterrents of corporate crime has led to a call for the imposition of more effective and varied criminal sanctions. Discussions of sanctions against the corporation have traditionally focused on a narrow field of civil sanctions, specifically fines and injunctive orders. This focus has been broadened in recent years by a number of Australian corporate criminologists who seek to expand the goals of criminal law and to elevate retribution as a legitimate goal of corporate criminal law. This broadened perspective brings into play sanctions that many consider inappropriate or ineffective in punishing or deterring street crime—such as incapacitation and execution—but may work well in the corporate criminal context.

Although individual corporate executives can be incapacitated for crimes against society, corporations willing to continue to flout the laws will merely substitute one executive for another. Thus, if a product safety control manager comes under an incapacitative order forbidding him or her from serving in such a position for three years, the corporation may merely substitute a manager of like mind in place of the exiled manager.

To overcome this substitution problem, legislatures and courts may turn to issuing incapacitation orders against the corporate entity. Courts may order companies to cease operating in areas where the company has shown repeated criminal conduct. In extreme cases, courts may impose an execution order, or death sentence. Since a corporation is a creation of the state, there is no reason why, in cases of egregious conduct, courts may not order the dissolution of the corporate entity. In 1983, for example, the Attorney General of Virginia asked the state's Corporation Commission to dissolve the charter of Croatan Books Inc., a firm reportedly convicted 69 times in five years for possessing obscene films or magazines. The dissolution was moved for on the grounds that the corporation had "continued to exceed or abuse the authority conferred upon it by law."[83]

It is generally agreed that rehabilitation has failed as an approach to controlling street crime. However, there is a growing consensus that it must be examined carefully as a way of gaining control of the corporate crime problem. As Fisse and Braithwaite have observed, it may be difficult to reorganize or rehabilitate a human psyche, but it is much easier to rearrange a corporation's standard operating procedures, defective control systems, inadequate communication mechanisms, and in general its internal structure. Australian investigators who have conducted most of the empirical research in this area conclude that rehabilitation works in the corporate sphere. Hopkins's study of the rehabilitation of corporate criminals in Australia found that most companies prosecuted under the consumer protection provisions of the Australian Trade Practices Act introduced at least some measures to ensure that the offense did not recur.[84] And Fisse and Braithwaite found similar patterns in their study of adverse publicity. Rehabilitation can be demanded by police agencies, through consent decrees and probation orders, as a condition of a suspended sentence or as a contingency of settlement. The police or the courts may thereby order a number of changes within the corporate organization, including changes in how information is exchanged and how decisions are made, as well as the creation of an internal ombudsman and accounting groups.

Court-sanctioned adverse publicity has great potential for bringing corporate criminal conduct under control. The recent quantitative study by Fisse and Braithwaite of 17 corporations involved in publicity crises found that large corporations care greatly about their reputations. The study concluded that corporations fear the sting of adverse publicity more than they fear the law itself.[85]

Corporate antisocial conduct is brought to the attention of the public through a number of channels, including consumer activist groups, investigative reporters, federal police agency enforcement actions, official inquiries, governmentally mandated disclosures, and international boycotts. In some instances a corporation is ordered to publicize its misdeeds as part of the sanction for a violation of law. In the J.P. Stevens case, for example, the company was ordered to give notice of anti-union violations by mail to its employees in North and South Carolina. In a securities case, a defendant was required to send its shareholders copies of the court's decision against it. And, in an FTC case against ITT Continental Baking, in which the company was accused of deceptive advertising for its Profile brand bread, the company agreed to a consent decree that required it to allocate 25 percent of its advertising budget for one year to a disclosure stating that "Profile is not effective for weight reduction."[86]

These instances involved civil and administrative proceedings, but there is a strong case to be made for court-ordered use of formal publicity orders as a sanction for convicted corporations. A 1970 draft of the U.S. National Commission on Reform of Federal Criminal Law (the Brown Commission) recommended:

When an organization is convicted of an offense, the court may, in addition to or in lieu of imposing other authorized sanctions . . . require the organization to give appropriate publicity to the conviction by notice to the class or classes of persons or sector of the public interested in or affected by the conviction, by advertising in designated areas or by designated media, or otherwise. . . .

Fisse and Braithwaite suggest two ways of implementing this recommendation: first, that publication of the details of an offense be made available as a court-ordered sentence against corporate offenders, and second, that pre-sentence or probation orders against corporate offenders should be used to require disclosure of organizational reforms and disciplinary action undertaken as a result of the offense.[87]

Still, some argue that corporations cannot be stigmatized by adverse publicity despite strong evidence and common sense suggesting the opposite. Surely corporate heads would turn and listen more attentively to law enforcement agents if, for example, Hooker Chemical Company were required to buy television ads to tell the nation about its pollution activities, or if the Ford Motor Company were required to run television ads informing the nation about how it marketed the unsafe Pinto, or if Grunenthal were required to tell the world about how it marketed thalidomide and how thalidomide affected its consumers. To use adverse publicity sanctions not just in remedial orders, but as punitive and educational measures, is one of the more effective and efficient ways of shaming corporate America out of its antisocial behavior and bringing it back within the bounds of legal commerce.

Another alternative corporate sentence is the equity fine. Professor John Coffee, dismayed by the failure of cash fines to effectively sanction corporate wrongdoing, has suggested that the corporation be fined not in cash, but in the equity securities of the corporation. Under Coffee's equity fine proposal, the convicted corporation would be required to authorize and issue such number of shares to a state's victim compensation fund as would have an expected market value equal to the cash fine necessary to deter illegal activity. The fund would then be able to liquidate the securities in whatever manner best maximized its return.

Coffee's equity fine proposal overcomes a number of the problems associated with cash fines. First, the equity fine better aligns the self-interest of managers with the interests of the corporation. When the corporation issues the shares designated for the victims' compensation fund, the per share market value would decline, thus reducing the value of stock options and other compensation available to the executives. Second, Coffee argues that a large block of marketable securities would make the corporation an inviting target for a takeover. Third, stockholders would have greater incentive to take a longer term view of the profit goals of the corporation and to insist on keeping operations within legal bounds. Fourth, the equity fine proposal overcomes the unfairness of cash fines in that the corporation would be less able to pass on the cost of the equity fine to workers and consumers. Finally, the deterrence trap problem associated with cash fines is overcome since the market value of the corporation exceeds its cash reserves. Under equity fines, much larger fines can be levied, fines large enough to deter giant companies from illegal behavior.[88]

Although community service orders against individual white-collar violators have attracted widespread attention and condemnation, little attention has been paid to the potential of community service orders in controlling corporate crime. As Fisse has observed, community service orders against the corporation can be invoked in a wide variety of legal settings: as a condition of probation, as a condition of mitigation of sentence, and as a condition of nonprosecution.

In the Allied Chemical/Kepone case, U.S. District Court Judge Robert Merhige fined Allied $13.24 million after the company pleaded no contest to 940 counts of water pollution. The amount of the fine was reduced to $5 million when the company agreed to spend $8,356,202 to establish the Virginia Environmental Endowment, a nonprofit group that would "fund scientific research projects and implement remedial projects and other programs to help alleviate problems that Kepone has created . . . and . . . enhance and improve the overall quality of the environment in Virginia."[89]

In *United States v. Olin Mathieson*, the corporate defendant, Olin, pleaded no contest to a charge of conspiring to ship 3,200 rifles to South Africa in violation of the trade embargo. U.S. District Court Judge Robert Zampano fined Olin Mathieson $45,000 after the company agreed to give $500,000 to set up the New Haven

Community Betterment Fund, a nonprofit group "to promote the general welfare of the greater New Haven area with gifts or grants to charitable organizations."[90]

Another notable example came in 1980, when FMC Corporation pleaded guilty to lying to the federal police (EPA) in 1975 and 1976 by reporting that it was discharging about 200 pounds per day of carbon tetrachloride into the Kanawha River in West Virginia when in reality it knew that the actual discharge was ten times that amount. As part of the plea agreement with U.S. police agents, FMC agreed to pay $1 million into the Virginia Environmental Endowment that had been created by the court order in the Allied/Kepone case.[91]

The community service sanctions in the Allied, Olin, and FMC cases were deductible, whereas fines are not—an advantage regarded favorably by corporate criminals. Fisse suggests making these sanctions expressly a sentence of punishment, thus disallowing tax deductibility and any patent or copyright protection from any product of a project of the community service.[92] But, by redirecting money fines to environmental, consumer, and other community and citizen action groups, judges can leverage the money, money usually lost in the shuffle at state and federal treasury departments, to assist the victims of the corporate criminal activity. Automobile corporate criminals could be directed to pay money to the auto safety groups, pharmaceutical corporate criminals could be directed to pay money to support health groups, and chemical corporate criminals could be directed to support environmental action groups. The deterrent and punitive effects of forcing companies to support their public policy adversaries cannot be overestimated.

And judges need not be limited to redirecting money fines to citizen groups. In the thalidomide case, Fisse suggests that the German manufacturer Grunenthal could have been required to set up production facilities to produce and supply artificial limbs, robotic devices, and other special aids.[93] In the Pinto case, Ford could have been required to set up regional burn treatment centers. Ralph Nader has suggested that "making a coal executive work in a coal mine for two years is better than putting him in a cushy jail."[94] The only limits to imaginative and effective community service orders are those binding the minds of legislators and sentencing judges.

What To Do? A 50-Point Law-and-Order Program to Curb Corporate Crime

Corporations and their executives, accustomed to getting away with illegal, immoral, and violent activity, will change only if the costs of that activity outweigh the benefits. Only a reconstruction of the federal and state corporate criminal justice systems, with strong laws enforced by a well-funded, effective police force, can control the excesses and abuses of centers of corporate power.

To this end, a 50-point program is proposed here to curb corporate crime. Some of these ideas have been considered by governing bodies and implemented in weaker forms, others considered and rejected out of hand, others ignored. This program focuses on generic problems of corporate crime—those dealing with law making, law breaking, law enforcing, and the sanctioning process. It does not discuss current substantive federal statutes (environmental, labor, consumer, health and safety) governing corporate behavior, each of which is in need of individual review with an eye toward strengthening the laws by plugging corporate-drilled loopholes.

Recent political history has shown that progressive lawmaking is initiated only when victims and an unencumbered citizenry organize to gain compensation for their injuries and protection against future corporate violence. The auto safety law would not have been passed had not auto victims had a strong voice in Washington to defeat the auto lobby and secure its passage. And those injured by hazardous products will not be protected from an alliance of corporate criminals seeking to pare back product liability laws unless they organize to fight the proposed revisions and to demand stronger laws.

The fight for law and order for corporations will not be a top-down fight but a bottom-up fight. Victims must join in an alliance with an enlightened citizenry to demand that the law be fair, equitable, and just; that "law and order" be not merely an empty phrase hurled at election time, but be applied fairly at all times to all citizens and corporations, including the most powerful ones.

This law-and-order program for corporations should help shape a citizens' agenda that will directly confront an inequitable justice system that consistently treats street thuggery as a criminal activity and corporate thuggery as business as usual.

✓ **1. Impose Upon Corporate Executives a Duty to Report Activities That May Cause Death or Injury.**

Require corporate managers to report to federal authorities a product or process that may cause death or serious injury. Legislation embodying this concept was introduced in 1979, by Representative George Miller (D.-Calif.) and 42 of his colleagues in the House of Representatives after the Love Canal, Ford Pinto, Kepone, and Firestone Tire disasters made national news. At the time, Miller said, "When someone makes a decision to conceal information about a product or an industrial process knowing full well that the product or process jeopardizes someone's life, health or safety, I believe a criminal act has occurred." Similar legislation has since been sponsored by Rep. John Conyers (D-Mich.). Had the Miller bill been law 30 years ago, those in the know at Hooker, Ford, Allied, and Firestone may have faced stiff prison sentences for failing to report the disasters in the making to the appropriate federal agencies.

✓ **2. Enact an Executive Responsibility Statute.**

If a corporate executive tells a staff aide, "Bribe the prime minister," and a bribe is given, that executive is criminally liable under the federal Foreign Corrupt Practices Act. But what of the executive who sets requirements that can be met only through illegal means, or who knows or has reason to know that illegal means are being used but fails to investigate? These cases are the more common and the more difficult to prove. Two U.S. Supreme Court cases, *U.S. v. Dotterweich* (320 US 277) and *U.S. v. Park* (421 US 658) have held that corporate executives can be held criminally liable for a violation of the Food and Drug Act regardless of their knowledge, intent, or direct participation. In *Park*, the president of a supermarket company was held criminally liable for allowing unsanitary conditions to persist in one of his company's food warehouses even though the building was in a different city from the company headquarters and Park had no personal daily involvement in managing the warehouse. The Court found that the Food, Drug, and Cosmetic Act "imposes not only a positive duty to seek out and remedy violations when they occur but also, and primarily, a duty to implement measures that will insure that violations will not occur."

The Court has been reluctant to extend *Park* to non-food and drug areas. Still, the principle of executive responsibility is an important and essential ingredient in any program to control corporate crime. Congress must pass a law making it a criminal offense for corporate supervisors to willfully or recklessly fail to oversee an assigned activity that results in criminal conduct.

✓ 3. Enact a Federal Homicide Statute.

In reaction to the failure of the federal government to control corporate abuses, state prosecutors have increasingly in recent years indicted corporations and their executives under state homicide statutes.[95] Most prominent of these cases have been the Film Recovery and Ford Motor cases mentioned above. Committed by individuals, murder clearly should be the province of the states. But committed by national and multinational corporations, murder demands at the least a national response. The Ford Pinto allegedly killed people—not just in northern Indiana, where the company was prosecuted and found not guilty of reckless homicide—but all around the country. And as the failed prosecution in that case demonstrated, the legal and political resources available to a multinational can easily and quickly overcome those available to a local prosecutor. To bring homicide charges against the likes of Manville, the tobacco companies or A. H. Robbins would require the resources available to federal prosecutors. Congress should enact a federal homicide statute to bring to justice those who kill on a mass scale.

✓ 4. Create a Centralized Corporate Crime Data Base.

In September 1980, the Department of Justice released a 485-page report titled *Data Sources on White Collar Law Breaking*[96] that confirmed the experiences of many researchers in the field of corporate crime: federal corporate crime police do not have centralized, easily accessible information about the field they are duty bound to police. The Environmental Protection Agency (EPA), for example, cannot tell a researcher the number of cases brought against any given corporation. To conduct such a search, the researcher must contact each of the regional EPA offices around the country, then tabulate the findings. The Securities and Exchange

Commission refers researchers to a *private company* to obtain a list of companies that have admitted improper foreign payments.

The Justice Department report's recommendation of a centralized data base on white-collar crime should be implemented (with separate categories for specific areas of corporate crime). Every month, the Federal Bureau of Investigation (FBI) releases to the public a compilation of street crime statistics from around the country that indicates the level of crime in major urban communities (e.g., burglary up 5 percent in Boston, robbery down 5 percent in Chicago) and nationwide (crime up 6 percent). The Uniform Crime Reporting System (UCRS), as it is known, is a compilation of street crimes in U.S. cities with populations exceeding 100,000 (approximately 170 cities). Local FBI offices compile the data.

The FBI should create a similar index for corporate crime (toxic dumping up 5 percent, marketing of hazardous products down 5 percent). Such a compilation will assist prosecutors, legislators, judges, and journalists in their efforts to expose and control corporate crime.

5. Require Publicly Held Corporations to Disclose Their Litigation Records.

Currently, the SEC requires all publicly held companies to disclose "any material legal proceedings, other than ordinary routine litigation incidental to the business. . . . "[97] Rarely do corporations, under this section of the SEC rules, comprehensively report problems with federal enforcement agents. The SEC should promulgate new, expanded rules requiring corporations to report all litigation with state, local, or federal government agencies, or with victims of corporate crime and negligence.

6. Strengthen Laws and Enforcement of Laws Governing Destruction of Documents.

Corporate destruction of documents is a serious problem getting very little attention. In 1973, lawyers for IBM, in the middle of a heated antitrust battle with the Justice Department, oversaw the destruction of hundreds of pages of a valuable index. A federal judge ordered IBM to reconstruct the data base, at an estimated cost of $3 million.[98] In 1971, several junk dealers stumbled across some boxes of General Motors microfilmed consumer complaint letters. The 100,000 microfilm clips of complaint letters dating from 1960 to 1964 included 544 complaints about fumes emitted from GM's Corvair—letters that could have been used against the company in subsequent liability litigation.[99] Corporate lawyers have become so cavalier that they now publicly discuss destruction of documents. John Fedders, chief of the Securities and Exchange Commission's (SEC's) enforcement division under Ronald Reagan, co-authored a law review article in 1980 titled "Document Retention and Destruction: Practical, Legal and Ethical Considerations," which described, in effect, a roadmap for lawyers seeking to destroy documents legally. At one point in the article, the authors wrote: "On occasion counsel will be shown a document which could expose the corporation to liability if it became available to adverse parties. If the document is not yet scheduled for destruction under the terms of the program, management may advocate waiver of the program to allow the document to be promptly destroyed."[100]

The law in this area must be tightened so that "sensitive" documents—that is, those that may cast light upon the guilt of the corporation—are protected for the benefit of the public. Corporate lawyers must give more weight to the public interest when considering the ethics of whether to destroy a document that might save their corporate client money or embarrassment but at the same time deny its victims just compensation or deny the public justice.

7. Adopt Reactive Corporate Fault as a More Reliable and Effective Method of Determining Corporate *Mens Rea* (State of Knowing).

As mentioned, Fisse defines reactive corporate fault as a corporation's fault in failing to undertake satisfactory preventive or corrective measures in response to the commission of an offense by personnel acting on behalf of the corporation. Traditionally, prosecutors have sought to graft the intent of an agent onto the corporation vicariously as a method of proving corporate intent. The corporate employee knew; therefore the corporation knew. Or, the prosecutor looks to see if there was a faulty standard operating procedure, or to see if together the intent in the minds of many managers added up to corporate intent. All of these methods have been traditionally difficult to prove. And these methods of vicarious corporate intent have been roundly criticized as unjust. The fact that an employee did it does not necessarily mean that the corporation did it or "knew" about it.

A more reliable and effective method is Fisse's "reactive corporate fault." Rather than look to evidence during or before the execution of the wrongful act, fault would be determined by looking at the corporation's reaction to the illegal act (does the corporation cover up or does it take measures to prevent repetition?). This is an innovative proposal that ought to be incorporated into the law of corporate fault.

8. Tighten Discretionary Justice Standards for Prosecution of Corporations.

In August 1983, the Justice Department filed a civil complaint against General Motors (that was dismissed in April 1987) seeking the recall of 1.1 million X-body cars because of faulty brake systems and imposing $4,027,000 in civil penalties. Citizen groups asserted that in the same case the Justice Department had the evidentiary basis for filing a parallel criminal suit charging GM with making false statements to the government, and should have done so.

In February 1984, the Justice Department settled its criminal case against Metropolitan Edison Company, the owner and operator of the Three Mile Island nuclear plant in Harrisburg, Pennsylvania, by allowing the company to plead no contest to six charges that it fudged the results of safety tests at the Three Mile Island facility. Local citizen groups, wanting the Justice Department to take the case to trial so that the public would learn exactly what happened at the facility, accused the department of engaging in a "cop-out."

These two cases, among others, raise questions about the constraints that govern a prosecutor's discretion when the defendant is a powerful corporation. For years, proposals have been floating through legal literature urging that discretionary justice be brought under the rule of law,[101] but few of them have been taken seriously by legislatures, especially those that eye criminal prosecutions of corporations. A law without effective enforcement is as good as no law at all. Congress should set mandatory prosecutorial guidelines for corporate crime cases.

9. Increase the Staffs and Budgets of the
Corporate Crime Police and Prosecutors.

In recent years, corporate criminals have secured cutbacks in the enforcement activities of federal enforcment agencies. President Reagan was elected to office on the slogan, "Let's get government off our backs," but as his policies have revealed, he meant "Let's get the police off the backs of the corporate criminals." He has worked to cripple the major policing agencies, including the Food and Drug Administration, the Environmental Protection Agency, and the Occupational Safety and Health Administration.[102] Budgets must be restored, enforcements staffs increased, and experienced police officers and prosecutors brought in to reinvigorate valuable dismantled programs.

10. Create a Corporate Crime Strike Force
at the Department of Justice.

As a complement to its "Organized Crime Task Force," the Justice Department should allocate the necessary funding for the creation of a "Corporate Crime Strike Force," to acknowledge the urgency of the problem and to focus talent and resources in a sustained manner. Corporate crime deserves resources at least equal to those devoted to "organized crime." Currently, the Justice Department has no unified program to deal with corporate crime.

11. Encourage Community Contact
by Corporate Crime Police.

Some police agencies, such as the National Highway Safety Administration, have installed toll-free 800 hotlines so that victims of automobile corporations may call Washington to report possible violations. Other police agencies should follow suit. More important, police officers should tour the country, educating citizens about the laws governing corporate America, teaching them how to spot a corporate criminal, to whom to report the activity, and how to seek redress. Police officials should also focus on educating the young about corporate crime. There is no reason why a street cop should seek access to an elementary school to speak to school children while at the same time an official from a regional EPA enforcement division wishing to speak to the children about water pollution should not.

12. Redefine the Rights of Corporations (They Should Not Have the Same Rights as Individuals).

Historically, rights were granted to individual defendants as a response to the overzealousness of powerful state prosecutors. Individuals have been granted the right to a jury trial, the right to privacy (from which arises a wide range of protected rights), and the right against self-incrimination. But do corporations, artificial entities created by pieces of paper, hold the same rights as flesh and blood individuals? The Supreme Court has held that "corporations can claim no equality with individuals in the enjoyment of a right to privacy. . . . They are endowed with public attributes. They have a collective impact on society, from which they derive the privilege of acting as artificial entities."[102A]

John Braithwaite has noted that "corporations cannot have a confession physically coerced out of them under bright lights in a police station. Corporations do not stand in the dock without the benefit of counsel. . . . The extreme *privation* suffered by individual victims of state oppression which *justifies* extreme protections of individual rights is not felt within the corporation."

Braithwaite also points out that in England and Australia prosecutors can engage in entrapment against a corporation, but such practices are illegal in the United States because of protections designed for individuals that are granted also to corporations. The rights of corporations must be redefined in light of the inequitable distribution of power. With an individual defendant, the prosecutor is the powerful figure, and the individual must be protected against abuse of that power. With a corporate defendant, the corporation is often the more powerful figure and, in many instances, the prosecutor must be protected against the abuse of the corporate power.[103]

13. Slow the Revolving Door.

One of the time-honored ways corporations use to capture police agencies is shuffling lawyers from the industry to the police, back to the industry, back to the police. Many police agencies have rules prohibiting a staff lawyer who used to work for a corporation from working on any case involving that corporation.

However, this type of rule is not good enough. Young lawyers today join enforcement staffs, not with an eye toward becoming career police agents, but with an eye toward "learning the ropes," so that they can jump to the corporate defense side and thereby greatly increase their salaries. Corporate crime police work has been denigrated, largely by corporate and political misinformation that degrades and demoralizes civil servants. President Reagan has done more than any prior president in this regard.

It would be unheard of for a narcotics officer to quit after four years to represent narcotics pushers, just to increase his salary. Federal police agencies should encourage careers in corporate crime police work and should enhance the stature of such positions in society. New rules should be put in place to prohibit police agencies from hiring from the ranks of the corporate defense bar.[104]

14. Create Neighborhood Watch Committees to Monitor Corporate Crime.

Local police agencies have effectively fostered the creation of neighborhood watch committees, where neighbors get together and are taught by local police how to monitor illegal activity in their neighborhood. Federal and state police should foster similar groups to watch for corporate criminal activity. Citizens could work, in conjunction with colleges, universities, and other scientific institutions, to test water and air around a factory for pollution, learn the laws governing consumer fraud and survey local merchants to check for compliance for fraud or false advertising, and check hiring practices of local companies for compliance with federal equal employment opportunity laws. Such citizen involvement would lend a needed hand to financially strapped police and prosecutors, while at the same time educating citizens in the workings of the law.

15. Change the Standard of Proof from "Beyond a Reasonable Doubt" to "On the Balance of Probabilities".

Imprisonment is the sanction that gave rise to the need to afford due process protections to individuals. It is seen as such a harsh sanction that individuals must have a wide array of rights to protect themselves from it. But corporations cannot be put in jail, so do they deserve the same protections, especially if the protections preclude a just decision in the case?

The issue is raised in terms of standard of proof. In the tetracycline criminal price fixing case, the corporate defendants were acquitted on the "beyond a reasonable doubt" standard, although the evidence could have met a "balance of the probabilities" standard. Braithwaite's argument for displacement of the "beyond a reasonable doubt" standard is convincing:

> In cases which involve scientific dispute, proof "beyond a reasonable doubt" is rarely, if ever, possible. Science deals in probabilities, not certainties. . . . When a remissible sanction such as a fine is the most severe penalty which can be imposed on a corporation, the case for proof beyond a reasonable doubt is weak. History is littered with shameful instances of innocent people who went to the gallows or suffered years of despair in prison only to have their innocence subsequently vindicated. Such instances justify insistence on proof beyond reasonable doubt. The state cannot compensate these people or their death or suffering. It can instantly compensate the wrongly fined corporation with a cheque for the value of the fine plus interest.[105]

16. Make Police Liable for Failure to Act and for Looking the Other Way.

In 1947, a mine disaster in Centralia, Illinois, claimed the lives of 11 miners. The director of the police agency legally responsible for mine safety in Illinois and his assistant had received more than a dozen reports from the department's own inspectors at the Centralia mine before the explosion. These reports outlined in detail the safety problems at the mine, yet the police officials simply forwarded the reports to the company and asked the company to comply with proper procedures. The company did not respond to the letter.

In Boston, in 1971, eight meat inspectors were convicted on charges of bribery and improper acceptance of gifts.[106]

Where corporations apply heavy-handed tactics (as in the case of bribery), or where a corporation is indifferent to legal requirements and the policing agency is similarly indifferent to the corporation's indifference, then an outside prosecutor must step in to make sure the job gets done. This type of policing the police should be institutionalized in the field of corporate crime police work, where the temptations not to prosecute are much greater than in other areas of police work.

17. Create an International Legal Structure and Police Network to Control Multinational Corporate Crime.

If a multinational corporation runs afoul of the laws of one country, it can move its products into the markets of others. Hazardous products banned in the United States are routinely dumped in countries where the laws are less stringent. New mechanisms must be created to halt this practice. The United Nations has proposed a transnational code to govern the operations of corporations as well as voluntary consumer guidelines for member nations to follow, but the United States, under the administration of Ronald Reagan, has worked to block passage.

The United Nations consumer code, for example, embodies the right to be protected against the marketing of hazardous goods, the right to be protected from fraudulent, deceptive, or restrictive business practices, the right to information necessary to make informed choices, and the freedom to organize consumer groups and to have their views represented.[107] Multinationals have the power to co-opt Third World governments, and only a strong international code can prevent the type of unethical practices, such as dumping, described in the profiles section of this book.

18. Encourage Private Attorneys General.

Private attorneys general is a phrase that refers to lawyers who represent victims of corporate wrongdoing. Their lawsuits against the corporation serve not only to gain compensation for the client, but also to assist police agents in enforcing the law. A corporation will be deterred from violating the law if its executives perceive possibly damaging litigation as a real threat. The Sherman Antitrust Act carries with it a triple damage provision that encourages lawyers representing individuals victimized by alleged antitrust behavior to sue the corporations. And trial lawyers representing victims of consumer products serve an important private attorney general function.

The triple damage provision is an inexpensive way to leverage prosecutorial power and should be included in other federal statutes governing corporate behavior.[108]

19. Facilitate Class Actions.

In a similar vein, class action lawsuits—lawsuits brought on behalf of a handful of named plaintiffs, but representing an entire class of victims—serve an important law enforcement function: deterrence. The lawyer agrees to take the case on a contingency basis. If the suit succeeds, the lawyer gets a percentage of the award or settlement; if it fails, the lawyer gets nothing. A class action allows thousands of individuals to pool their resources in an effort to meet the much greater resources of the corporate opponent. Currently there are serious roadblocks to successful class action lawsuits that must be legislatively excised so as to facilitate this effective redress and strengthen the private prosecutorial mechanism.[109]

20. Curb Abuse of the *Nolo Contendere* Plea.

A *nolo contendere* plea is in effect a guilty plea, but it cannot be used in a parallel or subsequent civil suit as evidence of wrongdoing. If a drug company, for example, pleads *nolo contendere* to violating federal food and drug laws by marketing an unsafe drug, then victims of that criminal act cannot use the plea as evidence in their case. Given the large damage awards handed down by juries against drug companies in these cases, it is clear that the threat of civil litigation is a much more serious deterrent to drug companies than the relatively minuscule criminal fines that may be imposed. The *nolo* plea only impedes the effective completion of these civil suits and thus hampers this highly effective enforcement mechanism. The primary purpose of this plea is to create an extra hurdle for civil litigation, and it should be either abolished or its use severely restricted.

21. End Abuse of Consent Decrees.

The vast majority of all federal civil cases brought against major corporations are settled with consent decrees through which the corporation neither admits nor denies violating the law, but consents to the sanction, which is a promise not to violate the law. The purpose of the consent decree is similar to that of the nolo plea: namely, to deny civil plaintiffs victimized by the corporate activity a finding of violation that can be used as evidence against the company in the civil litigation. Some SEC corporate defense lawyers openly expressed the view in the late 1970s that in the vast majority of cases brought by the SEC, the SEC had the goods and could prove its case, but nevertheless settled with a consent decree rather than going to court for a finding of violation and a public airing of the evidence.[110] Police and prosecutorial guidelines ought to be set up to define when a consent decree is appropriate and when it is not. Clearly it is not if the police "have the goods" on the corporation. Trials would be more costly than consent decree settlements, but the deterrent effect of a highly publicized trial might outweigh that of a score of consent decrees.

In addition, guidelines should be set up to govern the settlement process so that corporate defense lawyers don't exert excessive control over that process. In many instances today, for example, corporate defense lawyers are allowed to review the wording of the complaint before it is released to the press. This type of corporate public relations excess should not be allowed.

22. Convicted Companies Should Be Required to Notify Their Victims.

Unlike perpetrators of street crime, a corporation can commit a crime and the victim won't know it. If a bakery corporation, for example, illegally colludes with competitors to fix the price of bread at 32 cents when the price was 30 cents, there is little chance that a purchaser of bread will be made aware of the illegal nature of the price increase.

Convicted corporations should be required to notify their victims. This notification requirement gives the victims the opportunity to seek compensation. Furthermore it acts as a deterrent, by requiring the corporation to publicize its criminal activity and to tell the world, in effect, what it wishes no one to know.

23. Strictly Enforce Fine Collection Schedules.

Prosecutors must bring criminal contempt charges against corporations that fail to pay their fines promptly. At the time of the Buffalo Creek disaster (mentioned above), in which over 125 people lost their lives, the corporation had owed $1.5 million in fines, not a cent of which was paid. Similarly, in 1971, prior to a disaster in Blacksville, West Virginia, in which a fire took nine lives, the operator had been assessed for 379 violations, 178 of which were for electrical or trolley wire standards, and, of $76,330 assessed, only $31,090 had been paid.[111] A recent Senate hearing on the subject of unpaid fines revealed that from 1977 to 1983 the federal government collected only 55 percent of all criminal fines.

However debatable the fining of a corporation may be, the effect is greatly diminished if the fine goes uncollected. Corporations should be required to pay their fines promptly.

24. Add Citizen Bounty-Hunting Provisions to Federal Laws.

The Rivers and Harbors Act of 1899 makes it unlawful for anyone to pollute a navigable waterway of the United States (including rivers, lakes, streams, and harbors) without a permit from the U.S. Army Corps of Engineers. The law also provides that a citizen who reports a polluter will receive half of the fine if the polluter is convicted and fined. Thus, if a citizen reports a polluting company to the police and the government secures a conviction, and the company is fined $2,000, then the citizen collects $1,000. The Federal False Claims Act provides for a 25 percent finders fee going to the person who blows the whistle on corporations or individuals who defraud the government. This type of provision should be added to all federal laws governing corporate activity, in an effort to supplement federal enforcement agents and encourage an active citizenry in corporate crime control.[112]

25. Strengthen Laws Protecting Whistle-Blowers.

An employee of a corporation who witnesses wrongful, violent, or criminal corporate activity often must choose between his or her job and reporting the activity to the police. Because such a choice runs counter to the public policy of encouraging citizens to report criminal activity to the authorities, laws have been enacted to protect whistle-blowers who work for the government, and some states have passed laws to protect whistle-blowers who work in either the public or private sector. The federal government should step in to enact a protection statute for whistle-blowers that applies to all employees, be they public or private. That law should include a provision that forbids employers from discharging, threatening, or otherwise discriminating against an employee because that employee had reported or was about to report a violation of state, local, or federal law. This legislation should also include a comprehensive bill of rights protecting employees' rights of free speech against a powerful corporation bent on reprisal.[113]

26. Strengthen and Enforce Code of Ethics Governing Lawyers' Duties to the Public.

The American Bar Association's Code of Ethics imposes upon a lawyer the duty to represent a client zealously within the bounds of the law and at the same time an obligation to treat with consideration all persons involved in the legal process and to avoid the infliction of needless harm. What happens, though, when the interest of the corporate client collides with a wider public interest? For these instances, the ABA Code of Ethics imposes upon lawyers an obligation to raise the question and resign from the case. " . . . When an action in the best interest of a client seems to be unjust, [the lawyer] may ask his client for permission to forgo such action." The code also makes it clear that a lawyer's duty to a client does not lessen the lawyer's "concurrent obligation to treat with consideration all persons involved in the legal process and to avoid the infliction of needless harm." A lawyer must thus balance his duty to his client with his duties to the public at large.

The corporate lawyer sits in a position of power that can easily be, and often is, abused. The known instances where corporate lawyers have put the public interest above the interest of a fee-paying corporate client are notable for their scarcity. State legislatures should move to redress this serious problem by imposing strict public duties upon corporate lawyers. A first step would be to impose upon corporate lawyers an ethical obligation to disclose a corporate client's secrets to others when necessary to avoid assisting a criminal or fraudulent act by the client.[114]

27. Support and Defend RICO Against Corporate Attack. Expand It.

In 1970, the United States Congress passed the Racketeering Influenced Corrupt Organizations Act (RICO). RICO provides that any pattern of personal violence, the provision of illegal goods and services (drugs, prostitution), corruption in private or public life, and various forms of fraud within a ten-year period constitutes a crime under RICO punishable by a $25,000 fine, 20 years in prison, and the forfeiture of the business involved in the crime.

The federal government can file criminal charges under RICO, and any victim can sue under RICO'S civil provision and collect treble damages. RICO went relatively unnoticed by the financial press in the U.S. when it was being applied to "organized crime," but it became the center of attention once a number of blue chip corporations were sued under RICO. The securities, banking, and accounting industries have launched a nationwide effort to overturn or amend RICO, charging that the act was never aimed at "legitimate businesses," and that the statute is being abused by lawyers going after the big money of big corporations.

RICO is the most effective federal statute in place designed to curb corporate criminal recidivism. It should be defended against unfounded corporate attack, and should be broadened so that those who repeatedly violate federal regulatory statutes, including those that govern consumer product safety and occupational health, should be subject to RICO's triple damage and criminal penalties.

28. Strengthen and Defend Product Liabilty Laws.

As the criminal law currently stands, corporations can commit violent acts that injure thousands of innocent consumers, workers, and citizens, and yet not be effectively brought to criminal justice. Sensing this injustice, the states have developed laws under which victims can sue the corporate perpetrators to recover compensatory and punitive damages. Punitive damage provisions are especially important in the realm of these product liability laws because they are an effective substitute for an ineffective criminal mechanism to punish and deter corporate wrongdoing.

Corporate interests have organized on a national level to make it much more difficult for victims to sue and gain just compensation or punitive damages. The corporate sponsors of this federal legislation call it "product liability reform," but their proposal is aimed at weakening state laws designed to protect aggrieved victims in the workplace, marketplace, and community. The integrity of these state product liability laws must be defended against unfair attack by corporate criminals and their insurance carriers.

29. Legislate Stiffer Penalties for Convicted Corporate Executives.

Corporate executives are fearful of stiff criminal sanctions such as prison and heavy fines. But on the rare occasion where a corporate executive is convicted of violating the law, the penalties provided for by law are not severe enough to make the executive sit up and listen. For example, the Consumer Product Safety Act carries with it penalties of not more than $50,000 in fines, and not more than one year in prison. The Foreign Corrupt Practices Act, not more than $10,000 and not more than five years in prison; and the Occupational Safety and Health Act, not more than $10,000, and no more than six months in prison.

For serious violations of federal laws governing corporate executives, sanctions should be raised to a maximum of $1 million in fines and 15 years in prison. Minimums of 1 year in prison and a $200,000 fine should also be written into federal corporate laws for serious violations.

30. Bar Convicted Executives from Holding Similar Office.

In 1975, Fruehauf Corporation, its chairman, and its president were found guilty of conspiring to evade more than $12 million in federal taxes. Three years later, both the chairman and the president were forced to resign. Both argued that they should be reinstated. To support their argument, they pulled together a list of 20 corporate executives who had been indicted or implicated (many convicted) in crimes but had been allowed to retain their jobs. The president and chairman were eventually reinstated.[115]

A federal law, the Landrum-Griffin Act of 1959, prohibits convicted felons from holding union office for five years following conviction, and brokers, dealers, and lawyers can lose their licenses to practice if convicted of a felony. When then should an executive of a drug manufacturing company who has been convicted of violating federal food and drug laws be allowed to return to work in the drug industry? Enactment of a provision barring corporate executives from returning to their places of employment would have both general and specific deterrent effect.

31. Impose Upon the Judiciary White-Collar Crime Sentencing Standards.

Judges are reluctant to impose effective sentences on white-collar criminals. Such laxity is fundamentally unfair; it undermines faith in the criminal justice system, and it hampers prosecutorial efforts at controlling corporate crime. Especially in the area of white-collar sentences, where judges and defendants are usually white males from the same socioeconomic class with a certain class affinity, legislatures must step in to guarantee justice. Minimum sentences must be written into statutes governing serious violations of law. In addition, sentencing guidelines for judges in the case of lesser offenses must be written so as to protect against the lenient sentences currently endemic.

32. "Execute" Corporations in Serious Cases.

Legislatures should adopt provisions to strip corporations of their charters for serious corporate violations or for recidivist behavior. Some states already have such provisions, although they are rarely invoked. In 1983, for example, the attorney general of Virginia asked the State Corporation Commission to dissolve the charter of Croatan Books Inc., a firm convicted 69 times in five years of possessing obscene films or magazines, on the ground that the company had "continued to exceed or abuse the authority conferred upon it by law."[116] In 1983, the Justice Department effectively "executed" one company (see IBT profile) when it sought

and obtained the indictment and conviction of some of the laboratory testing firm's executives on testing fraud charges. The company's reputation was so damaged by the charges and trial that
it was driven out of business.

33. Impose Effective Probation on Corporate Criminals.

In some instances, putting a corporation on probation will serve
the ends of justice to a greater degree than requiring the corporation to serve its sentence. In 1972, for example, ARCO pleaded
nolo contendere to a federal charge of spilling oil into the Chicago
Sanitary and Ship Canal. The maximum fine under the Rivers and
Harbors Act was $2,500.

ARCO had previously been convicted of the same violation,
so the judge, recognizing that the fine would have little effect on
this multibillion-dollar oil company, suspended the sentence and
put the company on probation. As a condition of this probation,
the judge ordered the company to set up and complete, within
45 days, a program to handle the oil spillage.[117]

Judges may also use probation to cure institutional problems
within the company. They may, for example, order new management procedures, revise standard operating procedures, and create
new channels of communication within the company to ensure
compliance with laws.

34. Require Convicted Corporations
to Make Restitution to Their Victims.

Corporate criminals should be required to pay restitution to
victims of their crimes. Because corporations cannot be imprisoned
and because they can so easily absorb the fines currently being
imposed, new methods of crime control, such as requiring the company to pay for the damage inflicted, must be implemented as a
method of countering the ineffectiveness of traditional sanctioning methods.

In a similar vein, Brent Fisse suggests sanctions that facilitate
redress, such as ordering a corporation to help victims pursue civil
remedies. This might take the form of a punitive discovery order
requiring the company to turn over to civil litigants the company's
computer-based litigation support system.[118]

35. Impose Rehabilitative Sanctions on Corporations in Appropriate Circumstances.

As discussed above, it is much easier to rearrange the "psyche" of a corporation than to rearrange the psyche of an individual. Faulty standard operating procedures, ineffective communication systems, internal codes, written and unwritten, that suppress free speech within the corporation—these and other structural defects can be ordered rearranged or removed by sentencing judges who seek to prevent future criminal conduct by the corporation. Although rehabilitation of individuals is of dubious value, rehabilitation is a fundamentally sound goal in sanctioning corporations.

36. Impose Community Service Orders That Stick.

The failure of fines to curb corporate wrongdoing has created opportunities for judges to seek creative sanctioning. Community service orders and other behavioral sanctions against corporations and executives hold much promise as an effective supplement to fines. Legislatures should mandate minimum community service sentences, such as requiring the company to assist victims, ordering it to channel a certain percentage of future profits into educating the public about corporate crime and its control, or requiring the company to fund a local corporate crime prosecutor's office for a year. Sentencing judges have been noticeably lacking in imagination in this field, and they need to be prodded by legislatures committed to applying law and order to corporations.

Behavioral sanctions could also be imposed on individual corporate executives convicted of crimes. Convicted coal executives could be required to work in the mines for a year, to experience firsthand what their workers must endure. Convicted pharmaceutical executives might be required to serve in rehabilitation centers that serve children deformed as a result of medication their mothers took during pregnancy. Convicted auto executives could be ordered to work in the emergency room of a hospital for a year to experience the daily sight of humans injured or killed in auto accidents.

Sentencing guidelines should be implemented to prevent abuse of this sanctioning mechanism. Tax deductible donations to a company's favorite charity would, for example, be a less acceptable option.

37. Require a Percentage of Fines Be Paid to Support Independent Corporate Watchdogs.

In the wake of a string of revelations during the 1960s that corporate police such as the Federal Trade Commission and the Food and Drug Administration were coopted by corporate criminals, a number of private, nonprofit, independent watchdog groups have grown up to police the police and make sure they do their jobs. These groups usually run on a shoestring budget. They are nevertheless widely praised for their competent critiques and overall effectiveness.

Legislatures should require that a certain percentage of fines imposed on corporations go to support these groups. If a chemical company, for instance, is fined for dumping toxics in a river, part of that fine should be earmarked for an environmental watchdog group. Drug company fines would go to a watchdog group overseeing the pharmaceutical industry. Instead of the fine being mixed with general treasury funds, it could be specifically leveraged to keep the police, the offending corporations, and the industry on their toes and within the law.

38. Impose Equity Fines.

As discussed above, Professor John Coffee of Columbia University Law School has proposed the equity fine as a method of curbing corporate criminal behavior and as a substitute for the ineffective cash fine. As Coffee explains it, "When very severe cash fines need to be imposed on the corporation they should be imposed not in cash, but in the equity securities of the corporation. The convicted corporation should be required to authorize and issue such number of shares to the state's crime victim compensation fund as would have an expected market value equal to the cash fine necessary to deter illegal activity. Such funds should then be able to liquidate the securities in whatever manner maximizes its return."

With equity fines, much greater punishment could be imposed than with cash fines, since the market value of most corporations far exceeds the amount of cash the corporation is able to pay in cash fines. In 1983, a Canadian law commission recommended the adoption of the equity fine principle, and the United States should follow suit with an eye toward rectifying the ineffectiveness of cash fines.

39. Eliminate Country Club Prisons.

Elgin, Allenwood, Safford, Big Spring. These are the names of some of the country's Level 1 minimum security "country club prisons." Instead of fences, there are white lines to demarcate the "prison" from the free world. Inmates jog and play softball, tennis, and golf. Instead of padlocked rooms, there are sprawling lawns and manicured hedges. These are the homes of convicted corporate executives and other white-collar criminals unlucky enough to get caught by a system designed to let them off the hook.

The white-collar criminal should be sent to prison with the street criminal. The price-fixer should be housed next to the burglar, the company official whose drug company knowingly marketed unsafe drugs that killed people should be housed with other murderers. The bribe giver should be jailed with the corrupter of youth. To separate them, to put the white-collar criminal in a country club prison, is to lessen the severity of the sanction, to tell the criminal that corporate crime is really not as bad as street crime, that white-collar criminals are not really criminals at heart. Abolish country club prisons. A side benefit of ending this separation will be the improvement of prison conditions for all inmates. The white-collar criminals will insist on improvement.

40. Mandate Adverse Publicity Sanctions.

Adverse publicity is perhaps the most underutilized, underestimated sanction that effectively punishes corporate criminals and controls corporate crime. Corporations spend millions of dollars each year on what is known as "corporate image advertising"— advertising designed to make the company "look good" in the eyes of consumers, workers, citizens, and the public at large. Inevitably, they often seek to conceal and minimize publicity about their corporate criminal records.

In 1970, the U.S. National Commission on Reform of Criminal Laws proposed federal legislation that would impose adverse publicity sanctions on corporate criminals. The proposal read: "When an organization is convicted of an offense, the court may, in addition to or in lieu of imposing other authorized sanctions . . . require the organization to give appropriate publicity to the conviction by notice to the class or classes of persons or sector of the public interested in or affected by the conviction, by advertising in designated areas or by designated media, or otherwise . . . "[119]

Requiring Mobil to take out a *New York Times* ad presenting the company's criminal record would go a long way toward curbing similar crimes. Or requiring General Motors to publicize its crimes on television would be appropriate justice for a corporation that spends millions honing its public image through slick television ads. Adverse publicity sanctions are a potent tool that prosecutors and judges could use in their fight against corporate crime.

41. Limit Corporate Control Over the News Media.

Ever since Upton Sinclair and the muckrakers, journalists have been in the forefront of the corporate accountability movement. Journalists were instrumental in breaking many of the stories in the profile section of this book. For example, Morton Mintz of the *Washington Post* first wrote about the dangers of the Dalkon Shield. Bill Curtis broke the Agent Orange story when he was a reporter with a local television station in Chicago. And the London *Sunday Times* Insight Team led the campaign to force Distillers Ltd. to settle with the thalidomide victims. The type of investigative journalism that pries into corporate wrongdoing, however, is becoming more and more rare as the industry becomes more and more concentrated in the hands of a few corporations.

According to Ben H. Bagdikian, a professor of journalism at the University of California, Berkeley, most major American media today—newspapers, magazines, radio, television, books, and movies—are controlled by 50 very large corporations. Twenty corporations control more than half the 61 million daily newspapers sold every day; 20 corporations control more than half the revenues of the country's 11,000 magazines; 3 corporations control most of the revenues in radio; 11 corporations control most of the revenues in all kinds of books; and 4 corporations control most of the revenues in motion pictures.

In addition to outright ownership, corporations control media through heavy advertising budgets. The eye-opening statistics on the abject failure of the major magazines to investigate the tobacco industry indicate the extent of this influence (see Profile #36, Tobacco).

Congress must act to limit control of the media by large corporations. Such actions could include limiting the number of newspapers (based on circulation) that a corporation may own and setting guidelines for the democratic control of new media, such as cable.[120]

42. Increase Surveillance and Prosecution of False Statements and Perjury.

In 1980, the Public Citizen Litigation Group conducted a survey of corporations that engaged in what the group termed "crosstown hypocrisy." In one instance, B.F. Goodrich, General Tire and Rubber, and Goodyear filed sworn affidavits in the U.S. Supreme Court claiming that the benzene standard would shut down their tire manufacturing operations—and then either told their shareholders that the standard would have no material impact on their operations or told them nothing at all. In another example, VEPCO informed its shareholders that it could not estimate the cost of the proposed hazardous waste regulations; two weeks later VEPCO filed specific cost estimates with the Environmental Protection Agency. The report found 45 companies engaged in this type of hypocrisy.

This one survey indicates the scope of the problem of corporate lying, a problem given little attention by journalists, academics, and prosecutors. Corporate police should increase their surveillance of corporate lying.

43. Revise Business Ethics Curriculum.

Business ethics courses in America, by any standard, have been an abject failure. A survey published by the *Harvard Business Review* in the late 1970s found that half of the 1,700 corporation executives polled agreed with the statement "The American business executive tends to ignore the great ethical laws as they apply immediately to his work. He is preoccupied chiefly with gain." A 1975 survey conducted by Pitney Bowes found that 48 percent of some 500 top and middle managers said bribes should be paid in a foreign country if such practices are prevalent in that country.[121] A 1983 survey of 119 corporation codes of ethics found that the codes gave more attention to unethical conduct likely to decrease a firm's profits than to similar conduct that might increase profits. During the early 1980s, the Harvard Business School offered a course titled "Competitive Decision Making," in which students were encouraged to mislead, misrepresent, or blatantly lie — "strategic misrepresentation," the instructor called it — in an effort to reach agreement with an adversary group, such as a union. The highest grade in the course went to a student who believed that in business, morality was irrelevant and the question of ethics was no real issue because "that's the way the world is."

Business schools should see to it that students spend some part of their time with victims of corporate crimes. Reading hypothetical cases cannot match the experience of talking with a coal miner about black lung, or hearing from an automobile accident survivor about unsafe automobiles. State legislatures should set minimum competency requirements in business ethics.

44. Free Lawmaking Bodies from Corporate PAC Control.

Through a process of "legalized corruption," in the words of sociologist Amitai Etzioni, corporations are funneling millions of dollars into political coffers in an effort to define the law under which they must operate. This process has been well documented in recent years by numerous reports, books, and news articles.

Congress must act to reduce the costs of campaigning by allowing free media time for candidates for political office, limiting Political Action Committee (PAC) contributions to campaign funds, and authorizing the public financing of congressional campaigns.[122]

45. Discourage Investments in Criminally Recidivist Companies.

Once a reliable index of corporate criminality and social irresponsibility is compiled — preferably by the FBI, which has the resources to complete a comprehensive survey — pension funds, investment companies, and individual investors should be discouraged from investing in the worst companies on the list and encouraged to invest in the best companies. A number of investment companies (Calvert Social Investment, Dreyfus Third Century, Pax World Fund) already keep track of many companies and rank them based on social responsibility, but no one has yet compiled a corporate crime index.

Legislation should be passed prohibiting public pension funds from investing in criminal corporate entities.

46. Mandate Federal Chartering of Corporations.

Corporations are chartered by the states. In chartering a corporation, the state grants to it certain rights and privileges, and imposes certain duties and obligations. By demanding that corporations act responsibly and in a legal manner, states could go a long way, through the chartering process, toward bringing corporate abuses under control. The problem is that if, for example, New York decided to impose such duties upon corporations chartered in its state, the corporations would move to a state where the laws are less demanding. Today, most of the major corporations have fled to Delaware, a state with the least restrictive chartering law, a state that has been called the "Las Vegas of corporate chartering."

Given the giant size of the corporations being chartered in Delaware, it is fantasy to believe that states will be able to exert the necessary legal control over these companies. Congress should pass a federal chartering act for large corporations. Through the chartering mechanism, the federal government could use its power to grant, deny, revoke, and modify charters based on the legal record of the company. A company that is irresponsible and a criminal recidivist could have its charter revoked or modified.[122A]

47. Outlaw Job Blackmail.

Corporations often seek to avoid compliance with federal laws, especially environmental laws, by threatening to close a factory and leave town unless the environmental police back off. In 1980, for example, the Anaconda Copper Company announced it was "suspending operations indefinitely" at its Anaconda, Montana, smelter because, the company claimed, meeting environmental requirements for the plant were too costly. The announcement left 1,000 workers out of work. Residents of the small town turned their anger on environmental activists. Meeting with the governor's staff, some workers, following the Anaconda line, carried signs that read "Our Babies Can't Eat Clean Air."

Anaconda tried to paint the issue as one of jobs versus environment, when in fact the evidence is overwhelming, from this and other cases, that corporations use the threat of unemployment to gain relief from minimum environmental, health and safety standards, and other controls, irrespective of the facts of employment. Congress should outlaw this type of job blackmail, making it a criminal offense to threaten workers' jobs in the context of an environmental battle.[123]

48. Make It a Crime for a Corporation to Have a Faulty System for Ensuring Compliance with the Law.

Most corporations promulgate standard operating procedures (SOPs) for executives to use in implementing corporate strategy. Congress should make it illegal for a corporation to have an SOP that reasonably allows employees to execute their responsibilities in an illegal manner. SOPs might also require, for example, that a scientist who spots some flaw in a product or process should send such information to the chief executive officer or to the general counsel. By encouraging a free flow of information from all parts of the company structure to the top, the law relieves the executives of the oft invoked excuse, "I didn't know anything about this."

49. Prohibit Criminal Companies from Getting Government Grants, Licenses, or Contracts.

For many corporations, especially those in the defense industry, the government is the best customer. To obtain government grants or contracts, corporations must first meet certain federal requirements, but the government should use its economic purchasing power more effectively to bring corporate criminals into line. One way would be to deny government moneys to any corporation with a poor legal record. Standards would have to be set—again, probably through FBI statistics—to determine the legal, ethical, and social standing of corporations.

Currently, the Federal Communications Commission and the Nuclear Regulatory Commission both look at an applicant's corporate character, including its legal records, before considering whether to grant licenses. But the NRC has never defined its character requirement, and Congress is looking at imposing strict guidelines. All corporations seeking to do business with the federal government should be required to meet strict character requirements.

50. Expand Corporate and White-Collar Crime Programs of the National Institute for Justice and Bureau of Justice Statistics.

The National Institute for Justice (NIJ) is the leading criminal justice research agency in the country. Its mandate is to study all elements of the criminal justice system, with emphasis on preventing and reducing crime. The Bureau of Justice Statistics provides a variety of statistical services for the criminal justice community. Both are federal research agencies that have relegated corporate crime to a footnote in their programs. For each of the years 1982 through 1986, for example, NIJ's budget has been $19.4 million. And for each of those years, its budget for white-collar and corporate crime has been less than 1 percent of the annual budget, with zero dollars spent on white-collar and corporate crime in 1982 and 1986. And the National Crime Justice Reference Service, which has one of the world's largest data bases on research on criminal justice, has only 1.8 to 3 percent of its entries on white-collar and corporate crime. Congress should require that basic research into corporate crime be given equal footing with street crime.[124]

Notes

1. From the 36 profiles that follow this section.
2. *America the Poisoned,* by Lewis Regenstein. Acropolis Books, Washington, D.C., 1982, p. 45.
3. "Crime and Punishment," by Francis Flaherty. *Progressive,* August 1984.
4. "Rummel v. Estelle: Mockingbirds Among the Brethren," by Kenneth Lasson. 8 *American Criminal Law Review* 441 at 442, Winter 1980.
5. *The Limits of the Criminal Sanction,* by Herbert Packer. Stanford University Press, Stanford, California, 1968, p. 364.
6. "Criminal Charges on the Rise for Workplace Injuries, Deaths," by Rick Kendall. *Occupational Hazards,* December 1985, p. 49.
7. *Where the Law Ends,* by Christopher Stone. Harper Torchbooks, New York, 1975, p. 10.
8. *The Closed Enterprise System,* by Mark J. Green. Viking Compass, New York, 1972, p. 48.
9. *White-Collar Crime: The Uncut Version* (updated), by Edwin Sutherland. Yale University Press, New Haven, 1983, p. 54.
10. "Consent Decrees in Antitrust Enforcement: Some Thoughts and Proposals." 53 *Iowa Law Review* 938 at 988 (1968).
11. *White-Collar Crime,* Sutherland, p. 56.
12. Ibid., p. 58.
13. Ibid., p. 54.
14. "Who Is the Criminal?" by Paul W. Tappan. *American Sociological Review,* vol. 12 (1947) pp. 96–102.
15. *White-Collar Crime,* Sutherland, p. 46.
16. Ibid., p. 49.
17. *Illegal Corporate Behavior,* by Marshall Clinard. U.S. Department of Justice, Washington, D.C., October 1979, p. 19.
18. "Criminological Perspectives on Corporate Regulation: Review of Recent Research," by Gilbert Geis. Paper presented at conference on Contemporary Problems of Corporate Regulation, Hyatt Regency Hotel, San Antonio, November 3, 1983, p. 6.
19. "On Theory and Action for Corporate Crime Control," by John Braithwaite and Gilbert Geis. *Crime and Delinquency,* April 1982, p. 294.
20. "Reflections on Corporate Crime: Law in Search of Theory and Scholarship," by Leonard Orland. 17 *American Criminal Law Review* 506, Spring 1980.
21. Ibid., p. 508.
22. "How Lawless Are Big Companies?" *Fortune,* December 11, 1980.
23. "Corporate Crime: The Untold Story," *U.S. News & World Report,* September 6, 1982.

24. "Developments in the Law—Corporate Crime: Regulating Corporate Behavior Through Criminal Sanctions," 92 *Harvard Law Review* 1227, April 1979.

25. *Illegal Corporate Behavior,* Clinard, p. 14.

26. Ibid., p. 16.

27. "The Consequences of White-Collar Crime," by Robert F. Meier and James F. Short, Jr., in *Development of a Research Agenda on White Collar Crime,* November 1980, p. 29.

28. *Illegal Corporate Behavior,* Clinard, p. 16.

29. *Retreat From Safety: Reagan's Attack on America's Health,* by Joan Claybrook and the Staff of Public Citizen. Pantheon, New York, 1984, p. 60.

30. Ibid., p. 78.

31. *White-Collar Crime,* Sutherland, p. 15.

32. Ibid., p. 264.

33. 41 *Harvard Law Review* at 80 (1950).

34. *Illegal Corporate Behavior,* Clinard, p. 123.

35. Ibid., p. 81.

36. "How Lawless Are Big Companies?" *Fortune,* December 1, 1980, p. 57.

37. "Corporate Crime: The Untold Story," *U.S. News & World Report,* September 6, 1982.

38. See, for example, Posner, "Optimal Sentences for White-Collar Criminals," 17 *American Criminal Law Review* at 409; Becker, "Crime and Punishment: An Economic Approach," 76 *Journal of Political Economy* 169; Kadish, "Some Observations on the Use of Criminal Sanctions in Enforcing Economic Regulations," 30 *U Chicago Law Review* 423; "Developments in the Law—Corporate Crime: Regulating Corporate Behavior Through Criminal Sanctions," 92 *Harvard Law Review,* 1227, 1365–75; *The Limits of the Criminal Sanction,* by Herbert Packer, Stanford University Press, 1968, p. 361.

39. "On Theory and Action for Corporate Crime Control," Braithwaite and Geis, p. 292.

40. "Reconstructing Corporate Criminal Law: Deterrence, Retribution, Fault, and Sanctions," by Brent Fisse. 56 *Southern California Law Review* 1143.

41. "Developments in the Law—Corporate Crime: Regulating Corporate Behavior Through Criminal Sanctions," 92 *Harvard Law Review* 1227 at 1368.

42. *The Limits of the Criminal Sanction,* Packer (1968) pp. 361–62.

43. *The Impact of Publicity on Corporate Offenders,* by Brent Fisse and John Braithwaite. State University of New York Press, Albany, 1984, p. 232.

44. Robert Gordon, quoted in "Reconstructing Corporate Criminal Law," Fisse, at 1155.

45. "Reconstructing Corporate Criminal Law," Fisse, at 1156.

46. "Developments in the Law—Corporate Crime," 92 *Harvard Law Review* 1227 at 1241.

47. Ibid., at 1254.

48. "Reconstructing Corporate Criminal Law," Fisse, at 1191.

49. Ibid., at 1195.

50. Ibid., at 1198.

51. *Corporate Crime in the Pharmaceutical Industry*, by John Braithwaite. Routledge & Kegan Paul, London, 1984, p. 305.

52. "Deterring Corporate Crime: Adapting Legal Sanctions to Organizational Realities," Senior Thesis of David M. Howard, Princeton University, 1981, p. 80.

53. "Reflections on Corporate Crime," Orland, p. 518.

54. "Activist's Goodbye," *Washington Post*, July 17, 1984.

55. *Corporate Crime*, by Marshall Clinard and Peter Yeager. Free Press, New York, 1980, p. 124.

56. Ibid., p. 291.

57. *Where the Law Ends*, by Christopher Stone. Harper Torchbooks, New York, 1975, p. 65.

58. "Deterring Corporate Crime," by David Howard, Princeton Thesis, p. 89.

59. "Sentencing the White-Collar Offender," by Kenneth Mann, Stanton Wheeler, and Austin Sarat. 17 *American Criminal Law Review* 479 at 486, Spring 1980.

60. *Corporate Crime*, Clinard, p. 288.

61. Ibid.

62. "Sentencing the White-Collar Offender," Mann, Wheeler, and Sarat, p. 479.

63. Ibid., at 486.

64. Ibid., at 488.

65. Ibid., at 491.

66. "Deterring Corporate Crime," Howard, p. 88.

67. *Corporate Crime*, Clinard, p. 287.

68. "Deterring Corporate Crime," Howard, p. 93.

69. *Corporate Crime*, Clinard, p. 293.

70. "Deterring Corporate Crime," Howard, p. 94.

71. "Developments in the Law: Corporate Crime," 92 *Harvard Law Review* 1227 at 1365.

72. *Corporate Crime in the Pharmaceutical Industry*, Braithwaite, p. 331.

73. K. Elzinger and W. Breit, *The Antitrust Penalties*, (1976) quoted in "'No Soul to Damn: No Body to Kick' An Unscandalized Inquiry Into

the Problem of Corporate Punishment," by John C. Coffee, Jr. 79 *Michigan Law Review* 386 at 406, January 1981.

74. *To Punish or Persuade: Enforcement of Coal Mine Safety,* by John Braithwaite. SUNY Press, Albany, 1985.

75. *Where the Law Ends,* Stone, p. 57.

76. "No Soul to Damn," Coffee, at 389.

77. Ibid., at 390.

78. "Just Deserts," by John Braithwaite. 73 *Journal of Criminal Law and Criminology* 757.

79. "No Soul to Damn," Coffee, at 393.

80. Statement of Senator Charles Percy before Subcommittee on Energy, Nuclear Proliferation, and Government Processes of the Committee on Governmental Affairs, Hearing on Criminal Fine Collections, August 3, 1983.

81. Ibid.

82. *To Punish or Persuade,* Braithwaite, p. 89.

83. "Va. Moves to Get Rid of Bookstore," by Fred Hiatt and Molly Moore. *Washington Post,* January 21, 1983, p. 184.

84. "On Theory and Action for Corporate Crime Control," Braithwaite and Geis, p. 310.

85. *The Impact of Publicity on Corporate Offenders,* Fisse and Braithwaite, p. 249.

86. Ibid., p. 287.

87. Ibid., p. 312.

88. "No Soul To Damn," Coffee, p. 386.

89. "A Slap on the Wrist for the Kepone Mob," by Christopher Stone. *Business and Society Review,* Summer 1977, Number 22, p. 8.

90. "Community Service Sanctions Against Corporations," by Brent Fisse. 5 *Wisconsin Law Review* 970 at 974.

91. *Deterring Corporate Crime,* Howard, p. 34.

92. "Reconstructing Corporate Criminal Law," Fisse, at 1441.

93. "Community Service Sanctions," by Fisse, at 980.

94. "Deterring Corporate Crime," Howard, p. 95.

95. "Criminal Charges on the Rise for Workplace Injuries, Deaths," Kendall, p. 49.

96. *Data Sources on White-Collar Lawbreaking,* by Albert J. Reiss, Jr. and Albert D. Fiderman. U.S. Department of Justice, National Institute of Justice, Washington, D.C., September 1980.

97. Securities and Exchange Commission, Form 8-K, Item 3.

98. "Judge Asserts IBM Violated An Order," by Morton Mintz. *Washington Post,* March 7, 1973.

99. *Unsafe At Any Speed,* by Ralph Nader. Bantam Books, New York, May 1973, p. vii.

100. "Document Retention and Destruction: Practical, Legal, and

Ethical Considerations," by John Fedders and Lauryn Guttenplan. 56 *Notre Dame Lawyer* 5 at 20, 1980.

101. *Discretionary Justice: A Preliminary Inquiry,* by Kenneth Culp Davis. Louisiana State University Press, Baton Rouge, 1969.

102. For details on Reagan's cutbacks at the federal corporate crime police agencies, see: *Retreat from Safety: Reagan's Attack on America's Health,* by Joan Claybrook and the Staff of Public Citizen, Pantheon, New York, 1984; *A Season of Spoils: The Story of the Reagan Administration's Attack on the Environment,* by Jonathan Lash, Katherine Gillman, and David Sheridan, Pantheon, New York, 1984.

102A. *Duncan v. Louisiana,* 391 US 145 (1968).

103. *Corporate Crime in the Pharmaceutical Industry,* Braithwaite, p. 340.

104. "Officials Come and Go, Ethics Stay," by David Burnham. *New York Times,* August 31, 1986.

105. *Corporate Crime in the Pharmaceutical Industry,* Braithwaite, p. 342.

106. "Deterring Illegal Corporate Behavior in Complex Organizations," by J.W. Doig, D.E. Phillips, and T. Manson, in *Criminal Justice Ethics,* Winter/Spring 1984, p. 46.

107. "Consumer Guidelines New Bugaboo," *Charleston Gazette,* June 20, 1984.

108. For an interesting critique see, "Rescuing the Private Attorney General: Why the Model of the Lawyer as Bounty Hunter Is Not Working," by John C. Coffee, Jr. *Maryland Law Review,* vol. 42, no. 21, p. 215 (1983).

109. For a comprehensive reporter see "Class Action Reports: A Bi-Monthly of Private Attorney General and Public Interest Law," edited by Beverly Moore, Jr., 4900 Massachusetts Ave., N.W., Washington, D.C. 20016.

110. "Program of the Committee on Federal Regulation of Securities," 30 *Business Lawyer* 1303 at 1317 and 1335.

111. *To Punish or Persuade,* Braithwaite, p. 89.

112. *How to Stop Corporate Polluters and Make Money Doing It,* by William H. Brown. Bellerophon Books, San Francisco, (1972); see also, *Environmental Law,* by William H. Rodgers Jr. West Publishing Company, St. Paul, 1977, p. 396.

113. For ideas on an employee bill of rights see, *Taming the Giant Corporation,* by Ralph Nader, Mark Green, and Joel Seligman. W.W. Norton, New York, 1976, p. 180; also see "Statuary Protection of Whistle-blowers in the Federal Executive Branch," by Robert G. Vaughn. 1982, *University of Illinois Law Review* 615; *Truth and Consequence: Seven Who Would Not be Silenced,* by Greg Mitchell. Dembner, New York, 1981;

Whistle Blowing: Loyalty and Dissent in the Corporation, ed. by Alan F. Westin. McGraw-Hill, New York, 1981; and *Whistle Blowing,* ed. by Ralph Nader, Peter Petkas, and Kate Blackwell. Viking, New York 1972.

114. American Bar Association Model Code of Professional Responsibility, 1981, Ethical Consideration 7-9 and 7-10. For an overview of corporate lawyers in America, see *The Other Government: The Unseen Power of Washington Lawyers,* by Mark Green. Grossman/Viking, New York, 1975; *The Superlawyers: The Small and Powerful World of the Great Washington Law Firms,* by Joseph Goulden. Weigbright and Talley, New York, 1971; *Lawyers on Trial,* by Philip Stern. Times Books, New York, 1980.

115. *Corporate Crime,* Clinard and Yeager, p. 295.

116. "Va. Moves to Get Rid of Bookstores," by Fred Hiatt and Molly Moore, *The Washington Post,* January 21, 1983, p. 81.

117. *Where the Law Ends,* Stone, p. 184. "Corporate Contributions to Charity as a Condition of Probation under the Federal Probation Act." *Journal of Corporation Law,* Winter 1984, p. 243.

118. "Reconstructing Corporate Criminal Law," Fisse, at 1232.

119. *The Impact of Publicity on Corporate Offenders,* Fisse and Braithwaite, p. 312.

120. *The Media Monopoly,* by Ben H. Bagdikian. Beacon Press, Boston, 1983, p. 4.

121. "White-Collar Subversives," by Donald R. Cressey. *Center Magazine,* November/December 1978, p. 44.

122. *PACs Americana,* by Edward Roeder. Sunshine Services, Washington, D.C., October 1982.

122A. See *Taming the Giant Corporation,* by Ralph Nader, Mark Green, and Joel Seligman. Norton, New York, 1976.

123. *Fear At Work: Job Blackmail, Labor, and the Environment,* by Richard Kazis and Richard L. Grossman. Pilgrim Press, New York, 1982.

124. Personal communication, Terry Simpson, program analyst, National Institute for Justice, December 17, 1986. Personal communication, Carol Kaplan, chief, federal statistics branch, Bureau of Justice Statistics, December 18, 1986.

PART TWO
Profiles

A Note on the Profiles

To read about Agent Orange is to understand that the companies that produced and marketed that defoliant didn't much care about the effects on the exposed human population. To read about the Pinto is to learn that Ford Motor Company didn't emphasize building safety into its automobile because, as one Ford executive put it, "Safety doesn't sell." And to read about Love Canal is to be informed that Hooker Chemical & Plastics Company was indifferent to the effects of its toxic dumping on neighborhood communities.

Read separately, these profiles of corporate crime and violence show how in a technological age one corporation's wrongful conduct can adversely affect the health and well-being of, and put at great risk, thousands of workers, consumers, and neighbors and their environments. To read the profiles together is to see more than just isolated instances of errant corporate behavior. Patterns emerge, including destruction of documents, suppression of dissent within the corporate bureaucracy, and intricate cover-ups and stonewalls, which will aid public policy experts in designing strategies to control corporate crime. Patterns of victim behavior emerge that will aid future efforts to gain justice for victims from corporate wrongdoers.

A number of factors helped determine which of the hundreds of candidates for this section would be profiled. First of these was the nature and extent of the victimization. Second was the extent of the corporate knowledge. Did the company know the degree of risk of injury it was posing to the class of victims or was it merely reckless or negligent in the commission of the action that caused the injury? Also, what was the corporate reaction to the ensuing disaster? Did the company stonewall and delay or prevent compensation to the victims (as did Chemie Grunenthal in the thalidomide disaster, and J.P. Stevens in illegally thwarting a unionization effort)?

Those corporate crimes and acts of violence profiled here, while egregious enough, cannot in any sense be deemed the "worst." They are only "bad enough" and visible enough for plaintiff lawyers, corporate crime police, other government agencies, and investigative reporters to have ferreted out the documentary information.

1
Agent Orange

"Some of these executives from the chemical companies
belong in jail. We have veterans and children who have spent
years trying to cope with catastrophic disabilities without help.
Now that we know who is responsible, we want help for the
veterans and we want the people who sold them out to go to
prison for it. They're criminals. They knew."

—Michael Ryan, Vietnam veteran, 1982[1]

No RECTUM. NO URETHRA. Two uteri. Two vaginas. Four ovaries.
Minus one elbow. Minus one wrist. Spine problems. Muscle problems. Limp arm. Missing fingers. A hole in the heart. Two cervixes.

She was born that way. A beautiful baby, entering a world with
major defects throughout her body, defects that would keep her
in the hospital for three months, would force her to make in-
numerable return trips to the hospital for delicate operations to
keep her alive; defects that would keep her in diapers, and in a
wheelchair for the rest of her life.[2]

In *Kerry: Agent Orange and an American Family*, the Ryans
tell this story of their daughter who, despite her deformities, was
a lovable baby and could turn heads with the most adorable smile.
When she was born, her parents were understandably overcome
by a mixture of emotions. It was the first child for Maureen and
Michael Ryan, and they were both thrilled by the new addition
to their world. From the beginning, however, their happiness was
tempered by fear that the birth problems would jeopardize their
firstborn.

Not knowing the cause of Kerry's birth defects, Michael and Maureen at first blamed themselves. But the blame was difficult to accept, especially for Maureen, who considered herself to be somewhat of a "health nut" when it came to food and nutrition. Maureen figured that if she took care of herself during her pregnancy, she would at the same time be taking care of her baby. She could not have known that eating the purest of foods, drinking the most sparkling clean water, and breathing the freshest of air probably would not have saved her baby from the deformities that afflict Kerry today.

Kerry was conceived after her father returned from Vietnam, where he spent much of his time stationed in jungle areas that had been sprayed with a chemical known as Agent Orange. The army's goal was to defoliate large areas of Vietnamese forest with Agent Orange—especially forests in the areas believed to be hideouts for Viet Cong and North Vietnamese soldiers. By destroying their cover, the army hoped to destroy the enemy's hideouts. Agent Orange and other deadly chemicals were also sprayed on foodgrowing areas—land used to grow rice, melon, bananas, breadfruit, mango, and other crops. The idea was to destroy the food so the enemy couldn't eat.

Agent Orange was popular with the army's defoliation crews because it was so effective. A dose of the synthetic growth hormone would send tropical plants into a wild cancerous growth spree until they got so big they would explode into limp nothingness. Two-foot-long bananas, tree-sized weeds, and mangled mangroves would lie dead at the basin in hundreds of acres of mutilated forests, victims of Agent Orange. After the spraying, the jungles went silent. There were no more sounds of insects, birds, or other animals. Fish floated in the rivers. The soldiers labeled Agent Orange-sprayed forests, "the land of the dead."[3]

The aerial spray flight of the army's 309th Aerial Commando Squadron had seven aircraft and went out on spraying missions twice a day, six days a week. Between 1962 and 1970, the U.S Army, working under the label "Operation Hades," later known as "Operation Ranch Hand," dumped tons of Agent Orange and other killer chemicals onto six million acres of South Vietnam.[4] The sign above the ready room of the 309th Aerial Commando Squadron encouraged the spray flightmasters to do their jobs well. It read, "ONLY YOU CAN PREVENT FORESTS."[5]

The soldiers who sprayed the chemicals and patrolled the forests afterward remember well the sickly sweet smell that lingered in the atmosphere. They should have guessed that a chemical that could cause plants to grow fantastic cancerous growths and entire forests to die off in a matter of days might have dangerous consequences for their own future health. But it was wartime, and the men were occupied with thoughts of bullets, grenades, and shrapnel; of getting out of Vietnam alive. Even if they were aware of the dangers posed by the chemicals—which most of them weren't, since neither the army nor the chemical manufacturers had warned them of the possible damage that Agent Orange could inflict on their bodies and the bodies of their children—cancer, deformities, and genetic damage seemed remote given the immediate need to survive, and to leave Vietnam.

Early in the war, there were reports that Vietnamese peasants who were living in the sprayed areas and perhaps eating contaminated food and drinking contaminated water were getting ill and producing babies with gross birth deformities. Because these early reports were coming from Hanoi, they were quickly discounted by American military personnel as Communist propaganda..

Agent Orange was no ordinary defoliant. There were other effective jungle-killer chemicals that could force the enemy to seek new hideouts, but Agent Orange was a superagent with super ingredients. Its active ingredients were 2,4,5-T and 2,4-D, and with 2,4,5-T came a deadly sidekick contaminant, dioxin.

Today, dioxin is known as one of the most deadly manmade chemicals. Three ounces of dioxin placed in New York City's drinking water supply could wipe out the city's entire populace. "Dioxin is the most poisonous small molecule known to man. It is one of the most powerful carcinogens known," says Matthew Meselson, professor of biochemistry at Harvard. "We have not yet found any dosage at which it is safe, at which it has no observable effect . . . it is possible that dioxin is cumulative in our bodies. It is quite stable and is soluble in fat, but not water, and will build up in body fat."[6]

An estimated 130 pounds of dioxin was dumped on Vietnam before 1970, and some of that was inevitably brought home by two million GIs who sprayed or patrolled the dense jungle forests of South Vietnam and possibly ate contaminated food or drank contaminated water. Barry Commoner agrees with Meselson about the possibility that dioxin accumulates in the body, and that when dioxin-contaminated individuals lose weight, the dioxin breaks down and is carried into the bloodstream. Many Vietnam veterans have reported the now classic symptoms of dioxin poisoning: irrational emotional outbursts, numbing of the hands and feet, an acne-like rash covering the entire body, and sharp stomach pains. "It now appears that dioxin may be a kind of toxicological time bomb," Commoner observes, "and that people exposed to it may exhibit harmful symptoms [which] appear only years later."[7]

Since Vietnam, other parts of the world have learned firsthand of dioxin's toxic effects. In Niagara Falls, New York, a chemical company dumped tons of toxic chemicals, including dioxin, in landfills throughout the city, and deadly chemicals migrated out of the landfills, contaminating neighboring human populations and forcing the evacuation of hundreds of families. (See Profile #20, Love Canal.) In Seveso, Italy, when a chemical plant exploded, dioxin was spewed into the atmosphere; animals died, hundreds of acres of land were contaminated, people became ill, women suffered spontaneous abortions, and the towns for miles around were evacuated. In the northwestern corner of the United States, where the U.S. Forest Service sprayed dioxin-contaminated 2,4,5-T onto woodlands in Oregon, residents in the nearby town of Alsea complained of the high rate of miscarriages. A subsequent study of the area by the U.S. Environmental Protection Agency confirmed residents' fears. Alsea residents reported a high rate of miscarriages to EPA. Based on this and other evidence, the EPA banned most uses of 2,4,5-T in the United States.[8]

The EPA ban was handed down in 1979, ten years after the U.S. Army stopped using the defoliant in Vietnam under pressure from environmental groups in the United States, but Dow Chemical, the major manufacturer of 2,4,5-T in the United States, did not have to wait for the EPA studies or for the tragedies in Oregon, Love Canal, Seveso, and Vietnam to learn about the dangerous effects of the toxic dioxin on human population.

"Long before the advent of 2,4,5-T—in fact since the mid-nineteen thirties" writes Thomas Whiteside, in his book *The Pendulum and the Toxic Cloud,* "the Dow people had known that various polychlorinated derivatives of chlorophenols (as well as 2,4,5-T) had produced chloracne (a severe form of acne)-like symptoms among workers exposed to them. Dow's 2,4,5-trichlorophenol appears to have been no exception."[9] According to Whiteside, when

Dow began expanding its production of 2,4,5-T in 1964 to provide Agent Orange for Vietnam, 70 Dow employees who worked
at the Dow 2,4,5-T factory in Midland, Michigan, contracted cases
of chloracne, 12 of them severe. But the 1964 outbreak was only
one in a long line of case studies of 2,4,5-T contamination to human
populations.

According to documents revealed in 1983, during the civil litigation against the chemical manufacturers of Agent Orange, Dow
had for years been receiving reports of severe chloracne associated
with the manufacture of chlorophenols. In 1937, some of the 400
lumber workers using Dowicide H (tetrachlorophenol) developed
cysts, pustules (chloracne), urinary disturbances, skin lesions lasting
seven years, and marked hyperkeratosis. In 1949, 228 workers at
a Monsanto 2,4,5-T plant in Nitro, West Virginia, developed chloracne as the result of an industrial accident, and the chloracne continued to afflict workers at the plant for 20 years. In the words of
Monsanto's medical director, "I don't want to be cynical, but are
there any employees in the Department who don't have chloracne
already?"[10]

Also in 1949, 10 workers exposed in a West German plant during the manufacture of 2,4,5-trichlorophenol, the raw material from
which 2,4,5-T is made, developed neuralgic pains, heart disorders,
and chloracne. Four years later, at a 2,4,5-T plant owned by BASF
in Germany, 11 of the workers developed chloracne as a result of
the chemicals that spewed forth from the explosion of a plant reactor containing 2,4,5-T. Again in 1963, a 2,4,5-T factory owned by
N. V. Phillips of the Netherlands exploded, exposing 50 workers
to the chemical. These workers soon developed chloracne and
suffered damage to their internal organs and serious psychological
disturbances.[11]

In 1956, a number of workers in a Diamond Alkali (now Diamond Shamrock) plant that manufactured 2,4,5-T developed por-
phyria cutanea tarda, hyperpigmentation, and hirsutism. In 1954,
a number of workers at a C. H. Boehringer plant who were exposed
in the manufacture of 2,4,5-TCP and 2,4,5-T developed liver damage and chloracne.[12]

On April 15, 1970, Julius E. Johnson, vice president of research
for Dow, testified before a subcommittee of the U.S. Senate Committee on Commerce that the company knew about the dangers
of 2,4,5-T well before U.S. fighting troops were exposed to Agent

Orange. Johnson stated: "Since 1950 we have been keenly aware of the possibility of a highly toxic impurity being formed in 2,4,5-trichlorophenol as a side reaction under conditions of elevated processing temperatures. . . . We also knew that if the impurity was present in the 2,4,5-trichlorophenol it could be carried forward to the product, 2,4,5-T."[13]

Dow has consistently claimed that aside from chloracne, the company did not know of any harm to humans from dioxin. In March 1983, Paul Oreffice, president of Dow, appeared on NBC's *Today Show* and claimed that "there is absolutely no evidence of dioxin doing any damage to humans except for causing something that is called chloracne. It's a rash."

But in the spring of 1983, the *New York Times* reported that Dow documents made public during the court proceedings revealed that during 1965, at a time when the government was purchasing millions of pounds of Agent Orange, Dow's toxicology director wrote in an internal report that dioxin could be "exceptionally toxic" to humans and that the company's medical director warned "fatalities have been reported in the literature." The Dow documents also showed that Dow and other companies were concerned about the chloracne outbreaks and other evidence implicating dioxin but that the company failed to turn over the damaging information to the government. By 1970, when Dow did finally warn the Defense Department about the dangers of Agent Orange, the government declared that it was hearing about the problem for the first time.[14]

The Dow documents also revealed that a meeting of four chemical manufacturers was held on March 24, 1965, at Dow headquarters in Midland, Michigan to discuss the health hazards of dioxin. The *New York Times* reported in April 1983 that according to one of those attending the meeting, Dow did not want its findings about dioxin made public because the situation might "explode" and generate a new wave of government regulation of the chemical industry. A second scientist reported that at the meeting Dow officials had disclosed a study that showed that dioxin caused "severe" liver damage in rabbits.[15]

The Ryans and 16,000 other Vietnam veteran families went to federal court and sued Dow Chemical and six other chemical companies for billions of dollars in damages. Veterans groups estimate that of the 2.8 million U.S. soldiers who served in Vietnam, 40,000 veterans may eventually become ill or die from effects of the toxic chemicals dumped there. They may produce at least 2,000 children with deformities incurred because their fathers carried home the poisons in their bodies.

Dow Chemical and the other six chemical company defendants in the case denied any liability in the Agent Orange cases and unsuccessfully sought to blame the government for the chemically inflicted health problems. Dow sued the government, charging that if anyone was injured during Vietnam, it was the government's fault, not Dow's; and second, that since Dow was a war contractor, it was only following the government's orders.

Victor Yannacone, attorney for the Vietnam veterans in the Agent Orange case, called Dow's reasoning "utter nonsense." "The government contracted to get war materials," Yannacone argued, "but under no circumstances did the government contract to have its own men poisoned or killed."[16] More than 20,000 studies on the medical effects of 2,4,5-T provide strong evidence of the chemical's potent toxicity. A recent Swedish study of paper pulp, forestry, and sawmill workers found a highly significant fivefold excess relative risk for soft-tissue sarcomas in workers exposed primarily to 2,4,5-T and 2,4 D.[17]

In August 1982, an Illinois jury awarded nearly $58 million in damages to workers exposed to dioxin. The lawsuit stemmed from a chemical spill from a ruptured tank car in Sturgeon, Missouri, in January 1979. After the spill, workers complained of symptoms that ranged from dizziness and fatigue to impotence and loss of memory. For the first time in such a lawsuit, the jurors in this case concluded that dioxin was capable of and did cause the injury. "We wouldn't have awarded that kind of money if we didn't think dioxin was present and it has a harmful effect on people," one juror said after the trial.[18]

Nevertheless, Dow continued to argue in court and in the public forum that the company should not bear the responsibility that the vets are seeking to impose on them. One of the more revealing public defenses put forth by Dow came in the fall of 1979, when the Roman Catholic Archdiocese of Albany, a Dow stockholder, wrote to the company expressing concern over health effects attributed to Agent Orange. The archdiocese asked then Dow chairman Earle B. Barnes, "What steps, if any, is Dow Chemical taking to eliminate or minimize risks related to this product?" In response, Barnes claimed that "there is no product that we manufacture that we have more toxicology and health data on than 2,4,5-T and we consider it extremely safe."

"Unfortunately for the product," stated Barnes, "the U.S. government requisitioned its use in the Vietnam War to defoliate the jungle in the search for the Viet Cong. It therefore became a symbol of the Vietnam War that some people have become obsessed with destroying along with anything else relating to that unfortunate experience." So, according to Barnes, dioxin, made famous by the war, was "picked up by a lot of the extreme activists among the environmentalists. . . . These activists have learned the trick of the Hitler-type propaganda in Germany; that is, if you tell a lie often enough people will begin to believe it."

Barnes ended his response to the archdiocese by implying that marijuana growers in California were leading the drive against 2,4,5-T because the chemical was inadvertently destroying some of California's $900 million marijuana crop. " . . . there is a lot that doesn't always meet the eye in a single newspaper article," observed the chairman of the board of one of the world's largest chemical companies. "There are some very strong forces coming to do away with our agricultural chemical business."[19] In June 1983, Dow expanded greatly its public relations effort by announcing that it would spend $3 million on independent studies to try to show that there is no danger to humans from trace levels of dioxin.

Compared to the other six defendant chemical companies, Dow's was the "cleanest" Agent Orange—that is, it contained less dioxin than the others. Although Dow provided three-fourths of the Agent Orange to the United States for use in Vietnam, its share of the estimated $2.4 billion in damages to the veterans was only about 3 percent. Victor Yannacone, one of the attorneys representing the veterans, was about to settle the case with Dow on February 23, 1984, and then go to trial against the remaining six corporate defendants, but at the last minute, the Dow board of directors pulled out.[20]

On May 7, 1984, only hours before the consolidated Agent Orange case was to go to trial in a federal courtroom in New York, seven chemical companies, including Dow, agreed in an out-of-court settlement to pay $180 million to 16,000 veterans and their dependents. Many veterans who sought a public airing of the evidence against the manufacturers were disappointed with the settlement. "We wanted our day in court," former Marine Corps infantryman David P. Martin told reporters. "I want the truth to be told and the truth to come out."[21] "We were sold out," charged Rena Kopystenski, a spokesman for the National Vietnam Veterans Network. "The seven companies . . . got out of this for under $30 million apiece. That's not much for the thousands of lives and babies that they've destroyed." Yannacone agreed with Kopystenski, said it would be "unconscionable" for the legal team representing the plaintiffs to deduct their fees from such a "low amount," and promised to challenge the settlement. And syndicated columnist Colman McCarthy joined in with the dissenters, arguing that "Veterans are further demeaned if the word victory is attached to this settlement. The amount of money is small when spread out among 16,000 or more claimants. It is pin money for a company such as Dow which grossed $11 billion last year. Its payment is mostly covered by insurance. The day the settlement was announced, Dow's stock went up. If the word victory must be used, let it be applied to the Dow stockholders."[22]

Paul Reutershan didn't live to see the settlement—he died of cancer in December 1978. On Labor Day, 1977, Reutershan, a Vietnam veteran who came in close contact with the Agent Orange spraying operations while on tour in Vietnam, experienced sharp stomach pains. He thought it was food poisoning, but tests taken at the hospital in Connecticut revealed widespread abdominal cancer. Doctors told him he had only a few days to live. During the remaining days of his life, Reutershan toured the country, appeared on TV and radio talk shows, and tried to get the message across to his fellow Vietnam vets and to the American people that thousands of young men were injured in Vietnam by the chemical Agent Orange. He accused Dow Chemical and the United States government of his own murder, and he urged the American people to pressure the company and the government to compensate the vets for the damage inflicted on them and their families. "Agent Orange is killing me," he told audiences around the country, "and it's probably going to kill every person who came in contact with it in Vietnam."[23]

No criminal action has been brought against Dow Chemical or any other chemical company in connection with the manufacture of Agent Orange. The settlement of the civil case is currently on appeal to the U.S. Supreme Court.

Notes

1. *Kerry: Agent Orange and an American Family,* by Clifford Lindeker, with Michael and Maureen Ryan. St. Martin's Press, NY, 1982, p. 191.

2. *Kerry,* Lindeker, p. 108.

3. "The Agent Orange Time Bomb", by Matts Forbell. *Penthouse,* August 1979, p. 75.

4. Ibid.

5. *Kerry,* Lindeker, p. 46.

6. *Who's Poisoning America,* ed. by Ralph Nader, Ronald Brownstein, and John Richard. Sierra Club Books, San Francisco, 1982, p. 273.

7. "The Agent Orange Time Bomb," Forbell, p. 76.

8. *America the Poisoned,* by Lewis Regenstein. Acropolis Books, 1982, p. 53.

9. *The Pendulum and the Toxic Cloud,* by Thomas Whiteside. Yale University Press, New Haven, 1977, p. 25.

10. "Files Show Dioxin Makers Knew of Hazards," by Ralph Blumenthal. *New York Times,* July 6, 1983.

11. *The Pendulum and the Toxic Cloud,* Whiteside; *Elements of Risk,* by Cathy Trost. Times Books, 1984, p. 55.

12. "Plaintiffs' Opposition to Defendant The Dow Chemical Company's Motion for Summary Judgment on the Government Contract Defense," *In Re "Agent Orange" Product Liability Litigation,* United States District Court for the Eastern District of New York, p. 14.

13. Statement of Julius E. Johnson, vice president and director of research, Dow Chemical Company, before the Subcommittee on Energy, Natural Resources, and the Environment of the Senate Committee on Commerce, April 15, 1970.

14. "Files Show Dioxin Makers Knew of Hazards," Blumenthal.

15. "1965 Memo Shows Dow's Anxiety on Dioxin," by David Burnham. *New York Times,* April 4, 1983.

16. *Waiting for an Army to Die: The Tragedy of Agent Orange,* by Fred A. Wilcox. Random House, New York, 1983.

17. "Agent Orange Diseases: Problems of Causality, Burdens of Proof and Restitution," by Samuel S. Epstein. *Trial* magazine, November 1983, p. 91.

18. "State Jury Award of $58 Million in Dioxin Suit Hailed by Veterans," *Washington Post,* August 27, 1982.

19. Letter from Earle Barnes, chairman, Dow Chemical, to the Reverend Robert Roos, Chancellor, Archdiocese of Albany; November 1, 1979.

20. Interview with Victor Yannacone, May 9, 1984.

21. "Vietnam Veterans Divided by Agent Orange Battle," by Margot Hornblower. *Washington Post*, August 9, 1984.

22. "Agent Orange Outrage," by Colman McCarthy. *Washington Post*, May 20, 1984.

23. "The Agent Orange Time Bomb," Forbell, p. 75.

2
Bhopal

*"If there ever was a wretchedly undignified hideously helpless
form of mega-death after Hiroshima and Nagasaki, this is it."*

—Praful Bidwai, chemical engineer and investigative
reporter for the *Times of India*[1]

O N NOVEMBER 30, 1984, Anees Chishti, a journalist, went to Bhopal,
a city of 800,000 in central India, to study some aspects of Muslim
electoral behavior. He checked into the Nalanda, a small hotel in
the old city. He was probably one of the few journalists in Bhopal
on the morning of December 3, 1984. He told his story to the *Sunday Observer* of India.

I was trying to get one of the foreign stations on the radio
at about 2:30 a.m. when I felt some choking in my throat.
There was a burning sensation in the eye. I somehow
opened the door to my room. First, I thought it was a hotel
problem. I went out. I was running for some open space
where I could get some relief, but I could get relief nowhere.
When I came out I saw hordes of people moving towards
some direction. That was a ghastly experience. I saw ladies
almost undressed, straight out of the bed, children cling-
ing to their breasts, all wailing, weeping, some of them
vomiting, some of them vomiting blood, some falling down,
I now presume falling dead. . . . The sky was clear. As I was
passing, I could see the stars. I didn't smell anything, maybe

because of panic, but people were saying that it smelt of rotten almonds.[2]

As daylight broke, 20,000 persons were gathered at Bhopal's 1,000 bed Hamidia Hospital.[3] Praful Bidwai, a chemical engineer and journalist, described the situation three days later at the hospital.

> The scene is compelling in its display of death. There is something indescribable about the horror, the squalor, the sheer magnitude and force of death here. No one is counting numbers any longer. People are dying like flies. They are brought in, their chests heaving violently, their limbs trembling, their eyes blinking from photophobia. It will kill them in a few hours, more usually minutes.[4]

"It" was methyl isocyanate (MIC), a chemical used at the Union Carbide India Ltd. (UCIL) factory in Bhopal to manufacture pesticides. (Union Carbide Corporation, the Danbury, Connecticut, based multinational, owns 50.9 percent of UCIL.) The MIC production facility at the Union Carbide plant had been shut down for two months, but on the night of December 2, workers conducting routine maintenance on the unit noticed a leak. At 12:30 a.m. on December 3, the ground around one of the MIC storage tanks began to rumble. Water had entered the tank, triggering a chain reaction that created heat and pressure and led to the release of 40 tons of deadly gases into the atmosphere over Bhopal.[5]

The release of gas from the Union Carbide plant killed — conservatively — from 2,000 to 5,000 persons and injured 200,000 persons, at least 30,000 to 40,000 of them seriously, making it the world's worst industrial disaster.[6] The death figures may be low because many family members took away their dead for burial before they could be counted.[7] Many of the severely injured sustained respiratory ailments, permanent eye problems, and mental disorders. Medico Friend Circle, a Bhopal-based citizens group, conducted a survey in 1985 that found that rates of spontaneous abortions were higher among women who conceived shortly after the gas disaster than before. The group said that its findings indicate "a chronic exposure effect which could have a long-term effect on future fertility as well." In addition, a study conducted by Dr. V. R. Varma, an Indian-born pharmacologist based at McGill University in Montreal, found that about 40 percent of 865 pregnancies did not end in a live birth—much higher than what Varma claims is the normal rate of 11 percent.[8] In July 1985, Balendu Shukla, the provincial public health minister, said that six women gave birth to deformed babies after the gas leak. He linked the deformities to inhalation of MIC by the mothers.[9]

Two years after the disaster, the *Wall Street Journal* reported serious eye problems at Bhopal. The *Journal* reported that an ophthamologist at the Bhopal Eye Hospital, Dr. Lalit Mishra, was seeing 120 patients a day. While denying reports that some gas victims had gone blind, Mishra claimed that "there had been a gross change" in the eyesight of Bhopal residents since the leak.[10] Respiratory ailments, which diminish victims' capacity for strenuous activity, have contributed to psychological problems. Those ailments, combined with anxiety about possible long-term carcinogenic, mutagenic, or teratogenic effects, have increased the incidence of mental disorders, which are the second most important health consequence of the disaster—second only to respiratory problems, according to Dr. Varma.[11]

On December 4, the day after the gassing, Union Carbide chairman Warren Anderson, accompanied by other company officials, flew from the United States to India to inspect the disaster personally. Upon arrival in the Bhopal area, Anderson and two local Union Carbide officials were arrested and charged with criminal negligence. Six hours later, the three were released and ordered to pay a $2,000 bail, and Anderson was ordered to leave the country, which he planned to do in any event.[12] The charges were never pursued, which suggests that the arrests were made by the government to quell public outrage at the corporation, which became popularly known in Bhopal as "Killer Carbide," and at the government, which was widely perceived as ineffective in bringing medical relief to the victims.

Upon returning to the United States, Anderson told reporters that the purpose of his trip to India was to provide medical aid and seek the accident's cause. In a January 25, 1985, letter to shareholders, Anderson wrote, "All of us are deeply saddened by the tragedy, but proud of the way the Corporation responded." But as Stephen Adler pointed out in a firsthand report from Bhopal published in the April 1985 *American Lawyer,* Carbide's offer of

$1 million in disaster relief came to about $5 per victim, and the week after the accident, Carbide sent one shipment of medicine, sufficient for 300 to 400 persons.[13] Perhaps Anderson let out a more revealing truth when he told a reporter from *Chemical Week* magazine that one reason for his trip to Bhopal was, "You want to get together with the interested parties to say, let's not litigate."[14]

Anderson had good reasons for wanting to avoid the inevitable litigation. Even though Union Carbide repeatedly claimed that "the Indian company has nothing to do with the U.S. company," the facts indicate otherwise. Although the Bhopal plant was operated by UCIL, Union Carbide controlled UCIL.

The UCIL plant in Bhopal was storing MIC, the highly volatile and deadly gas used to make pesticides that leaked into the atmosphere on the morning of December 3, 1984. Installed at the plant was a refrigeration unit designed to keep the MIC storage tank at a temperature low enough to prevent runaway chemical reactions. But the unit was not working at the time of the accident, and the MIC in the storage tank was warmer than allowed by the plant's operating manual. "The refrigeration unit had been down over five months," Union Carbide officials admitted to a crowded March 20, 1985, press conference at Carbide's world headquarters.[15] The shutdown was a violation of plant procedures.[16]

With the refrigeration unit out of commission, it was crucial that instruments designed to measure the temperature and pressure of the gas in the storage tank be in good operating order. But the Temperature Indicator Alarm had been giving faulty readings for years. And the Pressure Indicator Control, which Bruce Agnew, editor of *Safety & Risk Management,* the magazine of the British Safety Council, likened to a "joke prop in a vintage Mickey Mouse movie," was similarly faulty.[17]

The plant also had an emergency scrubber system to neutralize gas in the event of a leak. But the scrubber system had been out of use for six weeks. The flare tower, designed as the final line of defense to burn off excess MIC, also had been closed down ten days before the fatal leak because, due to neglected maintenance, the line to the flare tower had corroded.[18]

To make matters worse, the workers operating this faulty equipment at the Bhopal plant were inadequately trained. The *New York Times* reported in January 1985 that the leak was triggered after "a worker whose training did not meet the plant's original standards was ordered by a novice supervisor to wash out a pipe that had not been properly sealed."[19] It was the mixture of water with the gas that triggered the chemical reaction that led to the gas leak.

"Everything that could possibly go wrong had gone wrong," Agnew observed. "Machinery failed; workers panicked; managers either took no decisions or took the wrong decisions."[20]

The structure of Union Carbide's relations with its subsidiaries indicates strict authority and control by the parent company. UCIL is listed on Union Carbide's consolidated balance sheet. Through its majority holding, Union Carbide had direct representation on the board of UCIL.

More important is the evidence indicating direct Union Carbide involvement in the design and operation of the Bhopal plant. According to Praful Bidwai's report of December 27, 1984, in the *Times of India,* Union Carbide designed the Bhopal plant and was responsible for inspecting and approving all major equipment installed in the factory. According to Bidwai, an engineer as well as a journalist, the Bhopal plant was "grossly underdesigned." He concluded, "Thus even if each piece of equipment had functioned as designed and the plant as a whole had been properly maintained and operated—which it evidently was not—it would still not have been possible to avert the disaster."[21]

In February 1985, Edward Munoz, a retired Union Carbide official and former managing director of UCIL, claimed in a sworn affidavit that in the early 1970s, Union Carbide insisted, over UCIL's objection, that large amounts of MIC be stored in Bhopal. In the early 1970s, Munoz "represented the Union Carbide India Ltd. position that only token storage [of the chemical at Bhopal] was necessary, preferably in small individual containers, based both on economic and safety considerations," according to the affidavit. But Union Carbide's corporate engineering group "imposed the view and ultimately made to be built [at Bhopal] large bulk storage tanks patterned on similar Union Carbide facilities at Institute, W. Va.," Munoz asserted in his affidavit.[22]

In the wake of the Bhopal disaster, a growing chorus of critics joined Munoz in disputing Union Carbide's view that "the Indian company [UCIL] has nothing to do with the U.S. company." A wide-ranging, seven-week investigation of the Bhopal disaster conducted by the *New York Times,* published in January 1985, concluded that Union Carbide "had the authority to exercise financial and technical control over its affiliate (UCIL) and the American parent used that right." The report quoted Kamal K. Pareek, senior project engineer during the building of the Bhopal plant's MIC installation: "Union Carbide had its finger on the pulse of the Bhopal plant all the time. They just didn't appreciate the information they were getting."[23]

An internal Union Carbide report supports this view. Dated May 1982, the report, submitted to Union Carbide by a team of American experts, points out major safety concerns at the Bhopal plant, including deficiencies in instrumentation and safety valves, lax maintenance procedures, and high turnover of operating and maintenance staff. The report, stamped "Business Confidential," warned that the plant presented "serious potential for sizeable releases of toxic materials." The U.S. team made numerous recommendations to rectify the deficiencies at the Bhopal plant, but according to reports from union activists, not one of the recommendations was ever implemented.[24]

After this report was sent from Union Carbide corporate headquarters to the Bhopal plant, union organizers in India appealed to U.S. management to improve safety conditions. Radhika Ramaseshan, writing in the Indian *Economic and Political Weekly,* reported that a letter was sent to the agricultural products division of Union Carbide in the United States, with a plea to appoint trained superintendents in the MIC plant. "The president was said to have replied in the negative," reported Ramaseshan, "in spite of the fact that the parent company had just then investigated the safety measures in the Bhopal plant and indicted the local management on every score."[25]

There were other warnings. Three months prior to the Bhopal gas leak, an internal Union Carbide memo warned that "a real potential for a serious incident exists" at Bhopal's sister plant in Institute, West Virginia, and that efforts to control the problem "would not be timely or effective enough to prevent catastrophic failure of the [storage] tank." The memo warned of a "runaway reaction" at the West Virginia facility.[26]

Union Carbide's culpability in the Bhopal gas leak is compounded by a history of serious accidents at the Bhopal plant. Between 1978 and 1984, there were six accidents at the plant that should have made clear to U.S. executives in Connecticut that something was grossly wrong in India:

- The alpha-napthol storage area had a huge fire on November 24, 1978, which could be controlled only after ten hours—it resulted in property damage of $5 million.
- Plant operator Mohammed Ashraf was killed by a phosgene gas leak on December 26, 1981.
- Another phosgene leak in January 1982 caused 28 injuries.
- Three electrical operators were severely burned while working on a control system panel on April 22, 1982.
- On the night of October 5, 1982, methyl isocynate escaped from a broken valve and seriously affected four workers. Several people living nearby also experienced burning in the eyes and breathing trouble due to the exposure.
- Two similar incidents were also reported in 1983.[27]

Although some residents of Bhopal were aware that pesticides were being produced at the factory, no one "had any idea that such a deadly poison was being used," according to one longtime resident. And the plant's chief medical officer, Dr. L. C. Loya, admitted that Carbide never told the community, except for a few within the medical community, of MIC's dangers.[28]

Carbide also failed to warn Bhopal's residents, many of whom lived in shantytowns surrounding the plant, immediately after the leak. The leak occurred about 12:30 A.M. on December 3, but most survivors don't recall an alarm until between 2:00 A.M. and 2:30 A.M. "The saabs of Union Carbide never sounded the siren," recalled one survivor. "If they had done so before or just after the gas leaked out, we would have known what to do. We'd at least have had a chance to run. We have had phosgene leaks and alarms in the past. I lost my wife and two sons only because they didn't warn us. . . . These people are criminals, butchers, worse than murderers."[29]

Soon after the accident, UCIL officials in Bhopal denied that MIC was hazardous. "The gas that leaked is only an irritant, it is not fatal," one UCIL official told reporters immediately after the leak,[30] but the MIC operating manual used at the Bhopal plant—adapted from a similar manual used at Bhopal's sister MIC plant in Institute, West Virginia—tells another story. The authors of the manual, five Indian engineers, make abundantly clear the dangers of MIC: "MIC's limited exposure can be fatal. The chemicals involved in its production are highly toxic and hazardous in nature. Even the big corporations have refrained from making this lethal chemical due to the complexity involved in the operation." The manual also instructed operators to "Keep circulation of storage tank contents continuously 'ON' through the refrigeration unit." As chairman Anderson admitted at his May 1985 press conference, the refrigeration unit was "down" for five months prior to the accident.[31]

On August 11, 1985, in Institute, West Virginia, 28 people, including six plant workers at the Union Carbide facility, were hospitalized overnight after the gaskets on a tank containing methylene chloride and aldicarb oxide ruptured, spewing several thousand pounds of the chemicals into the air. In March 1986, the company was fined $4,400 for violating occupational safety and health regulations in connection with the leak.[32] In April 1986, the company was fined a record $1.3 million for 221 alleged safety violations at the Carbide's Institute plant.[33]

Immediately following the Bhopal disaster, lawsuits on behalf of the victims and the government of India were filed across the United States against Union Carbide. But on May 12, 1986, federal judge John F. Keenan ruled that the lawsuits belonged not in the United States, but in India. The judge concluded that it would be more convenient and save United States taxpayers' money to have the Bhopal cases tried in India.

Before announcing his decision, Judge Keenan, in his words, "labored long and hard to promote settlement between the parties for over a year, to no avail." Indeed, Robert Hager, a lawyer representing 20 religious and public interest groups, argued in appealing the judge's decision, that the Bhopal victims had been "seriously prejudiced because Judge Keenan labored for a settlement too hard and too long." Arguing that "Carbide and its powerful Wall Street owners stood to lose probably $5 billion or more if the Bhopal case reached an American jury," Hager reasoned that "Carbide had to settle the case cheap, hide its assets, or get the case out of the U.S. courts to avoid or at least postpone potential bankruptcy. . . . [B]y succeeding in the last two, UCC saved its backers from what would have been one of Wall Street's worst losses in history . . . "

Hager charged that by permitting a year-long delay before making his decision, Judge Keenan gave Union Carbide the time to liquidate substantial assets and to make extraordinary payouts to its shareholders. This reduced its equity available for payment of any judgment eventually awarded the Bhopal victims. The payouts reduced equity from around $5 billion before the disaster to less than $700 million on the books by the end of 1985. "Carbide's depleted equity will now enable it to defend by means of bankruptcy, against any Indian judgment substantially in excess of its settlement offer [$350 million] without significant loss to the company's pre-Bhopal owners," Hager said.[34]

In addition to issues of compensation, the Bhopal disaster raised questions of criminal justice. In the United States, criminal homicide and reckless endangerment statutes have traditionally fallen within the jurisdiction of the states. Even though the state of Connecticut has been called on to launch a preliminary investigation to determine whether Union Carbide should be prosecuted under the state's homicide statute for criminally negligent homicide, the state has failed to investigate one of its most powerful corporations in connection with the deaths in Bhopal.[35]

Recent acts of corporate violence committed by large national and multinational corporations, such as those committed by Union Carbide in Bhopal and elsewhere around the world,[36] are creating a need for new legal mechanisms to distribute justice. In the United States, Congress should consider a federal homicide statute that would be applied to any company that committed acts of negligent, reckless, or intentional homicide across state or national boundaries. And at the United Nations, the world community must look carefully at setting and enforcing standards to control multinational corporate crime and violence, perhaps through a multinational treaty.

Notes

1. "The Poisoned City—Diary From Bhopal," by Praful Bidwai. Sunday Review, *Times of India,* December 16, 1984.

2. "A Night In Hell," by Dhiren Bhagat. *Sunday Observer* (undated) reprinted in *Bhopal: Industrial Genocide?,* by Arena Press, March 1985, p. 23.

3. *Behind the Poison Cloud: Union Carbide's Bhopal Massacre,* by Larry Everest. Banner Press, Chicago, 1985, p. 66.

4. "The Poisoned City—Diary from Bhopal," Bidwai.

5. *Behind the Poison Cloud: Union Carbide's Bhopal Massacre,* Everest, p. 12.

6. *The Bhopal Syndrome: Pesticide Manufacturing and the Third World,* by David Weir. IOCU Press, 1986, p. 20; also "Two Years After Bhopal's Gas Disaster, Lingering Effects Still Plague Its People," by Matt Miller. *Wall Street Journal,* December 5, 1986, p. 34.

7. "Bhopal Journal: The Voiceless Victims," by Stephen J. Adler. *American Lawyer,* April 1985, p. 129.

8. "Bhopal Disaster Casts Pall of Misery, Medical Uncertainty," by W. Joseph Campbell. *Hartford Courant,* November 30, 1986, p. 1.

9. "6 Deformed Babies in India Linked to Bhopal Gas Leak," *New York Times,* July 16, 1985.

10. "Two Years After Bhopal's Gas Disaster, Lingering Effects Still Plague Its People," by Matt Miller. *Wall Street Journal,* December 5, 1986, p. 34.

11. "Bhopal Disaster Casts Pall of Misery, Medical Uncertainty," Campbell, p. 1

12. "American Detained in India," by William Claiborne. *Washington Post,* December 8, 1984.

13. "Bhopal Journal: The Voiceless Victims," Adler, p. 131.

14. "Union Carbide Chief Quoted As Saying He Hoped India Visit Would Curb Suits," by Barry Meier. *Wall Street Journal,* January 7, 1985.

15. "Union Carbide's Inquiry Indicates Errors Led to India Plant Disaster," by Stuart Diamond. *New York Times,* March 21, 1985.

16. "The Bhopal Disaster: How It Happened," by Stuart Diamond. *New York Times,* January 28, 1985, p. 1.

17. "The Night Tank 610 Went Up," by Bruce Agnew. *Safety & Risk Management,* May 1985, p. 17.

18. Ibid.

19. "The Bhopal Disaster: How It Happened," Diamond, p. 1.

20. "The Night Tank 610 Went Up," Agnew, p. 17.

21. "Plant Design Badly Flawed," by Praful Bidwai. *Times of India,* December 27, 1984.

22. Affidavit of Edward Munoz, *In re Union Carbide Corp. Gas Plant Disaster at Bhopal, India, December 1984.* Dated January 28, 1985.

23. "U.S. Company Said to Have Control in Bhopal," *New York Times,* January 28, 1985.

24. "Search for a Scapegoat," *The Telegraph,* Editorial, December 8, 1984.

25. "Profit Against Safety," by Rahika Ramaseshan. *Economic and Political Weekly,* December 22–29, 1984.

26. "Union Carbide Had Been Told of Leak Danger," by Phillip Shabecoff. *New York Times,* January 25, 1985.

27. *No Place to Run: Local Realities and Global Issues of the Bhopal Disaster* by Anil Agarwal, Juliet Merrifield, and Rajesh Tandon. High-

lander Research and Education Center, New Market, Tennessee, 1985, p. 7.

28. *Behind the Poison Cloud: Union Carbide's Bhopal Massacre,* Everest, p. 51.

29. "The Poisoned City—Diary From Bhopal," Bidwai.

30. Ibid.

31. "The Bhopal Diaster: How It Happened," Diamond, p. 1.

32. "Union Carbide's Fine Reduced to $4,400 for Chemical Leak," *New York Times,* March 20, 1986.

33. "Union Carbide Fined $1.3 Million," by Michael Isikoff. *Washington Post,* April 2, 1986.

34. Brief of Amicus Curiae, *In re: Union Carbide Corporation Gas Plant Disaster at Bhopal, India in December, 1984.*

35. "Paying for Bhopal: Union Carbide's Campaign to Limit Its Liability," by Russell Mokhiber. *Multinational Monitor,* July 31, 1985.

36. Although Union Carbide had a reputation within the chemical industry for having a relatively clean and legal workplace, and environmental records, a closer look indicates otherwise. From brain cancer deaths among workers in Texas, to kidney disease among workers at a Carbide battery plant in Indonesia, Carbide's corporate character fails to live up to the Mr. Clean image created by the American business press. For more detail, see "Union Carbide: Not So Clean," *Multinational Monitor,* July 31, 1985, p. 4.

3
Black Lung

"No mule has gone through more. I breathed and swallered lots of dust. There's times I have spit things out of my lungs that looked 'most like black marbles."

—a 68-year old Kentucky miner who spent 45 years working underground mining coal[1]

ON November 20, 1968, 78 coal miners were asphyxiated when the mine in which they were working—in Farmington, West Virginia—exploded. For a brief, historic moment, the nation's attention focused on the disaster, the coal industry's failure to meet minimum safety standards, and the resulting carnage. The nation learned that in this century alone, 100,000 miners have been killed in mining accidents, and that since 1930, more than 1.5 million injuries have been reported. We also learned that in Western Europe, coal mining was a much safer occupation than in the United States, and that while their record was getting better, ours—under pressure from enemies of strict enforcement of the laws governing the operations of coal companies—was getting worse.[2]

Because of the way the U.S. media decide what is "news," information about pressing issues of public policy, health, safety, and justice are not widely disseminated until lives are threatened or extinguished in spectacular fashion. Thus, only when the Farmington coal mine exploded, burying 78 miners, did the nation learn of the need for strengthened mine safety laws, which were passed at state and federal levels within months of the accident.

If today such a coal mine disaster occurs, killing 11 miners, you undoubtedly will watch a news item about it on network television, listen to a radio report about it, or read about it on the front page of tomorrow morning's newspaper.

But today a coal mining disaster is occurring, taking the lives of 11 coal miners; tomorrow, 11 more will die. Yet there will be no headlines in the newspaper, and the network cameras will not swoop down on the Appalachian mining towns to interview the widows of the victims.

The United Mine Workers has estimated that 11 coal miners die every day from miner's asthma, silicosis, pneumoneuralmicroscopic-silicovolcanoconiosis, or simply "black lung"—a debilitating, incurable, respiratory disease that has killed at least 100,000 miners and disabled at least 265,000 coal miners in America.[3] The symptoms that afflict all miners to varying degrees are breathlessness, spitting up of phlegm, and prolonged coughing fits.

"At work, coal miners are covered with dust," says Lorin Kerr, director of occupational safety and health for the United Mine Workers of America (UMWA).

> It's in their hair, their clothes and their skin. It gets between their teeth and they swallow it. They suck so much of it into their lungs that until they die they never stop spitting up coal dust. Some cough so hard, they wonder if they have any lungs left. Gradually, the miners notice they are getting short of breath when they walk up hills. On the job they must stop work to catch their breath. Finally, just walking across the room at home is an effort.[4]

For years, coal mining corporations, and the company doctors they hired, denied that black lung was a *disease*, claiming it was only a normal, nondisabling affliction suffered by everyone who worked in the mines. This assertion led one Pennsylvania physician to conclude in 1935 that "As far as most of the men in this region are concerned, so called 'miner's asthma' is considered an *ordinary* condition that need cause no worry and therefore the profession has not troubled itself about its finer pathological associated clinical manifestations." (Emphasis added.)[5]

The commonly accepted definition of black lung would be determined not by impartial scientific research and analysis, but rather by the company in whose financial interest it was to find that the coughing, spitting, and breathlessness was just the way it was and would have to be if one was to live and work in the mines of Appalachia. In an expository article titled "Black Lung, The Social Production of Disease," Barbara Ellen Smith points out that in the Appalachian coal camps, the "company doctor was the only source of medical care." Although "the coal company controlled the employment of a doctor . . . the miners were required to pay for his services." As Smith observes, "The company doctors' accountability to the coal operators is one of the most obvious and fundamental reasons for the medical concepts of miners' occupational health developed developed during this [early twentieth century] period."[6]

To head off any organized effort of miners to gain compensation from the companies and to work toward prevention of coal dust–related injuries, the companies engaged in the widespread corporate ploy of "blaming the victim." Miners who complained of respiratory ailments were diagnosed as having cases of "malingering," "compensationitis," or "fear of the mines." As one company doctor explained, "Housing conditions, and hurtful forms of recreation, especially alcoholism, undoubtedly cause the major amount of sickness. The mine itself is not an unhealthful place to work."[7]

For decades, coal miners swallowed the logic of the companies' doctors along with the dust of the companies' mines. But by the late 1960s, when miners began to stand up for their rights to breathe dust-free air, they also began to stand up to their doctors. In January 1969, one miner spoke of coal dust and doctors to two reporters from the *New Republic*:

> That doctor [the Surgeon General] said over 100,000 of us have the damn disease and everyone knows that if you stay down there long enough, you get it, you get it worse and worse. And you heard him Corcoran (president of Consolidated Coal Company), say they had to do something to reduce the dust. But they didn't tell people what it *is*, what the disease we got *is*. How is someone here in Washington or in California or in New York supposed to know what they're talking about—that the mines are full of coal dust, and it gets into your lungs and eats them up, and then you die? Of course, when I first asked the company doctor if

anything was wrong, because I was having trouble breathing, he didn't even want to listen to my chest. He just came over to me from across the room and he said: "Look, if you want to stay working, you'd better not complain, you'd better not mention this." I looked at him as though he was a crook or something. Then I guess he just got mad, because he raised his voice at me: "Every miner has trouble with his breathing one time or another. So why should you start complaining? Don't you talk to your buddies? Haven't they all got the same troubles?" And he was right, there—we all do. And he was right with the last thing he told me, before I left: "Look, you're better off working than complaining. You'll die faster from not eating than from some coal dust in your lungs." You know what I said? I said, "You're right, doctor." You know why he's right? I could be on my deathbed—from not eating or from "black lung," either of them—and between the doctors like him, and all those lawyers they've got, and the bosses and the county courthouse people, I'd still not get a cent from the company or the welfare people or Washington or anyplace. And every miner knows that.[8]

The doctors' allegiance to the companies they served so well was not a purely American phenomenon. Dr. Donald Hunter, the famed British authority on occupational health, pointed out that although coal had been mined in England for 700 years, it was not until 1934 that British doctors recognized black lung as a fatal disease. "It must be admitted," wrote Dr. Hunter, "that medical men by their ill-informed complacency have a heavy load of responsibility to bear for this failure to discover the true state of affairs, a failure which constitutes what is probably the greatest disgrace in the history of British medicine."[9]

The British were "complacent," but they recognized and took action to prevent black lung disease a full 34 years before their American counterparts were forced to change course. It was not until 1968, after the explosion at Consolidated Coal mine no. 9 in West Virginia, that the American medical and political establishments were temporarily pried from the grip of the coal and energy conglomerates.

Led by Dr. Isadore Erwin (I.A.) Buff, a coal country people's doctor and activist, coal miners soon began to organize for safer mines, and compensation for black lung disease. Buff traveled the hollows of the Appalachian hills, speaking at community meetings, informing miners and their families that black lung is not an inevitable result of working in the mines, that the companies had the technology to lessen the dust levels, that such technologies were already in place in other countries, resulting in a lower rate of black lung disease and in compensation for those afflicted.

Buff was a man who spoke in long, slow, forceful sentences. His citizen activism grew out of his practice as a heart specialist. "They would send these men to me after they had collapsed in the mines," explained Buff. "They were supposed to have had an acute heart attack, but I would examine them and find they had lung failure. . . . I would tell these company doctors the men had lung trouble, but they wouldn't believe me. I was getting tired of it. There are literally thousands of coal miners in West Virginia who think they've had heart attacks who have never had one."[10]

Before larger and larger crowds, Buff would give stirring speeches in an attempt to arouse the miners to action. "Why are these horrible conditions allowed to exist?" he asked a group of 200 miners and their family members in Logan, West Virginia, in January 1969. "I'll tell you why. Most of this state is owned by ten giant corporations interested only in making money, whatever the human cost. You have got to organize and fight them or they will literally keep on killing you."[11]

The Logan rally at which Buff spoke was held to pressure the state legislature into enacting legislation that would compensate black lung victims for their injuries. On January 26, 1969, two weeks after the Logan rally, 3,000 miners converged on the state capitol in Charleston for the first statewide meeting of the newly formed West Virginia Black Lung Association. The crowd listened to militant speeches attacking the coal companies and the state government and unions for kowtowing to the state's corporate powers. Observers of West Virginia politics were shocked by the turnout. "It was the first time in the memory of most living West Virginia miners that workers in an industry noted for the fatalism and rural isolation of its men had banded together in such an organization," reported the *New York Times*.[12]

The coal corporations countered growing pressure from miners by once again blaming the victims. "Cigarette smoke is also dust," argued the West Virginia Coal Association. ". . . There is a need to have an all-out drive to eliminate cigarettes among smoking miners." The industry also argued that miners were already being adequately compensated for disabilities, and that if black lung were legislated into a separate category for compensation, the claims would threaten the industry's financial stability. ". . . the coal industry is now developing into the productive, proverbial goose," the industry association complained. "There are those [black lung organizers] who, greedy for their immediate desires, would open up this goose for a single golden egg [black lung benefits]."[13]

The Black Lung Association introduced a bill in the state legislature that would make black lung a compensable disease, but it was quickly blocked by those representatives supported by the coal industry. To protest the state's inaction, 40,000 miners walked out of the mines, and many of them marched to Charleston to pressure their representatives. The pressure worked, the legislature responded, and three weeks later, after the governor signed the black lung bill into law, the miners returned to work. It was the longest coal strike for workplace health and safety ever. The black lung movement kicked off similar organizing drives throughout coal country, and by 1971, four other coal states had enacted compensation legislation.

The miners felt strongly about the compensation issue, but dollar bills could not give them back their healthy lungs. Prevention became an equally important issue in the hills of Appalachia.

One disabled West Virginia miner echoed the sentiments of many miners when he said to Barbara Ellen Smith: "Where do we get the black lung from? The coal companies! They've had plenty of time to lessen the dust so nobody would get it. It's not an elaborate thing to keep it down: spray water. They just don't put enough of it on there. They don't want to maintain enough in materials and water to do that. . . ."[14]

A U.S. Senate report agreed, concluding that "The dreadful high incidence of black lung is an immediate consequence of the coal dust created by the increased production rates of the industry . . . the incidence of this disease can be completely prevented by implementing existing technology and undertaking the research necessary to reduce the levels of respirable dust. The problem lies not in the lack of technical competence but in the lack of will to invest in health and safety."[15]

With Rep. Ken Hechler (D-W. Va) taking the lead in the U.S. Congress, the black lung forces came to Washington in late 1968 and early 1969 and, with Washington-based public interest lawyers, lobbied through the Federal Coal Mine and Safety Act of 1969. That act set up a federal framework for compensating black lung victims and also set coal dust standards for the mines. During the heat of the legislative battle, the coal companies vigorously opposed the strict preventive measures of the legislation, which would set a respirable dust standard of 3 mg/m(3) from 1969 through 1972, after which time it would drop to 2 mg/m(3) (the current standard).

It is interesting to note, however, that the companies did not oppose the proposed federal compensation program. Coal corporations foresaw that if the miners were given money payments for their lost lung capacity, they would be less insistent on strict adherence to the provisions governing dust levels. More important, the barons of coal saw the federal compensation scheme as a method to keep injured miners from dragging the companies into court, where juries comprised of ordinary mining family members might look at the evidence showing that information about the dangers of black lung had been around for years, that miner's asthma was first described in 1922 as the lung disease occurring in coal miners, that the British made it a compensable disease in 1934, and that the coal companies did little to lessen the hazards to their workers. Such evidence would be the basis for punitive damage claims that might have resulted in million-dollar damage awards for the wrongful destruction of the plaintiff miners' lungs. The companies would rather have the miners' claims judged by bureaucrats than by the miners' peers.

While the 2 mg/m(3) standard is now law, there is convincing evidence that the standard is being widely disregarded. In September 1975, the Consolidated Coal Company, one of the largest coal corporations in the United States, was indicted for violating the 1969 law. In sworn testimony, Paul (Tex) Bobak, Consolidated Coal's man in charge of checking dust levels in company mines, told of systematic cheating, and of voiding air dust samples that came in higher than the federally mandated level.

The evidence of cheating pointed only to lower-level employees at Consolidated, but the cheating clearly benefited the entire company and its profits. As one Justice Department prosecutor explained, to have sent samples that registered above the legal limit would have brought about legal sanctions, and production delays. "Lost production is lost money," explained the prosecutor, "and there is probably a good deal of pressure on operating employees to keep that production up."[17] Lorin Kerr, for the UMW, charged that the Consolidated case was not an isolated instance. Voiding of samples with illegal readings was a practice of many operators, he claimed. "The miners have been saying [that] for a long long time," he added.

Since the 1969 law was passed, five coal companies have been convicted of submitting fraudulent dust samples to federal enforcement agents. In October 1980, Westmoreland Coal pleaded guilty to charges of destroying respirable dust samples and falsifying dust samples. In December 1982, Peabody Coal pleaded no contest to 13 counts of submitting fraudulent coal dust data. The company was fined $130,000.[18]

Internal United Mine Workers of America (UMW) documents obtained by the *Corporate Crime Reporter* in 1987 revealed that from October 1, 1985 to September 30, 1986 (fiscal year 1986), 80 coal mines had average annual coal dust concentrations in excess of the federally permissable limit of 2.0 milligrams per cubic meter (mg/m^3) and that 18 mines exceeded the statutory limit for each of the past three fiscal years.[19]

Most corporate violations of the coal dust standard are not prosecuted, but are sanctioned civilly with slap-on-the-wrist fines. In 1983, one-fifth of all mining sections in the country were found to be violating the dust standard one or more times, but the average fine for these violations was $117 per company. In one case, U.S. Steel's Morton mine in West Virginia was found to have been operating for 14 out of 20 months at dust levels sometimes triple the federal limit. The company was fined $140 for the 20-month period.[20]

Since 1969, the federal government and coal companies have paid more than $10 billion to more than 500,000 black lung victims and their families.[21] The Reagan administration, however, positioned the government to cut back black lung benefits. In October 1984, consumer advocate Ralph Nader and Davitt McAteer, director of the Occupational Safety and Health Law Center, charged the Reagan administration with concealing a "secret report" that outlined a plan for cutting back black lung benefits to miners and their survivors. The report attacks the statutory definition of pneumoconiosis and suggests that a strict medical definition be adopted instead. "By redefining Black Lung," says McAteer, "Reagan wants to cut out a large number of disabled miners and also cut back the amount paid by arguing that disability is only partial."[22]

While the federal and state reforms of the late sixties have brought some monetary relief to victims of black lung, the respiratory relief appears not to have followed. Indeed, recent studies have found that coal dust is beginning to afflict young miners in increasing numbers. In September 1984, the *Philadelphia Inquirer* reported that 6 percent of young people who had been in the mines less than ten years were already developing black lung, a rate four times the predicted number. Of 33,305 miners tested during the 1970s, 2,010 had some form of black lung.[23]

The concerns of today's miners resemble those of miners throughout the century — including a loss of the right to breathe. "Black lung is a cruel disease," said one West Virginia miner in a September 1978 interview, "a humiliating disease. It's when you can't do what you like to do; that's humiliating. I had to lay down my hammer and saw, and those were the things I got the most pleasure out of. The next thing I liked to do was work in my garden; now my garden's the biggest weed patch in Logan County. There were times in 1971 when I was still working that it was difficult for me to get to the bedroom when I was feeling bad. Now, of course, that's humiliating."[24]

"Should we all die a terrible death," asked another West Virginian, "to keep those companies going?"[25]

Notes

1. "Black Lung: A Story of Neglected People" by David Ross Stevens. *Louisville Courier-Journal*, January 26, 1969.

2. See generally, *To Punish or Persuade: Enforcement of Coal Mine Safety,* by John Braithwaite. State University of New York Press, Albany, New York, 1985.

3. "Black Lung," by Lorin E. Kerr. *Journal of Public Health Policy,* vol. 1, no. 1, March 1980, p. 57.

4. Ibid., p. 50.

5. "Black Lung: The Social Production of Disease," by Barbara Ellen Smith. *International Journal of Health Services,* vol. ii, no. 3, p. 346.

6. Ibid.

7. Ibid.

8. "Black Lung: Mining As a Way of Death," by Robert Coles and Harry Huge. *The New Republic,* January 25, 1969, p. 18.

9. Kerr, "Black Lung," p. 56.

10. *Death and the Mines,* by Brit Hume. Grossman, New York, 1971, p. 102.

11. "Coughing Miners Back Bills," by Hank Burchard. *Washington Post,* January 6, 1969.

12. "Miners Organize to Reduce Risks," by Ben A. Franklin. *New York Times,* January 27, 1969.

13. "The Hazards of Mining," *Charleston Gazette,* February 2, 1969, p. 6.

14. "Black Lung," Smith, p. 354.

15. Black Lung Benefits Reform Act and Black Lung Benefit Revenue Act of 1977, Committee on Education and Labor, House of Representatives, 96th Congress, February 1979, p. 1230.

16. "Black Lung," Kerr, p. 50.

17. "Are Coal Mine Operators Cheating on Black Lung," by Morton Mintz. *Washington Post,* March 18, 1979.

18. "Despite Reforms, Miners Still Get Black Lung," by Lucinda Fleeson. *Philadelphia Inquirer,* September 18, 1984, p. 1.

19. "Internal UMW Documents Reveal Coal Mines that Exceed Federal Coal Dust Standard," I (13) *Corporate Crime Reporter,* 3, July 6, 1987.

20. "Despite Reforms . . ." by Fleeson, p. 1.

21. "Black Lung Fact Sheet," by Davitt McAteer, Director, Occupational Safety and Health Law Center. October 1984.

22. *Secret Plan: Reagan to Cut Black Lung Benefits.* Press Release of the Occupational Safety and Health Law Center, Washington, D.C., October 11, 1984.

23. Ibid.

24. "Black Lung," Smith, p. 354.

25. Ibid.

4
Brown Lung

"The good Lord gives man the breath to breathe and I don't think the textile mills have the right to take it away. They sacrifice our lives for profits."

—Paul Cline, leader, Greenville, South Carolina Brown Lung Association[1]

WORKING WITH COTTON took Evelyn Lassiter's breath away. For 20 years, Lassiter had worked for the J.P. Stevens Company, until at the age of 45 she could not work another day. The cotton dust in the weave room of Stevens's Roanoke no. 2 mill was getting to her. She was constantly dizzy, and in pain. She found it hard to breathe, and when she spoke there was little volume to her voice.

Work in the cotton mills was demanding, and the workers were subjected to heat, noise, and cotton dust. But when she began, Lassiter was only 24 years old and her family was in need of a second income to help raise two children. "I just didn't think of working anywhere else except the cotton mills. There were so few other jobs elsewhere and the pay was about the best around for a woman. That's the only place I wanted to work," she recalls. "And after I got started, I didn't think about quitting. That's where my friends worked. Not that the work was easy . . . they try to give you twice as much work as you can handle. From the very beginning, they keep adding on more per day, trying to get you to do more than you really can."[2]

In the beginning, Lassiter kept pace with the company's demands. She was the top producer in the weave room, averaging about 97 percent of the maximum possible production. "During the first few years, I would run hard for them. I tried to do a good job. I don't know anyone at Stevens who was any better on a regular set of looms than I was. But I got a little more sensible as the years went on. Toward the end, I didn't care any more."

Eventually Lassiter discounted her early belief that she had a cold—the pains and coughs were too persistent to be colds. "It happened all so gradually," she says. "It just sneaks up on you. I knew I was having too many colds. I would lay off work for a few days, but a fresh one would start after I got back to the weave room. Even when the doctor told me I had bronchial pneumonia, I kept working because I didn't want to lose the pay or risk my job."

Night and day, the coughing and wheezing persisted, but mornings, when the lungs constricted tightly and the coughing was the heaviest, were the worst. "Usually my chest is much tighter in the morning," says Lassiter. "You just keep coughing until you think you got it up and out—if you can get it up at all."

In 1975, the year before she quit Stevens, Lassiter began seeing doctors. One doctor at Duke University told her that her air passages were "almost completely closed and that cotton dust was irritating my condition." A second doctor at the University of North Carolina took tests and determined that she "demonstrated gross expiratory wheezes in all lung fields." In one test a doctor lit a match and held it three inches in front of her face; he asked her to blow it out with the air from her lungs. She couldn't do it.

Lassiter decided to take sick leave for a couple of weeks and then to try to make a comeback at the mill. She felt she had no choice. If she didn't return, she would lose her job. But within three weeks of her return, breathing was extremely difficult. On the first day of her third week back, Lassiter quit. She could make it through only five hours of the day before she became unable to breathe. She decided never to return to work in a cotton mill.

"I just can't go back in there this way," she says. "I don't think I can do any more work like it ought to be done. The heat and the humidity . . . I just can't breathe. Five minutes after you arrive at work, every hair on your head is soaking wet. You pay $5 to get a hairdo and it's ruined as soon as you go to work. Sometimes you couldn't see three feet in front of you because of all the dust and lint blowing around."

Lassiter was never told about the dangers posed by breathing air with high levels of cotton dust. She was never told about brown lung. "When I first started, I just didn't think of it as brown lung. Nobody talked about brown lung in the mills. I just thought of it as a fresh cold."

But brown lung is more than just a cold. Known to scientists as byssinosis (from the Greek *byssos,* meaning cotton or flax), brown lung is a respiratory ailment that afflicts cotton workers. During the first year of exposure to cotton dust, a worker may begin to complain of slight breathlessness, and a tight feeling in the chest. One of the distinctive characteristics of brown lung is that the tight feeling in the chest initially occurs after a short absence from work, such as on the first day back after a weekend off. This post-weekend chest tightness is known as Monday fever. After a few more years of exposure to cotton dust, the brown lung symptoms become more frequent, with Monday fever hitting every Monday, not just on occasional Mondays. After about ten years of exposure, a byssinotic (brown lung victim) experiences unremitting breathlessness, as did Evelyn Lassiter. Even after quitting the job, the victim does not fully recover. For these brown lung victims, there is no such thing as a deep breath.

Although the health effects of brown lung had been known for more than 250 years, executives in the textile industry long ignored, then denied, the disease. According to one North Carolina health official, industry executives hadn't "heard of byssinosis, couldn't spell byssinosis, and didn't know what it was."[3] The medical director at Cannon Mills, one of the larger textile companies, wise-cracked that byssinosis cases were like something from outer space. "Seems like flying saucers," he told one reporter. "Heard about them but never seen one."[4]

But as early as 1713, an Italian physician, Bernadino Ramazzini, described the working conditions of flax and hemp workers: "For foul and poisonous dust flies out from these materials enters the mouth, then the throat and lungs, makes the workers cough incessantly, and by degrees brings on asthmatic troubles."

In the nineteenth century, French and English doctors noticed that cotton mill workers were afflicted with a respiratory disease they called "cotton spinners phthsis." In 1845, Belgian doctors who studied 2,000 cotton mill workers were the first to observe the weekend chest problems and labeled the disease "Monday chest tightness." Since then, there have been numerous reports of brown

lung from doctors around the world. As one congressional committee concluded recently, "the available scientific data clearly supports the existence of a relationship between cotton dust exposure
and acute byssinosis."[5]

In 1979, the U.S. Department of Labor estimated that nearly
560,000 workers were being exposed to cotton dust and that there
were 84,000 cases of byssinosis among active textile workers.[6] In
1980, the *Charlotte Observer* reported that 10,000 workers in the
Carolinas alone were exposed to levels of cotton dust that could
kill.[7] The Amalgamated Clothing and Textile Workers Union
(ACTWU) estimated that in 1983, 150,000 workers were exposed
to cotton dust. This decline from the 1979 figure was attributed
less to health improvements than to massive layoffs within the industry during the early 1980s.[8]

In response to this assault on the health of cotton mill workers,
the textile industry "has repeatedly tried to obstruct the studies,
deny the problem, and mislead the public with consistently false
reports of the glowing picture of health presented by its employees,"
according to the ACTWU. The union has documented how the
Georgia Textile Manufacturers Association, for example, deliberately attempted to obstruct the efforts of Dr. Bouhuys (then of
Emory University) to conduct his pioneering studies on byssinosis
in commercial textile mills in 1964, forcing him to finish his research
at the cotton mill in the Atlanta penitentiary. In testimony submitted to a September 1983 OSHA hearing on proposed amendments to OSHA's cotton dust standard, the ACTWU detailed how
"the industry used faulty studies, generally performed by its own
physicians, to show remarkably low prevalences of lung disease."[9]

The *American Textile Reporter*, an industry trade journal, went
to extremes in an editorial in 1969 denying the existence of the
disease: "We are particularly intrigued by the term 'byssinosis,' a
thing thought up by venal doctors who attended last year's ILO
meeting in Africa, where inferior races are bound to be inflicted
by new diseases more superior people defeated years ago." In a
similar vein, in 1979 Tennessee Governor Ray Blanton told a reporter, "Breathing cotton dust fiber is like breathing carrot juice—
it doesn't feel good, but it won't hurt you."[10]

In fact, the industry and its insurers knew the score on cotton
dust. Dr. Joseph Bosworth, a retired "loss prevention investigator"
for the leading workmens' compensation insurer for the U.S. tex-

tile industry, Liberty Mutual, testified in 1983 at a deposition in connection with a brown lung claim that instead of informing their workers of the risks of brown lung disease, the companies "ran from it . . . because it threatened them with a wholesale cost."[11]

The views of Governor Blanton and the *American Textile Reporter* were representative of the attitude the industry brought to the cotton dust controversy. Centered in the Carolinas, nine Fortune 500 textile firms, forming the core of the textile industry, rang up $17 billion in sales of cotton towels, blankets, and clothes in 1979. Burlington Industries, the leader of the industry, cleared $76.2 million in profits on sales of $2.7 billion.[12]

Ever since 1970, when Congress passed into law the Occupational Safety and Health (OSHA) Act, which mandated that the textile industry clean up its workplaces by lowering dust levels, the industry has been on the attack. The companies have publicly criticized the law, tried to weaken it, sought to weaken its enforcement, failed to pay fines when found in violation, and resisted compensation claims made by brown lung victims. Some companies have spent the necessary millions to lower dust levels and protect their workers, but they are in a minority in the industry.

In 1980, the *Charlotte Observer* reported that 101 of 128 mills in South Carolina, checked since inspections began in 1974, exceeded legal dust levels. In North Carolina, the *Observer* found that 128 of 210 mills inspected were in violation of the legal dust levels. And these violations were not mere technicalities. "A 1979 internal North Carolina labor department study of 148 inspections showed three-fourths of the companies exceeded legal dust limits by an average of nearly three times," the *Observer* reported.[13]

Despite reports of repeated and constant violations, enforcement of the cotton dust laws is weak or nonexistent, a failure of enforcement that is particularly acute at the state level. A 1975 report of the North Carolina Public Interest Research Group (NCPIRG), for example, found that inspections of plants by state officials were an "on again off again situation." No cotton dust inspections were conducted for the entire state during the first six months of 1975. And even when the state inspections found the companies in blatant violation, the sanctions imposed were ludicrously low. Cone Mills, which rang up sales of $617 million in 1978, was fined an average of $17.50 per violation; J.P. Stevens (1979 sales 1.8 billion), an average of $13.00; and Cannon Mills

(1978 sales, $547 million), an average of $11.00. Ten of the J.P. Stevens mills received no fines, despite the fact that some of these mills were cited for as many as 13 violations each.[14]

Between March 1980 and August 1983, the North Carolina Department of Labor inspected *every* cotton textile mill in the state. The Department found that in 1983, 19 percent of the employees inspected had no initial dust monitoring, 19 percent failed to use respirators in high-dust areas, 12 percent failed to maintain ventilation properly, 17 percent were not covered by a medical surveillance program, and 19 percent had no employee training. In hearings in November 1983 before the Subcommittee on Manpower and Housing of the House Committee on Government Operations, Eric Frumin, director of ACTW's Occupational Safety and Health Division, testified that these North Carolina enforcement statistics revealed that "the passage of time has not reduced the number of violations." "In 1983, *more than two years* after these requirements took effect, the rate of employer non-compliance with major requirements like medical surveillance remains the same or higher," Frumin reported. "Secondly, these continually high rates of non-compliance were found in a state where by 1983 it was common knowledge that an inspection was inevitable in the near future. With the virtual exemption resulting from Federal enforcement policies in Georgia and Alabama, the rate of non-compliance is much worse."[15]

When they weren't engaged in violating the law, the major textile companies were working to ensure that more protective standards were not adopted. After OSHA announced in 1972 that it would act to regulate five toxic substances, including cotton dust, the textile industry went on the offensive to make certain the standard would not pinch company profits.

George Guenther, a former textile mill owner from Pennsylvania who held a high post in the Labor Department during the Nixon administration, epitomized much of the industry's attitude toward law and order as it applied to textile corporations. In 1974, Guenther wrote a memorandum to his boss, the Under-Secretary of Labor, Laurence H. Silberman, suggesting in effect that the administration weaken the cotton dust law in return for campaign contributions to Nixon's reelection campaign. Guenther's memo, marked CONFIDENTIAL, urged the White House to promote "the great potential of OSHA as a sales point for fundraising and general support by employers" and promised that "no highly controversial standards" would be proposed by OSHA or NIOSH until after the election. A new cotton dust standard was not proposed until 1976.[16]

Nixon's chief fundraiser, Maurice Stans, also urged textile executives to contribute to the Nixon reelection campaign, and the industry responded gratefully with one million dollars. A good chunk of this, $363,122.50 in checks and cash, was delivered to Stans by Roger Milliken, president of a major textile company that bore his name, only hours before a law took effect requiring public disclosure of campaign contributions. An additional $10,000 came from Frederick Dent, president of Mayfair Mills. One month after Nixon was reelected, Dent was named Secretary of Commerce, a post crucial to the tariff-sensitive textile industry.[17]

In December 1976, OSHA proposed a 200 ug/m3 standard for cotton dust. After receiving comments on its proposed standard, holding a series of hearings, and reviewing medical studies, OSHA issued its final standard in June 1978. For three years, the industry kept the 1978 standard bottled up in the courts on the ground that it could not be justified under a cost-benefit analysis. On June 17, 1981, in *ATMI v. Donovan* the U.S. Supreme Court rejected the industry's arguments and upheld the standard.[18]

During the entire cotton dust standard episode, the industry's considerable clout was being felt throughout Washington. One week before OSHA issued its final 1978 standard, President Jimmy Carter's economic advisers, including Charles Schultz, Barry Bosworth, and the Regulatory Analysis Group, urged that the standard be delayed until less inflationary alternatives were considered. Bosworth's Rube Goldberg idea was to strap respirators onto the workers. Consumer and labor groups protested to President Carter that, as OSHA noted, "wearing respirators for even a short time is fatiguing, uncomfortable, and stressful, especially in a hot, humid textile mill. Respirators are especially unsuited for workers who cannot bear the extra resistance of such devices precisely because they suffer from respiratory problems." Carter eventually backed the 200ug/m3 standard, although the industry was given four extra years to comply.[19]

The Reagan administration took its swipe at the cotton dust standard, with Vice President George Bush's Task Force for Regulatory Relief leading the attack. Under pressure from Bush's group, in March 1981, OSHA issued a rulemaking procedure declaring its purpose to reconsider the standard from a cost-benefit perspective. The Supreme Court decision halted a Reagan OSHA move to destroy the standard, but OSHA came back with a second rulemaking in February 1982 designed to sidestep the Supreme Court decision. It was announced that "new health data" about byssinosis warranted reconsideration of the cotton dust standard.[20] In June 1983, OSHA proposed easing some parts of the rule and retaining others. ACTW called the move to weaken the rule "unfortunate and unnecessary."[21] In December 1985, OSHA issued final amendments to the cotton dust rule, amendments that did not severely damage the existing standard, according to the ACTWU, but added little to workers' safety.[22]

At the state and local levels, the industry has worked hard to deny compensation to victims of brown lung. During 1979, for example, the South Carolina Textile Manufacturers Association (SCTMA), a trade group representing 75 cotton firms, led a successful fight to defeat state legislation that has made it easier for brown lung victims to win compensation. The SCTMA Good Government Fund spent $30,584 on more than a hundred candidates for local and state offices during the 1978 election campaign. In North Carolina, the industry didn't have to spend money to get what it wanted. For 1980, the chairman of the state senate committee most closely involved with textile legislation was a retired textile executive and former chairman of the North Carolina Textile Manufacturers Association.[23]

In the Carolinas, the companies pay workmens' compensation claims, and the textile companies have fought off brown lung claims successfully for years. In 1980, of an estimated 10,000 workers potentially eligible for brown lung compensation only 1,100 had filed, and of that number only 320 had been approved. In the Carolinas these settlements averaged $13,000 to $14,000, but the average worker lost more in wages than he gained in compensation. A state Department of Labor study of 270 Carolina workers who filed brown lung claims showed that the average employee lost seven years of work due to brown lung—years in which the worker would have earned $56,000.[24]

James "Shorty" Fisher was one such worker. Fisher had worked for 43 years in a cotton mill before three doctors certified that he was too sick to work. One of the doctors diagnosed brown lung, but the industrial commission that heard Fisher's claim ordered the company to pay him a meager $600, of which $150 went to Fisher's lawyers. In 1980, Fisher could barely breathe and believed that he was shortchanged by the commissioners who heard his case. "I didn't know about [the process]," Fisher reflects, "I just took what they gave me."[25]

The textile companies are also actively, and in many instances illegally, engaged in an effort to keep unions out of the Carolinas, the nation's least unionized states. In a span of less than ten years, the National Labor Relations Board (NLRB) had cited J. P. Stevens for unfair labor practices 22 times. When unions win elections, some companies just shut down and leave town. This happened in South Carolina in 1956 when a Deering-Milliken plant shut down just six days after 556 millworkers voted to join a union. (The U.S. Supreme Court later ruled that the closing was illegal, and ordered the company to pay the workers lost wages.)

The result of this concerted industry activity is weak law and little justice. Originally designed to protect the workers' health and safety, the law remains weak or gets weaker, enforcement remains weak or gets weaker, the health of workers deteriorates, and when they become disabled, workers are denied adequate compensation for their injuries.

Although this pattern of lawbreakers seeking to weaken the law and its enforcement is the norm within the textile industry, there are commendable exceptions. In July 1977, the SCOSH cited the Riegel Textile Corporation for cotton dust violation in one of its cotton mills. Rather than run to Washington to plead for regulatory relief, the company decided to abide by the law. Within a month of the citation, Riegel notified OSHA that it was spending $5 million to clean up its act—and it did. "Nobody with common sense can argue that it isn't beneficial to clean up a work place," Robert Coleman, Riegel's chairman, told the *Charlotte Observer*. "But it's also money well spent regardless of whether we meet the OSHA standard or not. It provides a more attractive workplace, and that allows us to attract workers more easily in a labor market that's getting increasingly tighter."[26]

A 1983 ACTWU study entitled "The Economic Impact of the Cotton Dust Standard" compared the economic performance of seven major textile companies that had largely complied with the standard against that of the textile industry as a whole. The profitability of the seven companies compared with that of the industry improved by 22 percent between 1978 and 1981, the period during which industry had invested most heavily in dust controls.[27]

All of Evelyn Lassiter's doctors have told her that her shortness of breath will not improve. Brown lung is an irreversible disease. "I don't get out much anymore," she says. "I used to see my friends when I went bowling and I used to dance a little. I can't do those anymore. And I used to like to water ski but I haven't been able to do that for years. The water does something to me . . . it makes my lungs feel like they are filling up with water. I can't play softball anymore . . . no bicycling . . . I can't even pitch horseshoes. I used to like to ride a motorcycle, but I can't take the wind anymore."

Looking back over her life, Lassiter is firm in questioning her initial decision to enter the milll.

"I ask myself why the devil did I have to go to work in that cotton mill."[28]

Notes

1. "Brown Lung, A Case of Deadly Neglect," part 7, *Charlotte Observer,* February 9, 1980, p. 1.
2. *A Breathtaking Experience,* by John Bell, unpublished manuscript (all Evelyn Lassiter quotes taken from here.)
3. Ibid., p. 43.
4. Ibid.
5. "A Review of the Scientific and Technological Issues in the Regulation of Cotton Dust in Primary Cotton Textile Industry." Report by the Committee on Science and Technology together with minority views, U.S. House of Representatives, May 24, 1983. p. 9.
6. U.S. Department of Labor, *Report to the Congress: Cotton Dust: Review of Alternative Technical Standards and Control Technologies,* p. 1 (May 1979). See also, Testimony of the Amalgamated Clothing and Textile Workers Union, AFL-CIO, on the Notice of Proposed Rulemaking for the Cotton Dust Standard before the Occupational Safety and Health Administration, U.S. Department of Labor, Docket Number H-052E, Washington, D.C., September 9, 1983, p. 1.
7. "Brown Lung: A Case of Deadly Neglect, *Charlotte Observer,* February 3, 1980, p. 1.
8. Personal communication, Eric Frumin, ACTWU. December 16, 1986.
9. Testimony of the ACTWU, AFL-CIO, on the Notice of Proposed Rulemaking, September 9, 1983, p. 1.

10. Quoted in *Business War on the Law*, by Mark Green and Norman Waitzman. The Corporate Accountability Research Group, Washington, D.C., 1981, p. 107.

11. "Death by Cotton Dust," by Richard Guasrasci, *Corporate Violence: Injury and Death for Profit*, ed. by Stuart L. Hills. Rowman & Littlefield, Totowa, New Jersey, 1987, p. 76.

12. *Everybody's Business*, edited by Milton Moskowitz, Michael Katz, and Robert Levering. Harper & Row, New York, 1980, p. 133.

13. "Brown Lung: A Case of Deadly Neglect," *Charlotte Observer*, February 3, 1980, p. 20A.

14. On fines, *A Breathtaking Experience*, Bell, p. 311; on sales, "Brown Lung: A Case of Deadly Neglect," *Charlotte Observer*, February 3, 1980, p. 19A.

15. Testimony of Eric Frumin, director of occupational safety and health, Amalgamated Clothing and Textile Workers Union, AFL-CIO, before the Subcommittee on Manpower and Housing, House Committee on Government Operations, on the Enforcement of the OSHA Standards for Cotton Dust. November 9, 1983, Washington, D.C., p. 4.

16. *A Breathtaking Experience*, Bell, p. 246.

17. "Brown Lung: A Case of Deadly Neglect," *Charlotte Observer*, February 7, 1980, p. 11A.

18. "A Review of the Scientific and Technological Issues in the Regulation of Cotton Dust in Primary Cotton Textile Industry," Report by the Committee on Science and Technology together with Minority Views, May 24, 1983.

19. *Business War on the Law*, Green and Waitzman, p. 109.

20. "A Review of the Scientific and Technological Issues in the Regulation of Cotton Dust in Primary Cotton Textile Industry," Report by the Committee on Science and Technology together with Minority View, May 24, 1983, p. 6.

21. "U.S. Proposes Easing Some Rules on Cotton Dust," by Seth King. *New York Times*, June 8, 1983.

22. Personal communication, Frumin.

23. "Brown Lung: A Case of Deadly Neglect," *Charlotte Observer*, February 7, 1980, p. 11a.

24. Ibid.

25. "Brown Lung: A Case of Deadly Neglect," *Charlotte Observer*, February 5, 1980, p. 6a.

26. "Brown Lung: A Case of Deadly Neglect," *Charlotte Observer*, February 3, 1980, p. 20a.

27. Personal communication, Frumin.

28. *A Breathtaking Experience*, Bell, p. 19.

5
Buffalo Creek

"You know what it's like? It's like you were watching the best movie ever made and it stops for a commercial or something like that. And the commercial goes on and on and on ... "

—survivor describing life after Buffalo Creek disaster[1]

STARTING AT THE TOP of the mountain where three tiny waterways converge to form Buffalo Creek, the water trickles down the hollow past the tiny coal towns of Kistler, Fanco, Becco, and Pardee, and 12 others, including Man, some 17 miles downstream, where Buffalo Creek empties into the Guyandotte River. Nestled in the western edge of the Appalachian mountains in West Virginia, Buffalo Creek hollow was home to 5,000 rugged Appalachian mountaineers—people who had a deep pride in home and neighborhood, who were committed to hard work and a rejection of every kind of welfare. The people of the hollow enjoyed a peaceful life fishing, hunting, raising large families, and enjoying the clean air and fresh water.

With the coming of the coal companies in the 1920s, all of that changed. The farmers became miners and the coal dust replaced the fresh air. Black lung became a preoccupation and a killer. The corporations saw Appalachia not as land to live and build a community on but as land to dig, and saw, and shovel and strip and then to abandon.

Buffalo Creek hollow had its own coal company, the Buffalo

Mining Company, owned by the New York City-based Pittston Corporation, one of the largest coal companies in the country. In addition to worrying about the health hazards encountered daily in the mines, the people of Buffalo Creek had another concern — Buffalo Mining's waste products. Waste was a big problem for Buffalo Mining. With every four tons the company dug out of the ground came one ton of "slag" or "gob" — a black mixture of mine dust, shale, clay, and other impurities.

Traditionally, the coal companies would deposit their wastes at the most convenient locales, dumping them at the side of the mountain, in the middle of a river, or at the base of a mountain hollow. Buffalo Mining chose the top of Buffalo Creek hollow and dumped its slag right into the middle of the waters of Middle Creek, one of the three streams that feed Buffalo Creek. The company began dumping there as early as 1957, and by 1972, it was depositing a thousand tons of slag a day right into Middle Fork, right at the top of the mountain, right within eyesight of the 5,000 residents of the hollow below. The tons of slag clogged up Middle Fork and formed a gigantic bank of waste more than 200 feet deep, 600 feet wide, and 1,500 feet long.

The company also had a liquid waste problem. Huge quantities of water were needed to prepare a ton of coal for shipment, and Buffalo Mining used more than half a million gallons of water per day to clean the thousands of tons of coal it mined daily. The traditional practice of the companies was to pump this polluted waste water wherever convenient, usually into a nearby stream or river. With the advent of a new environmental awareness during the 1960s, however, the coal companies were expected to hold onto this waste water at least until some of the impurities had settled out. Buffalo Mining responded by dumping its liquid waste behind the dam created by its solid wastes. To the company, the Buffalo Creek dam appeared to be an inexpensive solution to a potentially costly problem.

In his book *The Buffalo Creek Disaster*, attorney Gerald M. Stern tells the story of Maggie Rhodes. Whenever it rained in Buffalo Creek hollow, Maggie Rhodes would wonder about Buffalo Mining's dam and whether it was strong enough to hold 132 million gallons of water. "I could not rest whenever it would cloud up to rain," she said. "When that would happen, I would take food and bed clothing and pack up the car and go and stay at Jean Cook's house in Lorado [a neighboring town]. I did this on several occasions, whenever there would be rain or a storm."

Maggie Rhodes's fear of a dam failure was born out of experience. "It was about ten on a cold night in March 1967," she recalled.

> I was watching television with my sister. The rest of the family was asleep. The front door was shut. I heard someone screaming. I ran to the porch. The creek was to its banks and was roaring. It was making so much noise I could not understand what the person was hollering, so I hollered back. The only word I heard the person hollering was the word "dam." Part of Buffalo Mining dam located at the top of the hollow had washed out and some of the water rushed down toward the towns below.

Rhodes immediately gathered her family together and headed up the mountain. "The water was in the road in front of our house. It was up to my waist as I ran leading my children. People were screaming, but there was no crying."

Even though no one was killed or seriously injured during the 1967 partial dam collapse, the event left a lasting impression on Maggie Rhodes. By the spring of the next year, Buffalo Mining had built a second dam behind the first, and eventually had enough wastes to build a third dam behind the second, but Maggie Rhodes was not comforted by numbers. She contacted Steve Dasovich, Buffalo Mining's local man in charge. "Steve Dasovich knew I was afraid of the dams on Middle Fork. I had a conversation with him about that after he joined the Buffalo Mining Company," she recalls. "Steve just told me there was no danger. He just laughed at us, made fun of us. One of these times he even laughed at me about losing my shoes during the 1967 flood. He was laughing about me running barefoot through Ozzie Adkins's cornfield."

Maggie Rhodes did not share Steve Dasovich's sense of humor. Nor did the other residents of Saunders (Rhodes's hometown), which was the first town below the Buffalo Mining Company's dam. If the dams burst, Saunders would be the first to go.[2]

Since Buffalo Mining was not responding to the pleas put forward by Saunders residents, Mrs. Pearl Woodrum, one of those residents, decided to take things into her own hands. In February 1968, she wrote what proved to be a prophetic letter to Arch Moore, the governor of West Virginia:

Dear Sir:

I live 3 miles above Lorado. I'm writing you about a big dam of water above us. The coal co. has dumped a big pile of slug about 4 or 5 hundred feet high. The water behind it is about 400 feet deep and it is like a river. It is endangering our homes and lives. There are over 20 families here and they own their homes. Please send some one here to see the water and see how dangerous it is. Every time it rains it scares everyone to death. We are all afraid we will be washed away and drowned. They just keep dumping slate and making it more dangerous everyday.

Please let me hear from you at once and please for God's sake have the dump and waters destroyed. Our lives are in danger.[3]

The governor sent several of his state representatives to Buffalo Creek where they were met by Buffalo Mining's Dasovich. Dasovich pacified the state officials by promising to create a "new dam" behind the first two. Dasovich drew a one-page "sketch" of the new dam for the state representatives. He consulted no civil engineers, nor any books. In fact, Dasovich later admitted that "there were no engineering calculations whatsoever on Middle Fork."[4]

It rained hard for a few days before February 26, 1972, but on that day in Appalachia, at 8 A.M., it was quiet. "There was such a cold stillness. There was no words, no dogs, no nothing. It felt like you could reach out and slice the stillness,"[5] remembers one resident of Amherstdale, a town halfway down the hollow. At that same moment, 8 A.M., when everything was still in Amherstdale, Buffalo Mining's slag dam situated nine miles above Amherstdale collapsed, sending a black torrent of 132 million gallons of water and a million tons of solid waste roaring through the breach. The gigantic wave set off a series of explosions as it thundered down the valley like a mass of rolling lava—a "mud wave," as one engineer put it—on a roller coaster ride of destruction aimed to disturb the stillness at Amherstdale and demolish everything in its path.

"It was about a hundred and fifty feet above where the water came out," reported the eyewitness closest to the dam collapse. "It was burning there and when the water hit the fire, it shot right through the air about two hundred feet high, right through the air. There was a lot of dust and black smoke. And when we looked back down there [toward Saunders] and the water was down and the smoke had cleared up we couldn't see nary a thing, not a living thing, nothing standing."[6]

The mud wave totally demolished Saunders. It didn't just crush the houses, and the cars, and the church; it took everything with it. With a wall 30 feet high, it swept the town clean. A picture of Saunders after the flood looks like any of a hundred strip-mined, uninhabited, desolate, Appalachian hillsides.

Saunders was only the first in line. The wave continued on down the hollow. "This water," explained one survivor, "when it came down through there, it acted real funny. It would go this way on this side of the hill and take a house out, take one house out of all the rows and then go back the other way. It would just go from one hillside to another." Another eyewitness also found it hard to describe in conventional terms. "I cannot explain that water as being water," she said. "It looked like a black ocean where the ground had opened up and it was coming in big waves and it was coming in a rolling position. If you had thrown a milk carton out in the river—that's the way the homes went out, like they were nothing. The water seemed like the demon itself. It came, it destroyed, it left."[7]

Another survivor who viewed the water from about a third of the way down the hollow, looked up and "saw the houses coming. They just looked like toy boats on the water and they was abusting and hitting against each other and bringing the lines down there. But what scared me out of my mind was that debris up against the bridge going sky high. I went to screaming."[8]

By the time the black wave reached the mouth of Buffalo Creek, 17 miles down the hollow, 125 people were dead and 4,000 of Buffalo Creek's 5,000 residents were left homeless. The survivors, in shock and afraid to move, huddled together in small groups on the hillside. "There wasn't anything to do but just sit there," said one. "We looked out over that dark hollow down there and it just looked so lonesome. It just looked like it was God-forsaken. Dark. That was the lonesomest, saddest place that anybody ever looked at."[9]

Some moved from hill to hill looking for lost family members. One survivor, a 15-year-old girl, told sociologist Kai T. Erikson:

everybody was wandering around and asking if you had seen so-and-so. . . . I never saw a time like it. People would just stop to go to the bathroom right beside the railroad because there wasn't anywhere to go and dogs that had been washed down and weren't dead were running up to you and they were wet. We walked up to the bridge at Proctor (about halfway down the hollow) and a bulldozer was starting to clear the debris from the bridge there. The bulldozer picked a little girl up, and when he saw he had her on, he dropped her off because it cut her back and her back was still pink. Her face was tore up so bad they couldn't tell who it was. Then we saw a hand under her, sticking up through the debris.[10]

As the debris was bulldozed into large piles to be burned, as the dispossessed were resettled into mobile homes provided by the federal government, and as an attempt was being made to identify the dead, news reports of the Buffalo Creek disaster shot across the United States. Upon receiving the reports, executives at Pittston corporate headquarters on Park Avenue in New York City began to act on what had become, in corporate parlance, both a public relations and a financial problem.

On the public relations front, Pittston at first attempted to shirk its responsibility by pointing its corporate finger to the sky. The company asserted that the "break in the dam was caused by flooding" and was therefore "an Act of God" (flood, hurricane, tornado, cyclone). If under law, it was determined that the flood was indeed an act of God, then Pittston would be relieved of any financial liability.

The people of Buffalo Creek hollow, thinking back to the times they had complained about the dam, were not at all pleased by the report that Pittston was trying to pass the buck upstairs. "I didn't see God running any bulldozer," said one. "It's murder! The big shots want to call it an Act of God. It's a lie. They've told a lie on God, and they shouldn't have done that. God didn't do this. He wouldn't do that." Another survivor understood Pittston's motivation. "You can blame the Almighty all right," he said, "the Almighty dollar."

Robert Weedall, West Virginia's state climatologist, understood the meaning of "act of God" and knew that there were other potentially appropriate legal phrases. "Act of God is a legal term," he said. "There are other legal terms—terms like 'involuntary manslaughter because of stupidity' and 'criminal negligence'."[11]

Talking about "criminal negligence" and "involuntary man-slaughter" and proving them were two different things — especially in West Virginia, especially against the nation's fourth-largest coal company. Many in the hollow believed that the coal companies controlled the entire state. It was also assumed that getting effective legal representation would be impossible since all the coal companies also controlled the "respectable" law firms.

Nevertheless, the people wanted Pittston to pay for the loss of their family members, for the loss of their property, for the loss of their communities, and for the damages, both physical and psychological, to themselves. Within two weeks, the survivors formed the Buffalo Creek Citizens Committee and began to search outside the state for legal help, for a strong law firm that the companies could not scare off or buy off. They happened across Arnold and Porter, a large corporate law firm in Washington, D.C. Arnold and Porter had the resources necessary to take on one of the nation's largest energy corporations. Pittston, however, had jumped to a head start.

Even before the survivors had moved to organize their fight for compensation, Pittston representatives were canvassing the hollow offering money settlements to the dazed survivors if they would agree not to take Pittston to court.[12] Many accepted this offer without understanding fully the extent of Pittston's culpability, the nature of the legal process, or their chances of recovering a large money judgment if they joined with other survivors in a lawsuit. Pittston, on the other hand, surely understood what insurance companies knew as a rule of the game — that the lowest settlements usually come when they are made immediately after any disaster.

Realizing that they had to act quickly to counter Pittston's early move, the Citizens Committee accelerated its program and was able to contact 615 survivors before Pittston's representative could get to them. Together they filed a suit against the company in federal court in West Virginia, charging that Pittston's negligence and reckless disregard for the safety of the people of Buffalo Creek hollow caused death, and destruction to property, and damaged the health of those who survived. The plaintiffs demanded $64 million in compensation.

Just two days before the residents filed their lawsuit, the governor released the report of the West Virginia Ad Hoc Commission of Inquiry into the Buffalo Creek flood. The commission found that "The Pittston company, through its officials, has shown flagrant disregard for the safety of residents of Buffalo Creek and other persons who live near coal-refuse impoundments. This attitude appears to be prevalent through much of the coal industry." At the suggestion of this commission, a special grand jury was convened, but on a "mighty close vote,"[13] no indictment was handed down.

Pittston surely had adequate notice that coal waste refuse piles were extremely dangerous. On October 21, 1966, a 300-foot-high coal slag mound in Aberfan, Wales, weakened by a natural spring beneath it, collapsed, and the resulting two-million-ton torrent of rock, coal, and mud cascaded onto an elementary school below, killing 145 persons, including 116 children.[14]

The Aberfan disaster triggered investigations in this country into similar coal refuse piles. In 1967, a federal investigator visited the Buffalo Creek dam and determined that the dam was "subject to a large washout on the north side from overflow of the lake." Soon thereafter, the washout that so terrified Maggie Rhodes and so amused Buffalo Mining's representative proved the feds correct.

Indeed, as far back as 1926, *Coal Age*, the industry weekly, reported that "where refuse is dumped in a hollow which is the drain for an appreciable watershed in hilly or mountainous country, trouble can be expected unless some provision is made to take care of the water."[15] The article suggested that one such provision was the placement of a concrete pipe under the pile "so that there will be no damning of the water nor percolation through the bottom of the pile." Following this advice, a West Virginia inspector who checked Dam 3 at Buffalo Creek wrote to the company on a number of occasions observing that the dam "needed an emergency spillway." Pittston was warned again in 1971, when a 150- to 200-foot section of Dam 3 gave way, spilling debris into the waters behind Dam 2. Despite this failure and numerous warnings by the state inspectors, Pittston did not build an emergency spillway for Dam 3.[16]

After the disaster, Garth Fuquay of the U.S. Army Corps of Engineers found that "the basic concept of Dam 3 was not acceptable from an engineering standpoint." At Senate hearings convened to investigate the cause of the flood, Fuquay noted that the successful operation of Dam 3 "depended on uncontrolled seepage;

unless some happy accident occurred whereby Mother Nature took care of this fundamental error of conception, the dam was doomed to failure from the time the first load of refuse was dumped."[17]

Only two days before the dam collapsed, Pittston's second in command, John Klebbish, along with a number of his associates, visited Buffalo Creek hollow. According to Klebbish, as the group was driving past the dam, Klebbish asked the local company supervisor if he had an emergency overflow in the pond behind the dam. The supervisor said no. "Well," Klebbish came back, "don't you think you ought to be getting one in?" Klebbish doesn't remember the supervisor's answering the question. No emergency spillway was installed at Dam 3.[18]

As the evidence against Pittston mounted, the company backed off its "Act of God defense." Well into the discovery phase of the lawsuit, the president of Pittston confided to the *Charlotte Observer* that "the impoundment was man-made and machine made, and of course, it was the cause of the disaster."[19] Although Pittston's president had thus shifted the blame from God to technology, he was not yet willing to accept personal or corporate responsibility for the disaster.

Don Jones, a Pittston employee, had prepared a memorandum intended to advise Pittston officials of proposed federal regulations on the subject of waste piles. Jones warned in the memo that the federal regulations would "forbid the closing off of any stream or the impoundment of water" by refuse-pile dams. The memo was written one year before the disastrous collapse at Buffalo Creek.

As was customary procedure within the corporation, Jones showed the memo to his superior, Mr. Spotte. Spotte ordered Jones not to send out the memo, so Jones went back across the street after the conversation, "took the letters out of the envelopes, and put them back in the files." On February 28, 1972, two days after the Buffalo Creek disaster, Jones went to his files, pulled the memos out, and sent them to all concerned. This time he didn't consult his superiors. But this time it was too late.[20]

In *The Buffalo Creek Disaster*, Stern points to additional evidence that Pittston knew at least nine months before the dam broke that the company was in violation of a specific federal safety standard governing dams.[21] For Pittston, however, this was not an unusual position. From the time of passage of the Coal Mine Health and Safety Act in 1969 through October of 1973, Pittston had been assessed over $2 million in fines for alleged violation of federal law.[22]

In the days before the disaster, as the rains came down on Buffalo Creek hollow, residents worried about the dam. Some left their homes and gathered in a nearby schoolhouse, where they thought they would be safer. They put a message through to Ben Tudor, the superintendent at the Buffalo Mining Company. Tudor said that everything was all right, but Jack Kent, the supervisor of strip mining at the company, was worried about the water behind the dam. The night before the collapse, Kent stayed up all night, watching as the water moved to the top of the dam. At around 5 A.M., three hours before the break, Kent called Steve Dasovich, told him that water was rising at the rate of three inches an hour, and urged him to go to the dam.

Dasovich drove to the dam and ordered Kent to put two pipes behind the dam to drain the water. But it was too late for the pipes. Dasovich then proceeded to the schoolhouse where he told the huddled townspeople that they didn't "have anything to be concerned about."[23] At 7:30 A.M., Dasovich got on the phone to the sheriff to "impress upon him that the situation was not alarming and if anyone gave him that information, it was overly done."

At 8:00 A.M., the dam collapsed.

Three years after the Buffalo Creek disaster, survivors were still living in makeshift huts and a team of 60 psychiatrists, psychologists, and social workers concluded that Buffalo Creek valley was virtually "a village of the damned." "We found continued anxiety and fear focusing now on nights when there is rain or stormy conditions," reported Dr. James Titchener, an associate professor of psychiatry and study team leader. "The people are now defensive, constantly on guard, and their lives have become geared to existence and survival. They have lost all interest, ambitions, and sexual desires. Before the flood, the community was one that enjoyed hunting, shooting, and fishing. Those were their hobbies. Now they just sit almost lifeless in front of TV sets, not really watching programs, but afraid to do anything else."[24]

Six hundred and twenty-five survivors of Buffalo Creek settled their $64 million lawsuit against Pittston out of court for $13.5 million—$5.5 million for property losses and in wrongful death payments and $8 million for their mental suffering as survivors whose valley community was destroyed by the company's recklessness.[25] The state of West Virginia, in a separate action, sued Pittston for $100 million and settled out of court for $1,000,001.[26]

The settlement raised important questions of legal compensation for corporate violence. Was $13.5 million an adequate settlement given the loss of life and community? How much was the Buffalo Creek community worth? "We did lose a community," reflected one survivor,

> and I mean it was a good community. Everybody was close, everybody knowed everybody. But now everybody is alone. They act like they're lost. They've lost their homes and their way of life, the one they liked, the one they was used to. All the houses are gone, every one of them. The people are gone, scattered. You don't know who your neighbor is going to be. You can't go next door and talk. You can't do that no more; there's no next door. You can't laugh with friends. You can't do that anymore, because there's no friends around to laugh with. That don't happen no more. There's nobody around to even holler and say "Hi," and you can't help miss that.[27]

Notes

1. *Everything in Its Path: Destruction of Community in the Buffalo Creek Flood*, by Kai T. Erikson. Touchstone, New York, 1976, p. 47.

2. *The Buffalo Creek Disaster*, by Gerald M. Stern. Vintage, New York, 1976, p. 157.

3. Ibid., p. 159; and *Buffalo Creek (W. Va.) Disaster*, 1972, Hearing before the Subcommittee on Labor of the Committee on Labor and Public Welfare, U.S. Senate, 92d Cong., 2d sess., on Buffalo Creek Disaster, May 30 and 31, 1972, App. A, part 1, p. 1346.

4. *The Buffalo Creek Disaster*, Stern, p. 161.

5. *Everything in Its Path*, Erikson, p. 29.

6. Ibid.

7. Ibid., p. 30.

8. Ibid., p. 32.

9. Ibid., p. 42.

10. Ibid., p. 41.

11. "The Pittston Mentality: Manslaughter on Buffalo Creek," by Thomas N. Bethell and Davitt McAteer. *Washington Monthly,* May 1972.

12. "After the Flood," by Mary Walton. *Harpers,* March 1973, p. 83.

13. *The Buffalo Creek Disaster,* Stern, p. 74.

14. "After the Flood," Walton, p. 80.

15. *The Buffalo Creek Disaster,* Stern, p. 141.

16. Ibid., p. 161.

17. *Buffalo Creek (W. Va.) Disaster,* 1972, Hearings, App. A, part 1, p. 224.

18. *The Buffalo Creek Disaster,* Stern, p. 148.

19. Ibid., p. 187.

20. Ibid., p. 188.

21. Ibid., p. 169.

22. Ibid., p. 191.

23. Ibid., p. 272; and *Buffalo Creek (W. Va.) Disaster,* 1972, Hearings, App. A, part 1, p. 304 et. seq.

24. "A Flood's Legacy of Fear," *Washington Post,* May 24, 1975.

25. "Disaster," by Gerald M. Stern. *New York Times,* February 27, 1976.

26. "Pittston Settles Suit in W. Va. Flood, Will Pay $1,000,001," *Wall Street Journal,* January 17, 1977, p. 30.

27. *Everything in Its Path,* Erikson, p. 196.

6
Corvair

"We are not going to do anything. We are going to ride this out."

—William Hamilton, General Motors VP for public relations, in response to a fellow GM executive who wanted to know what GM was going to do about defective Corvairs[1]

On the side of the Santa Barbara roadway, Rose Pierini was bleeding profusely. She had been driving her 1961 Chevrolet Corvair, traveling 35 miles per hour in a 35 mph zone. "All of a sudden," reported John Bortolozzo, the California highway patrolman who witnessed the accident, "the vehicle made a sharp cut to the left and swerved over." Bortolozzo, later joined by two other patrolmen, rushed to help Pierini and tried to stop the bleeding. "Something went wrong with my steering," she told the patrolmen.[2]

The accident cost Rose Pierini her left arm. It cost General Motors $70,000. That's how much the giant automaker paid to settle the lawsuit Pierini brought against GM, a lawsuit claiming that the Corvair she was driving was defective. One of hundreds of similar lawsuits brought by Corvair victims, it was the first installment of millions of dollars that GM would pay those victims to prevent their cases from going to trial. GM's goal was to avoid having a jury of twelve men and women decide how much an arm is worth, and, more important, to prevent internal company documents from getting out, documents that could damage GM's legal position in the courtroom and its reputation in the outside world.

The Corvair was introduced to the U.S. market in September of 1959, to a wave of critical acclaim. Its styling was sporty, its engineering was new, and the combination caught the eye of auto writers bored by the monotony of Detroit's big cars. The acclaim soon turned to disdain as those automotive writers, who judge their subjects by driving them, found that the Corvair's unique combination of rear-engine and swing-axle suspension made the car extremely difficult to control in certain highway situations. "The classic Corvair accident," wrote Denise McCluggage, a sports driver and writer, "is a quick spin in a turn and swoosh!—off the road backwards. Or, perhaps, if half-corrective measures are applied, the backward motion is arrested, the tires claw at the pavement and the car is sent darting across the road to the other side."

Another auto writer wrote that the Corvair "can be a handful if the driver doesn't understand its peculiarity," and a third suggested that the rear weight bias and independent springing together "give the car rather unsettling properties at higher speeds. Take cornering for example. The rear starts to swing outward. The rear tires dig in but the shift in weight places them at rather odd angles relative to the pavement. These angles are great enough to increase steering force, and suddenly, the car is negotiating a tighter curve than intended. The phenomenon of oversteer has intruded into the scene."[3]

Small auto accessory companies began making extra money by selling stabilizing equipment to Corvair owners who were lucky enough to be aware of the inherent defects early enough to correct those defects. Rose Pierini was not so lucky. She was caught by surprise that summer day when "something happened to the steering." Hundreds of other Corvair drivers and passengers around the country suffered similar or worse fates. Many were seriously injured. Others became single-digit fatalities, contributing to the total of 50,000 killed each year on America's highways.

It is not known how many persons were killed or injured at the wheel of the defectively designed Corvair. It is known that, whatever the number, much of the carnage was preventable. During the four model years from 1960 to 1964, General Motors marketed 1,124,076 Corvairs. And before GM put the first Corvairs into the hands of unsuspecting drivers, serious questions about the Corvair's safety were raised at executive levels of the corporation.

In the highly acclaimed *On a Clear Day You Can See General*

Motors, J. Patrick Wright gives John DeLorean's first-hand account of the struggle within GM's upper echelons over the decision to market the Corvair. According to DeLorean, who was a GM vice president before resigning in 1973, "The questionable safety of the car caused a massive internal fight among GM's engineers over whether the car should be built with another form of suspension." The pro-Corvair forces, led by Ed Cole, the father of the Corvair, were "enthralled with the idea of building the first modern, rear-engine, American car." They felt that the safety risks of the controversial swing-axle suspension were "minimal." Charles Chayne, GM vice president for engineering, led a group of top executives who argued that the Corvair should be kept out of production— or, alternatively, that the suspension system be changed to make the car safer. But Ed Cole was the company's most effective salesman, and since Ed Cole wanted the Corvair, GM would produce the Corvair. One engineer, in explaining why GM discounted negative safety reports on the Corvair, put it succinctly, "Cole's mind was made up."[4]

Those negative safety reports were not easy to discount. Secret internal GM proving-ground tests, made public ten years after the Corvair was first produced, show conclusively that General Motors was aware of the Corvair's instability. In one test, conducted in June 1959, a Corvair flipped over as the driver attempted to maneuver a J-turn at 30 mph. In later tests, conducted in 1962–63, GM found that modest modifications of the Corvair's suspension improved stability.

Even before the first test was ever conducted on a Corvair, GM was warned of the dangers inherent in the concept of a rear-engine automobile. In 1956, more than three years before the first Corvair rolled off the production line and one year before the Corvair project was launched, Maurice Olley, then head of research and development at Chevrolet—and a specialist in handling characteristics of automobiles—warned of the dangers inherent in Corvair-type swing-axle suspension. "The ordinary swing axle," wrote Olley, in a patent application filed on May 18, 1956, "under severe lateral forces produced by cornering, tends to lift the rear end of the vehicle so that both wheels assume severe positive (tilt inward) camber positions to such an extent that the vehicle not only 'oversteers' but actually tends to roll over. In addition, the effect is non-linear and increases vehicle handling characteristics."[5]

In 1953, Olley had publicly expressed his concerns about the dangers inherent in rear-engine vehicles, whatever the suspension. He labeled such vehicles "a poor bargain," and said that they could not handle safely in wind even at moderate speeds. He called the heavy-ended vehicles "a collision risk, as the mass of the engine is in the rear."[6]

General Motors ignored or discounted these warnings. "Ed Cole's mind was made up." The company's main concern was "target rate of return," not safety. The goal of the Corvair project was to build a smaller, lighter, fuel-efficient, six-passenger car that would ride comfortably. And once the car was on the production line, modification was difficult to implement. In 1961, for example, Bunkie Knudsen became president of the Chevrolet division, which produced the Corvair. Knudsen, aware of the turn-over potential in the Corvair, "insisted," according to DeLorean, that "he be given corporate authorization to install a stabilizing bar in the rear to counteract the natural tendencies of the Corvair to flip off the road." The estimated cost of this change to each buyer was $15. Knudsen's superiors refused his request as "too expensive."

Knudsen would not take no for an answer. He threatened to resign from the corporation unless the stabilizing devices were implemented, and GM executives, fearful of negative publicity that would undoubtedly accompany such a resignation, agreed to the change. But the change did not come about until the 1964 model year.

In the meantime, more than a million Corvairs were on the road, taking their toll. "The results were disastrous," observes DeLorean. "I don't think any one car before or since produced as gruesome a record on the highway as the Corvair. It was designed and promoted to the spirit and flair of young people. It was sold in part as a sports car. Young Corvair owners, therefore, were trying to bend their car around curves at high speeds and were killing themselves in alarming numbers."[7]

Some of these young Corvair owners were the sons and daughters of GM executives. The general manager of the Cadillac division was convinced that the designed-in defects of the car were responsible for the death of his son, who was killed in a Corvair. The son of Cy Osborne, an executive VP at GM, suffered irreparable brain damage as a result of a Corvair accident. Ernie Kovacs, the famous comedian, was killed in a Corvair.[8]

Within months after the first Corvair rolled off the production line, GM began receiving complaints from disgruntled customers. Their complaints revealed that stability was not the only problem inherent in the sporty Corvair. From 1960 to 1964, GM received 544 complaints about Corvair fumes, 143 of which specifically described engine exhaust fumes entering the passenger compartment. Not only did Corvair occupants risk death or injury because of the instability caused by the rear-engine, swing-axle design, but they also risked brain damage or asphyxiation from carbon monoxide fumes that could enter the passenger compartment from a leaking engine through the heater.

John Petry took the risk and lost. In 1972, Edward Wolf, Petry's Philadelphia attorney, sued General Motors, claiming that Petry suffered permanent brain damage as a result of driving long distances in his leaking 1961 Corvair station wagon. At first, General Motors claimed that it did not know that the Corvair heater was dangerous. But within months, a GM executive close to the case came forth with a different version.

Under questioning from Wolf, the General Motors engineer in charge of the Corvair engine design admitted, that (1) any malfunction of the engine that permitted the emission of carbon monoxide would result in carbon monoxide's being carried by the heating system into the passenger compartment; (2) General Motors knew that it was not possible to design with certainty an engine that would not malfunction and leak carbon monoxide; (3) General Motors had considered the possible danger of carbon monoxide leakage from the engine and had therefore upgraded the quality of the engine seals and exhaust manifolds; and (4) General Motors had considered but had not adopted a shield device to prevent contact between engine cooling air and passenger compartment warming air.[9]

The explosive nature of this testimony in light of GM's original assertion that it knew nothing forced GM to negotiate with Petry. The multinational giant offered $125,000 to settle the case, but only if Petry and his attorney agreed to a wide range of conditions that would protect GM from other Corvair victims who wished to sue. GM demanded that Wolf sell the company all his depositions, all information from expert witnesses, his entire file, and Petry's Corvair. Wolf, his law firm, and his client would have to agree not to talk or write about the case. Finally, GM demanded that Wolf change the original complaint from design defect to manufacturing defect. GM wanted the world to believe that the defect in Petry's Corvair was an isolated mechanical defect, not something inherent in the design.[10] Wolf's firm agreed to the settlement and GM's demands with the added consideration that GM pay all court costs.[11]

In addition to the complaints about Corvair fumes, during the same four-year period (1960–64), GM received tens of thousands of other complaints relating to the trouble-plagued automobile. The existence of these complaints would have never been publicly known had it not been for a couple of alert suburban Detroit junk dealers. They stumbled across 19 boxes of microfilmed Corvair owner complaints—complaints GM management ordered destroyed. "When the Fourteenth Floor [where GM's executive suites are located at GM headquarters building in Detroit] found out," DeLorean reported, "it went into panic and we at Chevrolet were ordered to buy the microfilm back and have it destroyed."

DeLorean objected to this order, arguing that a public company had no right to destroy business-related documents. In addition, the junk dealers, who knew the difference between Junk and junk, were asking GM $20,000 for the microfilm. DeLorean considered this "blackmail," and refused to follow the order from his superiors to buy back the complaints.

When consumer groups showed interest in getting their hands on the documents, GM took quick action to override DeLorean's objections. The fourteenth floor ordered the Customer Relations department to accept the junk dealers' offer. The junk dealers reportedly received their $20,000 asking price from GM, the complaints were turned over to GM, and GM's scrapping procedure was revised to prevent future exposure of company documents.[12]

Corvair complaint letters were the least of GM's worries. More important was the flood of lawsuits brought by Corvair occupants injured, many in eerie one-car accidents. GM spent millions of dollars defending these lawsuits and compensating the survivors of these Corvair "accidents."

Others inside the industry, including current Chrysler chairman Lee Iacocca, agreed that the Corvair was unsafe. " . . . GM has had its fiascos, too, like the Corvair," wrote Iacocca in his best-selling autobiography. "Here I find myself in rare agreement with Ralph Nader: the Corvair really was unsafe. The Vega and the Corvair were both terrible cars, but GM is so big and powerful that it can withstand a disaster or two without suffering any major damage."[13]

From Ford Motor Company, Iacocca's former employer, came similar criticism. On October 1, 1959, a presentation was made to the Ford executive committee detailing the handling of a wide range of Fords and other makes of cars. A film was shown to the executive committee with the following explanation:

> The handling and stability of the Falcon (Ford) are excellent. The Corvair with its rear heavyweight distribution shows marked instability under conditions of severe cornering and passing. While the driver will not encounter difficulty under most normal driving conditions, there are frequently encountered emergency conditions such as slippery pavement or emergency maneuvering in which the driver cannot maintain control over the vehicle. The Corvair falls considerably short of our (Ford) handling.[14]

In 1982, from Capitol Hill, the late Representative John L. Burton (D.-Calif.), then chairman of the House Government Activities and Transportation Subcommittee of the Committee on Government Operations and a man who followed issues of auto safety closely, gave the following summary of the Corvair episode:

> From a safety point of view, the evidence is clear, overwhelming, and convincing: General Motors manufactured and marketed 1.2 million unsafe Corvairs for the 1960, 1961, 1962, and 1963 model years, knew about the inherent safety defects, yet did nothing to correct them. From the point of view of honesty and integrity, the evidence is also clear, overwhelming, and convincing: General Motors has sought to conceal and suppress evidence showing that the Corvair was unsafe, and that GM did little to remedy a situation that was causing unnecessary death and injury on the highway. Taken as a whole, the record shows that in manufacturing and marketing the Corvair, GM acted in reckless disregard of human life.[15]

Evidence from GM's own files shows that the Corvair was not a safe vehicle, that GM executives knew it was not a safe vehicle, yet nevertheless proceeded to produce, market, and sell the Corvair to thousands of unsuspecting customers. Despite this record, GM defended its ill-fated subcompact to the end. No GM executive went to jail, nor was the company finded. Indeed, today in America it is perfectly "legal" for a corporation to, in certain circumstances, endanger the lives of millions of Americans by marketing hazardous products to unsuspecting consumers as GM did with the Corvair.

Despite this evidence, the National Highway Traffic Safety Administration in 1972 found that "handling and stability of the Corvair does not result in abnormal potential for loss of control or rollover." A subsequent Senate Subcommittee on Executive Reorganization in 1973, chaired by Senator Abraham Ribicoff (D.-Conn.) uncritically accepted the conclusions of the NHTSA report. Both the NHTSA report and the Ribicoff report came under heavy criticism from members of Congress and Ralph Nader's staff.

Nader's staff issued a detailed rebuttal, charging that the Ribicoff report "read like a GM brief." The rebuttal reported that "little of the [Ribicoff] staff report's supporting materials have been made public, most of its investigation has been conducted in secret, and GM and DOT (Department of Transportation) have reviewed a draft of the [Ribicoff] report, making suggestions and corrections prior to its release."[16] Congressman Burton blasted the Ribicoff report, charging that its acceptance of NHTSA findings, coupled with "an overriding obsession with secrecy, raises important questions of impartial judgment and bias." (Burton pointed out that all of the Ribicoff staff documents from GM, which included 80 depositions, have been sealed and stored at the National Archives until the year 2000.) Burton also charged that the Ribicoff staff refused to consider as relevant the most damning evidence against GM and the Corvair—the preproducton GM proving-ground reports that detailed how Corvairs flipped over while maneuvering J-turns at moderate speeds.[17]

The lesson of the Corvair is simple: if corporate executives are allowed to operate in an environment devoid of effective criminal sanctions, they will act lawlessly. Lawmakers throughout the country must move to close the current opening in the law that allows corporations to market products that endanger human life. Strong sanctions must be imposed on corporate evecutives who knowingly market these products without informing an appropriate public agency. The alternative is the continuation of a preventable public slaughter with the increased public costs of litigation, medical treatment, and disability payments that inevitably follow.

Notes

1. *Memo to Ralph Nader* from Carl Nash, Joan Claybrook, and Mark Green. Subject: The Staff Report On Corvair Stability Controversy, March 23, 1973, in *Congressional Record*, March 28, 1973, p. S 6059.

2. *Unsafe at Any Speed*, by Ralph Nader. Bantam, New York, 1973.

3. All quoted in *Unsafe*, Nader, p. 7.

4. *On a Clear Day You Can See General Motors: John Z. DeLorean's Look Inside the Automotive Giant*, by J. Patrick Wright. Avon Books, New York, 1979, p. 65.

5. *Unsafe*, Nader, p. 34. See also Hon. John L. Burton of California in the House of Representatives, *Congressional Record*, December 16, 1982, Extension of Remarks, p. E 5270.

6. *Unsafe*, Nader, p. 15.

7. *On a Clear Day*, Wright, p. 66.

8. Ibid.

9. Hon. John L. Burton of California in the House of Representatives, *Congressional Record*, Extension of Remarks, December 16, 1982, p. E 5270.

10. Ibid.

11. Telephone conversation with Edward Wolf, January 7, 1985.

12. *On a Clear Day*, p. 61.

13. *Iacocca: An Autobiography*, by Lee Iacocca with William Novak. Bantam, New York, 1984, p. 161.

14. Hon. John L. Burton of California in the House of Representatives, December 16, 1982, Extension of Remarks, p. E 5270.

15. Ibid.

16. *Memo to Ralph Nader* from Nash, Claybrook, and Green. March 23, 1973, p. S 6059.

17. Hon. John J. Burton of California in the House of Representatives, December 16, 1982, Extension of Remarks, p. E 5270.

7
DBCP

". . . something like [sterility] is scary. I'm working out there. I wanted kids, man. You talk about the long-term effects. You're talking about one right there—that's pretty close to my heart, man, you know, because I wanted to have me a couple, you know? And something like that, man, even thinking about something like that and even thinking about those kids could come out wrong—it just gives me the cold chills, you know?"

—worker at Occidental Chemical plant, Lathrop, California, 1977[1]

DI. BROMO. CHLORO. PROPANE. The workers at Occidental Chemical's fertilizer plant outside of Lathrop, California, knew it as DBCP. It was one of 200 different pesticides handled by these workers and marketed by their employer, Occidental Chemical Corporation. This one, DBCP, was used to control the tiny nematode worms that attack the roots of fruits and vegetables in southern California. By producing DBCP, Occidental attacked more than just the tiny nematode. Dust, gases, and fumes drifted from the factory onto neighboring plots of land. "My dad used to have a pig farm right down there," reported one resident to two young filmmakers documenting the DBCP disaster, pointing to the land. "The fumes would come over, fly over, and get into the water, and these pigs were drinking his water and it was killing his pigs, so they [the company] bought him out. It was killing this guy's alfalfa over here, so they bought him out. It was getting in Ralph's—he owns the dairy right over there—they were noticing it in the milk, so they bought him out."

Inside the factory the situation was worse. There was the nausea and headaches suffered by the workers. "You work in some of these poisons," said one Occidental worker, "and when you come home you just feel nauseated. You wake up the next day with headaches or, you know, just a slight case of poisoning." Over the long term, working on the inside affected all the senses to varying degrees—especially the sense of smell. "I don't seem to be able to smell as good as I used to be able to," said one worker. "It used to be that I'd be there at work and I'd take a week's vacation and by that time my sense of smell would clear up and I'd be able to smell things again. Now it doesn't make any difference whether I take a week off or two weeks off; I still can't smell anything."

Cathy Trost, a *Wall Street Journal* reporter and author of *Elements of Risk: The Chemical Industry and Its Threat to America*, reports that the workers stood upon platforms over 1,000-gallon containers known as batch tanks so that they could monitor the mixing of the DBCP with diluting chemicals. To the side of the tanks, other workers would measure the finished DBCP product as it poured into cans for sale. There was no ventiliation system to disperse the fumes from the chemicals. Workers were supposed to wear rubber gloves, but the rule was rarely enforced, and most workers wore no gloves when handling DBCP.[2]

Most of the men who worked at the plant probably figured out that anything that caused headaches and nausea and substantially destroyed any sense of smell had a good possibility of inflicting a greater health danger. They were forced, however, to choose between their jobs and their health. "People say, 'well, you're foolish,'" reported one worker from the Lathrop plant. "'You oughta quit. You're gonna die.' I kind of realize that too, that it has shortened my lifespan and I think it's going to shorten everybody's lifespan that works out there, but right now my main concern in life is raising my kids so I have to weigh the bad against the good and I've been out there ten and a half years and that's what keeps me going back day after day."

Indeed, many of the 26 workers saw the choice between their health and their jobs as no choice at all. "If you need a job," said one older worker, "you get up around my age, you're forty-eight years old—who's gonna hire you? And you've got a whole bunch of people out there like that. Where are you going to go?"

Many stayed on at the Occidental plant in Lathrop, mixing chemicals for pesticides to kill the little bugs that attack fruit trees and vegetables. Most suffered from more than just run-of-the-mill headache, or nausea, or loss of smell. Spots began to appear on their bodies. "These spots," said one worker, "are getting worse and I sure hope they don't eventually cover the rest of my body. I've really been concerned about it. I've been going to the doctor for over a year now—see what they can do for me to slow it down."

Even the spots were relegated to mere nuisance status compared with what DBCP was doing to the workers' abilities to produce children. For years, workers suspected that something in the plant was causing sterility among them but no one had proof. Some of them might have been thinking about it, but few would openly discuss their abilities to procreate, to produce fertile sperm. They would talk around it, rarely saying the word *sterility*. One of the workers put it this way: "I can't think of the last time that anyone there had a baby. Who was the last one? Ted? And that's been three years, four years ago? Three or four years ago. And the majority of the guys working out there are all under forty. A lot of them are twenty or so, in their early twenties—so you take it from there." One man recalls that when he started working at the Occidental facility, he heard disturbing rumors about the men who worked in the plant. "They said anybody that worked in that department for more than two years couldn't produce children. And I haven't."

These distressing stories were told to two young California investigative filmmakers, David Davis and Josh Hanig, who heard of the problems at the chemical facility and visited Lathrop to compile their award-winning documentary film, *Song of the Canary.* After speaking with the workers, they came to believe that DBCP was making the workers sterile, but no one would go on record to confirm this. The company was not willing to do the tests that might have proved that the work environment was making its workers sterile. The filmmakers approached the union, but local union officials told them that sterility tests were too expensive. So Hanig and Davis took the initiative, went to a local lab, and arranged for sterility tests for some of the workers who were concerned. The tests cost the filmmakers $100 and confirmed their fears. All seven workers tested were sterile.

The filmmakers immediately reported the results of their tests to the local union and to the Occupational Safety and Health Administration (OSHA), which then ordered Occidental to shut down the Agricultural Chemicals Division of its Lathrop facility. With network news media converging on Lathrop, Occidental spokesmen were putting out the word that they didn't know the cause of the sterility in the men. One company spokesman said that until a week before he had never seen or heard of a report linking DBCP to sterility in lab animals.[3] Later tests showed that of the 114 workers exposed at the Occidental plant, 35 were infertile.

The news out of Lathrop triggered studies at other DBCP manufacturing plants around the country, studies that confirm the potent human toxicity of the pesticide. At the Dow Chemical plant in Magnolia, Arkansas, 62 of the 86 employees tested were found to be sterile or to have very low sperm counts. At the Velsicol Company plant in El Dorado, Arkansas, about half of the 24 workers who handled DBCP were found to have abnormally low sperm counts. At a Shell plant in Alabama, sterility was also found among workers who handled DBCP.[4]

These high sterility rates should not, however, have come as a surprise to the chemical companies that manufactured the pesticides. For 20 years, from 1957 through 1977, Dow and Shell, two of the nation's largest petrochemical producers, manufactured DBCP, even though during the mid-1950s the companies had strong indications that this pesticide caused sterility in animals. Shell began tests on DBCP at the University of California's San Francisco Medical Center in 1952. The Center gave its findings to Shell in 1954, including a discussion of shrinking testicles and of sterility in the test animals. Dow conducted similar tests and the results of both studies were reported in the *Journal of Toxicology and Applied Pharmacology* in 1961. This report found that "Excessive exposure to the vapors resulted in damage to the liver, kidneys, and various tissues, including sperm cells and seminiferous tubules, dermis, bronchioles, renal collecting tubules, lens and cornea, and the alimentary canal."[5]

The authors studied tests that exposed DBCP vapors at a level of 12 parts per million to 40 rats, and found that 40 to 50 percent of the exposed rats died. It was the effects of DBCP on the testes that caused the authors to note that "The most striking observation at autopsy was severe atrophy and degeneration of the testes of all species [rats, guinea pigs, rabbits, and monkeys]. In the rats, this was characterized by degenerative changes in the seminiferous tubules [where sperm is produced], an increase in Sertoli cells [which nourish growing sperm], reduction in the number of sperm cells, and development of abnormal forms of sperm cells."[6]

In addition to sterility problems, studies have shown DBCP to cause cancer in test animals including stomach cancer in both sexes of rats and mice and mammary tumors in rats.[7]

The filmmakers were disturbed by what they found and told the world about it in their film *Song of the Canary*. (A voice at the beginning of the film explained the title: "For years coal miners took caged canaries into the mines to detect deadly carbon monoxide gas. By collapsing and sometimes dying the canaries warned of the danger that otherwise would have crept up undetected.") During production of the film, Hanig and Davis took their cameras to Occidental's managerial suite where they interviewed a company official.

Q: What was your initial feeling when you first found out that in fact these men were sterile?

OCCIDENTAL OFFICIAL: Shock. We had no idea. I had no idea at all that we had any kind of process here in our plant operations that could do such a thing to a human being.

Q: But hadn't a study been done by Dow Chemical back in 1961 that indicated that DBCP did cause sterility in rats?

OCCIDENTAL OFFICIAL: Well, there was a study funded by Dow—the Torkelson study, and *it did not show sterility in rats*. What it did show was that with very high doses of DBCP you could get *testicular atrophy*, if you will, the shriveling of the testicles. I've talked to two scientists who are familiar with that work and they both say, "Heck, we just didn't draw the conclusion that there'd be sterility from the fact that the testicles were shriveling up." (Emphasis added.)

This distinction between shriveling up of testicles and sterility was of little solace to the sterile workers. "It's too bad that they're having to use people as guinea pigs," one worker said. "That's the way I feel. You can work here and not have any children or you can work somewhere else and then have children. But they didn't give us a choice. Sure, I volunteered to go to work out there but I didn't know this was going to happen."[8]

Although the victims expected little protection from Occidental, some expected more from the government and were disappointed. OSHA is authorized to regulate chemicals in the workplace. If a company uses chemicals that endanger the workers, in a manner that violates the law, OSHA, the federal cop in this instance, can enforce the law against the company. Where was OSHA when the workers at Lathrop were being exposed to DBCP?

Knowing that there are federal standards governing the safe use of only 500 of the 250,000 chemicals used throughout the country, Davis and Hanig took their cameras to record the comments of a California OSHA official, Bill Steffan:

Q: What about the ones [chemicals] that have not been tested, about which we know nothing? What is the department's position on those?

OSHA OFFICIAL: Well, the ones that have standards are the ones we have problems with and that's why they have standards for the 500.

Q: With DBCP there's no standard and there's a problem, it seems.

OSHA OFFICIAL: There will be a standard because we've got a problem. And that's the way its been working.[9]

The federal policy governing chemicals in the workplace was defined thus: With no problem, there was no standard, and with no standard, there was no protection. Once the problem surfaces, the protection, if it comes, comes too late for those on the front line. Since today the vast majority of chemicals have no standards, it can be said that the chemical industry is to a large degree lawless. Few workers within the industry harbor any illusion of getting protection from the federal police force. One chemical worker from San Jose, California, after viewing *Song of the Canary* and seeing the effects on his fellow workers, observed, "If I got fucked up and I didn't get a large cash settlement, I'd take care of myself," he said. "Or I'd hire someone. The government and OSHA is shit."[10]

In August 1977, OSHA asked all manufacturers of DBCP to halt production voluntarily. News of the high rates of sterility heightened public concern about continued use of the pesticide and in 1977 the EPA was pressured into effectively banning major uses of the chemical. Soon thereafter, Dow and Shell announced that they were halting production.

The U.S. production halt didn't stop the DBCP merchants — production simply shifted across the border to two plants in Mexico, whence it was imported by the Amvac Corporation of Los Angeles. Amvac also began production in the United States and was charged with various health and safety violations. In February 1979 the company was fined $3,520. After learning of Amvac's activities, the EPA in October 1979 formally cancelled DBCP's registration for all remaining uses, in all states except Hawaii.

The Hawaiian exception was a political victory for the pineapple growers of the state, but DBCP's effect on Hawaiian workers was just as devastating as its effect on workers in the rest of the country. One study showed that 40 percent of the state's pineapple workers had dangerously low sperm counts.[11] In addition, evidence persists that DBCP is being used on products in less developed countries around the world — products that sometimes make it back onto the U.S. market.[12]

As the chemical companies searched for other unsuspecting countries in which they could manufacture DBCP, the fruit and vegetable growers in the United States were beginning a campaign to get the chemical back on the market. In an effort to push the news of sterile workers onto the back pages, the growers issued dire warning that without DBCP, food prices would take a sharp rise. The news from Lathrop, Magnolia, and Mobile, however, had already attracted national media attention and would not fade away. Indeed, new questions were being raised about DBCP. If DBCP caused sterility and cancer among workers, as it apparently did, then what about the effect on the consumers who ate the DBCP–

laden fruit? What about the farmworkers who sprayed the DBCP on the fruit trees and vegetables?

Ralph Lightstone, an attorney with California Rural Legal Assistance (CRLA), a group that represents farmworkers, once lived on a ranch where DBCP was used. "I saw how it was handled," reported Lightstone. "It was dripped into the irrigation water. The streets are always flooded with irrigation water because it runs for 24 hours. Irrigators get wet. Kids play in it."[13]

The fruit growers understood this danger to young children and were not oblivious to dangers posed to older workers using DBCP. The National Peach Council, for example, an association representing 6,300 peach growers in 35 states, admitted that DBCP might cause sterility, but suggested that sterility wasn't all that bad. In a letter to OSHA, Peach Council executive secretary Robert K. Phillips told OSHA administrator Eula Bingham that by banning DBCP from the marketplace, Bingham "may have overreacted." He suggested that older workers who do not want children and persons who would like to get around religious bans against birth control be allowed to handle DBCP. "If possible sterility is the main problem," Phillips asked, "couldn't workers who were old enough that they no longer wanted to have children accept such positions voluntarily? Or could workers be advised of the situation, and some might volunteer for such work posts as an alternative to planned surgery for a vasectomy or tubal ligation, or as a means of getting around religious bans on birth control when they want no more children." Moreover, Phillips claimed that DBCP did not cause cancer in human beings.[14]

And Hooker Chemical Company wanted back in, too. After the EPA ban, Hooker officials wrote a two-page memo discussing the possibility of reentering the DBCP market should the ban be lifted. In determining the risk involved, the internal memo looked at a number of factors:

- Determine the normal temporary or permanent sterility rate in the general population. Also the normal cancer rate for the type of tumor DBCP is suspected of causing.
- Assume that 50 percent of the normal rate for those exposed may file claims; determine the number of potential claims for cancer and sterility.

• Estimate the probable average judgment or settlement which would result from a claim; calculate the potential liability.[15]

Eventually, 57 DBCP workers brought suit against Occidental, Dow, Shell, and the University of California. Most of the plaintiffs alleged fertility and genetic damages and fear of cancer and birth defects. Three cancer claims and one wrongful death action were also brought. The cases were consolidated in a single suit in San Francisco federal court. In October 1982, Occidental agreed to pay $425,000 to settle 25 claims against the company. Much of the money went to pay lawyers. The widow of an Occidental employee who had died of brain cancer settled her separate wrongful death action against the company for a reported $750,000. Other cases were settled in pretrial conference.

By December 7, 1982, only seven plaintiffs remained, as *Arnett v. Dow*, the DBCP case, went to trial. Occidental, the University of California, and a university researcher also named as a defendant had settled out of the case, leaving only Dow and Shell as defendants. The plaintiffs charged that Dow and Shell knew about the toxic effects of DBCP on testicles of lab animals during the 1950s, that they failed to warn workers of the hazards of DBCP, and that they conspired to suppress the test results by convincing the government of the adequacy of watered-down labels. After hearing five months of testimony, a jury awarded the DBCP workers $4.9 million in damages. One worker received $2 million for sterility and $25,000 for fear of cancer. A second received $1 million for sterility, $37,500 for fear of cancer, and $10,000 for fear of birth defects. His wife received $100,000 for loss of consortium and $20,000 for fear of birth defects.[16]

After working as a supervisor at the Occidental plant for 15 years, John Kreitzer died of cancer. Esther Kreitzer, his wife, believed that "chemicals had a lot to do" with John's death. She puts the blame squarely on corporate shoulders. "You can say anything you want to," she tells a visitor, "but large corporations, Occidental Chemical for one — one of the largest, that's all they're in business for. They're in business to make money, you know, regardless as to what happens to my life or Jack's life or anybody else's life that works out there."

Esther Kreitzer believes that workers can and should fight to protect their health. "If you stay in that plant and put up a fight, some type of fight, you're going to be able to help things out, but if you get up and leave it, they're going to keep on doing the same thing over and over again. Their number one priority will still be money until somebody puts their foot down and says, 'Hey, you're going to quit killing these people — you're going to quit giving them cancer.'"[17]

Notes

1. Quotes from Lathrop workers and residents taken from transcript of film *Song of the Canary.* New Day Films, 1554 6th St., #1, Berkeley, CA, 94710.

2. *Elements of Risk: The Chemical Industry and Its Threat to America,* by Cathy Trost. New York Times Books, New York, 1984, p. 199.

3. Ibid., p. 223.

4. *America the Poisoned,* by Lewis Regenstein. Acropolis Books, p. 317.

5. "Firms Had Sterility Data on Pesticide," *Washington Post,* August 23, 1977.

6. *Elements of Risk,* Trost, p. 42.

7. *America the Poisoned,* Regenstein, p. 321.

8. *Song of the Canary* transcript, p. 13.

9. Ibid.

10. "The Sterility Scandal," by Daniel Ben-Horin. *Mother Jones,* May 1979, p. 54.

11. *America the Poisoned,* Regenstein, p. 324.

12. *Circle of Poison,* by David Weir and Mark Shapiro. Institute for Food and Developmental Policy, San Francisco, 1981, p. 20.

13. "The Sterility Scandal," Ben-Horin, p. 61.

14. "Peach Growers Suggest that Those Who Don't Want Children Handle Pesticide that Can Cause Sterility," *New York Times,* September 27, 1977, p. 18.

15. "Chemical Dumping as a Way of Life," by Matt Tallmer. *Progressive,* November 1981, pp. 35–42.

16. *Elements of Risk,* Trost, pp. 277–90.

17. *Song of the Canary,* p. 18.

8
Dalkon Shield

"There is not a damn thing wrong with the Dalkon Shield. Ninety percent of these gals, Christ, you ought to read their histories . . . Its unreal. The number of men they screw would knock you off your seat."

—corporate defense lawyer putting forth the view that uterine infection is caused by frequent sexual contact rather than by use of an intrauterine device known as the Dalkon Shield[1]

IN 1973, CARIE PALMER was a young mother of two. Palmer wanted more children—two or three more. The two that she had were boys, and Palmer wanted to try for a girl. She also wanted to space her children out a little more, so she began searching for an effective and safe contraceptive. Palmer was afraid of the widely used birth control pill because of what she had read concerning pill-induced strokes. She asked her doctor for an alternative to the pill, and he suggested an intrauterine device (IUD).

IUDs became popular during the mid-sixties, as the dangers associated with the pill became widely known. An IUD is a thumbnail-size device of metal or plastic that is inserted into the uterus to prevent conception. Medical device manufacturers have marketed a wide range of IUDs; they came in different shapes and had names such as Lippes Loop, Saf-T-Coil, Comet, Butterfly, Multiloop, and Ahmed.

Carie Palmer's doctor had just recently come across literature promoting the Dalkon Shield, an IUD manufactured by the A.H. Robins company of Richmond, Virginia, hailed by the company as having the "lowest pregnancy rate," as the "Modern, Superior IUD," and as "safe." Since Palmer's doctor had very little knowledge or experience with the Dalkon Shield, he was left to rely to a great extent on Robins's claims of effectiveness and safety.

Unfortunately for Palmer, Robins was wrong on both counts. In July of 1973, despite the fact that earlier in the year her doctor had inserted a Dalkon Shield in her uterus, Palmer became pregnant. At that time, standard medical practice held that if a woman became pregnant while using an IUD, the IUD should not be removed. It was thought that the newly conceived fetus and the Dalkon Shield could both occupy the uterus at the same time. The fetus would be protected from the rough edged-IUD by the amniotic sac. The sac and the IUD would simply come out at the time of birth, with the afterbirth. That was the theory.

While Palmer's pregnancy was uncomplicated for the first 16 weeks, the 17th proved disastrous. On November 16, everything was going well, and for the first time Palmer heard her baby's heartbeat. Then, two days later, at about 2:00 p.m., while Palmer was working at her part-time job, she began feeling terrible, and soon thereafter called her doctor. Immediately, her doctor ordered her to the emergency room of the hospital where she was found to have a very high white blood cell count and a fever. There were signs that Palmer would abort the baby, and she was diagnosed as having the flu.

Palmer was admitted to the hospital, and as daytime turned to night, her condition worsened. At 2:00 a.m. the next day, Palmer lost her baby, and then went into septic shock. She rapidly became critically ill. Her doctors were giving her massive blood transfusions and drugs designed to stimulate her blood pressure, but she failed to respond. Her blood pressure dropped dramatically, first to 60/20 then to 50/40. Eventually doctors stabilized her condition, then attempted to find out what was wrong.

A needle was inserted into the abdominal cavity and came back full of blood. After getting consent from Palmer's husband, the doctors decided to do exploratory abdominal surgery. They opened her up and found a quart of free blood originating from no obvious source. This indicated to the doctors that Palmer's blood clotting abilities had been totally exhausted. She was oozing blood internally through her organs. Again, the doctors went to Mr. Palmer to get his consent. This time they wanted to remove her tubes and ovaries—an emergency hysterectomy. Again, Mr. Palmer agreed. The operation was done in order to save her life.[2]

A.H. Robins distributed an estimated 4.5 million Shields in 80 countries. The Shields injured thousands of women, most of them suffering from life-threatening pelvic inflammatory disease (PID), which also impaired or destroyed the ability to bear children. Shield-induced PID killed at least 18 women in the United States alone. Of the estimated 110,000 women who conceived while wearing the Shield, probably 66,000 miscarried—most as a result of spontaneous abortions. Others suffered infected miscarriages known as septic spontaneous abortions. And hundreds of women gave birth prematurely to stillborn children or to children with birth defects including blindness, cerebral palsy, and mental retardation.[3]

Hugh J. Davis, M.D., assistant professor of obstetrics and gynecology at Johns Hopkins University, in Baltimore, was coinventor of the Dalkon Shield. He has been described as a tall neat man with an "overwhelming heart."[4] He viewed pregnancy as "a social evil—contributing to poverty, unhappiness and unrest," and was dedicated to finding an effective alternative to the much-criticized pill. While Davis looked at contraception from a medical angle, his coinventor, Irwin S. "Win" Lerner, saw it more from an inventor's point of view. Lerner, an engineer and inventor, met Davis in 1964 and they grew to be close friends. Together they researched and designed and produced the Dalkon Shield (the brand name "Dalkon" came from the amalgam of three names, Davis, Lerner, and Cohn. Robert E. Cohn, of Hartford, Connecticut, was the team's attorney). Other IUDs then on the market had problems — they caused pains, cramps, and bleeding, were insufficiently reliable, or they didn't stay in place. Davis and Lerner discussed these problems and attempted to design solutions. To prevent the IUD from dropping out of the uterus, they designed the Shield in a disk shape with barbed tentacles on the edges.

In January 1970, Davis testified before the Senate committee investigating alleged dangers of oral contraceptives. Davis told the committee, chaired by Gaylord Nelson (D.-Wis.), about new intrauterine contraceptive devices that offered virtually 100 percent protection against pregnancy without the risks of oral contraceptive pills. Davis was asked whether or not he held any commercial interest in any of the intrauterine devices. "I hold no recent patent on any intrauterine device," Davis answered. In fact, at the time, Davis held a 35 percent interest in the Dalkon Corporation. (Lerner owned 55 percent, Cohn 10 percent.)[5]

By August 1968, the first Dalkon Shields arrived at Davis's clinic at Johns Hopkins. The clinic was located in one of Baltimore's poorer neighborhoods and Davis tested his Dalkon Shield on its black and latino residents. In 12 months, Davis inserted about 640 Shields, and observed the results. In February 1970, with the prestigious Johns Hopkins name behind him, he reported the results in the *American Journal of Obstetrics and Gynecology*. The study caused a stir in the Ob/Gyn community. Of the 640 women who used the Shield, claimed Davis, only 5 became pregnant, or an astonishingly low rate of 1.1 percent. Davis concluded that "taken altogether, the superior performance of the shield intrauterine device makes this technique a first choice method of conception control."[6]

The Dalkon Shield became an immediate hit, but things might have been different had Hugh Davis provided a little more background information. First, nowhere in the article did Davis reveal his financial interest in the company. It is unclear whether Davis's financial interest in the Shield affected his research, but it necessarily forced him into a position not conducive to impartiality—a fundamental prerequisite for all scientific research, especially when the outcome may affect the lives of millions of human beings. Some observers have also questioned the reliability of any pregnancy study like this one, in which there was an average of only 5.5 months of testing per woman, when an accepted testing period was twelve months.

But standing alone, Davis's article made the Shield look good to thousands of physicians and family planning clinics. To take advantage of the publicity generated by the article, Davis, Lerner, and Cohn—and the Dalkon Corporation's first salesman, Thad Earl—began pushing the IUD at medical conventions around the country. At one such convention in Ohio, Earl, who was himself an M.D., ran into a salesman for A. H. Robins Company. Robins, a drug manufacturer, was perhaps best known to the American consuming public through its everyday products such as Chapstick, Robitussin cough syrup, and Sergeant's flea collar. The company was eager to enter the lucrative IUD field and saw a chance in the Dalkon Shield for greater profits. A meeting was set up in Richmond, where Robins purchased the patent rights for $750,000 from Davis, Lerner, Earl, and Cohn. Robins agreed to pay the four partners—by this time Earl was a partner—10 percent royalties on all gross sales of the Shield in the United States and Canada. The better Shields sold, the richer the four would get. Robins also agreed to pay yearly consulting fees: $30,000 a year for three years to Earl, $20,000 a year for five years to Davis, and a total of $150,000 to Lerner.[7]

As the deal was being cut, Robins medical director, Dr. Frederick Clark, Jr., flew to Baltimore to check on Davis's health data and Clark found that of the 832 patients tested, 26 had become pregnant. Davis had claimed a 1.1 percent rate, but Clark's findings indicated a rate of 3.1 percent pregnancy rate. Clark reported his findings in a memo dated June 9, 1970, to the company files. Two days later, Dr. Jack Freund, a vice president of the company, wrote another memo in which he expressed concern that the time span of Davis's study was not long enough to project with confidence to the population as a whole and that Davis's later data showed a pregnancy rate higher than that reported initially to Robins.[8]

Knowing of this discrepancy between Davis's widely publicized 1.1 percent pregnancy rate and what it later had reason to believe was a higher rate, on June 12, 1970, Robins nevertheless consummated the purchase. In October 1970, the company made five changes in the design of the Dalkon Shield before sending it onto the market under the company's name. Despite the company's finding that Davis's claim of 1.1 percent was misleading, and despite inadequate testing, the company went ahead and marketed the Shield with claims of "lowest pregnancy rate . . . 1.1 percent," "The Modern Superior IUD," "safe," "prevents pregnancy without any effect on the body, blood, or brain," and "nearly as effective as the birth control pill."[9]

Prior to marketing, Robins consulted William S. Floyd, an associate professor of Ob/Gyn at Wayne State University in Detroit. During the premarket tests, Dr. Floyd warned Robins that the device was not superior, that the pregnancy rate would be not 1.1 percent as claimed, but closer to 5 percent, and that Davis's published study was biased. Nevertheless, Robins procured approximately 199,000 copies of the Davis paper for dissemination to physicians.[10]

In September 1971, nine months after the market launch, Robins began a two-year baboon safety study. The results: one out of eight baboons "perished," and uterine perforation was found in 30 percent of the baboon population. Robins never revealed the results of this study.[11]

To promote the Shield, Robins placed ads in medical journals, some of which featured a flying uterus with a Dalkon Shield nestled inside. Some of the information generated by this promotional campaign was misleading. One widely disseminated misleading statement was that clinical trials at Johns Hopkins had shown a 1.1 percent pregnancy rate.

But the deceptive sales pitch was effective, and within a few years, 2.2 million women were walking around with Dalkon Shields inside them. Robins had captured roughly 45 percent of the IUD market. From a device that cost only pennies to make but was sold to the doctor for $4.35, the company was reaping a high rate of return. Robins stock shot through Wall Street's ceiling, rising 20 points, to a high of 40¾ during the three years after the Shield was first marketed.[12]

With the profits came the complaints. Women complained about difficulty of insertion, difficulty with removal, pain and bleeding, perforations (sometimes the Shield would perforate the uterus, whence it would enter the abdominal cavity), high pregnancy rates and occasional infections. The greatest danger came when the women became pregnant despite using the Shield. The fundamental proposition that a foreign object can safely be implanted into a womb to prevent pregnancy—a proposition that underlies the marketing of all IUDs—was, and continues to be, at best debatable. But once a woman accepted an IUD into her body, and in particular the Dalkon Shield, she accepted the risk, perhaps unknowingly, that if she became pregnant, her problems would be compounded. Soon after the Shield hit the market, it became clear that the crab-shaped Shield and a fetus were incompatible neighbors within the confines of the womb.

In February 1971, six weeks after Robins began selling the Shield, a doctor wrote to the company: "I have just inserted my tenth Dalkon Shield and have found the procedure to be the most traumatic manipulation ever perpetrated upon womanhood. . . . I have ordered all shields out of my office and will do the same in all clinics with which I am affiliated." One gynecologist, as soon as she saw the crab-shaped Shield, refused to use it. "When the Dalkon Shield appeared on the scene, we rejected its use on my say-so. Why? Well, it's a gruesome-looking device that I would not allow to be installed in myself, that's why."[13]

If a woman became pregnant, the doctor was not to try to remove the Shield, but following this advice did not guarantee a safe pregnancy. Many pregnant Dalkon Shield wearers did not go to full term without severe problems. Some developed severe infections during the mid-trimester. Others died.

The burgeoning problem of spontaneous septic abortions or infected miscarriages was brought to Robins's attention in the summer of 1972 by Thad Earl, the Dalkon Shield's original salesman. As noted, Earl was a Robins consultant and had a royalty interest in the Robins sales of the Shield. He was also selected by Robins as one of ten doctors around the country to run continuing studies on the Dalkon Shield after it had been put on the market. Earl had spoken with many doctors who told him that they had witnessed mid-trimester spontaneous septic abortions in women using the Shield. Earl himself observed the syndrome in his own patients. On June 23, 1972, Earl notified Robins, in a letter that read, in part:

> The next situation I have found is with women becoming pregnant and if the Shield is left in place the women abort at three and one-half to five months and become septic. I am advising physicians that the device should be removed as soon as a diagnosis of pregnancy is made. Numerous physicians have noted this. In my [patients'] six pregnancies, I removed one and she carried full term, the rest all aborted and became septic. I, therefore, feel it is hazardous to leave the device in and I advised that it be removed. I realize that this is a small statistic but I feel we should correlate this data with other investigators across the country, because most men [doctors] are experiencing the same problems.[14]

In addition to Earl's eye-opening report, Robins received independent communications from doctors around the country reporting spontaneous septic abortions. But for 18 months after Earl's memo, Robins did little to warn doctors or patients of the Shield's apparent dangers. Robins did not launch a full-scale investigation. For 18 months the company sat on these reports and doctors continued to insert the Shield into thousands of women. Many of those women became pregnant, and many, like Carrie Palmer, became seriously ill.

During the late months of 1973, Dr. Donald Christian, of the University of Arizona, was researching and writing about the Dalkon Shield septic abortion problem. Only upon learning about the imminent publication of Christian's reports was Robins prodded into action. The company called a "septic abortion conference" in Richmond, Virginia, and invited 12 doctors to attend, including some from the company's own advisory panel. Earl, who had recently sent off his warning memo to Robins, was not invited. Nor was Christian. Earl's June 23, 1972, letter was withheld from the conferees. During the conference, a vote was taken as to whether the Dalkon Shield was uniquely related to second trimester spontaneous septic abortions. Five voted yes, five voted no, and two abstained.[15]

Robins did not need a "septic abortion conference," or a vote of doctors, to learn of the dangers of the Shield. It already had in its possession Earl's memo and other complaints from doctors around the country. One Robins memo dated June 29, 1970 from R. W. Nickless, management coordinator for pharmaceutical products, informed of the "wicking" properties of the string. The tail-string of the Dalkon Shield, which is made of about 400 tiny strands encased in a nylon sheath, hangs out of the uterus so a woman can check to see if the Shield is still in place. Wicking would mean facilitating the movement of bacteria from the outside into the uterus.

A second memo from Roy Smith, a Robins executive, shows that three days *before* Robins bought the Shield, Smith raised ethical reservations about selling an IUD that would leach copper into a woman's body.[16] Dr. Ellen Preston, the company's liaison with physicians, expressed concern about wicking as early as 1971, in a memo to her boss, Dr. Clark. Her fears were confirmed months later when independent tests indicated that bacteria from the vagina would enter the open end of the tailstring and "wick" upward through the string. During pregnancy, the tailstring and accumulated bacteria would be drawn into the previously sterile womb, increasing chances of a spontaneous abortion in the second trimester. Others who studied the Shield theorized that the barbs that circle the crab-shaped Shield would catch onto the uterine lining, creating a place where infection could start.

In his book *At Any Cost*, an in-depth account of the Dalkon Shield, Morton Mintz reports how Robins executives were "repeatedly warned of the string's wicking properties, but they failed or refused to listen. Instead, they stonewalled, deceived, covered up, and covered up the cover ups. And in doing so they inflicted on women a worldwide epidemic of pelvic infections."

At one point, E. Wayne Crowder, a quality control supervisor in the Shield manufacturing plant in Richmond, warned his supervisor, Julian W. Ross, about the wicking problem. Crowder recalls how "I told [Ross] that I couldn't, in good conscience, not say something about something I felt could cause infections. And he said that my conscience did not pay my salary. . . . He referred to my persistent 'insubordination' [and said that] if I valued my job I would do as I was told."[17]

Finally, in May 1974, almost two years after Earl had warned the company about the septic abortion Shield syndrome, Robins sent out a "Dear Doctor" letter advising the medical profession of the risk of leaving the Dalkon Shield inside the womb in the event of pregnancy. The letter recommended that women who became pregnant while wearing the Shield be given therapeutic abortions. The Robins letter closely paralleled the warning raised by Earl in his letter of June 1972.[18]

On the heels of this announcement, things turned sour for the Shield and for Robins. The Planned Parenthood Federation sent a memo to its member clinics suggesting that they cease prescribing the Shield. The Federation reported that 26.4 percent of Dalkon Shield users in their clinics experienced severe cramps and bleeding.[19] On June 27, 1974, at the request of the Food and Drug Administration (FDA), Robins suspended distribution of the device, and an FDA advisory panel later recommended that "the moratorium on commercial distribution of the Dalkon Shield remain in effect pending accumulation of definitive data." Six years later, in September 1980, as the lawsuits against Robins mounted, the company urged physicians to remove the Shield from women still wearing it.[20]

Nearly 15,000 Shield users have sued Robins to seek justice. Robins has so far settled about 6,900 of the cases for more than

$200 million.[21] A few plaintiffs, like Carrie Palmer, have chosen to take their chances before a jury. At trial, the company has in some instances sought to defend itself by shifting the blame to the victims. In these instances, Robins attorneys argued that the women's injuries could conceivably have been caused by sources other than the Shield, such as frequent sexual intercourse with multiple partners. Robins has won some of these cases by subjecting the women plaintiffs to intense questioning about their sexual histories. "They made her look like a whore," complained one plaintiff's attorney who lost a case to Robins. "It was all innuendo."[22]

Sexual innuendos were only one tactic in the Robins war of dirty tricks waged against Shield victims suing the company for compensation. Lying was another, as was destruction of key documents. Throughout more than ten years of litigation, the attorneys for the Shield users alleged that Robins had effectively avoided discovery of relevant documents by improperly hiding behind the attorney/client privilege and work product doctrine.

In response to these complaints, on February 8, 1984, Judge Miles Lord, hearing some 400 Shield cases in his federal courtroom in Minneapolis, Minnesota, ordered that the Robins documents be viewed by someone other than Robins's attorneys to see which documents were legitimately covered by the attorney/client privilege or the work product doctrine. Judge Lord issued a second order prohibiting any party or their attorney from damaging, mutilating, or destroying any document having potential relevance to the consolidated cases being heard by the judge.[23]

On February 29, 1984, Lord, not reticent in condemning immoral and illegal behavior, corporate or individual, lashed out against Robins in what is destined to become a classic in the history of judicial reprimand. After approving a $4.6 million settlement of seven product liability cases involving the Shield, Lord summoned to his courtroom E. Claiborne Robins, Jr., the company president, Carl D. Lunsford, senior vice president for research and development, and William A. Forrest, Jr., vice president and general counsel. He gave each of the men a statement that he said he hoped "burns its mark into your souls." When one of the Robins attorneys objected to Lord's questioning of the three executives and asked that the proceeding be halted, Lord read the statement aloud.[24] He accused the company of "corporate irresponsibility at its meanest."

"Under your direction," Lord intoned, as the three executives sat silently and a number of plaintiffs wept, "your company has in fact continued to allow women, tens of thousands of them, to wear this device—a deadly depth charge in their wombs, ready to explode at any time. . . . You have taken the bottom line as your guiding beacon and the low road as your route." Lord also chastised the company for its questioning of the plaintiffs. "You inquired into their sexual practices," Lord said. "You exposed these women— and ruined families and reputations and careers—in order to intimidate those who would raise their voices against you."[25]

Robins filed an immediate complaint with the Eighth Circuit Court of Appeals. The company charged that Lord was against it from the beginning, sought to have him sanctioned, and sought to have his remarks stricken from the record.[26] Robins charged the judge with "a gross abuse of judicial discretion and power. . . . Contrary to the court's accusation, the company believes it has acted responsibly in the handling of the Dalkon Shield."[27] Robins hired former attorney general Griffin Bell to represent it, and Lord brought in former attorney general Ramsey Clark to defend him against the Robins charges. Hearings were held in late 1984, and on November 2 a three-judge federal panel of the Eighth Circuit ordered Lord's statement expunged from the record.[28]

Lord's statement, in addition to touching off a furor about corporate and judicial ethics, triggered the conscience of Roger L. Tuttle. Tuttle worked as a lawyer for Robins from 1971 until 1976. In July and August 1984, he testified under oath that he had been ordered to arrange the destruction of sensitive documents relating to the Dalkon Shield case.[29] A second former Robins attorney, Harris W. Wagenseil, controlled about 20 boxes of Dalkon Shield documents stored in his home. In a May 25, 1984, letter, Robins notified the court that the documents had been thrown out in a "general spring cleaning."

Other unusual testimony came forth in the wake of the widely reported Lord lecture. Patricia Lashley, a legal assistant to vice president and general counsel William Forrest, testified in April 1984 that notes of a key meeting of Robins executives to discuss the Shield could not be found in the file where she kept them. She could not explain the reason for the disappearance. Similarly, on February 28, 1984, Lashley revealed for the first time the fact that the Robins Septic Abortion Conference was tape recorded. These tapes have never been made public.[30]

The reports of missing documents and thrown-out documents raised the suspicion that Robins was trying to hide something. Rather than cooperate with the judge in a process of open discovery, Robins decided instead to seek to remove Lord from the bench. Plaintiffs' attorneys, in turn, sought to have Robins sanctioned for violating Judge Lord's February 28 Non-Destruct order.

In 1979, when Robins entered the courtroom against Carie Palmer, the company had to leave its dirty tricks and its "blame the victim" defense at the door. For Carie Palmer, Robins's twin claim that the Dalkon Shield was both effective and safe proved disastrously wrong. The Shield failed to prevent her pregnancy and, she believed, caused the death of her baby and then caused her severe injury and loss of her reproductive capacity. After her operation, Palmer suffered long-term problems including hormonal replacement problems and lower abdominal pain due to scarring. She also suffered enormous depression over the loss of her baby and her inability to have more children.

In the Palmer case, Robins argued that the Shield was no worse and no better than any other IUD, that any mistakes it made were innocent mistakes based on simple bureaucratic errors in filing, and that it didn't understand what people were trying to tell it about the dangers of the Shield. This third argument was made when Carie Palmer's attorney entered Thad Earl's early warning letter into evidence. But the jury was not convinced by Robins's arguments and awarded Palmer $600,000 to compensate her for injuries and $6.2 million to punish Robins.[31] The $6.2 million award dealt a severe blow to Robins because it signaled to other lawyers that Robins could be beaten.

Thousands of Dalkon Shield lawsuits have been filed against Robins and only a handful have gone to trial. Robins has settled the vast majority out of court for amounts ranging from $250 to $1.375 million. By June 30, 1984, in those cases that did go to trial, juries had awarded punitive damages in eight cases totaling $17.2 million. Once a promising money-maker, the Dalkon Shield in the end cost the company dearly. Robins estimated payouts to Shield victims would hit $1 billion by the year 2002. On August 21, 1985, Robins asked a federal judge to let it reorganize under Chapter 11 of the Bankruptcy Code. Victims' attorneys immediately blasted the filing as a "sham" and "unjustified" action that would protect it from future claims of victims of the Shield. The decision on bankruptcy is pending.[32]

In October 1987 U.S. District Court Judge Robert Mehrige, Jr. found A.H. Robins Co., and its president and chief executive officer, E. Clairborne Robins, Jr., in criminal contempt of court because of what Judge Merhige called "deliberate defiance" of a court order to recover millions of dollars in improper payments that were made after the firm went bankrupt in August 1985. Judge Merhige fined the pharmaceutical's president $10,000, saying that he had to remedy an attitude that produced "excuse after excuse after excuse."

A citation of the Richmond, Virginia-based Robins for civil and criminal contempt had been sought by the Dalkon Shield Claimants' Committee, a group that represents thousands of women who claim they were injured by the Shield. The Shield victims' group argued that the company had unilaterally decided to terminate the program to recover improper payments "although they had no right to stop." According to court documents, Robins failed to recover about $3.7 million.

It was the revelations of the Dalkon Shield-induced injuries that led to the passage of the Medical Device Amendments of 1976. Prior to 1976, device manufacturers, including Robins, were under no obligation to submit to the government pre-marketing tests on safety or effectiveness. Had the 1976 law been in effect at the creation of the Shield, this disaster might not have happened.

Notes

1. "Piercing the Dalkon Shield," *National Law Journal*, June 16, 1980, p. 13.
2. Letter from Douglas E. Bragg (Palmer attorney) to Hon. Jim R. Carrigan, Colorado Supreme Court, August 1, 1979.
3. *At Any Cost: Corporate Greed, Women, and the Dalkon Shield*, by Morton Mintz. Pantheon, New York, 1985, p. 3.
4. "A Case of Corporate Malpractice," by Mark Dowie and Tracy Johnson. *Mother Jones*, November 1976, p. 37.
5. Ibid. See also *At Any Cost*, Mintz, p. 37.
6. *At Any Cost*, Mintz, p. 31.
7. "The Dalkon Shield Story," by Aaron Levine. Unpublished manuscript, p. 20.
8. Letter from Bragg to Carrigan, p. 4.
9. Ibid.

10. "The Dalkon Shield Story," Levine, p. 23.

11. Ibid., p. 24.

12. "Dalkon Shield Starts Losing in Court," *American Lawyer*, July 1980.

13. "Criminals by Any Other Names," by Russell Mokhiber. *Washington Monthly*, January 1986, p. 40.

14. Bragg letter, p. 5, also "The Dalkon Shield Story," Levine, p. 30.

15. Bragg letter, p. 6.

16. *At Any Cost*, Mintz, p. 61.

17. Ibid., p. 141.

18. "A Case of Corporate Malpractice," Dowie and Johnson, p. 48.

19. Ibid.

20. "Maker of Dalkon Shield Urges Removal of Devices From Women Having Them," *Wall Street Journal*, September 26, 1980.

21. "Bizarre Twist in Lawsuits on Contraceptive Is Provided by Ex-A.H. Robins Attorney," *Wall Street Journal*, August 3, 1984.

22. "Piercing the Dalkon Shield," *National Law Journal*, June 16, 1980, p. 13.

23. "Notice of Motion and Motion for an Order Imposing Sanctions on Defendant A.H. Robins and Appointing Special Masters to Supervise Discovery," in *Mary Bolender v. A.H. Robins, Inc.*, Civil No. 3-80-341, pp. 1-3.

24. "U.S. Judge Assails Officers of Dalkon Shield Maker," by Morton Mintz. *The Washington Post*, March 2, 1984, p. A4.

25. *At Any Cost*, Mintz, p. 264.

26. "Jurist's Tactics Hasten the Pace of Litigation in Dalkon Shield Case," by Mary Williams Walsh. *Wall Street Journal*, September 14, 1984.

27. "U.S. Judge Assails Officers of Dalkon Shield Maker," *Washington Post*, March 2, 1984.

28. *At Any Cost*, Mintz, p. 236.

29. "Jurist's Tactics Hasten The Pace of Litigation in Dalkon Shield Case," Walsh.

30. Notice of Motion and Motion for an Order . . . , *Bolender v. A.H. Robins*, p. 10 et. seq.

31. Bragg letter, p. 1.

32. *At Any Cost*, Mintz, p. 245.

33. "A.H. Robins, Chief Executive, Found in Criminal Contempt," *Corporate Crime Reporter* 26 (7), October 19, 1987.

9
DC 10

"On my left, over a distance of four hundred or five hundred
meters, trees were hacked and mangled, most of them charred
but not burnt. Pieces of metal, brightly colored electric wires,
and clothes were littered all over the ground. In front of me,
in the valley, the trees were even more severely hacked and the
wreckage even greater. There were fragments of bodies and
pieces of flesh that were hardly recognizable. In front of me,
not far from where I stood, there were two hands clasping
each other, a man's hand tightly holding a woman's hand, two
hands which withstood disintegration . . ."

—Captain Jacques Lannier, commander of the
Senlis District of the French Gendarmerie Nationale,
describing scene outside of Paris on March 3, 1974
after Turkish Airlines flight 981 slammed into the
forest of Ermenonville[1]

THIS CRASH SITE WAS especially gruesome. As at most airplane crash
sites, there were the bodies, or the parts of the bodies, but here
there were more bodies than ever before. On March 3, 1974, 346
persons boarded Turkish Airlines flight 981, a DC-10 jumbo jet,
for the short trip from Paris to London. Nine minutes after takeoff
from Orly Airport, the plane's rear cargo door blew open, the aircraft decompressed rapidly, the floor caved in, and the 300-ton
DC-10, traveling at 475 mph, slammed into the forest of Ermenonville, 35 miles northeast of Paris. There were no survivors.

At the time, this was the worst crash in the history of aviation.[2] The 18 children who died included a one-month old baby. There were 30 college students, 21 engineers, 3 architects, 1 priest, 4 doctors, 2 nurses, 8 teachers, 3 accountants, and 3 lawyers. Dr. Charles Bowley of Sheffield was an internationally recognized authority on blood transfusion. Dr. Patrick Hutton was principal scientific officer at the British Atomic Weapons Research Establishment. Hubert "Jake" Davies and Geoffrey Brigstock were Britain's two chief experts on the law of the sea. Jim Conway was the secretary of Britain's second largest union, the Amalgamated Union of Electrical Workers (AUEW).[3] All were killed.

The impact of the crash left not one body intact. "Although a few heads were still attached to chests, a great many bodies were limbless, bellies were ripped open, and their contents emptied," reported Captain Lannier. "Everywhere, the scene was nightmarish; the Forest of Ermenonville had been turned into a battlefield, it was Verdun after the bloodiest battle."[4]

All crash scenes have bodies, ghastly tales, and grotesque endings, and in some cases, the pain of the family members and friends of the victims is somewhat mitigated by the thought that the carnage was the result of some sort of unavoidable accident, a fluke, or an act of God.

The DC-10 that crashed outside Paris, however, was different. This crash was preventable, foreseeable, and predictable—in fact, it was specifically predicted months before it happened. The 346 passengers aboard flight 981 died senseless deaths.

The DC-10 was McDonnell Douglas's entry into the race to capture the lucrative market of the new generation of large airplanes known as jumbo jets. During the 1960s, Douglas entered the high-stakes competition against two formidable rivals—Lockheed, with its L-1011 Tristar, and Boeing, with its 747. The costs of competing in this race were staggering: to develop the 747, Boeing committed $750 million, 90 percent of the corporation's net worth. McDonnell Douglas estimated development costs to be $1 billion. The competition was fierce and all three companies were pushed to the brink of financial disaster.

On August 7, 1968, Douglas chose Convair, a subsidiary of General Dynamics, to design the fuselage and doors for the DC-10. Convair was chosen not only because of the financial stability of its parent, but also because of its excellent reputation for structural design. Douglas executives immediately began handing out specifications. They told Convair that weight should be saved wherever possible, and that one pound of weight should be thought of as costing $100. In November 1968, Douglas instructed the Convair engineers to use electric actuators, rather than hydraulic cylinders, to drive the cargo door latches. Some engineers at Convair, in particular F.D. "Dan" Applegate, were not receptive to the idea. For starters, hydraulic cylinders for the latches would be intrinsically safer than electric actuators, they argued.

The Convair engineers, after studying potential hazards inherent in the Douglas design for the cargo door, drew up a draft Failure Mode and Effects Analysis (FMEA)—a document required by the Federal Aviation Administration (FAA) before it will certify an airplane. Convair's FMEA listed nine possible failure sequences that could lead to a Class IV hazard, a hazard involving danger to life. One of these nine described the possible situation where, given Douglas's suggested design, "the door will open—resulting in sudden depressurization and possibly structural failure of floor; also damage to empennage [tail assembly] by expelled cargo and/or detached door. *Class IV hazard in flight.*"[5] This draft FMEA was forwarded to Douglas.

As lead manufacturer, Douglas was responsible for certification of the DC-10, but Convair's FMEA was never shown to the FAA by Douglas. The FMEAs submitted to the FAA by Douglas did not mention the possibility of a hazard involving danger to life arising from malfunction of the lower cargo doors.

In May 1970, nine months after Convair had warned Douglas of the potential of a cargo door blowout, Douglas began ground tests of the DC-10 at its Long Beach, California, production facility, in preparation for its maiden flight scheduled for that August. One test was designed to check the air-conditioning system and involved the pressurization of the cabin. In the midst of this test, and without warning, the forward lower cargo door blew open and a large section of the cabin floor collapsed.

The fact that the cabin floor collapsed was especially pertinent to the design of the DC-10. In the event of any real midair accident, the crew of most aircraft, if they had control over the wings and tail, would have a fair chance of navigating their craft to safety. That chance would depend, of course, on the amount of damage done to the fuselage, the central body of the plane. The control cables of the DC-10, however, run from the cockpit to the tail, through the center of the plane, under the cabin floor. A midair accident that involved the collapse of the DC-10's cabin floor would in all probability sever the control cables and make it necessary to try to land the plane by manipulating the thrust from the three engines.

Despite the dangers inherent in the DC-10's design, and the warnings raised by the Convair engineers, and the Long Beach accident, Douglas appeared intent on sweeping all counterindications under the corporate rug. Douglas blamed the Long Beach accident on the "human failure" of the mechanic who closed the door. It made a slight modification in the design of the cargo door that added little or nothing to the safety factor. In fact, not even all the engineers at the Douglas production facility agreed with the efficacy of this slight modification. H.B. "Spud" Riggs wrote that the design concept of this new modification was "less than desirable" and suggested possible improvements to ensure the future safety of the aircraft. None of Riggs's suggestions were incorporated by Douglas into the DC-10, nor was his memo forwarded to the FAA.

The FAA, of course, doesn't have the manpower to check every part or safety system of all planes manufactured in the United States. It therefore appoints to every manufacturing plant a Designated Engineering Representative (DER). DERs are paid for by the company and their job is to ascertain that the plane meets Federal Airworthiness Regulations. Of the 42,950 inspections made of the DC-10, *roughly one-fourth were carried out by FAA personnel, with the remainder, including the check on the cargo door, assigned to McDonnell Douglas-paid DERs.* On July 29, 1971, almost three years after the Convair engineers warned about the cargo door, and one year after the Long Beach blowout, the FAA certified the DC-10 for safety.

McDonnell Douglas was given an additional warning about the designed-in danger of its DC-10 cargo door, and this came in the form of a near catastrophe over Detroit, Michigan. American Airlines flight 96 took off from Detroit's Wayne County Airport bound for Buffalo and New York, carrying 56 passengers. Captain Bryce McCormick lifted his DC-10 through the clouds over Lake Erie and pointed it east toward Buffalo. Five minutes after takeoff, flying 11,500 feet over Windsor, Ontario, McCormick heard a loud bang. It sounded, he said, like a book being brought down on a table very loudly. The aircraft was filled immediately with a dust storm, the earphones were ripped from his head, and the aircraft began to decelerate and yaw drastically to the right. The autopilot had disengaged itself.

The loud bang, as McCormock was to learn later, was the sound of the cargo door blowout, followed by the collapse of the cabin floor. McCormick went for the controls, but most were knocked out of commission. The collapse of the cabin floor had disabled most of the control for the tail surface and center engine. The plane was falling steadily, its nose dropping to the horizon, and the plane was about to head into a severe nose dive when McCormick grabbed the wing engine throttles and pushed them forward. The engines responded with a burst of power and the DC-10 leveled out.

Using the differential power of the wing engines, McCormick turned the big plane around and guided it back to Detroit. The DC-10 touched down at Wayne County Airport traveling at 186 miles per hour. After touchdown, the DC-10 lurched toward the terminal, but McCormick was able to pull it to a halt—half on the infield grass, half on concrete, a mile and a half from the end of the runway. With quick thinking and fast action, McCormick had averted a major catastrophe.[6]

The day after this incident over Windsor, the FAA began an investigation of the DC-10 by asking McDonnell Douglas officials if there had been any previous problems with the cargo doors. Company officials acknowledged only that there were a few "minor problems" and they failed to hand over the operating reports of the airline. This attitude disturbed the regional FAA officer handling the case, who then had to "raise a fuss to get the reports." McDonnell Douglas finally agreed to turn them over to the FAA, and in examining them, officials found that in the ten months that the DC-10 had been in service, there had been approximately a hundred instances of cargo doors failing to close properly. The FAA western regional office immediately began drafting an airworthiness directive (AD) that would have forced McDonnell Douglas to fix the cargo doors.

As the regional FAA cops discovered, enforcing the law against McDonnell Douglas would not be easy. Early one morning, while the ADs were being drafted, the head of the western regional FAA office, Arvin O. Basnight, received a call from Jackson McGowen, president of the Douglas division of McDonnell Douglas. McGowen told Basnight that he had spoken with Basnight's boss in Washington, FAA administrator John Shaffer. Shaffer and McGowen had "reviewed" the work that McDonnell Douglas had done on beefing up the DC-10 door system, the manufacturer was cooperating with the FAA, and there was no reason to issue the customary airworthiness directive. Basnight immediately got on the phone to Washington to confirm what McGowen told him. It was true. There would be no airworthiness directive.

In all the 30 years that he worked for the government, Basnight had never before felt compelled to do what he did after his conversation with his superiors. He sat down and wrote a 1,500-word memorandum to the file recording the events of the preceding days. It read in part, "Mr. Shaffer . . . had told Mr. McGowan that the corrective measures could be undertaken as a product of a Gentleman's Agreement, thereby not requiring the issuance of an FAA Airworthiness Directive."[7]

The difference between the issuance or nonissuance of an AD was the difference between law enforcement and no law enforcement. The gentleman's agreement between FAA's Shaffer and Douglas's McGowen meant, in effect, that there would be no law enforcement. McDonnell Douglas was left to its own devices and internal mechanisms to make and implement the necessary design changes on all its DC-10s. In fact, the company came up with a plan that might well have avoided the disaster outside Paris. Douglas issued Service Bulletins to airlines flying DC-10s, ordering them to implement the plan to modify the cargo door so that it would not blow out in midair. Unfortunately, one crucial Service Bulletin, SB 52-37, was printed on plain white paper, which implied that this was a routine service bulletin; there was no indication that the change was vital to the safety of the aircraft. As a result, many of the directives were carried out late or improperly or both.

Dan Applegate, the Convair engineer who questioned Douglas's original cargo door design, was not at all pleased with the FAA–McDonnell Douglas agreement. On June 27, 1972, 15 days after that understanding was reached, Applegate wrote a long memorandum to his superiors that began, "The potential for long-term Convair liability on the DC-10 has caused me increasing concern for several reasons." The memo outlined in detail Applegate's objections to the way McDonnell Douglas was handling the cargo door safety problem. Applegate was worried that the "progressive degradation of the fundamental safety of the cargo door latch system since 1968 has exposed us to increasing liability claims." On the American Airlines mishap over Windsor, he noted that it was "only chance that the airplane was not lost."

As for Douglas's proposed remedy, Applegate was not convinced that even if implemented it would ensure the safety of the airplane. "Douglas has again studied alternative corrective action," he wrote, "and appears to be applying more 'band-aids.'" Applegate also criticized Douglas for the design of its cabin floor, which he described as a "fundamental deficiency." In commenting on the Long Beach test incident, Applegate observed that the DC-10 "demonstrated an inherent susceptibility to catastrophic failure when exposed to explosive decompression of the cargo compartment."

He concluded his memo with a prophetic warning and a recommendation: *"It seems to me inevitable,"* he wrote, *"that in the twenty years ahead of us, DC-10 cargo doors will come open and I would expect this to usually result in the loss of an airplane.* It is recommended that overtures be made at the highest management level to persuade Douglas to immediately make a decision to incorporate changes in the DC-10 which will correct the fundamental cabin floor catastrophic failure mode." (Emphasis added.)[8]

Applegate's memo reached top-level Convair management, but apparently never made it to McDonnell Douglas or to the FAA. Applegate's immediate superior, J.B. Hurt, wrote a reply memo recognizing that "we have an interesting legal and moral problem," but suggesting that no approach be made to Douglas. At a meeting of Convair executives it was decided that Applegate's memo would not leave the company. "After all," said Hurt afterward, "most of the statements made by Applegate were considered to be well-known to Douglas."[9]

On March 3, 1974, less than two years after Applegate wrote his memo, Turkish Airways flight 981 left Paris bound for London. A few minutes into the flight, when the DC-10 was at about 13,000 feet, the cargo door blew out, the cabin floor collapsed, and the crew lost control of the aircraft. The on-board recording told the story of the final few seconds in the cockpit (the names are those of the Turkish Airline crew members):

VOICES: oop Aw Aw.

A klaxon goes off. Plus nine seconds.

BERKOZ: What happened?

ULSMAN: The cabin blew out.

Eleven seconds.

BERKOZ: Are you sure?

Sixteen seconds.

BERKOZ: Bring it up, pull her nose up.

ULSMAN: I can't bring it up—she doesn't respond.

Twenty-three seconds.

AN UNIDENTIFIED VOICE (PROBABLY OXER): Nothing is left.

Klaxon sounds, warning that the plane has gone over the "never exceed" speed.

Thirty-two seconds.

BERKOZ: Hydraulics?

ANOTHER VOICE: "We have lost it . . . oops oops."

Fifty-four seconds.

BERKOZ: "Speed."

Sixty-one seconds.

BERKOZ: "Oops."

There is no further speech.

Seventy-seven seconds.

Sound of initial impact.

McDonnell Douglas and General Dynamics settled more than 300 lawsuits out of court and paid damages estimated at $80 million.[10] In July 1975, the FAA ordered the modification of all DC-10 cargo doors and of all DC-10, TriStar, and 747 floors.[11] The delay cost the lives of 346 people.

Notes

1. *Destination Disaster,* by Paul Eddy, Elaine Potter, and Bruce Page. Quadrangle, New York, 1976, p. 6.
2. *Darkest Hours,* by Jay Robert Nash. Wallaby, New York, 1977, p. 572.
3. *Destination Disaster,* Eddy et al., p. 246.
4. Ibid., p. 11.
5. Ibid., p. 178.
6. *Lawsuit,* by Stuart M. Speiser. Horizon Press, New York, 1980, p. 421.
7. *Destination Disaster,* Eddy et al., p. 153; also *Lawsuit,* Speiser, p. 423.
8. Ibid., p. 178.
9. Ibid., p. 187.
10. "Last Suit Is Settled Arising from Crash of Turkish Air DC-10 Near Paris," *Wall Street Journal,* November 30, 1977, p. 26.
11. *Destination Disaster,* Eddy et al., p. 164.

10
DES

"In my naïveté, I had believed that the drug companies were humanitarian institutions. I had really believed that. Gradually I was realizing that the pharmaceutical industry is made up of large corporations and like any large corporation, they are in the business to make money. Profits are their ultimate goal. The fact that their business happens to be in the field of human health is virtually irrelevant."

—Joyce Bichler, DES daughter[1]

"APART FROM BEING in love and struggling desperately with chemistry and calculus, I suddenly had something else on my mind," says Joyce Bichler about her first semester in college, in her book *DES Daughter*. "Since I had started college I had noticed that my periods had become very irregular. Instead of having four days of bleeding, it was more like seven or eight. My menstrual cycle seemed to be completing itself every three weeks instead of four, and the bleeding was lasting longer and longer."

At first Bichler attributed her irregular cycle to the trials and traumas of being a first-year university student. She had just left home for the first time in her life, she was trying to keep up with a hectic academic schedule, and she was in love. A little irregularity in the menstrual cycle was understandable, she thought.

At the end of the semester, however, while home from Christmas break, Bichler had no weeks at all between her periods. "I was bleeding almost constantly," she recalls. "I was going through a jumbo-sized box of tampons in just ten days. I still tried not to be alarmed. I still told myself that this irregularity was caused by the changes in my life and that it would eventually get back to being normal all by itself. But as much as I tried to deny it, the fear was there. I was terrified that there was something seriously wrong with me. I just wasn't ready to face it yet." Bichler hid the box of tampons in the back of her closet so her mother wouldn't notice how quickly they disappeared.

By the time Bichler returned to college for the spring semester, she was practically hemorrhaging. She called the university health office and made an appointment for the next day. "That night, I couldn't sleep," she recalled. "I lay in bed worrying. Part of me was sure something was seriously wrong, and part of me was hoping desperately that everything would be all right." Frustrated by her inability to sleep, Bichler turned on the light and picked up a medical journal (her roommate was pre-med). "I turned the pages only to discover an article about cervical cancer. To my horror, it described the exact symptoms I had—in particular the ever-increasing bleeding." Bichler threw the journal on the floor. A stream of thoughts, questions, and fears began running through her mind. "Cancer? I could not believe that could happen to me."

Nineteen-forty-seven was a bad year for Joyce Bichler. She was not born until 1955, and she didn't experience the profuse bleeding until 1972, but 1947 was the year she would remember. It was in 1947 that the Food and Drug Administration (FDA) allowed drug manufacturers, led by Eli Lilly & Company, to market the drug diethylstilbestrol (DES) for use by pregnant women. Eight years later, Mrs. Bichler, three months pregnant with Joyce, was told to take DES to avoid a possible miscarriage. Mrs. Bichler followed the doctor's instructions and took the pills for twelve days. Joyce was born an apparently healthy baby, but the DES pills that her mother took affected Joyce, not her mother, and affected her not at birth, but 18 years later.

DES, the world's first synthetic estrogen (female hormone) was discovered by Dr. Charles Dodds in 1938. Dodds took out no patent on the drug, but gave it as a "gift" to the world—and to the world's drug companies. These companies, with visions of millions of postmenopausal women creating a multimillion-dollar estrogen replacement market, accepted Dodds's gift and began plotting to market the drug for as many uses as possible.[2]

An Eli Lilly researcher, Don Carlos Hines, took Dodds's gift and ran with it to the FDA for approval. But in 1939, the FDA rejected Lilly's application because the testing had not been adequate. Hines, realizing that several other major pharmaceutical companies were also working to get DES approved, approached these companies, including Abbott and Squibb, with the idea of forming a joint research committee to pool information. This would expedite gaining quick approval from the FDA. The committee was formed and the companies shared the results of the research, but each company filed an independent application with the FDA.[3]

By 1941, the coordinated effort began to pay off. The FDA approved DES to inhibit lactation in women who did not want to breast-feed their babies, for men who had prostate cancer, and for postmenopausal women as an estrogen replacement.

The drug companies, however, believed that women who had a tendency to miscarry would also benefit from extra doses of DES. The excitement within the industry over this possible use of synthetic estrogen was enormous. One researcher proclaimed that DES would make a normal pregnancy even more normal. The excitement, however, obscured the danger warnings coming from independent researchers.

Even at the time DES was first synthesized in 1938, it was found to be carcinogenic in laboratory animals.[4] Lilly's Hines was aware of DES's cancer potential, but since he considered the risk not "significant," his joint committee continued to work for quick FDA approval. Early studies of DES in the 1930s and early 1940s had shown that the drug was a teratogen (a teratogen is a drug that crosses through the placental barrier and causes harmful effects to the offspring). A 1939 Northwestern University study found that DES produced structural changes in sexual organs. A 1939 University of Liverpool study showed that DES may induce uterine cancer in humans. A 1939 Lilly study found that DES produced mammary cancer in mice. A 1942 Lilly study showed DES to be 12 times as active as estrogen by oral administration. A 1942 Georgetown University study found that DES induced breast tumors in rats. Between 1932 and 1947, over 24 articles appeared in the literature identifying DES, along with estrogen, as a carcinogen.[5] Some medical journals warned people to beware of DES because of its toxic effects and potential for causing cancer.

In December 1939, for example, the Council on Pharmacy and

Chemistry warned, in the *Journal of the American Medical Association,* that "Because the product [DES] is so potent and because the possibility of harm must be recognized, the Council is of the opinion that it should not be recognized for general use or for inclusion in *New and Nonofficial Remedies* at the present time and that its use by the general medical profession should not be undertaken until further studies have led to a better understanding of such a drug." Again, in the following year, the *Journal* warned in an editorial about the growing evidence linking estrogens with cancer: "Malignant growths of the mammary gland and the uterus have been induced in rodents with estrogens by numerous investigators. . . . Recently two significant reports have appeared which should indicate the possible dangers of administration of estrogen . . . It would be unwise to consider that there is safety in using small doses of estrogen, since it is quite possible that the same harm may be obtained through the use of small doses of estrogen over a long period of time."[6]

Joyce Bichler survived the day the doctors removed her uterus and vagina to save her from the cancer that was eating away at her body. She survived it with enough strength to confront one of the nation's largest pharmaceutical companies in a legal battle that would last eight years and set landmark legal and social precedents in the fields of drug safety and women's health. In 1972, Bichler sued Eli Lilly, claiming that DES was inadequately tested by the drug companies before it was marketed, that DES caused Bichler's cancer, and that Lilly, because it was one of the largest early manufacturers of the drug, must assume responsibility for Bichler's injuries.

Some DES victims, unable to prove that it was Lilly that had produced the DES that they or their mothers consumed, are proceeding against Lilly on what one plaintiffs' attorney has called the "Carney Theory." This approach was conceived based on the testimony of Robert Carney, then Lilly's president, in 1960, at congressional hearings 11 years before the FDA banned DES for pregnant women.

> CONGRESSMAN MOSS: What percentage of Stilbestrol consumed in this country is produced by Eli Lilly?
>
> PRESIDENT CARNEY: Maybe as high as 75 percent.[7]

In the spring of 1979, Bichler took her case before a jury of six citizens of the Bronx, a borough of New York City: a black businessman, a young black male bank teller, a young black woman who worked in a nursery school, a middle-aged black woman nurse, a middle-aged white male post office worker, and a middle-aged white mother whose daughter was a nurse. As the first witness, Bichler's attorney called Dr. Allen Goldman, an expert in the field of tetralogy. Goldman testified that while the drug companies, led by Lilly, did do their own testing of DES, they had failed to test the drug adequately. For instance, DES had never been tested on pregnant animals before being given to pregnant women. Goldman had long been astonished by this. If the tests had been done on pregnant mice, their offspring would show cancer of the cervix and vagina. Exactly this result was shown by a study done years later.

Goldman reviewed the medical literature on DES. Prior to the marketing of DES there existed numerous separate factors, which, taken as a whole, could have and should have alerted a reasonably prudent pharmaceutical company to the need for animal testing and the danger of promoting DES for pregnant women without undertaking such testing.[8]

As Bichler listened to Goldman's testimony, she clenched her fists. "I had known that the drug companies had done incompetent research," she says, "but I hadn't realized that they had been quite as irresponsible as this respected doctor was saying. They hadn't bothered to do a simple and necessary test that would have prevented all the pain and suffering that I and others had to endure. They had just used pregnant women as guinea pigs."[9]

Given that during the 1940s, the FDA did no independent testing of its own to determine whether a drug was safe or effective, instead relying on research carried out by the drug companies themselves, it followed that the FDA would eventually approve DES for use by pregnant women, as it did in 1947. But the FDA's reliance on drug company data may not have been the only reason that it discounted warnings about the safety of the drug.[10]

Another reason may have been Dr. Theodore Klump. Klump had been chief of the Drug Division of the FDA at the time DES was approved and was instrumental in getting the drug on the market. Klump testified about the FDA's testing procedures, or lack thereof, and told of how the agency relied on drug industry data. Before he left the stand, Bichler's attorney asked him how much money he made at the FDA. Kump replied that he made $6,000 a year. The attorney then asked how much he made the year he left the FDA. Klump shifted uncomfortably in his seat. He said that he left to become president of Winthrop Laboratories, a company that had filed for DES approval, at a salary of $30,000 a year.[11]

Bichler's attorneys also presented evidence that in 1953, six years after the FDA had approved DES for use by pregnant women, Dr. William J. Dieckmann of the University of Chicago conducted a controlled study on the effect of DES on pregnant women. Dieckmann did not believe that any of the previous drug company tests on effectiveness had been scientifically accurate. The results of Dieckmann's study showed that contrary to Lilly's claims, DES was not effective in preventing miscarriages.[12] A number of similar studies that Lilly left out of its promotional campaign for DES preceded Dieckmann's and raised similar questions as to the efficacy of DES. These included a 1947 University of Chicago study revealing no changes in the number of miscarriages caused by DES administration, a 1949 University of Edinburg study finding that DES causes no change, and a 1952 Columbia University study finding DES to be a dismal failure.[13]

Thus, by 1954, when a pregnant Mrs. Bichler swallowed the white DES tablets to "save her baby," it was known that the risks associated with DES were high, that DES was a teratogen and it was known that DES could cause cancer. Moreover, the 1953 Dieckmann study presented evidence that DES did not prevent miscarriages. The risks were high, the benefits questionable. Yet Eli Lilly continued to manufacture the drug and promote its use for pregnant women, until the FDA finally banned DES for such use in 1971.

Still, Lilly admitted no responsibility. Lilly's attorneys argued that adequate testing had been done on DES, that had it not been for the drug, Joyce Bichler would never have been born. Lilly also claimed that despite the recently mounting evidence to the contrary, DES does not cause cancer and it certainly did not cause Bichler's cancer. But the jury was not convinced.

At the end of the trial, the judge instructed the jury to answer six questions, all of which would have to be answered in Bichler's favor in order for Bichler to prevail. After three days of deliberation, the six men and women from the Bronx returned to the court-room to deliver their verdict.

The foreman stood. The judge read the questions. "Was DES safe for miscarriage purposes in 1953?" The foreman answered, "No, 5–1 (the vote of the jurors)." The questioning continued:

> JUDGE: Did DES cause Joyce Bichler's vaginal and cervical cancer?
>
> FOREMAN: Yes, 5 with one abstention.
>
> JUDGE: In 1953, should a reasonably prudent drug manufacturer have foreseen that DES might cause cancer in the offspring of pregnant women who took it?
>
> FOREMAN: Yes, 6–0.
>
> JUDGE: Foreseeing that DES might cause cancer in the offspring of pregnant women who took it, would a prudent manufacturer have tested it on pregnant mice before marketing it?
>
> FOREMAN: Yes, 6–0.
>
> JUDGE: If DES had been tested on pregnant mice, would the tests have shown that DES caused cancer in the offspring?
>
> FOREMAN: Yes, 6–0.
>
> JUDGE: Would a prudent manufacturer have marketed DES for miscarriage purposes had it known that it caused cancer in the offspring of pregnant mice?
>
> FOREMAN: No, 6–0.
>
> JUDGE: Did the defendant Eli Lilly and the other drug manufacturers act in concert with each other in the testing and marketing of DES for miscarriage purposes?
>
> FOREMAN: Yes, 6–0.
>
> JUDGE: How much do you award Ms. Bichler?
>
> FOREMAN: $500,000.[14]

DES was taken by hundreds of thousands of pregnant women from 1940 until 1971, when it was banned by the FDA for use by pregnant women. From 1945 to 1955, a time of peak DES usage, between half a million and two million women received DES, and as many as four to six million Americans (mothers, daughters, sons) may have been exposed to the drug during pregnancy.[15] Between 60 and 90 percent of daughters born to women who took DES during their pregnancies were found to have exhibited changes in their vagina or cervix. In some DES daughters, the vagina, cervix, and uterus showed structural changes. Approximately one in a thousand DES daughters develop a cancer known as adenocarcinoma, which usually starts on the cervix or vagina. DES daughters aren't the only ones affected, however. DES sons face an increased chance of having fertility problems and testicular abnormalities.[16]

Today more than 6,000 named plaintiffs in 40 states have brought more than 600 lawsuits against drug companies that manufactured and marketed DES. On February 11, 1983, Eli Lilly agreed to pay 21-year-old Barbara Watson $250,000 in cash and $30,000 a year for life to settle her DES suit against the company. Watson's attorney estimates the settlement could cost Lilly $1.7 million. On March 24, 1982, a Philadelphia jury awarded DES daughter Judith Axler $2.2 million in her suit against E.R. Squibb & Sons. Axler developed clear-cell cancer and is now unable to have children.

All of this was preventable. Had the drug companies adequately tested their drug and had the FDA been more vigilant, DES might not have been approved for use by pregnant women in 1947, and Joyce Bichler and hundreds of other DES daughters and sons would have been spared their suffering. DES was a preventable tragedy.

"It never should have happened," Bichler told the Bronx jury, "it never should have happened to me or to anyone else."[17]

Notes

1. *DES Daughter,* by Joyce Bichler. Avon Books, New York: 1981. All quotes from Bichler from this book.
2. "The Synthetic Compound Diethylstilbestrol (DES) 1938–1941: The Social Construction of A Medical Treatment," Dissertation by Susan E. Bell, Ph.D., Brandeis University, May 1980, p. 28.
3. *DES Daughter,* Bichler, p. 137.
4. *DES: The Bitter Pill,* by Robert Meyers. Seaview/Putnam, New York, 1983, p. 61.
5. "Plaintiff's Pretrial Statement," *Barbara Ann Watson v. Eli Lilly & Company,* Superior Court of the District of Columbia, Civil Division, Civil Action Number 16183–80, by Aaron Levine, Attorney for the Plaintiff, p. 4.
6. "The Synthetic Compound Diethylstilbestrol (DES) 1938–1941," Bell, p. 135.
7. "Gilding the Lilly: A DES Update," by Aaron Levine. *Trial,* December 1984, p. 19.
8. "Plaintiff's Second Amended 26(b)(4) Statement," in *Myrtle Breeden et al. v. Eli Lilly & Company et al.,* U.S. District Court for the District of Columbia, Civil Action No. 81–0718, by Aaron Levine, counsel for the plaintiffs.
9. *DES Daughter,* Bichler, p. 135.
10. *DES: The Bitter Pill,* Meyers, p. 75.
11. *DES Daughter,* Bichler, p. 142.
12. *DES: The Bitter Pill,* Meyers, pp. 86, 219. In March 1976, three women who were part of the Dieckmann study sued the University of Chicago, charging battery and claiming that they were given DES without their knowledge or consent. The women charged that the university had effectively lied to them by telling them that they were taking "vitamin pills" and by not telling them for five years that they had been exposed to DES. In 1981, the university agreed to pay $225,000 to the women, to provide medical examinations to the men and women exposed to DES during the Dieckman study, and to notify nearly 1,000 people born to women in the study about the availability of treatment. See also, *DES: The Complete Story,* by Cynthia Latinman Orenberg. St. Martin's Press, New York, 1981, p. 29.
13. "Plaintiff's Pretrial Statement," *Barbara Ann Watson v. Eli Lilly & Company,* p. 9.
14. *DES Daughter,* Bichler, p. 180.
15. "The Synthetic Compound Diethylstilbestrol (DES) 1938–1941," Bell, p. 1.
16. *DES: The Bitter Pill,* Meyers, p. 143 et seq.
17. Ibid., p. 153.

11
Dumping Overseas

"The first responsibility is the company which commits the crime deliberately. They know what a drug is about, they know what they have to write about in America, in the United States, and they do the opposite in other countries. They omit contra-indications [what the drug should not be used for], they omit side-effects indications, they enlarge the spectrum of indications [what the drug should be used for], they falsify, scientifically falsify the image of the drug in order to make each drug a natural candidate to be a best selling [drug]. They optimize the conditions, and in order to do this they falsify. They are the main responsible [party] because they are conscious of the crime."

—Bernardo Kucinski, Brazilian journalist and expert on multinational pharmaceutical corporations in South America[1]

AMINOPYRINE AND DIPYRON are inexpensive drugs marketed to combat headaches. Both can cause a serious and sometimes fatal blood disease called agranulocytosis, a disease that results in an abrupt drop in the patient's white blood cell count. In the United States, Carol Gates would never have had the chance to purchase these drugs to ease a headache. The Food and Drug Administration has banned both of them except as a last resort to treat fever in terminal cancer patients.

While traveling in Africa, Carol Gates fell ill. "I felt very tired and uncomfortable, and I had quite a few headaches," reported Gates, "so I went to the chemist and bought some Cibalgin." Gates swallowed the Cibalgin pills—pills that contained aminopyrine. "They seemed to work," Gates said. "They killed the pain. And then after a few days I began to vomit and I had a very sore throat. The headaches came back. At the end of the week I was so weak and so ill that I couldn't walk. I could hardly talk because the whole of my mouth was covered with sores. I couldn't swallow. I obviously couldn't chew anything."[2]

Despite the known fact that aminopyrine can cause a serious blood disease and that the FDA banned it for that reason, the corporations that manufacture this and other drugs banned in the United States sell them to other countries, including third world countries where governments and medical personnel may be more susceptible to corporate pressures to accept such drugs. Drug companies are by no means the only culprits in this international trafficking in hazardous products. They are joined in force by chemical companies, medical device manufacturers, and even pajama makers.

In the United States it is illegal to sell a wide range of drugs, pesticides, medical devices, and other consumer products that may cause disease, injury, or death. DBCP, a pesticide used to destroy a worm that attacks certain fruit trees, may not be used in the United States except for very limited purposes because it was found to cause cancer in test animals and to make people sterile. It is the law that children's pajamas treated with 2,3-dibromoprophyl (TRIS), a fire-retardant chemical that has been linked to kidney cancer in children, shall not be sold in the United States. As Carol Gates learned after she suffered an adverse reaction from the Cibalgin she purchased and used in Africa, it is illegal in the United States to sell any drug containing aminopyrine with limited exceptions.

Companies such as those that produce Cibalgin, DBCP, and TRIS-treated pajamas know the U.S. government has concluded that their products may injure, or have injured, U.S. consumers, and that therefore they may not sell those products in the United States. These corporations also know that people in the less developed countries likewise risk injury, disease, or death if they use or are exposed to the condemned products. Nevertheless, corporations whose products are condemned or banned in this country routinely take those products and sell them in other, less developed parts of the world.

Every year, millions of dollars worth of untested pesticides, contaminated or expired drugs, and banned industrial chemicals leave the United States for sale abroad—to often unsuspecting foreign customers.[3] "The hypocrisy, the duplicity of saying that what we have found out in this country is too dangerous for us but it's okay to dump it on Third World people is startling," observes David Weir, of the Center for Investigative Reporting, who wrote the book *Circle of Poison* about the export of hazardous goods.[4]

One example of dumping was performed by the A.H. Robins Company during the early 1970s. In 1971, Robins was marketing the Dalkon Shield, an intrauterine device (IUD), in the United States. Soon thereafter, Robins began receiving complaints from women who used the Shield and doctors who prescribed it. According to Mark Dowie and Tracy Johnson, in an article published in *Mother Jones* magazine ("A Case of Corporate Malpractice," November 1976), women who used the Shield complained of inflammatory disease (an infection of the uterus that can require weeks of bedrest and antibiotic treatment), septicemia (blood poisoning), pregnancies resulting in spontaneous abortions, ectopic (tubal) pregnancies, and perforations of the uterus. In some cases, the damage necessitated a hysterectomy, and there were some medical reports, according to Dowie and Johnson, of Dalkon Shields "ripping their way through the walls of the uterus and being found floating free in the abdominal cavity far from the uterus." In total, the Dalkon Shield caused over 200,000 cases of serious uterine infections in this country by 1974, and 18 deaths have been reported as clearly attributable to the Shield.[5]

As early as 1971, the dangers posed by the Dalkon Shield were being brought to the attention of Robins. "I have found the procedure to be the most traumatic manipulation ever perpetrated on womenhood," wrote one physician to the company in February 1971, "and I have inserted thousands of other varieties."[6] Assuming that Dalkon Shield sales in the United States would decline dramatically as soon as the adverse effects became public knowledge, Robins moved to market its product in the third world.

Robins dumped, with assistance from the U.S. Agency for International Development (AID), thousands of the suspect Shields in 42 countries around the world. To entice AID's Office of Population into spending some of its $125 million contraceptive budget on Dalkon Shields—according to *Mother Jones*—Robins offered AID a discount of 48 percent if the agency agreed to buy the Shield in bulk packages—unsterilized. AID accepted this offer despite the fact that one of the greatest dangers of using an IUD is the risk of infecting the uterus.

Robins attempted to dismiss this danger by claiming that practitioners in less developed countries were expected to sterilize the Shields by soaking them in a disinfectant solution, but the company attached only one set of instructions to each package of 1,000 Shields that it sent out. Although the Shields were destined for countries such as Ethiopia and Malaysia, the instructions were written only in English, French, and Spanish. According to gynecologists interviewed by *Mother Jones*, the insertion of an unsterilized IUD that had merely been soaked in a disinfectant would possibly be grounds for a malpractice suit in this country. In addition to the fact that it is dangerous to insert an unsterilized object into the human womb, reports from the countries where the Shield was being dumped indicated that the Shield was not performing effectively as a contraceptive. Robins claimed a pregnancy rate of 1.1 percent, but third world clinics were reporting rates as high as 14.8 percent.[7]

By 1974, reports of the dangers of the Shield had built to a crescendo and the U.S. Food and Drug Administration (FDA), although it had no authority to control medical devices, held hearings on the dangers of the Dalkon Shield. With a national spotlight focused on its product and on the company's name, Robins, at the urging of the FDA, withdrew the Shield from the world market. One year later, AID was forced to issue an international recall of the Shield from the third world countries, but the effectiveness of that recall order is in doubt. AID could not recall the 44,000 Shields already implanted in third world women by the time the order was issued. It had no way of stopping Robins from privately dumping its leftover stock of Dalkon Shields. One AID official has charged that as late as June 1979, the Dalkon Shield was still being inserted into women in Pakistan, India, and possibly South Africa.[8]

Many people in the third world—because of undeveloped medical infrastructures, weak or nonexistent consumer protection laws, and governments controlled or influenced by multinational corporations—are unable to protect themselves against abuses such as the unscrupulous dumping practices epitomized by Robins's export of the Dalkon Shield. Many U.S. companies take advantage of this disparity; few exploit it as effectively as do those in the chemical and pharmaceutical industries.

U.S. chemical companies ship overseas at least 150 million pounds a year of pesticides that are totally prohibited, severely restricted, or never registered for use in this country. While data on the effects of this practice are incomplete, evidence indicates a problem of major proportions. The World Health Organization (WHO) estimated in 1973 that 250,000 pesticide poisonings, 6,700 of which are fatal, occur each year in the third world. The Oxford Committee on Famine Relief (Oxfam) estimated in 1982 that the toll had risen to 375,000 poisonings with a resulting 10,000 deaths each year.[9]

The U.S. Environmental Protection Agency (EPA) banned all crop uses of DDT in 1972 and of Dieldrin in 1974. DDT causes reproductive failures in birds and both DDT and Dieldrin kill fish, cause tumors in animals, and build up in the food chain and ultimately into the fatty tissue of humans. Neither the ban nor the evidence of adverse health and environmental effects stopped the Montrose Chemical Corporation from selling DDT to 21 overseas importers in 18 months from early 1979 to November 1980.[10]

DDT levels in cows' milk in Guatemala is 90 times as high as that allowed in the United States. People in Nicaragua and Guatemala carry over 31 times as much DDT in their blood as people in the United States.[11] In milk from nursing mothers in those countries, DDT has been found at levels as high as 200 times greater than the average DDT level in women in the United States. Dieldrin and DDT were being sold and used near Lake Nakura, Kenya, as late as 1980. A million flamingos used to swim in Lake Nakura, attracting tourists from all over the world. Now there are few birds and fewer tourists. Some local residents believe that the decline of the flamingos is due to the DDT and Dieldrin found in the waters of Nakura.[12]

In 1980, in a small town in Malaysia, Cha Ket, a consumer advocate, surveyed the availability of 2,4,5-T in local general stores. He told his story to Robert Richter, producer of the highly acclaimed two-part Public Broadcasting Service television series "Pesticides and Pills: For Export Only." In 1979, the EPA banned 2,4,5-T for most uses in the United States because it contains a substance called dioxin, one of the most deadly manmade poisons. Dioxin causes cancer and birth deformities in test animals at extremely low doses. Agent Orange, the defoliant used in Vietnam, contains 2,4,5-T. "I entered one store to ask whether they sell 2,4,5-T," reported Cha Ket, "and I found that they sell 2,4,5-T in bottles, and those bottles were kept next to bottles that contain sauce. They do not have any label. The sauce label has been torn off. We Malaysians do not know much about such products. It has been marketed by multinational companies for the sake of profit and they sell it in the rural area which does not know much about toxic chemicals."[13]

Heptachlor, chlordane, endrin, and many other pesticides are dangerous to human beings because they cause cancer or birth deformities in test animals, or endanger the environment. Like DDT and Dieldrin, these pesticides are banned or their use is severely restricted in the United States and in Europe. They are, however, routinely sold throughout the third world, where their indiscriminate use has raised the constant specter of pesticide poisoning. Gerardo Delgado, a union leader in Costa Rica, expressed concern for the safety of his fellow workers who were being constantly bombarded by airplanes dumping DDT, Dieldrin, and Kepone on the banana plantations. "Every time that the pesticides are used," Delgado told Richter,

> many people are poisoned. There are even cases of workers who have died due to the use of pesticides. The problem with aerial spraying is that not only are the plantations sprayed, but also the workers who are on the plantations and also the children who come to bring their food. Even at the edge of the plantations at the workers' houses, the substance is also sprayed. So spraying the banana plantation includes spraying the workers, their homes, and their families.[14]

In Brazil, a scandal erupted when it was revealed that tomatoes were being treated with mercury compounds. Mercury is a poison that attacks the nervous system. A very high percentage of the workers in cane fields in the state of Rio de Janeiro were poisoned by mercury. Jose Lutzenberger, a leader of the environmental movement in Brazil, charged in 1980 that despite these mass poisonings, mercury was still being used. "The big international outfits that produce and sell these products know what's happening," Lutzenberger told Richter, "and they know that in the case of tomatoes, for instance, where mercury compounds are even against the law, they know that they are selling it where it is being used against the law."[15]

Brazil, however, was not the first country to experience mercury poisoning. In 1971, cargoes of American barley and Mexican wheat arrived in Al Basrah, Iraq, treated with methylmercury, a fungicide prohibited for use in the United States and elsewhere. The grain, intended as seed only, had been chemically treated to prevent rot and had been sprayed with a bright pink dye to indicate the presence of the mercury solution. The shipments had been clearly marked in Spanish and English, but not in Arabic, the language of Iraq. The grain, stolen from dockside, was sold to hundreds of thousands of Iraqis. An American newsman estimated that "as many as 6,000 may have died and perhaps 100,000 were injured" as result of the mass poisoning.[16]

From 1971 through 1976, the Velsicol Chemical Company produced and exported the pesticide leptophos (trade name: Phosvel) to developing countries, including Colombia, Egypt, and Indonesia. Leptophos was never registered by the Environmental Protection Agency for use in the United States. Leptophos has been shown to produce delayed but lasting nervous system damage to humans. In Egypt, where it was used to kill insects on cotton, the pesticide was blamed for the deaths of several farmers and at least 1,200 water buffalo. Despite this evidence, Velsicol continued to market leptophos as a safe pesticide. Not until 1976, when workers at the company's Texas manufacturing plants began to show symptoms of severe neurological damage, was production of the pesticide in the United States halted.[17]

The chemical companies argue that there are compelling reasons to export dangerous chemicals overseas. All they are doing, they say, is helping to feed a hungry world. Third world peoples have critical malnutrition problems, they argue, and pesticides will make food more plentiful for them. But, recent investigations show that up to 70 percent of all the pesticides used in third world countries are not applied to food for local consumption. "At least 50 percent and up to 70 percent are instead applied to export crops," reports David Weir, applied "to food that we eat, not people in the Third World, to cocoa, to coffee, to bananas, tapioca, all sorts of luxury crops, to non-food items like cotton, and especially in Central America, to rubber."[18]

This dumping of dangerous pesticides overseas eventually comes home to haunt consumers in the United States. The FDA estimates, through spot checks, that 10 percent of our imported food is contaminated with illegal residues of banned pesticides.

Weir challenges this figure as being too low, claiming that "The FDA's most commonly used analytical method does not even check for 70 percent of the almost 900 food tolerances for cancer-causing pesticides." (A tolerance is the amount of a pesticide allowed in any particular food product.) Citing U.S. General Accounting Office (GAO) reports, Weir reports that "over 15 percent of the beans and 13 percent of the peppers imported from Mexico, during one recent period, were found to violate FDA pesticide residue standards. Nearly half the imported green coffee beans contain levels of pesticides that are banned from the United States, and imported beef from Central America often contains pesticide contamination."[19] A GAO report released in December 1986 found that things had gotten worse since Weir's analysis. The GAO found that the FDA tests almost no domestically grown food for pesticides and prevents the sale of little of the adulterated food it does find.[20]

For sheer lack of responsibility in this area, few industries can match the chemical industry. The pharmaceutical industry, however, is a worthy competitor. Some of the largest pharmaceutical companies in the world are today in the business of supplying third world countries with drugs that are banned or severely restricted in the West. People in the third world today buy almost $3 billion worth of medicine every year from Western pharmaceutical companies.

Until 1986, U.S. laws regulating drugs differed from those regulating pesticides in one important aspect: U.S. pharmaceutical companies were barred from exporting drugs that are banned or not registered in this country. No law prohibits overseas sales of pesticides that cannot be sold in the U.S. In 1986, U.S. drug companies succeeded in weakening the law that now allows the export to 21 countries of drugs not yet approved for use in the U.S. The prohibition on the export of hazardous drugs, however, was easily sidestepped. "Unless the package bursts open on the dock," observed one drug company executive, "you have no chance of being caught."[21]

Some companies avoid this risk of getting caught and bypass the law entirely by building production facilities in the third world—close to their intended markets. One Eli Lilly executive admitted as much when he testified in 1974 before the subcommittee on health of the Senate Committee on Labor and Public Welfare that the current law banning exports of harmful drugs "causes, unnecessarily, the export of capital, technology, and jobs."[22]

A current example of the drug industry's disregard for the health and well-being of its consumers involves Upjohn's contraceptive, Depo-Provera, a drug that, when injected into a woman's arm, prevents conception for three to six weeks. This long-lasting effect puts Depo into the "wonder drug" category for heavily populated third world countries. However, due to a long list of side effects, complications, and potential hazards, Depo has not been approved for marketing in the United States. It causes "irregular bleeding disturbances" that have been described as "menstrual chaos." It also causes cancer in the reproductive organs of test animals and reduces the human body's resistance to infection. If injected into a pregnant woman, it can cause birth defects.[23]

For 11 years, Upjohn, the manufacturer of Depo, has been pushing the FDA to approve the drug for use in this country. The FDA, aware of the dangers of Depo and the supporting data, has adamantly refused. In 1978, the FDA notified Upjohn of its final decision that Depo was "not approvable" in the United States. Again, in 1984, an FDA board of inquiry recommended that the commissioner not approve the drug for use in the United States.

Although these decisions effectively barred Upjohn from shipping Depo out of the United States, they did not bar the company from producing it in its Belgian subsidiary. Today in 80 countries around the world it is possible to buy Depo over-the-counter with no prescription. There is little public information on exactly how much Depo is being used by the women of the world, but for many women who are being injected with the drug there have been reports of amenorrhea (lack of menstrual periods) and profuse bleeding.[24]

Perhaps the most blatant example of this type of marketing involves the drug clioquinol. Ciba-Geigy, the giant Swiss multinational, marketed clioquinol throughout the United States and Japan during the late 1960s as a cure for severe diarrhea. The drug quickly became associated with a disease known as SMON (subacute myelo-optic neuropathy). Known for its serious neurotoxic effects on the spinal cord, the nerves of the body surfaces, and the optic nerve, this disease struck at least 10,000 persons in Japan alone.

These Japanese SMON victims and their supporters took to the streets of Tokyo in mass demonstrations and demanded that Ciba pull the drug off the market. They also took to the courthouse, sued the company, and have since recovered $456 million in compensatory damages. Although the demonstrations and the lawsuits effectively forced Ciba to pull clioquinol from the Japanese market, they had little effect on the company's marketing strategy in the rest of the world. Ciba continued to push clioquinol in Latin America, Africa, and much of Asia. The drug was sold under a number of different brand names, and each country had different information about indications (when to use the product) and contraindications (when not to use the product). In some countries there was no information at all.

Arturo Lomelli, the director of Mexico's Consumers Union, has charged that Ciba sold clioquinol under 13 different brand names around the world. "This shows us the lack of ethics on the part of this lab [Ciba] . . . [T]o provide thirteen different sets of instructions for the same product, under the assumption that there are basic differences in people when there is only one mankind." In Mexico, according to Lomelli, the company provided no instructions whatsoever. "We call this the fourteenth set of instructions," he explains, "the nonexistent one. On this fourteenth package there are no indications regarding its purpose, the limitations of its use and the side effects that it may cause, or what the dose should be. It is sold like candy. And we know it is a medicine that has already caused injury and death to thousands of people in Japan."[25] John Braithwaite, an Australian criminologist specializing in the corporate sector who has studied the pharmaceutical industry, observed that "in light of the SMON disaster it is a gross abuse to use clioquinol for simple diarrhea."[26] In March 1985, Ciba halted worldwide sales of the drug.[27]

Depo-Provera and clioquinol are only two of a host of banned, condemned, or restricted drugs that have been dumped on the third world. Chloroform agents, for example, used as preservatives and for flavoring, are banned in the West because they have been found to cause liver and heart damage in humans. Yet they are sold freely in the third world as an additive in cough mixtures and in toothpaste.[28] Panalba, an antibiotic, has been banned in the United States for more than ten years because one out of five patients who took it had an allergic reaction to it, yet it sells freely in Brazil.[29]

Chloramphenicol is the drug of choice for treatment of typhoid fever around the world. Unfortunately, in some patients it causes a serious and sometimes fatal blood disease called aplastic anemia. Many believe that this risk is one that should be accepted in the case of a patient who may die from typhoid. However, Dr. Milton Silverman, author of the investigative study *Prescription for Death,* believes that the drug is being misused in third world countries. "We found out in Latin America that this drug was being promoted and used for such trivial illnesses as acne and athlete's foot," Silverman observed, "and for practically any infection you might want to name without warnings being given to the physician."[30]

To escape stringent U.S. occupational safety and health laws, U.S. corporations sometimes take advantage of the ultimate corporate dump and operate factories overseas. Union Carbide operated a battery plant on the outskirts of Jakarta, Indonesia, that Bob Wyrick—in his ten-part series "Hazards for Exports," in *Newsday,* in 1981—labeled "a monument to worker exploitation." At one point more than half the work force of 750 were diagnosed as having a kidney disease linked to mercury exposure. During the mid-1970s, according to Wyrick, a Nicaragua-based chlorine and caustic-soda corporation was discharging poisonous mercury into Lake Managua. The U.S.-based Pennwalt Company, which owned 40 percent of the Nicaraguan company, had decided in 1972 to install pollution control equipment at a similar plant in Kentucky. The Nicaraguan corporation, on which Pennwalt exerted considerable influence, decided in 1978 to declare its shareholders a $3 million-dollar dividend instead of spending $650,000 for a pollution control system. "It was . . . observed by board members that this course of action would best protect the interests of shareholders in light of the unsettled political climate that then existed in Nicaragua," wrote Peter J. McCarthy, Pennwalt's director of advertising and public relations.[31]

Multinational corporations defend the dumping of hazardous products in the third world by claiming that each country is competent and responsible for determining its own policies on the export and import of hazardous products. So, if the government of Guatemala wishes to subject its people to a drug that the United States considers dangerous, then the manufacturer should not feel constrained just because some Western country has banned the drug. This viewpoint was put forth by a senior American executive who believed that the *corporation* knew when a drug was safe, and once the *corporation* was satisfied with the drug's safety, then the drug would be marketed, regardless of what the United States or any other Western government might say. "If Guatemala will let us in first because they have no regulations," the executive told criminologist John Braithwaite, "then we will get it registered in Guatemala in the first six months."[32]

This raises an interesting question: "Why does Guatemala have no regulations?" As Braithwaite observes, one must question the liberal democratic ideal of national sovereignty "when one is talking about undemocratic regimes who . . . make their decisions about the pharmaceutical industry on the strength of bribes."[33] Indeed, due to corruption and other pressures from multinationals, most third world countries have been unable to stop the flow of dangerous products. Jose Lutzenberger, the Brazilian environmental leader, has seen these pressures at work. "Unfortunately, the multinational corporations, whether from the U.S. or Europe, are so strong that they manage to transform the [Brazilian] Department of Plant Protection, in our Ministry of Agriculture into a true subsidiary of them," Lutzenberger observed recently. "Those people take orders from them and carry them out. So we have the case of products that are prohibited in their countries of origin being freely promoted here."[34]

Some third world countries are attempting to combat the influence of the multinational pharmaceutical corporations by starting drug companies of their own. The World Health Organization (WHO) is moving to implement a voluntary code of conduct governing dumping practices. The multinationals, however, are defending what they perceive as their inherent rights to sell freely whatever and wherever they choose. They enlisted the help of Ronald Reagan's administration to defeat consumer and third world initiatives to curb corporate abuses in these areas.

In one of his first acts as president, Reagan rescinded former President Jimmy Carter's 34-day-old executive order that would have curbed export abuses by (1) improving the export notice procedures already required by other laws; (2) calling for the annual publication of a summary of U.S. government actions banning or severely restricting substances for domestic use; (3) directing the State Department and other federal agencies to participate in the development of international hazardous alert systems; and (4) establishing procedures whereby formal export licensing controls would be placed upon a very limited number of "extremely hazardous substances" that represented a serious threat to human health or the environment, the export of which would threaten U.S. foreign policy interests.[35]

In late 1984, the multinationals went after the UN's proposed WHO guidelines on hazardous exports. Led by U.S. ambassador Jeanne J. Kirkpatrick, who labeled the code "global paternalism," they had the code bottled up in the UN committee system.

Anwar Fazal, former president of the International Organization of Consumer Unions, based in Malaysia, believes that changes favoring consumers, if they come, are going to come slowly. "Greed is a very very important aspect of this whole problem," observes Fazal, "and to overcome the powers of the multinationals, citizen groups must spring up around the world to alert the people about these problems." Brazil's Lutzenberger agrees. "Personally, we are fighting the best we can against this scandal," says Lutzenberger, "but on our side we have only a very reduced number of people who are all idealists fighting in their free time, and with their own means, and without any help . . . on the other side, the companies have armies of well-paid technicians, many of them paid in foreign currencies, so it really is a tremendous fight still that we have. So what we need is more consciousness, more people fighting."[36]

Notes

1. "Pesticides and Pills: For Export Only," by Robert Richter. Part Two: Pharmaceuticals, Transcript of television broadcast aired on Public Broadcasting Service, October 7, 1981, p. 20.

2. Ibid., p. 13.

3. "Banned at Home, Exported Abroad: The Control of Hazardous Exports," Remarks of S. Jacob Scherr. Natural Resources Defense Council, Science and Technology Workshop, Agenda for the Eighties Conference, New York, New York, August 26, 1980, p. 1.

4. "Pesticides and Pills: For Export Only," by Robert Richter. Part One: Pesticides. Transcript of television broadcast on Public Broadcasting Service, October 5, 1981, p. 3.

5. "The Corporate Crime of the Century," by Mark Dowie. *Mother Jones*, November 1979, p. 28.

6. "The Charge: Gynocide," by Barbara Ehrenreich, Mark Dowie, and Stephen Minkin. *Mother Jones*, November 1979, p. 28.

7. Ibid., p. 29.

8. Ibid., p. 30.

9. "Hazardous Exports: United States and International Policy Devel-

opments," by S. Jacob Scherr, Senior Staff Attorney, Natural Resources Defense Council, June 1984, unpublished paper, p. 6.

10. *Pills, Pesticides, and Profits: The International Trade in Toxic Substances,* Ruth Norris, ed. North River Press, Croton-on-Hudson, New York, p. 21.

11. *Circles of Poison: Pesticides and People in a Hungry World,* by David Weir and Mark Shapiro. Institute for Food and Development Policy, San Francisco, 1981, p. 13.

12. "Pesticides and Pills: For Export Only," Richter. Part One, Pesticides, p. 4.

13. Ibid., p. 5.

14. Ibid., p. 11.

15. Ibid., p. 12.

16. *Darkest Hours,* by Robert Jay Nash. Pocket Books, New York, 1977, p. 16; see also, "How the Pink Death Came to Iraq," by Ed Hughes. *Sunday Times of India,* September 9, 1973, pp. 17–19.

17. "U.S. Made Poisons Hurt More Than Just Pests," by Bob Wyrick. *Newsday,* December 14, 1981.

18. "Pesticides and Pills: For Export Only," Richter. Part One: Pesticides, p. 14.

19. *Circle of Poison,* Weir and Shapiro, p. 28.

20. "Report Says FDA Checks Few Foods For Pesticides," *Wall Street Journal,* December 4, 1986.

21. *Corporate Crime in the Pharmaceutical Industry,* by John Braithwaite. Routledge & Keegan Paul, London, 1984, p. 262.

22. Ibid., p. 260.

23. "The Charge: Gynocide," Ehrenreich et al., p. 34.

24. Ibid.

25. "Pesticides and Pills: For Export Only," Richter. Part Two: Pharmaceuticals, p. 2.

26. *Corporate Crime in the Pharmaceutical Industry,* Braithwaite, p. 253.

27. Personal communication, Milton Silverman, December 17, 1986.

28. "Pesticides and Pills: For Export Only," Richter. Part Two: Pharmaceuticals, p. 5.

29. Ibid.

30. Ibid., p. 12.

31. "Chemical Plant's Poison Inflames a Nation," by Bob Wyrick. *Newsday,* December 21, 1981.

32. *Corporate Crime in the Pharmaceutical Industry,* Braithwaite, p. 262.

33. Ibid., p. 264.

34. "Pesticides and Pills: For Export Only," Richter. Part One: Pesticides, p. 7.

35. "Hazardous Exports: United States and International Policy Developments," by S. Jacob Scherr, June 1984, unpublished paper.

36. "Pesticides and Pills: For Export Only," Richter. Part One: Pesticides, p. 16.

12
Firestone

"The Firestone Tire and Rubber Co. is and has been for some time in a position to avoid the devastating toll of human destruction which it knew its tires could cause. In the exercise of clear and conscious choice, it nonetheless permitted this destruction to take place."

> —John E. Moss, Chairman, Subcommittee on Oversight and Investigations of the Committee on Interstate and Foreign Commerce, U.S. House of Representatives, May 18, 1978[1]

It WAS NEW YEAR'S EVE DAY, 1987. Moira Johnston and Dinny Perry, two mothers, were in the front seat of Perry's large Ford LTD station wagon. Three of their children, Woolsey, Christy, and Matthew, were in the rear. Johnston was driving at the speed limit, 55 mph, sometimes less, on her way home from Death Valley, California. Every time the speedometer crept over 50, she would feel a vibration. She thought of the tires, but discounted any fear. She remembered reading somewhere that "Tires don't blow out anymore, they just ooze air."

It was three in the afternoon, they were still driving home, and Perry was becoming nervous. The vibrations reminded her of similar vibrations she felt six months earlier. At that time she took the car into the shop. Her left front tire had a bulge. She bought a new tire to replace the old one. Now, six months later, the vibrations were back again. On the way to Death Valley, Perry and

Johnston had pulled into a Union 76 station, where the gas station attendant spotted a small bump on the right front tire. He replaced it with a spare. Johnston pulled back onto the highway. Soon the vibrations were getting worse.

Perry insisted that Johnston pull into a gas station to check the tires. Johnston pulled into a Texaco station. The attendant looked at the tires. He saw no visible bulges. Johnston noticed that the sidewalls were bulging, but the station attendant assured her that such were the characteristics of steel-belted radials. Johnston and Perry decided to drive on.

Woolsey, one of the children sitting in the back, read aloud. The Ford station wagon moved on down the highway, hovering around the speed limit. Then, all of a sudden, the children were shaken by an explosive boom. Woolsey stopped reading. The rear end of the car was "thrust into a violent and uncontrolled skid," according to Johnston. In her article "Hell on Wheels" (*New West Magazine,* May 8, 1978), Moira Johnston recounts what happened next.

> The rear end of the car whipped back and forth across the road, hurling us, at nearly 55 miles an hour, toward the shoulder and then toward the dividing strip. The children caught their breaths in a spontaneous gasp, then stared in catatonic silence as disaster sped toward them. Woolsey was thinking, A bomb . . . earthquake . . . the tire's been shot . . . we're going to crash! Matthew tried to grab Christie as she banged against the right door. With the will to survive that sweeps the brain and body in high crisis, I desperately tried to retrieve any experience that could save us. Ice! Drive it like ice. Don't fight it. Steer into the skid . . . Steer into the skid. I didn't know that I was saying over and over, "Oh God, oh God, oh God." I could only hear Dinny yelling, "Don't hit the brakes. Don't hit the brakes!" as the car went mad. I saw a cement curb coming at us, and knew with simmering clarity that we would hit it and all hell would break loose."[2]

Luckily, the car did not hit the dividing strip, and it slowly began to stop shaking and Johnston guided it carefully onto the shoulder. Everybody piled out of the car and ran to the rear to see what had happened. The right rear tire had ripped apart in an explosive blowout, putting the car into a state of critical uncontrollable instability. "You're lucky," said a passing motorist who stopped to give assistance. "They usually flip."

No one in Johnston's car was injured as a result of the blowout. The Neal family was not so lucky. On June 15, 1974, Louis and Cornelia and their daughter Floretta Neal were riding in their Ford Thunderbird near Las Vegas, Nevada. While traveling on the highway, one of their radial tires suddenly blew out. The Thunderbird flipped out of control. When it came to rest, Louis and Cornelia were dead. Floretta was permanently crippled.[3]

Others suffered similar fates. In June of 1977, near Venice, Florida, J. David was traveling the speed limit, 55 mph, when one of his Firestone 500 tires separated and blew out. David's 1976 Chrysler Cordoba flipped over and ejected David out of the car. He did not survive the crash.[4] Peggy Clement and her daughter Crystal were traveling in their late-model Monza in June of 1977 outside of Loris, South Carolina, when their rear tire blew out. The car swerved into oncoming traffic and smashed into a second car. Peggy Clement died instantly. Her daughter died the morning after the crash.

Throughout the country during the mid-1970s, Firestone 500 radial tires were blowing out, propelling the cars to which they were attached off the highway, into highway barriers, or into oncoming traffic. Thousands of accidents, hundreds of injuries, and at least 34 fatalities resulted.[5]

The Center for Auto Safety (hereafter Center), a Washington-based clearinghouse founded by Ralph Nader, first noticed the Firestone 500 blowout pattern in early 1976. When the high complaint rate continued into 1977, the Center began an intensive review of all the tire complaints it had received. It also forwarded its data to the National Highway Traffic Safety Administration (NHTSA), the federal police agents who are supposed to police tire manufacturers and blow the whistle when a company is allowing defective tires into the stream of commerce.

The Center's review of its tire complaint data revealed a disturbing pattern. Half of the tire letters complained about Firestone tires, a rate that was three times the average, based on Firestone's 1976 market share. Alarmed by this statistic, Clarence Ditlow, the director of the Center, addressed a letter to Mario DiFederico, the president of Firestone, in which Ditlow pointed out that nearly all of the Firestone complaints concerned the Firestone 500 steel-belted radial. "Since the problem is almost entirely with your highly advertised steel-belted radial," Ditlow wrote, "one has to ask what would happen if Firestone cut its $28,000,000 advertising budget for 1976 in half and spent the money on quality control."[6]

Ditlow furnished Firestone with copies of some of the complaints and urged DiFederico to recall all the defective Firestone tires. DiFederico did not answer Ditlow's letter, and his failure to answer marked the beginning of one of the most prolonged stonewalls in recent corporate history—a stonewall that led one writer to label Firestone the Richard Nixon of the tire companies.[7]

As early as 1972, five years before Ditlow's letter to Firestone, the company was aware of extensive failure problems with their "500" belted radial tires. "We are in danger of being cut off by Chevrolet because of separation failures," wrote Firestone's Thomas Robertson to DiFrederico, then vice president for tire production, on November 2, 1972.[8] In addition to this damning memo, Firestone had in its possession data that indicated that many of its customers were returning the radials to dealers for various reasons. In 1973, 5.48 percent of the company's entire 1972 production of one million tires were returned to the company.[9]

Another early indication that something was seriously wrong with the "500" tires came in 1975, when the company tests indicated that some of its steel-belted radials failed to measure up to acceptable standards after a year or two of storage. According to "Deep Tread," an anonymous source within Firestone who leaked the test results to government officials and to reporters, 26 of 46 of the tires failed Firestone's test. In a second tire separation test, none of the 34 tires tested even came close to meeting Firestone's own minimum standard of lasting 15,000 miles, with 16 suffering tread distortions within 55 miles. The longest any of the tires lasted was 1,385 miles.[10]

By November 1977, when the Center for Auto Safety wrote to DiFrederico, informing him of a "sharp increase in the number of consumer complaints relating to Firestone tires in the past year," Firestone officials should have not been surprised. For five years they had kept the steel-belted radial problem out of the spotlight. During this time, a growing number of victimized drivers, and the dealers to whom they complained, shared Firestone's knowledge of the grave nature of the 500 problem. The word was destined to get out.

Ditlow's letter had forced the issue, and the struggle to get the facts into the open had begun. DiFrederico headed the battle to keep the damning evidence from making its way into the hands of consumers, federal law enforcement agencies, and product liability attorneys.

Most of all, Firestone had reason to fear the attorneys. People across America were being seriously injured or killed when their Firestone 500s failed, and the product liability attorneys sensed a gold mine. The resulting damage suits would cost Firestone millions of dollars in liability payments and threaten the company's financial well-being.

A public airing of the 500 problem might also bring in federal law enforcement officials to demand a recall. Firestone had produced 23.5 million 500 radials, and 13 million were still on the road in 1978. Perhaps 2 million of those would be exempted from any recall, leaving 11 million tires that Firestone would have to replace — at a cost of at least $275 million. There were, in addition, the replacement costs for private brands that Firestone made for Montgomery Ward and Shell. Only one year after reporting a total of $110.2 million net income, Firestone executives were faced with a total recall bill of over $300 million. A federally mandated recall would go a long way toward erasing Firestone profits for at least several months.

Firestone took the bottom-line approach and decided to stonewall, hoping to muffle Ditlow and to prevent a recall. In earlier battles, the company's stonewall had worked well. The government took Firestone to court, demanding that it recall certain of its radial tires for safety reasons. Firestone fought one such effort started by the National Highway Traffic Safety Administration in 1974, and succeeded in limiting the recall to a mere 400,000 radial tires, claiming a temporary production problem at a single plant in Illinois. Firestone was forced to recall a total of 10,425 tires on three earlier occasions — also, the company claimed, because of production problems. Firestone insisted that the problem was a limited one, involving not more than a few thousand tires.

In some ways, corporate and political stonewalls are alike. Both are doomed to failure in a democratic society where access to information is relatively open. But corporate and political stonewalls differ in one crucial aspect. Political stonewalls may inflict severe damage to such concepts as "truth" or "democratic values" or "justice," but corporate stonewalls usually result directly in the injury or death of human beings. Thus, when Nixon lied about his activities in Watergate, some charged that he was doing serious damage to our "democratic institutions." When Firestone officials knew millions of Americans were riding on unsafe Firestone tires, yet did nothing to remove those tires from the market—and, in fact, actively fought to prevent their removal from the market—they were jeopardizing lives.

The Center for Auto Safety wasn't the only group receiving complaints from disgruntled Firestone customers. Hundreds of Firestone dealers from around the country were reporting high rates of adjustments. Robert Buchanen, a veteran Firestone dealer from Aiken, South Carolina, had come to expect an adjustment rate of two to four percent. But for three years (1974–77), Buchanen found himself shipping 73 percent of the radial 500s back to Firestone headquarters—tires that customers had brought in for replacements.[11] A dealer from Modesto, California, told a House committee investigating the Firestone tires that his adjustment rate for the Firestone 500 was hovering at 65 percent. He also told the committee that he had twice brought the 500 problem to top Firestone management's attention, and that he was assured that the problem "would be taken care of." The problem wasn't taken care of—until the government forced Firestone to recall its tires—and the dealers took the heat from the customers. "Our image was slipping," he told the House committee. "People were attacking the dealership—blaming us."[12]

In Washington, federal enforcement officials were reviewing thousands of complaints from unhappy Firestone customers. NHTSA, the federal auto safety agency, received 6,000 complaints detailing 14,000 separate tire failures.[13] In an attempt to better understand the problem, NHTSA sent out questionnaires to 87,153 consumers of steel-belted radial tires.

The results were bad news for Firestone: the survey found that owners of Firestone tires were more likely to have multiple tire failures than owners of other makes of radials. Michelin had the lowest percentage of consumers complaining about their tires (1.1 percent), and Firestone had the highest—46.4 percent.

When Firestone learned about the results of the NHTSA survey, it sought to have the findings shielded from the public. However, when customers around the country read about Firestone's effort to prevent NHTSA from making the results public, many became suspicious. Congressman John Moss, then chairman of the Subcommittee on Oversight and Investigation of the House Committee on Interstate and Foreign Commerce, announced that he would hold hearings on the Firestone 500 tire.

With Firestone in court arguing that the survey results shouldn't be made public, NHTSA "inadvertently" gave the Center for Auto Safety the entire survey package in response to a Freedom of Information request. Ditlow immediately released the results to the press. "Consumers have a right to know the likelihood of their riding on defective steel-belted radials that could fail and cause an accident," Ditlow said, in justifying his action. "Accordingly, we are releasing this information for which their tax dollars paid so that consumers can be alerted to the potential dangers of tires they buy or use."[14]

The NHTSA survey hit the papers the next morning and stirred Firestone customers to demand that law enforcement officials take action to get the 500s off the road. Firestone had other ideas. The company began to dump its lemon 500s onto markets throughout the country at clearance prices. *Fortune* magazine reported that "new tires were sold in Miami and Birmingham at half the list price." The company explained that this was a routine procedure when phasing out any line of tire, but others were skeptical. "The company should have anticipated that the government's investigation would eventually get lots of publicity," commented *Fortune*, "and that the sale would then appear—whether justly or not—as a desperate effort to unload damaged goods."[15] Ditlow was less charitable. He called the Firestone dump "a callous display of corporate disregard for human life."[16]

NHTSA was eager to force Firestone to get its 500s off the road, but Firestone was not cooperating with the agency's mandated concern for highway safety. For instance, NHTSA asked for copies of any and all complaints about failures of Firestone radials, for a list of all lawsuits against Firestone arising from these failures, and for a detailed account of any changes in the methods used to manufacture radials. Firestone refused to provide the information. NHTSA had to go to court to pry the information out of the company. In the meantime, thousands of Americans were barreling down highways on Firestone tires, unknowingly risking their lives.

NHTSA eventually overcame Firestone's legal obstacles and ordered a recall of approximately 18 million Firestone tires, but the company's delaying tactics prolonged the risk for thousands more Americans on the highways. John Moss, whose committee investigated the Firestone fiasco, decried the company's intransigence. "The Firestone Tire and Rubber Co. is and has been for some time in a position to avoid the devastating toll of human destruction which it knew its tires could cause," Moss wrote in the committee's final report. "In the exercise of clear and conscious choice, it nonetheless permitted this destruction to take place."

The Moss committee reported that Firestone 500 separations had caused thousands of accidents, hundreds of injuries, and 34 known fatalities. Yet no Firestone official went to jail. And in 1980, the company was fined a token $50,000 for selling a defective product.[17]

The Firestone showdown emphasized the need for a national corporate crime bill that would impose criminal sanctions on those corporate executives who knowingly marketed dangerous products. At the time of the Firestone affair, Chairman Moss commented that it was "unfortunate" that the National Highway Traffic Safety Act of 1966 did not provide for "criminal penalties to address this episode and others like it which might occur."[18]

In 1980, Congress had the opportunity to plug this hole in the corporate criminal law but failed to act, after being heavily pressured by business lobbies led by the U.S. Chamber of Commerce. Today, the Firestone caper could happen again: there is still no law on the books to effectively deter those corporate executives who are governed by the bottom line and by a very narrow code of ethics. Neither can be relied on to protect the health and safety of the American public.

Notes

1. *The Safety of Firestone 500 Steel-Belted Radial Tires,* Report Together with Additional and Dissenting Views by the Subcommittee on Oversight and Investigations of the Committee on Interstate and Foreign Commerce. U.S. House of Representatives, 95th Cong., 2d Sess., August 16, 1978, p. 53.

2. "Hell on Wheels," by Moira Johnston. *New West,* May 8, 1978.

3. "Killer Tires," by David Hess. *Ohio Magazine,*

4. *The Safety of Firestone Steel-Belted Radial Tires,* Subcommittee report, testimony of Samuel J. Tolsom, officer, Florida State Highway Patrol.

5. "Killer Tires," Hess.

6. Letter from Ditlow to DiFederico, November 29, 1977.

7. *Everybody's Business, An Almanac,* ed. by Moskowitz, Katz, and Livering. Harper & Row, 1980, p. 286.

8. "Firestone Officials Knew of Tire Faults in '72," by Larry Kramer. *Washington Post*

9. *Corporate Crime,* Report of the Subcommittee on Crime, U.S. House of Representatives, May 1980, p. 7.

10. "Killer Tires," Hess, p. 46.

11. "Safety of Firestone Steel-Belted Radial 500 Tires," Hearings before the Subcommittee on Oversight and Investigations of the Committee on Interstate and Foreign Commerce, U.S. House of Representatives, May 19, 22, 23, and July 10, 1978, p. 69. According to the House of Representatives Subcommittee on Crime, the "adjustment rate" is the percentage of tires produced by a company that it accepts back from customers because of some problem with the tires that occurs before their useful tread is worn. The customer is allowed a credit (or "adjustment") for the remaining tread life, to be applied to the purchase of replacement tires. Tires are adjusted for reasons other than failures, including "policy adjustments" or adjustments to keep customers satisfied. A tire's failure rate is therefore some fraction of the adjustment rate.

12. "Killer Tires," Hess.

13. "Lessons From the Firestone Fracas," by Arthur M. Louis. *Fortune,* August 28, 1978, p. 45.

14. Center for Auto Safety, Press Release, March 31, 1978.

15. *Fortune,* April 26, 1978, p. 45.

16. "New Action on the Killer Tires," by Moira Johnston. *New West,* June 19, 1978.

17. Personal communication, Clarence Ditlow, director, Center for Auto Safety, November 19, 1986.

18. *The Safety of Firestone 500 Steel-Belted Radial Tires,* Subcommittee report, p. 53.

19. *Corporate Crime,* Report of the Subcommittee on Crime, May 1980, p. 7.

13
Ford and Emissions Testing

"Well I guess if you're going to cheat you should never put it on computers."

— Ford Motor Company executive during staff meeting convened to discuss company's criminal behavior[1]

Harley copp can tell you the engineering details of every car ever produced in the United States since 1946. He is an automotive genius, and for 31 years he applied that genius to the benefit of the Ford Motor Company. At Ford, Copp spent long hours experimenting with, designing, and test-driving Pintos, Capris, Corvairs, and Mustangs. During his first 20 years at Ford, Copp's love for his work and the professional attitude he brought to the job made him a star within the company. Copp zoomed up the corporate ladder, on his way to becoming the director of technical service for one of the world's multinational giants.

Henry Ford II was pleased to have this auto whiz kid in his corner. Copp was held up to others as an example of how hard work and loyalty to the company would eventually pay off. But the admiration was not unstinting, because Copp held strong views on automobile safety—not a very popular topic with either Ford or the industry. The auto companies, Ford included, often put styling and performance ahead of safety. Styling sold cars; safety did not. Copp's concern for safety was a nuisance, albeit a harmless one. Copp was designing automobiles that were selling well and making the company millions of dollars. His "eccentric" views on safety would never find their way onto the production line, so the Ford executives listened and laughed off his theories.[2]

In 1966, the laughter stopped. The federal government passed a law requiring the auto companies to meet safety standards before putting their automobiles onto the highways. A few years later, the government passed another law that limited the amount of pollutants that automobiles might emit into the atmosphere. The companies opposed the passage of both laws and have resisted their enforcement ever since. They don't much like to be told by anyone how they should build their automobiles.

No longer was Ford dealing with the eccentric suggestions of a mere employee about auto safety and auto pollution. Now, Ford was dealing with the law, law enforcement, courts, judges, lawyers, fines, consent decrees, and the possibility of jail for its executives.

In 1959, when Harley Copp was out on the Ford test track test-driving GM's sporty Corvair, he noticed that the car had a tendency to roll over in a slow turn due to a rear-end suspension defect. On reporting his observations to his superiors, Copp was assured that the Corvair defect would be reported to the government and to General Motors. Twelve years later, Copp found out that he had been deceived. His report was never forwarded to GM or to the government. Copp took direct action, and mailed off the report to Senator Warren Magnuson (D.-Wash.), an auto safety advocate in Congress. Magnuson wrote to the company warning that it would be illegal to fire Copp. The company did the next best thing—it let Copp stagnate on the middle rungs of the corporate ladder, stopping all future promotions. From that point on, a formerly respected Copp was held in disgrace by some top Ford executives. Either Copp had to give up his safety advocacy or leave the company. The views he had espoused in the early years of the Corvair controversy, while tolerated at the time, had become totally unacceptable.

The clincher came in the early 1970s. The battlefield was not auto safety, but air pollution. Under the Clean Air Act, Ford was required to test its auto engines for emissions and to submit the results of those tests to the Environmental Protection Agency (EPA). Ford was not required to test cars off the assembly line but instead was required to test prototype vehicles prior to mass production. The results of the emissions tests conducted on these vehicles were then submitted to the EPA. If the tests met the federal pollution standard, then the EPA would grant a certificate of conformity, and Ford could proceed to market the automobile.

Ford executives despised this law, as they despised most health and safety laws that came out of Washington. Company officials spent hundreds of hours in the legislative and administrative arenas of the capital trying to defeat or curtail the Clean Air Act. "Ford spent more money fighting the law than they did trying to comply with the law," Copp observes.[3] The result was a half-hearted attempt at compliance that resulted in a haphazard system of engine certification.

In 1970, Ford experienced delays in testing heavy-duty gasoline engines and asked the EPA to grant conditional certification of its engines, after which Ford would fulfill its obligations. On January 11, 1971, the EPA agreed and issued a conditional certification, but 11 days later it revoked the certification for two of those engines because they failed to meet federal pollution standards.

That was only the first instance where Ford's hostility to the Clean Air Act placed the company in conflict with federal authorities. In a second instance, Ford shipped about 200,000 1972 model vehicles to its dealers before EPA had certified the vehicles. The EPA considered this an illegal act and turned over its files to the Justice Department for prosecution. The case never went to trial. Ford settled the case with a consent decree and a $10,000 wrist-slap fine, a fine that amounted to five cents per vehicle.[4]

By the time Ford began testing its 1973 models, the company had already run afoul of the law more than once. Although Ford's disorderly process of certification made errors predictable, what happened in 1973 was an eye-opener even to such seasoned engineering veterans as Harley Copp.

At the time, Copp was operations director of Ford's Engineering Technical Services, which included some of the company's computer operations. Jim Struck, director of Engine Engineering — who was in charge of the certification testing — complained to Copp about the computer division's inadequate support for Engine Engineering. Copp, who had been working for a year and a half to upgrade Ford's computer services, was a bit piqued by Struck's complaint. Nevertheless, he took it seriously and ordered a full report. "I figured that this was just another one of Struck's complaints,"

Copp recalls, "but I told my people that I wanted an audit of every program that we're doing for them, that I wanted a statement of the program and I wanted a description of what we're doing. Tell me everything we're doing for engine engineering and for the emissions certification process. I asked that it be done in a week."

Three days later, one of Copp's people, Bill Hieney, telephoned Copp and reported that he had discovered a problem.

"What's the problem?" Copp asked.

"I'd rather talk to you about it in person," Hieney replied.

In Copp's office, Hieney explained that the check on the computer had turned up two computer programs for the EPA certification of 1973 engines.

At first, Copp did not understand what Hieney meant by "two computer programs."

"One is for the government," Hieney said, "and one is for Ford."

Now the picture became clear. "It turned out," Copp explained in an interview, "that Ford had an 'us' and a 'them' file. Ford was putting into the government computer ['them'] file only the adjustments that were permitted under law. And in the Ford file ['us'] they were putting all of the adjustments, both legal and illegal—cleaning plugs, timing, and the various other illegal adjustments were going into the Ford file."

The Ford employees who knew about the illegal adjustments referred to the operation as "lemon juice." "When you write on a piece of white paper with lemon juice, you can't read it," Copp explains. "But if you put it over heat you can read it over a candle. It used to be a way of writing secret messages."

Copp immediately recognized the legal consequences for himself, his associates, and the company. He took a number of people from his division and, with computer printout in hand, met face to face with a Ford vice president and reported what he had found out the previous week. The official listened to Copp's presentation, then asked Copp to investigate the matter further. "There's got to be some reasons for this," the vice president told Copp.

"This is clearly a violation of the law," Copp retorted.

But the vice president was noncommittal. "Let's get into it some more," he told Copp before the group left.

Copp left the office with the feeling that he was getting straight-armed, that the official "didn't want to face up to it." One week later, the vice president sent Copp a response. "It was basically that 'everybody cheats and that if it got out it would chop the Ford Motor Company down,'" recalls Copp. This was hardly an adequate response. So Copp returned to the vice president's office, printout in hand, and again presented a copy of the printout.

"My problem, Harley, is that I don't know what to do with this," the official said, without embarrassment.

Copp, after an instant, knew just what to do with it: "I'd call everybody at home before the end of this day or this week and make sure everybody was aware of it. I'd get it to the government. I'd get everybody involved that had anything to do with it."

Within a week, Ford was in Washington, admitting to the EPA that "irregularities" had occurred during the certification process for 1973 Ford engines. But it was too late.

After being notified by Ford of the rigged pollution tests, EPA immediately ruled that the engines could not be certified and turned the case over to the Justice Department for investigation. When the feds arrived in Dearborn, Michigan, they interviewed many of the persons involved in the case. They did not interview Harley Copp.

"After I wrote a letter to my superiors outlining the dual reporting system, and before the Justice Department investigation," Copp explains, "I was visited by a Ford lawyer I knew had been a patent attorney for years during my design days. He was clearly the man they picked out to ask me some questions."

"Harley," the lawyer said, "the letter you wrote was pretty strong."

"What was strong about it?" Copp asked.

"Well, you said it was like 'bandits guarding the bank.'"

"That's right," Copp replied.

"Well, that's pretty strong language," the lawyer charged.

"It might be," retorted Copp, "but that's the way it was."

The Ford lawyer asked Copp where his files were. Copp obediently took the lawyer to his outer office and pointed to the files.

"Do you have a list of everyone who received a copy of your letter?" the lawyer asked Copp.

Copp said he did, and asked his secretary to bring it in. She brought in the list and the extra copies of the letter. The lawyer glanced at the list, and the extra copies, then handed them back to the secretary. The lawyer then followed the secretary out of the office and watched her refile the list and the extra copies of the damaging letter.

"A week later," Copp recalls, "I asked my secretary for the file. She came in absolutely white-faced. The file was gone. Stolen! I told my secretary never to say anything in the office that she wouldn't say to Henry Ford or to Henry Nolte (vice president and general counsel). She asked me why and I said I'm just asking you not to do it. So she beckoned me to come out in the hall, where she told me that she had made a copy of my letter upstairs. She showed it to me. I said, 'That's great!'"

But Copp would never see that copy of the letter again. "She said she lost it," Copp says in disgust. "My own secretary."

Did the Justice Department have a copy of the original Copp letter? No, says Harley Copp. The Justice Department had what purported to be a letter from Copp to his superiors, but it wasn't Copp's letter. Copp claims that he saw the Justice Department files, and that all the documents were numbered. Copp's letter was unnumbered. And it was a fake. It was rewritten. His signature was not on it. "They were smart enough not to try to sign my signature to it," Copp remarks.

According to Copp, only after the company stole the copies of the original "smoking gun" letter and replaced it with a fake in company files—files that would eventually end up in Washington at the Justice Department—only then did Ford go to the EPA in Washington and admit to "irregularities" in its emissions testing. The agency immediately ruled that Ford's vehicles could not be certified and the company was sent back to redo the tests, this time without "irregularities," under a shorter but more stringent testing procedure. The EPA eventually certified the '73 Ford vehicles.[6]

But Ford's "irregularities" did not go unnoticed on Capitol Hill. Senator Edmund Muskie (D.-Me.), then chairman of the Senate Subcommittee on Air and Water Pollution, called for an investigation by the General Accounting Office.

During the recertification process, Henry Ford, in a speech in Washington, D.C., admitted that "some of our people withheld maintenance information that should have been submitted to the government in our application for certifications of 1973 model test vehicles." But Ford contradicted Copp's version of who reported what when. "As soon as I and other members of top management learned of this failure to report," Ford told his Washington audience, "we promptly notified the Environmental Protection Agency and withdrew our applications for certification."[7] Ford also admitted to "discrepancies" in the 1972 model certification process, discrepancies that, he said, were "promptly reported to the EPA."

Henry Ford tried to counter the impression that his company was a habitual law violator. "After nearly 70 years in business," he said, "Ford Motor Company has a great many firmly established policies. One of those policies, obviously, is to adhere strictly to all the government rules and regulations affecting our business. Clearly, that policy was not followed." So, in Henry Ford's view, the fraudulent reports were aberrations from a policy of obedience to the law. He was willing to accept responsibility for the criminal acts of his company. "As chief executive officer of the company," Ford told his audience, "I must take the ultimate responsibility for what has happened."

Luckily for Henry Ford, the law was not equipped to deliver the justice Ford claimed he was willing to accept. The Justice Department did charge the Ford Motor Company with both criminal and civil violations of the Clean Air Act. The company pleaded no contest (in effect, an admission of guilt) to 350 separate counts, and the judge imposed the maximum penalty — $3.5 million in the criminal case and $3.5 million in the civil case, for a record total of $7 million in fines.

Despite these fines, Copp maintains that "Ford got off easy." Environmental and consumer groups were similarly displeased with the outcome. "The $7 million settlement was an exchange for not imposing criminal penalties on Ford officials who had willfully falsified records submitted to EPA or who had approved such falsification," charged Clarence Ditlow, of the Center for Auto Safety. Ditlow and consumer advocate Ralph Nader charged that Ford shareholders were being forced to pay for "the crimes of Ford officials." Fines were not enough to deter corporate crime, Ditlow claimed. "The only effective deterrent against the criminal activity of corporate executives is the criminal sanction — imprisonment. . . . When will the Justice Department apply the same rule of law to the corporate criminal as it does to the criminal on the streets?"

The Ford emissions tests and his efforts to disclose the practice was Copp's last stand. No other automobile manufacturer will hire this renowned automotive genius. "There's a club," Copp observes, "Once you're ostracized by one, you're ostracized by all."

Notes

1. Telephone interview with Harley Copp. March 7, 1982.

2. "Pinto Madness," Mark Dowie. *Mother Jones,* Sept/Oct 1977.

3. Telephone interview with Copp.

4. *Examination Into the Adequacy of the Environmental Protection Agency's Motor Vehicle Certification Activities,* June 12, 1972, p. 3.

5. Telephone interview with Copp.

6. "Court Fines Ford $7 Million in Suit On Pollution Test," *New York Times,* February 14, 1973, p. 1.

7. *Text of Henry Ford Speech at International Conference on Transportation and Environment,* May 31, 1972.

14
General Electric Price Fix

"More goods for more people at less price."

—General Electric motto, late 1950s

RALPH CORDINER, PRESIDENT of the General Electric Company during the 1950s, didn't like a piece of legislation that Senator Joseph O'Mahoney of Wyoming had introduced in the Congress of the United States. The bill, known as S. 215, was designed to increase competition in those industries where a few companies controlled a majority share of the market. The senator believed that in heavily concentrated industries there was a temptation for the few dominant companies to rig prices and eliminate competition, forcing consumers to pay artificially high prices. The senator also believed that the antitrust remedies available to the government and to competitors were weak and ineffective. O'Mahoney's S. 215 would require public review of proposed price increases in those industries where a few companies controlled large shares of the market.

GE and a handful of other companies controlled the majority of the electrical equipment industry and would be affected by the senator's bill, if it became law. GE president Cordiner's dislike of S. 215 led him to Washington, in May of 1959, to testify against it.

Under oath, Cordiner told a Senate antitrust subcommittee that even where a few companies controlled multimillion-dollar industries, "in all instances the price is completely subject to the force of competition in the marketplace."[1]

During the same year, two GE officers, Cordiner's associates and underlings, were meeting at the luxurious Homestead Hotel, in Hot Springs, Virginia, to set the prices of the company's low-voltage power circuit breakers. At this and numerous other similar meetings, prices were rigged, market shares were divided up between GE and a handful of other controlling companies, smaller competitors were thwarted or crushed, the price of low-voltage power circuit breakers was kept artificially high, and the free market was controlled in this $9 million a year market.

Senator Estes Kefauver (D.-Tenn.), chairing the Senate Anti-trust and Monopoly Committee, listened skeptically to Cordiner's proclamation that competition was rampant, even in those industries controlled by a few firms. The senator had noticed an article printed in the local section of the *Knoxville News-Sentinel* on the Tennessee Valley Authority's (TVA) practice of using a bidding procedure to purchase equipment. Kefauver knew that many local governments and public bodies had instituted a sealed bid procedure to get the best price on their purchases. For example, the TVA, a large purchaser of heavy electrical equipment, would announce that it wanted to purchase a hydro turbine generator. Each turbine manufacturer would slip its best price into an envelope, and then send it to the TVA. The Authority would then buy its generator from the lowest competent bidder. This sealed bid procedure was designed to ensure that competitors would give the TVA and other purchasers their best prices.

The *News-Sentinel* article, however, indicated that something fishy was going on back in Knoxville. "Some American manufacturers," the paper reported, "primarily in the electrical field, have regularly submitted identical bids on TVA purchases of equipment and materials."[2] In one instance, TVA issued an order for four power transformers and received seven bids, five of which read:

General Electric (Rome, Ga.)	$62,872
Allis-Chalmers (Pittsburgh, Pa.)	$62,872
Pennsylvania Electric (Cannonsburg, Pa.)	$62,872
Westinghouse (Sharon, Pa.)	$62,872
Wagner (St. Louis, Mo.)	$62,872

In a second power transformer order, four out of six bids received read as follows:

General Electric (Rome, Ga.)	$93,844
Pennsylvania Electric (Cannonsburg, Pa.)	$93,844
Wagner (St. Louis, Mo.)	$93,844
Westinghouse (Sharon, Pa.)	$93,844

On a bid for a piece of equipment called "potential transformers," only three bids were received:

General Electric (Holyoke, Mass.)	$4,368
Westinghouse (Sharon, Pa.)	$4,368
Allis-Chalmers (Pittsburgh, Pa.)	$4,368

Kefauver was not amused by these lists of identical prices.[3] How could competing companies, making independent determinations of the best price on electrical hardware, arrive at identical prices, down to the last dollar? The senator was determined to find out. So in September 1959, he took his antitrust committee on the road to Knoxville, Tennessee.[4] The first witness in Knoxville was Paul Fahey, director of TVA's Division of Materials. Fahey revealed that eight electrical companies, including GE and the Thomas Company, had placed bids on an order for 4,200 insulators. Each of the eight companies bid $12,936. Fahey was asked if he knew "how General Electric knew at the time they submitted their bid that the Thomas Company was going to make the same bid?"

"No sir," Fahey answered.

"How do you think it happens?" Senator Kefauver asked.

"I don't know," Fahey responded.

"So far as you're concerned," committee counsel Paul Rand Dixon asked, "your procedures call for them to be done secretly?"

"Yes," Fahey answered. "Sealed bids are required, which are, of course, secret until opened at the bid opening."

Fahey was not at a loss for examples of identical bidding from the big corporate manufacturers of electrical equipment. He submitted to the subcommittee the record of a purchasing contract for an item known as carrier current equipment. There were only two bidders:

General Electric	Syracuse, NY	$2,768
Westinghouse	Bloomington, Ind.	
	Halethorpe Md.	$2,768

Counsel Dixon was intrigued by this new piece of evidence. "Mr. Fahey," he asked, "on this type of material, carrier current equipment, I have several summary sheets. I note from each one of them that, by and large, GE and Westinghouse are the only bidders."

"They are the only manufacturers that we know of on this type of equipment," Fahey responded.

"In other words," inquired Dixon, "there are only two manufacturers of this equipment in the country, and each time they bid, they bid identically."

"Yes."

"You are at their mercy," Kefauver asked, "whatever they want to charge?"

"That is correct," replied Fahey.

"What can you do about it?" the senator asked.

"There is apparently little that we can do about it," Fahey replied.[5]

The Knoxville hearings also revealed that although prices for radios, stoves, and refrigerators had stayed down because of the many companies in active competition with one another, prices for heavy industrial equipment, the type needed by the TVA and other utilities to produce electricity, had moved up 50 percent in the eight years since 1951.

Kefauver was convinced that one of the major causes of inflation in this country was administered prices — prices set by a few powerful corporations in industries where competition was eliminated or controlled. "Administered prices," explained the senator, "prices not responding to the law of supply and demand, have had considerable to do with the inflation that we have in the country today. Inflation is a thing that every man, woman and child in America is presently aware of. Inflation gnaws at the vitals of any nation."[6]

Paul Fahey believed that there was little TVA could do about the identical prices he was receiving from the large corporations which produced the heavy electrical equipment he needed, but Senator Kefauver knew that the government could act. In fact, a few months before the Kefauver antitrust committee hearings in Knoxville, the Justice Department began investigating the entire pricing structure of the electrical equipment industry. By the time Kefauver arrived in Knoxville for the hearings, secret grand juries had been impaneled in Philadelphia, and by the time the Philadelphia grand juries concluded their deliberations, they would hand down 20 indictments charging 239 corporations and 45 of their top management executives with conspiring to fix prices, rig bids, and divide markets on electrical equipment valued at $1.75 billion annually. It was the biggest criminal antitrust case in U.S. history.[7]

The defendants included companies with big names—Westinghouse, Allis-Chalmers, Federal Pacific, and Cordiner's GE. Executives from these and other indicted companies met surreptitiously in hotel rooms throughout eastern North America to fix prices and eliminate competition. These corporate executives devised elaborate schemes to conceal the illegal nature of their activities—to cover their tracks. Meetings were known as "choir practices"; companies were not called by their corporate names, but instead by code numbers. GE's code number was 1; Westinghouse, 2; Allis-Chalmers, 3; Federal Pacific, 7. When calling a conspirator at home, the question would be asked, "This is Bob, what is 7's bid?" The executives used blank envelopes, which were sent to their homes where they were to be immediately destroyed. On the way to their conspiratorial meeting at the hotel room, they would purposefully avoid greeting each other in the hotel lobbies and dining rooms.[8]

Expense accounts were falsified so that any future investigators would have a difficult time tracking down the dates and places of the meetings. If, for example, an executive was going from Pittsfield, Massachusetts, to meet with his fellow conspirators in Pittsburgh, Pennsylvania, he would fill in the expense account to make it look as if he had gone instead to a city of equivalent distance— Baltimore, or Washington, for instance.[9]

As for the bid rigging itself, the companies agreed on a plan which could have been governed by the maxim "To each according to its market share." One of the indictments (Criminal/Docket No. 20234), for example, charged that "the bid invitations were allocated in such a manner as to provide each manufacturer with an agreed upon percentage of the total sealed bids as follows:

General Electric	42%
Westinghouse	38%
Allis-Chalmers	11%
ITE	9%

Using these and other devices, the executives agreed not to compete with one another; to prop up prices for electrical equipment at artificially high levels, and at the same time ensure each company its proportionate share of the business[10].

It is generally acknowledged that violations of the antitrust laws, whether prosecuted or not, are not unusual in many industries throughout the country. Few, however, would go as far as F.F. Loock, president of the Allen Bradley Company, one of the corporations indicted by a Philadelphia grand jury for price fixing. About the meeting attended by the conspirators to set prices, Loock commented: "No one attending the gatherings was so stupid that he didn't know that the meetings were in violation of the law. But it is the only way a business can be run. It is free enterprise."[11]

In this antitrust case, unlike so many unprovable others, the Justice Department knew that it had the evidence to prove that the defendants were in flagrant violation of the law. At first, however, attorneys for the largest companies went before Judge J. Cullen Ganey in Federal District Court in Philadelphia and entered pleas of not guilty, or of nolo contendere. Judge Ganey expressed displeasure with this stonewalling in the face of overwhelming evidence compiled by the Justice Department attorneys. He sternly reminded the corporate attorneys that the case was a "criminal proceeding," to which most of them were not yet accustomed. "I certainly hope," said the judge, "[that] these pleas being entered here are the result of a considered deliberate judgment." He warned the attorneys that he would not be lenient in his sentencing if the companies pleaded not guilty and were later proven guilty[12]. As the company attorneys considered changing their pleas to pleas of guilty, national media attention focused on the individual executives, especially the seven men who held the highest positions of responsibility—the vice-presidents and division managers who were unlucky enough to be indicted along with their company. They became known as the "Unlucky Seven."

These were men who had reached the pinnacles of power in modern America—clean-living, church-going, family men making upward of $135,000 a year (in 1959) along with prestige, country clubs, and power. Now they were facing thousands of dollars of fines and jail terms. Some observers thought that these men were being made the scapegoats for the corporation and for their superiors. Nonetheless, they had chosen freely to "get along by going along," and the decision would cost them dearly. They pleaded guilty to the charges against them.

Eventually, all of the corporate defendants, taking into consideration Judge Ganey's warnings about strict sentencing and taking a second look at the evidence, decided to change their not guilty and nolo pleas to pleas of guilty.

On Monday, February 6, 1961, a cold morning in Philadelphia, the defendants made their way up to the courtroom for sentencing. "I want to say a few words before I impose sentence," the judge told those in the crowded courtroom, "and I want to make certain observations concerning these bills of indictments. They cover some forty-eight individual defendants [three were later dropped] and thirty-two corporations, which comprise virtually every large manufacturer of electrical equipment in the industry."

In his opening remarks, the judge observed that this was no ordinary corporate crime.

> The conduct of the corporate and individual defendants alike . . . has flagrantly mocked the image of the economic system of free enterprise which we profess to the country and it has destroyed the model, it seems to me, which we offer today as a free world alternative to state control, to socialism, and eventual dictatorship. Some extent of the vastness of the schemes for price-fixing, bid-rigging, and job allocations can be gleaned from the fact that the annual corporate sales covered by these bills of indictment represent $1.75 billion. Their pervasiveness, likewise, may be judged by the fact that the sales herewith are concerned with a variety of products. They were made not only to private utilities throughout the country, but by sealed bids to federal, state, and municipal governments.

The judge believed that the real blame for this crime lay with those outside the courtroom that day. "This court has spent long hours in what it hopes is a fair appraisal of a most difficult task," he said. "In reaching that judgment, it is not at all unmindful that the real blame is to be laid at the doorstep of the corporate defendants and those who guide and direct their policy." (GE's president Cordiner, who made pious statements before the congressional committee about the sanctity of the free enterprise system, was not indicted by the Philadelphia grand juries.)

With that, Judge Ganey handed down the sentences. The corporate defendants were sentenced to fines totaling $1,924,500, including a $372,500 fine against Westinghouse, and a $437,500 fine against GE. In level tones, the judge read the sentence for the executives. A gray-haired Westinghouse vice president, J.H. Chiles Jr., vestryman of St. John's Episcopal Church in Sharon, Pennsylvania, was given 30 days in prison and a $2,000 fine; William S. Ginn, a $135,000 a year vice president of GE (indicted in two conspiracies), 30 days and a $12,500 fine; and George Burens, GE vice president, 30 days and a $4,000 fine.

"There goes my whole life," said Burens, a 40-year veteran with GE. "Who's going to want to hire a jailbird?" he asked as he waited in the hallway to telephone his wife. "What am I going to tell my children?"[13]

Notes

1. *The Gentlemen Conspirators*, by John Fuller. Grove Press, 1962, p. 34.
2. Ibid., p. 27.
3. Ibid., p. 46.
4. "The Impacted Philosophers," by John Brooks. *New Yorker*, May 26, 1962, p. 45.
5. *The Gentlemen Conspirators*, Fuller, p. 40.
6. Ibid., p. 49.
7. "The Incredible Electrical Conspiracy," by Richard Alan Smith. *Fortune*, April 1961.
8. Ibid., p. 137.
9. *The Gentlemen Conspirators*, Fuller, p. 81.
10. "The Incredible Electrical Conspiracy," Smith, p. 172.
11. *The Gentlemen Conspirators*, Fuller, p. 9.
12. Ibid., p. 83.
13. "The Incredible Electrical Conspiracy," Smith, p. 175.

15
GM Rips Out the Tracks

"Motorization drastically altered the quality of life in southern California. Today, Los Angeles is an ecological wasteland: the trees are dying from petrochemical smog; the orange groves have been paved over by 399 miles of freeways; the air is a septic tank into which 4 million cars, half of them built by General Motors, pump 13,000 tons of pollutants daily."

—Bradford Snell, transportation consultant, testifying before Senate subcommittee on Antitrust and Monopoly, March 1974

THIRTY-FIVE YEARS AGO, a citizen of Los Angeles could breathe clean air. Today, that is not possible—especially when the sun rises, or when the sun sets. When the sun rises, millions of workers are driving or riding on buses into Los Angeles from Glendale, or Burbank, or Pasadena, or San Bernardino, or one of the 56 other cities which together comprise the Greater Los Angeles Metropolitan Area. When the sun sets, the millions drive or ride back to their homes. Every day, the cars and buses involved in this two-way transfer/shuffle/hysteria dump thousands of tons of hydrocarbons and nitrous oxides into the air—air that goes into millions of human lungs. For 206 days in 1978, air pollution readings in Los Angeles violated national air quality standards.[1] The result is increased disease among the residents of the Los Angeles basin. In addition to the obvious heart and lung dangers, recent studies suggest an association between high atmospheric levels of nitrous oxides and a high frequency of cancers in all parts of the body, including the breast and the lung.[2]

During the 1930s, the Los Angeles air was clean all 365 days of the year. Today, millions of cars and buses with internal combustion engines clog hundreds of miles of superhighways. Thirty-five years ago, 3,000 quiet, pollution-free electric trains transported 80 million people annually throughout the sprawling metropolis. Los Angeles was no hick town, either, but a fully developed city, a city developed by the trains, not by the automobile, and it prospered in a cleaner environment.

The clean, efficient, electric train system, then owned by the Pacific Electric utility company, was the world's largest interurban electric railway system. Branching from Los Angeles east to San Bernardino, and south to Santa Ana, it carried thousands of commuters between Los Angeles and the area's 56 separately incorporated cities. Today this railway no longer exists. The tracks have been ripped out or paved over, the train cars destroyed; smog has replaced clean air.

Some say that the people of Los Angeles chose the automobile over the trains, chose paved highways over palm trees, chose smog over clean air—all for the freedom and mobility associated with automobile travel. In fact, the people of Los Angeles had no say in the matter. As with more than 100 electric transit systems in 45 cities around the country, the Los Angeles railway was eliminated to make way for gasoline-powered, rubber-laden automobiles and buses. It was destroyed by those very companies that would benefit most from its destruction: oil, tire, and automobile companies, led by General Motors.

Then, as today, General Motors was the largest automobile manufacturer in the country. The industry was in a vulnerable position: it was not clear that the four-wheeled buggy would become the transportation method of choice for a nation in the midst of its worst economic depression. The electric railway system of the 1930s posed a threat to the automobile industry's dream of selling a car to every family in America. The industry knew that without efficient rail systems, city-dwellers around the country would be forced to find alternative means of transportation. So GM, determined to sell more automobiles and buses, decided to destroy the rail systems.

The campaign was kicked off in 1932 when, as one GM general counsel later put it, the corporation "decided that the only way his new market for [city] buses could be created was for [GM] to finance the conversion from streetcars to buses in some small cities."[3] On June 29, 1932, the GM-bus executive committee formally resolved that "to develop motorized transportation, our company should initiate a program of this nature and authorize the incorporation of a holding company with capital of $300,000." The United Cities Motor Transit company (UCMT) was born.

UCMT's sole reason for being was to buy out electric streetcar companies, convert them to GM motorbus operations, and then sell the properties back to the local companies, which agreed to buy only GM bus replacements. Springfield, Ohio, and Saginaw and Kalamzoo, Michigan, were UCMT's first targets. In each case, according to one GM official, the company "successfully motorized the city, turned the management over to other interests, and liquidated its investments."

When GM moved to implement its plan in Portland, Oregon, however, the American Transit Association stepped in and said stop. The ATA saw GM as playing a self-serving role as a bus manufacturer, in apparently attempting to motorize Portland's electric streetcar system. The ATA censured GM for its activity in Portland, and shortly thereafter UCMT was dissolved.

The death of UCMT, however, did not mean the end of GM's plan to eliminate many more electric railway systems. ATA's public censure of the company only forced GM to go underground. Rather than setting up its own company, GM worked with an outside company, the Omnibus Corporation, and instead of focusing in on midsize cities like Saginaw and Kalamzoo, GM set its sights on the biggest prize: New York City.

Through management interlocks, GM was able to exert substantial influence over Omnibus. John A. Ritchie, for example, served as both chairman of GM's bus division and president of Omnibus during the period that the companies worked to rid New York of its streetcar transportation system. According to Bradford Snell, a transportation consultant and mass transit expert, the conversion of the New York City streetcar system to GM buses was accomplished in only 18 months and "has been recognized subsequently as the turning point in the electric railway industry."[4]

GM, however, was not content with New York City alone. The company had destroyed the largest streetcar system in the world, and was now after hundreds of other systems around the country. Coincidentally, GM's need for a front company to handle this dirty work meshed well with the personal and proprietary goals of E. Roy Fitzgerald.

During the 1920s, Fitzgerald and his brother started a bus company that serviced the two miles between the towns of Eveleth and Leonidas, Minnesota. As the Fitzgerald business began to grow, it attracted the eye of GM executives working on the company's rip-out-the-tracks campaign. In 1933, a GM salesman approached the Fitzgeralds and suggested that they buy the transit franchise in Galesburg, Illinois. GM offered to assist them in financing the deal if the Fitzgeralds would agree to replace the Galesburg streetcars with GM buses. The Fitzgeralds agreed.

Galesburg was only the first stop for Fitzgerald and GM. Other Illinois towns soon fell victim to GM's predatory ways. Within months, Fitzgerald found himself in Detroit, in the executive offices of the General Motors headquarters building, negotiating a deal for his biggest yet: East St. Louis, Illinois.

Like the streetcar systems that his company was destroying, Fitzgerald's modus operandi was clean, swift, and efficient. "They discontinued operating streetcars in the city one night," Fitzgerald reported, "and we started operating modern buses . . . the next day."[5] One day East St. Louis had streetcars and fresh air; the next day, GM buses and fumes. One by one, streetcar systems around the country fell victim to GM's crowbar. East St. Louis was followed by Tulsa, Oklahoma; then Jackson, Mississippi; and then Montgomery, Alabama. Fitzgerald was never interested in buying streetcar companies and operating them as streetcar companies. He would buy a city's streetcar company only "if a deal could be made with the city for complete bus operations — we were not interested in operating streetcars." By 1936, Port Arthur, Texas, and Cedar Rapids, Iowa, had the GM/Fitzgerald stamp on their streets — the tracks were ripped up, paved over, or left to waste.

By this time, E. Roy Fitzgerald was heading a big business, and he again went to Detroit to seek advice and consultation. This time he met with GM division president I.B. Babcock and the company's sales manager, Herbert Listman. Out of this meeting grew National City Lines, Inc. (NCL), a GM front company that would finish the job started by the GM/Omnibus and GM/Fitzgerald associations. GM sought to finance the endeavor with bank loans and a public stock sale, but the financial community balked. NCL was able to raise only $1.9 million, not nearly the amount needed to do serious damage to the hundreds of rail systems targeted for destruction. After failing in this first attempt to raise the necessary funds, GM and Fitzgerald met again in Detroit to discuss alternative financing methods.

Who would be the natural beneficiaries of their illegal acts? With the demise of the city rail systems and the subsequent advent of automobiles and buses, the obvious beneficiaries of a potential multibillion-dollar windfall would be the auto companies (they would sell more cars), the oil companies (they would sell more gasoline), and the tire companies (they would sell more tires). Greyhound, the intercity bus company, agreed to participate in a nationwide venture to eliminate the mass transit systems, but only if others agreed to participate. The group approached B.F. Goodrich Company, the tire company, but Goodrich declined to join the conspiracy. Firestone, on the other hand, agreed to join.

By mid-1937, even with these added partners, financing the NCL operation was still a major problem. One Greyhound executive reported to GM that he talked to investment houses, stockbrokers, and private capital brokers, but he "couldn't get the money."[6] There was pressure to find additional conspirators — conspirators with free cash on hand. The oil companies immediately became prime candidates for the partnership.

Standard Oil of California was the first company approached. "We could see . . . from our standpoint," testified one Standard Oil executive at a conspiracy trial held in 1949, "[that] it was going to create a market for our product — gasoline, lubricating oils, and greases. . . . If the Fitzgeralds were able to accomplish anything along this line [destroying rail systems] on the Pacific coast, the other people would do it, and that would open up even more markets for us."

Following this rationale, Standard Oil agreed to join the conspiracy, as did Mack Truck, a manufacturer of buses and GM's primary competitor for bus sales. The NCL adventure was ready to go.

Officers from Mack, GM, and Standard Oil met in the Chicago offices of Greyhound to decide on strategy. They agreed that Fitzgerald's operations would buy at least 42.5 percent of their buses from Mack and the same percentage from GM, with the remainder divided up on a "need" basis. By the end of the meeting, the conspirators had agreed to invest close to $10 million in the scheme.

At trial, where GM and its fellow conspirators were charged with violating the nation's antitrust laws in a conspiracy to restrain trade, Fitzgerald testified that he thought the defendants had invested such large amounts of money because the new bus lines promised to make big money for the investors. Fitzgerald's view, however, was not endorsed by an executive from Mack, who joined the Standard Oil executive in putting forth the theory that the companies invested with NCL, not for profits to be made from immediate bus sales, but from sales of their products after the rail systems had been eliminated. In an internal Mack Company memo, the executive wrote of "probable loss" on the bus-line stock, a loss that would be "more than justified" by "the business and gross profit flowing out of this move in the years to come."

NCL operated in the GM/Fitzgerald mold: acquisition, motorization, and resale. Resale was a key element in the entire financing scheme, for it assured GM that the group's capital was continually being reinvested in the motorization of more and more cities. In addition, there was little possibility that the cities would be able to convert back to electrical transportation. As transportation consultant Snell pointed out in his congressional testimony in 1974, GM imposed on the local transit companies contracts that prohibited purchase of ". . . any new equipment using fuel or means of propulsion other than gas."[7]

By 1940, GM and company were ready to move in on the sprawling electric railway system in southern California. Pacific City Lines (PCL), an affiliate of NCL, began to acquire and scrap portions of the $100 million Pacific Electric system, including rail lines from Los Angeles to Glendale, Burbank, Pasadena, and San Bernardino.[8] Another NCL affiliate (American City Lines) moved on downtown Los Angeles, removed the rail system, and motorized the city. With that, according to Snell, "Los Angeles may have lost its best hope for rapid transit and a smog free metropolitan area."

By the early 1960s, with the people of the Los Angeles basin laboring under the smog-related effects of GM's crime, the city was seeking ways to raise $500 million to rebuild a rail system "to supersede its present inadequate network of bus lines." But by 1973, building a rail system in southern California had become just another pipe dream. The cost of constructing the proposed 116-mile rail system had skyrocketed to a prohibitive $6.6 billion.[9] Today, there is no mass transit rail system in Los Angeles. The people must make their way in buses and cars. "The Pacific Electric," wrote George Hilton, a professor of economics at UCLA, "could have comprised the nucleus of a highly efficient rapid transit system which would have contributed greatly to lessening the tremendous traffic and smog problems that develop from population growth.[10]

Before a Senate hearing in 1974, San Francisco mayor Joseph Alioto lamented the loss of his city's electric mass transit system. "We had in the San Francisco bay area . . . something we called the Key system," Alioto testified. "It had 180 electric streetcars, and it had 50 rather sleek and fumeless electric passenger trains." Alioto related how, in 1946, NCL came in and "two days after they acquired the system, they announced that they were going to convert the system to buses, and within a very short period of time that company . . . did in fact purchase 200 General Motors buses."

In 1954, eight years after the acquisition and at a time when San Francisco was contemplating building a Bay Area Rapid Transit System (BART), NCL and its associate companies announced their intention of abandoning the remaining electric rail system that ran across the bridge. Alioto was, at the time, surprised by this development. "It is very difficult to escape the inference, in light of the total context, that they did this for the very purpose of slowing up and perhaps making impossible the development of our BART system," Alioto told Congress. "Nevertheless, regardless of the motive, the fact is clear. They pulled up the track. Now for BART we have had to spend $200 million to create that same corridor in the form of a tube on the bed of the bay."[11]

By 1949, GM had been involved in the replacement of more than 100 electric systems with GM buses in more than 45 cities including New York, Philadelphia, Baltimore, St. Louis, Oakland, Salt Lake City, and Los Angeles. In April of that year, a Chicago grand jury indicted and a jury convicted GM, Standard Oil of California, Firestone, and E. Roy Fitzgerald, among others, for criminally conspiring to replace electric transportation with gas- and diesel-powered buses and to monopolize the sale of buses and related products to transportation companies throughout the country.

GM and the other convicted companies were fined $5,000 each. Fitzgerald and the other guilty offenders paid fines of $1 each. Not one of the convicted individuals was sent to jail.

Former mayor Alioto, surveying the damages of these criminal acts on the state of California, summed up his Senate testimony with an insightful paraphrase. "What is good for General Motors is not necessarily good for the country," Alioto told the senators. "In the field of transportation, what has been good for General Motors has, in fact, been very, very bad for the country."[12]

Notes

1. *Environmental Quality,* 11th Annual Report by the Council of Environmental Quality, 1980, p. 146.

2. *The Politics of Cancer,* by Samuel S. Epstein. Anchor Press, Garden City, New York, 1979, p. 285.

3. "The Industrial Reorganization Act," Hearings before the Subcommittee on Antitrust and Monopoly, of the Committee on the Judiciary United States Senate, 93rd Cong., 2d sess. on S. 1167 Part 4a— Appendix to Part 4, "American Ground Transport," by Bradford Snell, p. A-30.

4. Ibid.

5. "The Great Transportation Conspiracy," by Jonathan Kwitny. *Harpers,* February 1981, p. 18.

6. Ibid.

7. "The Industrial Reorganization Act," Hearings. Snell, p. A-31.

8. Ibid.

9. Ibid., p. A-32.

10. Ibid., p. A-31.

11. "The Industrial Reorganization Act," Hearings before the Subcommittee on Antitrust and Monopoly of the Committee on the Judiciary, US Senate, 93rd Cong., 2d sess. on S. 1167, Part 3, *Ground Transportation Industries,* Feb 26, 27, 28, March 1, 1974, p. 1787.

12. Ibid., p. 1784.

16
IBT

"The fact that there were problems in a business is not a crime. Every business has problems. Some businesses have very serious problems. Some businesses go under. That is not a crime.

But if you have problems in your business and you lie to cover up the problems, and you lie to your clients who are paying you to conduct studies, and you lie to the government agencies who are responsible for regulating your business, then you are committing a crime, and if the business you are in is the business of testing the safety of drugs and chemicals and you lie and cover up problems that you have, then you are committing an extraordinarily serious crime, and that is what this case is about."

> —U.S. Attorney Scott Lassar in closing argument before a federal jury in Chicago in *U.S. v. Keplinger,* September 1983[1]

ONE OF THE PROBLEMS with Industrial Bio-Test Laboratories (IBT) corporation was an animal feeding room in IBT's Northbrook, Illinois, facility—a room the IBT technicians there called "the swamp." IBT's business was to use animals to test for safety a wide range of chemicals from drugs to pesticides to food additives. In 1970, IBT installed an automatic watering system in one of its feeding rooms, a system designed to fill drinking water bottles and flush animal wastes from hundreds of rodent cages. The system malfunctioned often. Faulty nozzles would run nonstop. Animals would get wet. Water would accumulate in four-inch pools on the floor. The humidity in the room was high. The temperature was low. Mice drowned. Rats died of exposure. Dead rats and mice decomposed so rapidly in the misty swamp that their bodies reportedly "oozed through wire cage bottoms and lay in purple puddles on the dropping trays."[2]

At other times within the IBT compound, mice and rats would escape their cages and run wild through the IBT complex. Animal technicians would track them down and spray the escapees with chloroform. "The animals were very wild," reported one technician. "They would run from humans. So our only chance was to slow them down with chloroform."[3]

The spectacle of drowning mice, dead rats, and humans chasing rodents might have been perversely entertaining to some, were IBT in the entertainment business. But IBT was in the business of safeguarding the health of millions of Americans who would come in contact with pesticides, insecticides, food additives, in deodorants, and thousands of other chemical compounds that IBT tested for safety in its 25-year existence—testing upon which federal authorities relied in deciding whether to allow the manufacturing companies to expose the American population to these ingredients.

The conditions in the swamp were only the most sensational symptoms of a company out of control, where scientific accuracy and the public health were sacrificed to satisfy the short-term bottom-line demands of IBT and its corporate clients.

IBT was no two-bit company. Founded in 1953 by Joseph Calandra, a 35-year-old graduate of the Northwestern University School of Medicine, the company was off to a running start by landing a number of federal government contracts, including an $8 million Pentagon contract to conduct a long-term study involving the feeding of irradiated beef to mice and rats. By the mid-1960s, IBT revenues hit an estimated $2 million a year. IBT was purchased in 1966 from Calandra by Nalco Chemicals, an Oak Brook, Illinois, chemical specialties firm for a reported $4.5 million, but Calandra remained at the helm.

The environmental movement of the late 1960s resulted in stronger laws governing the testing and manufacture of potentially hazardous products. These laws translated into boom times for the hundreds of companies in the scientific testing industry, including IBT, which had maneuvered itself to become one of the largest independent laboratories in the field. Offering cheaper rates than most established firms, IBT was flooded with contracts from major American chemical and pharmaceutical companies seeking to have their products independently tested for safety.

IBT found it difficult to handle the boom business. Mobile trailers were set up outside the main facility to handle the overflow. The turnover of animal technicians was high and their salaries were low. According to one IBT technician, in 1972 there were 5 technicians doing more work than 20 technicians were doing in 1977. According to another, there were only 5 technicians in IBT's Rodent Department responsible for the cleaning and care of 10,000 to 15,000 animals.[4]

IBT's competitive rates overshadowed the company's less public growth problems, and the business flowed. In 1969, Syntex Corporation, a pharmaceutical manufacturer based in Palo Alto, California, contracted with IBT to test a new antiarthritis drug, Naprosyn. Syntex was enthusiastic about Naprosyn because it did not, it believed, carry the same side effects as similar drugs. In order to get a new drug application through federal (FDA) police officials, Syntex needed a long-term rodent study. The company requested bids from independent testing laboratories, and IBT came back the low bidder.

Such long-term health effect studies are crucial for this type of drug since humans are destined, if the drug is approved for market, to use it daily over long periods of time. If the drug affected the rats negatively, chances are it would also cause damage to its human consumers.

In October 1976, at the end of the 18-month tests of Naprosyn on rats, Phillip Smith, a 25-year-old IBT technician, was assigned to write the report. But when Smith and the manager of the lab, Ron Greco, went to look for the final blood and urine data, they found that due to a mix-up, the data apparently had never been collected before the rats were sacrificed. Phil Smith wrote the report in rough draft, but he left the blood and urine data section blank. Smith then took his draft report to Paul Wright, the head of IBT's Rodent Toxicity Section. "As near as I can tell," Smith told Wright, "the blood and urine tests were not done."[5]

Instead of reporting to Syntex that a mix-up had occurred, that the long-term study would have to be conducted over again, IBT decided on a different path. The new study would have taken years to complete, and Syntex undoubtedly would not have been pleased with the news. When Smith saw a final copy of the report, he noticed that the spaces he left blank were filled in in the handwriting of Wright and James B. Plank, senior group leader for rat toxicology. Page after page of fabricated data—30 pages worth, according to the government. Someone even signed his name to the document.

In November 1971, IBT mailed the report to Syntex. Within weeks, Syntex replied in a stern letter to IBT president Calandra. "From past experience I am convinced that the report would be rejected by regulatory agencies in the United States, United Kingdom, Canada, and Germany," wrote Syntex's Dr. Robert Hill. "Would you please see the report is corrected and returned at the earliest?"[6]

Two IBT staffers charged with reworking the report looked for the blood and urine data, but couldn't find them. They mentioned this to IBT's manager of toxicology, Moreno Keplinger. "I'll take care of it," Keplinger replied. A revised IBT report on Naprosyn was sent to Syntex and eventually mailed to the FDA, which soon thereafter granted Syntex its long-awaited registration. Syntex subsequently repeated the rat feeding study.

Four years later, one of the nation's leading pathologists, Dr. Adrian Gross, then an employee of the FDA, began investigating testing reports submitted to the agency. Gross looked at IBT's report on Naprosyn. He noticed that the number of rats that had developed tumors and the numbers that had died during the Naprosyn study were underreported. Of the 160 rats entered in the study, according to Gross, pathological examinations were conducted on only 30.[7]

Gross continued his search, examining other IBT studies. He found serious problems with one that IBT conducted for Monsanto on a chemical called Triclocarbon (TCC), a common ingredient used widely in deodorant soaps, and with a study on two now widely used herbicides, Sencor and Nemacur. Gross and the FDA referred the case to the Justice Department for criminal prosecution.

By January 1977, Gross was concerned that given what he already knew of IBT, any action against the testing company had to be taken quickly. "Given IBT's track record of not being entirely candid with us, as well as their current embarrassing situation," Gross wrote to his superiors at the FDA, "and given the potential for great economic loss to them if additional bad news surfaces . . . IBT personnel might destroy incriminating records." Indeed by the time the U.S. Attorney in Chicago had convened his grand jury, many IBT documents had been shredded. In 1983, *Mother Jones* magazine reported that in February and April of 1976, and again in June 1977, IBT shredded hundreds of studies. "Before the shredding was over," reported author Douglas Foster, "seven long-term studies on the cancer-causing potential of cyclamates, the artificial sweetener; herbicides; and substances used in plastics were destroyed."[8]

Despite this wholesale destruction of documents, enough IBT paper escaped the shredder to incriminate the company and its personnel. According to these documents and testimony given by IBT employees, IBT's study for Monsanto of the deodorant ingredient TCC ran into problems when it ran into the swamp. The study called for feeding the TCC to 210 rats in the swamp. The conditions there were so bad, though, that if the rats were dying from TCC, you'd never know it because they'd probably die from exposure first. The technicians drew up their own special code to record the history of the swamp. One code word was "TBD/ TDA." It meant, "too badly decomposed/technician destroyed animal." According to one IBT technician, the death rate of rats in the swamp was two to three times higher than in other rooms.[9]

Over a period of months, Paul Wright, head of IBT's Rodent Toxicity Section, was told about the problems in the swamp. Phil Smith often saw him in the swamp during the testing period. Smith told Wright that the system was malfunctioning and they needed to do something to correct it, but Wright responded simply, "Well, let's give the system a chance."

When Manny Reyna, an IBT animal technician, was confronted with this answer, he responded, "That is totally wrong. You don't experiment on two-year studies." Instead of scrapping the study and starting over in a dry environment, IBT lied about the death rate in the swamp, added into the study animals that had not been fed test material from the beginning of the study, and commingled data from them with data from animals that had been fed the test material from the beginning.

The swamp and the cover-up that followed was one problem with the TCC study. The other problem was IBT pathologist Donovan Gordon. Gordon presented a problem because upon examining the male rats given the lowest dose he found that TCC caused testicular lesions in those rats. IBT acted as if it wasn't Gordon's TCC findings that presented problems, but Gordon himself. IBT officials began meeting with him in an effort to get him to change his findings.

In the course of the TCC study, Paul Wright, who began the study as head of Rodent Toxicology, left IBT for another employer, Monsanto, IBT's client, the corporation that was seeking FDA approval for TCC. At Monsanto, Wright worked on the same project—TCC. On October 11, 1972, a few days after Wright left IBT to join Monsanto, Gordon attended a meeting of Monsanto scientists to discuss an upcoming Monsanto presentation before an FDA panel that had jurisdiction over the TCC application. Gordon later accompanied Monsanto to the FDA and reportedly failed to raise the issue of treatment-related effects he had found.[10]

Wright, in his new capacity at Monsanto (the corporation that advertises that "without chemicals, life itself would be impossible"), began writing to IBT asking that IBT look at more test animals in the hope, according to the government prosecutors, that Gordon would change his findings about TCC and testicular lesions in rats. Gordon looked at more test animals but failed to fulfill Monsanto's hope, and instead found more testicular lesions.

In October 1973, Monsanto's Wright went over Gordon's head and met with Calandra and other top IBT officials. Wright was reportedly extremely upset with Gordon's findings and argued that the effects could be triggered by age, nutrition, and the conditions of the rats. He urged IBT top brass to convince Gordon to change his conclusions.[11] A series of meetings between IBT officials and Gordon brought no better results. Then Calandra directed Gordon to meet with an outside independent pathologist to discuss his conclusions. The outside consultant agreed with Gordon that there was a treatment-related effect on the rats.[12]

Finally, in January 1976, Calandra called Gordon into his office and told him that he, Calandra, was going to remove Gordon's findings from the report and substitute his own, namely that "decomposition precluded meaningful evaluation of the testicular tissues." This was far from the truth. Gordon knew it then, but he nevertheless signed the report, under direction from Calandra. "I did not want to leave IBT at the time, so I succumbed to my boss' interpretation . . . even though I knew he had not examined the slides," Gordon said later.[13]

    IBT eventually mailed the report to Monsanto and Monsanto then mailed the report to the FDA. The police agency, in turn eventually approved higher levels of the compound for deodorant soaps.

    Similar deceits were perpetrated by IBT in connection with its testing of the herbicide Sencor and the insecticide Nemacur. The evidence on testing of Sencor/Nemacur, TCC, and Naprosyn constituted the basis upon which, in May 1981, a federal grand jury in Chicago, following a five-year federal investigation, indicted Dr. Joseph Calandra, Dr. Paul Wright, and two other IBT officials on criminal charges of conducting and distributing fake scientific research and then attempting to cover up the scheme.

    At trial, evidence of the mess at the swamp, Gordon's problem with the testicular lesions, and Wright's flip-flop from IBT to Monsanto during the TCC study was presented to the jury. The key government witness turned out to be Merrill Thompson, a Chicago lawyer hired in 1976 by the Nalco company, IBT's parent. Thompson testified that after working with IBT for almost a year, he refused to accompany IBT officials into an FDA investigation to answer questions about several IBT studies submitted to the government. "As I got into it and worked on these things more," Thompson told the six men and six women of the jury, "and found out more, and worked with IBT people more, and looked at the evidence of other practices within the industry, I decided I couldn't defend IBT's practices."[14]

    On October 21, 1983, after hearing six months of testimony that filled more than 15,000 pages of court transcript, the jury in the IBT case, after deliberating eleven days, convicted three IBT officers of fabricating key safety tests. Convicted were Moreno L. Keplinger, 53, former head of toxicology, on two counts of mail fraud and four counts of making false statements. He was sentenced to one year in prison. Wright was convicted of one count of mail fraud and three counts of making false statements and was sentenced to six months in prison. Plank was convicted of two counts of mail fraud and three counts of making false statements and was also given a six-month jail term.[15]

    IBT was not a defendant in the case. According to Scott Lassar, of the U.S. Attorney's office in Chicago, the government cut a deal with IBT. The feds agreed not to bring charges against the corporation in return for IBT's not invoking its claim of attorney-client privilege. This opened the way for Merrill Thompson, formerly IBT's attorney, to testify at the trial and help convict the three IBT executives.[16]

The jury foreman in the IBT case expressed posttrial shock at the defendants' behavior. "They were dealing with chemicals that could cause cancer and could cause other problems," he told reporters. "To have done the things they did is almost unimaginable."[17]

Indications are that IBT is not alone in the industry. In October 1983, federal officials announced that they had found problems with scientific procedures of Gulf South Research Institute, a large independent lab in Louisiana.[18] A 1980 Federal Trade Commission report identified 157 cases of compromised and deceptive product standards and testing lab actions.[19] A federal investigation of G.D. Searle found deficiencies in safety tests performed by the company of its own products.[20]

The harm done to the American populace by IBT can never be accurately measured.

What can be said is that the IBT revelations have ripped a gaping hole in the safety net that politicians promised was guarding American consumers from the high-risk abyss of chemical exposure. The repair work will have to be done by federal prosecutors taking chemical and pharmaceutical companies and their client testing companies into court, putting the facts before juries of citizens around the country, and letting the people decide the criminal nature of their activities.

Notes

1. *U.S v. Keplinger,* closing argument by U.S. Attorney Scott Lassar, transcript, p. 17009.
2. "Faking It, The Case Against Industrial Bio-Test Laboratories," by Keith Schneider. *Amicus Journal,* Spring 1983, p. 14.
3. Ibid., p. 17.
4. *U.S. v. Keplinger,* Lassar closing arguments, pp. 17008–9.
5. Ibid., 17013.
6. "Faking It," Schneider, p. 22.
7. "Illusion of Safety," by Douglas Foster. *Mother Jones,* June/July, 1983. Reprinted separately.

8. Ibid.

9. Lassar, p. 17034.

10. "Faking It," Schneider, p. 23.

11. Ibid., p. 24.

12. Lassar, p. 17058.

13. "Faking It," Schneider, p. 25.

14. "Government Exaggeration Charged in Trial of Lab Officials," *New York Times*, October 1, 1983, p. 28.

15. "Ex-Officials of Chemical Testing Lab Found Guilty of Falsifying Results," *Washington Post*, October 22, 1983, p. A7. Also telephone conversation with Scott Lassar, November 5, 1986.

16. Telephone conversation with Lassar, December 7, 1983.

17. "How Many Product Safety Tests are Invalid?" *Sacramento Bee*, October 23, 1983, p. A20.

18. "IBT Guilty," by Keith Schneider. *Amicus Journal*, Fall 1983, p. 4.

19. "Illusion of Safety," Foster, *Mother Jones*.

20. "Drug Testing at Searle," in *The Impact of Publicity on Corporate Offenders*, by Brent Fisse and John Braithwaite. State University of New York Press, 1983, p. 136.

17
J.P. Stevens

"An 'embarrassment to the business community.'"

—*Fortune* magazine, 1978, describing J.P. Stevens Co.[1]

IN 1963, SHIRLEY HOBBS was employed at J.P. Stevens cotton plant in Roanoke Rapids, South Carolina. Her job was to sort napkins into "firsts" and "seconds." Hobbs was good at what she did, and on an average day, she could sort and count 8,500 napkins. On October 6, 1963, she wrote a letter to J.P. Stevens informing the company that she had joined the union's organizing committee. Three days later, Shirley Hobbs was summoned by the company supervisor, who told her that she was being discharged for having been several napkins short in her count.

Months before Shirley Hobbs allegedly undercounted her napkins, James Walden decided to become one of the first J.P. Stevens employees to join the Textile Workers Union of America (TWUA). Soon company officials posted his name on a shop wall, and one week later James Walden was fired for "tying doubles" in his work materials. No one in 20 years had been fired for "tying doubles" at Stevens. The day after Walden was fired, three of his coworkers told J.P. Stevens management that they had offered their resignation to the union. The three were then told that they would have to prove themselves by disclosing information on union activities.

Had Walden and Hobbs known the fate of five of their coworkers from Stevens's Republic No. 2, in Great Falls, South Carolina, they may have never dared join the TWUA. Idolene Steel,

Charles Knight, Arthur Knight, and two others were the first five Stevens workers to join TWUA in 1963. Their names were subsequently posted on the company bulletin board by mill managers and the next day all five were discharged. According to the company, Wright and Steel lost their jobs for failing to clean their equipment properly. There was no evidence that any Stevens worker had ever been fired for this reason before. Knight lost his job for allegedly having neglected to piece together the ends of certain materials. Knight later testified that he knew of no other worker who had been fired on these grounds.[2]

In 1963, when J.P. Stevens first learned that the workers were planning to organize a union at Stevens's Roanoke Rapids mill, executives posted a notice on company bulletin boards declaring that the company would oppose the union "by every proper means and prevent its coming into existence."[3] In the following decade the notice was borne out, with one exception: Stevens opposed the union by every means, proper and improper, legal and illegal, and prevented the union from coming into existence for almost 15 years.

Nonunion mills were nothing new to the southern textile workers, who historically were plagued by dangerous working conditions, stretched-out work days and weeks, and low pay. In 1963, when the TWUA targeted Stevens, none of the 600,000 textile workers in the South were unionized, despite frequent attempts to organize them. But the difference between J.P. Stevens and the other large textile manufacturers was that Stevens prevented unionization by using tactics in blatant violation of the law, while other equally antiunion companies at least gave lip service to such provisions as Section 8(a)3 of the National Labor Relations Act, which prohibited employers from discriminating against workers who support a union.

From 1963 through 1980, Stevens was cited 21 times by the National Labor Relations Board (NLRB)—the federal police agency on the labor beat—for hundreds of violations of federal labor law. In 136 cases, Stevens was found in violation of the law. Virtually all of the findings of violations were upheld by the U.S. Court of Appeals, and the U.S. Supreme Court ruled against Stevens three times.[4] As the Steels, Hobbses, Waldens, Knights and other early unionizers learned, Stevens's most effective tactic was to fire union supporters during their organizing drives, a tactic that clearly violated NLRB Sec. 8(a)3. Stevens was also engaged in threatening plant closings, economic reprisals, coercive interrogation of workers, denial of overtime to union supporters, altering working conditions discriminatorily, electronic spying on organizers, downgrading jobs of union members, and firing workers who testified before the NLRB.

The company's strategy and tactics reflected the beliefs stubbornly held by the Stevens family and president Robert Stevens. Fervently antiunion, Stevens believed organized labor was a threat to the free enterprise system and decided from the beginning to "fight like hell" against the TWUA organizing drive. And Stevens's sidekick, the attorney who represented the company before the federal police and federal courts, was Whiteford Blakeney, a 74-year-old Harvard-educated, North Carolina-born, tough guy who has been called by a fellow lawyer "an old style Southern resister," and an "adamant conservative" who "hates unions."

Together, Blakeney and Stevens set the company on a collision course with the federal cops and the federal courts. Stevens was hauled into court so many times, and on such a regular basis, that federal police authorities had a difficult time keeping up with the paperwork. "It was like nothing we have ever seen at the board (NLRB)," commented Reed Johnston, a federal enforcement officer based in Winston-Salem, North Carolina, to the *American Lawyer's* Steven Brill. "Every day the union was filing a new charge of unfair practices—you know, disciminatory firing—against Stevens. Hell, this company was firing people the same day they signed a union card. Doing it blatantly. Posting their names would scare others."[5]

When the Stevens cases eventually reached the courts (such cases can drag on for as long as four years), the judges imposed one of the stiffer sanctions available under the law—forcing the company to make payment to workers who were illegally fired. By 1976, Stevens had been forced to pay these workers $1.3 million in back wages. Yet, despite this cash drain on Stevens's resources, the company could look at its overall balance sheet and still safely conclude that "crime pays." Journalist Brill makes the point lucidly in "Labor Outlaws," his searing exposé of the Stevens affair. The back awards were

> clear proof of the soundness of Blakeney's and the company's strategy. Nothing dampened the union's efforts faster

than the immediate firing of those who signed on first and tried to become in-plant leaders. Even adding a hypothetical $2 million in legal fees to the $1.3 million in back pay awards, the $3.3 million Stevens spent between 1963 and 1976 fighting off the union totaled much less than half of what it would have had to pay for just a one-cent-per hour increase in plant workers' wages that a union might have won.[6]

J.P. Stevens obviously acted in the belief that the benefits of a union-free environment greatly outweighed the cost of breaking the law. In 1971, the U.S. Court of Appeals, in ruling on one of the myriad of Stevens cases, underlined the cost factor in a Stevens decision to remove a union supporter:

In fact, one of the employees so discharged had been illegally terminated before, was reinstated by our prior order, but was then illegally discharged again. We regard this pattern of flagrantly contemptuous conduct most seriously. Our system of justice cannot survive if litigants are seized with the notion that they can ignore the lawful orders of a court simply because they may disagree with them. In addition, the record here strongly justifies the inference that these respondents deliberately took their chances in ignoring our decrees because they thought it profitable for them to do so.[7]

As the second largest corporation in the textile industry (employing at the time 43,500 persons), with 1980 sales of $1.8 billion and profits of $47.7 million, Stevens wielded a big economic stick in the textile-dependent Carolinas. By keeping the union out, thus keeping wages low, Stevens contributed significantly to the depression of income levels of the residents of the Carolinas and to their overall impoverishment.

Without organized pressure, workers had little hope that Stevens's riches would ever trickle down. In a report titled *Earnings Gap: A Study of Earnings of North Carolinians,* a group of researchers at the University of North Carolina found that a gap of $21.34 a week existed between the average weekly earnings of North Carolina production workers in 1971 and the U.S. average. As of December 1975, the gap had widened to $54.67 a week. "Since North Carolina is the least unionized state in the nation and has right-to-work legislation," the report concluded, "the significant impact of these factors produces the lowest wage rate in the United States."[8]

By fortifying and widening North Carolina's wage gap, Stevens's illegal union-busting schemes perpetuated the state's relative poverty. Infant health, education and housing in the Carolinas lagged far behind the national average.[9]

Working at a Stevens plant meant not only smaller paychecks but also increased health risks. Individual workers had little choice but to breathe the cotton dust that filled the plants in which they worked. Groups of organized workers would demand that the company install new technologies to protect them from brown lung disease or from having their arms or fingers maimed in the mills. Because of the company's antiunion drive, however, Stevens employees traditionally had no say in safety and health conditions at their plants. During the organizing drive, one of the key demands was that the company agree to maintain a safety and health committee at each plant.

The company, however, was of no mind to listen to "demands" from "workers." Since 1963, when the first Stevens worker signed the first union card and was fired for it, Stevens had fired scores of union sympathizers. Under the strong-armed direction of its attorney, the company had pursued a hard-line policy to prevent the union from taking hold in the textile industry's second largest company. Whiteford Blakeney saw to it that nothing, not even the law, stood in the way of a union-free Stevens. In commenting on the company's attitude to a set of negotiations at the Roanoke Rapids plant, one federal court found that "the record as a whole indicates that the respondent [Stevens] approached these negotiations with all the tractability and open-mindedness of Sherman at the outskirts of Atlanta."[10]

The union organizers hired a competent team of attorneys to prevent Stephens from illegally nullifying the workers' demand for a voice in determining wages, seniority, and health and safety policies, but it gradually became clear that the law offered scant protection from a powerful corporation that was determined not to obey. The Roanoke Rapids organizing drive was illustrative. On August 28, 1974, after 11 years of organizing efforts, a majority of the 3,500 workers voted for a union to represent their interests before J.P. Stevens. The company continued to violate the law by refusing to bargain in good faith, by threatening changes in working conditions, by refusing to reinstate discharged workers, and by making unilateral changes in working conditions at the plant. The federal cops told Stevens to stop these actions and warned that if they did not, the company would be held in contempt, and possibly fined. Conceivably, Stevens executives would go to jail.[11]

But these were only possibilities. Little came to pass. No Stevens executive, for example, was ever sent to jail.

The number and weight of the violations that were piling up against Stevens forced union organizers to use new tactics. The lawyers for the workers were reporting the company to the police, the police were filing cases, the company was being found in violation of the law, and that was the end of it. Effective sanctions were not being imposed and Stevens remained all powerful, still able to impose its will.

By 1976, 13 years after the first union card was signed at J.P. Stevens, union organizers, still without a contract, commenced a two-pronged attack to force the company to the bargaining table. First, organizers agreed to launch a nationwide consumer boycott of J.P. Stevens products, focusing on major retail stores such as Woolworth's and Macy's. At Woolworth lunch counters, seats were occupied by union supporters who refused to move and refused to purchase any food.[12] The boycott was announced at the first meeting of the newly formed American Clothing and Textile Workers Union (ACTWU—a merger between TWUA and ACWA) by AFL-CIO president George Meany, who called Stevens "the nation's No. 1 labor law violator." Meany lambasted the company and told the delegates that the boycott could bring "this outlaw company to the bargaining table."[13]

During 1978, when the consumer boycott of Stevens was at its peak, the Stevens earnings from its home furnishings division (sheets and towels) were down from 34 percent to 29 percent. This drop came at a time when sales at some of Stevens's other divisions, such as its aircraft rental division, were booming.[14]

On the second front, organizers began what they called a "corporate campaign"—an effort to inform the corporate community around the country of the nature of Stevens's acts. The goals were to pressure financial institutions not to loan money to Stevens, and to embarrass outside directors into resigning from the Stevens board of directors.

The union organizers first studied the interlocking directorates that linked Stevens and other Fortune 500 companies. They found that a Stevens board member sat on the board of New York Life Insurance Company and that a New York Life Insurance Company board member sat on the board of Stevens. The organizers also found that the chairman of the board of Avon (the cosmetics firm) also sat on the board at Stevens. By publicizing Stevens's scofflaw record and by linking Avon and New York Life to that record, the corporate campaign posed corporate lawbreaking as an issue of social responsibility and by so doing pressured the Avon and New York Life directors off the Stevens board. The Stevens executive also resigned from the board of New York Life. New York Life's chairman, Ralph Manning Brown, upon resigning from the Stevens board, explained that

> The union's involvement of New York Life in the Stevens controversy places me in a position of conflict between the interest of New York Life and Stevens. Under the circumstances, I must consider the interests of New York Life to be paramount. Therefore, with deep regret, I am resigning from the Board of J.P. Stevens. I am equally regretful that Mr. Finley [the Stevens executive on the New York Life board] has felt compelled to resign from the Board of New York Life. He has acted because his sense of duty and responsibility to New York Life left him no alternative.[15]

In a 1978 speech before the Washington State Labor Council Convention, Ray Rogers, the director of the corporate campaign against Stevens, explained the success of the effort and why such an effort is a key tactic for similar grassroots efforts to counter corporate power:

> People have asked me if Corporate America, banks and insurance companies, won't band together to put a stop to the Corporate Campaign. I'll tell you why they can't. You have to understand the nature of power relationships in the corporate community. Up until now the banks and insurance companies in Corporate America have been an impenetrable bastion of power. There is no doubt in my mind that when Manufacturers Hanover was being confronted

by the union that all of the other banks got together and said, "Look . . . don't you give in to those damn unions. Don't get rid of the directors on your board because if you do you are going to set an awful precedent. Nobody has ever been able to confront us successfully and we don't want it to happen now." I have no doubt in my mind that the Manufacturers Hanover board of directors said, "Don't worry because we will never give in." Manufacturers Hanover was figuring that the whole thing would blow over. But they soon realized that it wasn't going to blow over.

I never asked any labor union or anybody else to threaten or boycott or to pull a penny out of Manufacturers Hanover. But when the labor unions realized these intimate links existed between Manufacturers Hanover and J.P. Stevens, they did what they thought they had to do. *Newsweek* and other publications mentioned that the bank was facing a $1 billion pullout of union funds. That is raw economic power. It is confronting power with power and that is what unions have to do with these big financial institutions.[16]

With the consumer boycott gaining national attention and pinching Stevens's revenues, with the corporate campaign gaining three early knockout victories, and with *Norma Rae*—a first-run movie starring Sally Field as a Stevens textile worker, opening in theaters around the country—Stevens began feeling the heat. In the fall of 1980, the corporate campaign moved from Avon and New York Life to what its organizers considered its biggest target: Metropolitan Life Insurance Company. In 1980, Metropolitan was one of Stevens's largest creditors, holding 40 percent of the textile company's $226 million long-term debt. The corporate campaign sought to take over this large insurance company by running its own independent slate of candidates for Metropolitan's board of directors. However, in late September, 1980, before the Metropolitan Life campaign got off the ground, Richard Shinn, Metropolitan's chairman, met with Whitney Stevens. Neither admitted that the meeting had anything to do with the takeover attempt at Metropolitan. "I merely wanted to find out how the negotiations were going," Shinn told the *Wall Street Journal.*[17]

Within days of Shinn's meeting with Stevens, J.P. Stevens came to a settlement agreement with the union. After a 17-year struggle,

Stevens agreed to a historic 82-page contract that covered 3,500 workers in ten Stevens plants in the Carolinas and Alabama. The contract gave the workers the right to disagree with management without putting their jobs on the line. Stevens also agreed to maintain a safety and health committee in each plant, and to negotiate on the issue of job standards, including the traditionally unfair practices of speed-ups and stretch-outs.

"Now we have the right to go up to a supervisor and say, 'This is wrong. No, it's not like that,'" observed Mary Robinson, a spinner at the Boylston Plant near Montgomery, Alabama. "We never had that before. Now we can say, 'You can't do that. You've got to go by the contract.'"[18]

In October 1983, J.P. Stevens settled all outstanding charges of unfair labor practices by agreeing to pay $1.2 million to the union. At the time, the number of Stevens employees who were organized and covered was only about 3,800 out of 40,000 workers.[19]

The Stevens organizing effort left citizens questioning a legal system that for years had failed to protect the powerless from the arrogance of the powerful and had allowed a proven recidivist back into the community after numerous violations of federal law. To the question: "Should a recidivist labor law violator be allowed to prowl the Carolina hills and profit thereby?" the legal system answered with a resounding "yes."

Notes

1. *Everybody's Business, An Almanac,* ed. by Milton Moskowitz, Michael Katz, and Robert Levering. Harper & Row, Cambridge, Mass., 1980, p. 140.

2. *A Breathtaking Experience,* by Bell. Unpublished manuscript, chap. 3, p. 108.

3. Ibid., p. 107.

4. *The Impact of Publicity on Corporate Offenders,* by Brent Fisse and John Braithwaite. State University of New York Press, Albany, New York, 1983, p. 13.

5. "Labor Outlaws,' by Steven Brill. *American Lawyer,* April 1980, p. 17.

6. Ibid., p. 18.

7. *The Impact of Publicity On Corporate Offenders,* Fisse and Braithwaite, p. 16.

8. *"J.P. Stevens and the Impoverishment of the Carolinas,"* J.P. Stevens Fact Sheet, ACTWU, AFL-CIO.

9. Ibid.

10. "Labor Outlaws," Brill, p. 21.

11. "J.P. Stevens Scofflaw Record: 16 Years of Defying Courts," American Clothing and Textile Workers Union, May 1979.

12. *The Impact of Publicity on Corporate Offenders*, Fisse and Braithwaite, p. 14.

13. "A Union at J.P. Stevens," by Tom Harriman. *The American Federationist*, December 1980.

14. *The Impact of Publicity on Corporate Offenders*, Fisse and Braithwaite, p. 17.

15. "Forced Off the Board: The ACTWU Corporate Campaign Against J.P. Stevens," *Directors and Boards*, Summer 1979: 16–36, p. 19.

16. *The Impact of Publicity on Corporate Offenders*, Fisse and Braithwaite, p. 22.

17. "A Union at J.P. Stevens," Harriman.

18. Ibid.

19. "Stevens Settles All Unfair Labor Charges with $1.2 Million," *New York Times*, October 21, 1983.

18
Kepone

"My hands started shaking real bad. I could not drink a cup of coffee without pouring it on me and my balance was not that good on my feet. When I walked I would stagger . . . I lost a lot of weight. Maybe about 10 or 15 pounds and I had pains in the stomach. I could feel the weakness from that."

> —Thurman Dykes, of Hopewell, Virginia, employee of a chemical plant that manufactured Kepone, testifying before the Senate subcommittee on agricultural research, January 1976[1]

W HEN THURMAN DYKES first began working with Kepone, his coworkers warned him. "Everyone I seen had the shakes," Dykes recalled about his first days at the plant. "They said 'Wait until you get the shakes.' I thought it was a joke. They ran around and said, 'You are going to get them.'"[2]

Within weeks, Dykes too, began shaking. But the shakes were only the most visible sign of the damage that Kepone, a highly potent pesticide, was inflicting on the workers who produced it in a tiny manufacturing plant run out of an old converted gas station in Hopewell, Virginia, "the chemical capital of the south." Dale Gilbert, another Kepone worker, suffered from a headache that persisted for a year and a half. His joints stiffened and he became sterile.

At one time, Dale Gilbert was the head of his household, providing for his wife and children. But Kepone forced Gilbert out of work and altered his role in his family. "Prior to this time, Dale had been the primary figure in our family," recalled Gilbert's wife, Jan, "and then it went to me. I didn't think it would be, but it was actually a bigger shock for Dale. He was totally stripped not only of his responsibility, but his ability to handle responsibility. I could feel a lot of grief he went through over his inability to support the family, and to handle financial matters and to simply handle the responsibilities of a parent and husband."

Gilbert was humbled by the Kepone experience. "People think of the word disabled," Gilbert told a reporter, "and they think, 'he doesn't get up and go to work,' but that's only the tip of the iceberg. . . . I'll tell you, it's quite ego-shattering. I've always since I was a kid had my own responsibility, making money. . . . And all of a sudden, you can't go out and rake leaves. That's a terrible thing. I don't think you can describe it unless you go through it."[3]

More than a hundred chemical workers went through "it," and the majority of them suffered from the shakes. In addition, many were diagnosed as having neurological abnormalities, rashes, and other clinical illnesses compatible with exposure to the pesticide Kepone. At one point, 29 workers were hospitalized for treatment, with 15 to 20 listed as having significant disabilities.[4]

"It" was work, but not ordinary work. Going through "it" meant working in a chemical sweatshop, with a deadly pesticide, and without proper protection from chemical contamination. In July 1975, the state of Virginia's epidemiologist, Dr. Robert S. Jackson, began an investigation of the Life Sciences operation in Hopewell. Jackson called Life Sciences for permission to inspect the workers coming off the afternoon shift. The company agreed. "The first man I saw was a 23-year-old," Jackson reported, "who was so sick he was unable to stand due to unsteadiness, was suffering severe chest pains, and on physical examination had severe tremors, abnormal eye movements, was disoriented and quite ill." Jackson immediately ordered this worker into a local hospital.[5]

After examining other workers with similar symptoms of Kepone contamination, Jackson headed for the plant. Once inside he found "massive building, air, and ground contamination with a white-gray brown substance which I was told was Kepone." A strong chemical odor permeated the plant environment and irritated the inspector's eyes. He asked if there were respirators and was shown three white plastic dust protective devices buried under a mound of papers and dust on a corner desk. "One had a broken strap, and they were all covered with dust." Jackson later testified. "It was clear they had not been used in some time." Nowhere in the plant was there a single sign or placard warning that Kepone was a hazardous substance.[6]

Under Virginia law, Jackson was authorized and obligated to protect the health of the citizens of the commonwealth, and he acted quickly. Just 24 hours after he examined his first patient in Hopewell, Jackson ordered the Life Sciences plant closed.

By then, the Kepone had already done its damage. Not only were the workers contaminated but, because Life Sciences was equally cavalier about the health of the community, unknown numbers of Virginians were unnecessarily exposed to the toxic pesticide. Shortly after it began producing Kepone, the company was found to be operating without the required Virginia air pollution discharge permit.[7] The plant was emitting sulfur trioxide, a Kepone ingredient, into the air.

The emissions from the Life Sciences plant got so bad that the building could not be seen by the operator of a gas station across the highway. His vision was blocked by thick white clouds, clouds that slowed traffic on the heavily traveled Route 10. The operator of a neighboring ice house reported that the Kepone dust left a film on his desk and, at one point, a noxious cloud drove him off the loading dock and into his office. A survey of neighboring residents located 40 people with Kepone in their blood.[8]

Not only were Kepone emissions spewing into the air, but at the same time, Kepone wastes were being dumped into the Hopewell municipal sewage system, to be treated at the sewage treatment plant. Cleaned effluent would then presumably spill into Baileys Creek, thereafter flowing into Baileys Bay, the James River, the Chesapeake Bay, and into the Atlantic Ocean. On the best of days, the Life Sciences plant would dump only one pound of Kepone per day into the sewer system, but there were days when much more went down the drain. One company supervisor recalls the dumping of 800 pounds of Kepone into the sewers in one day.

In theory, the bacteria at the sewage treatment plant would cleanse the effluent before it entered the James River. But the Kepone proved the stronger, and by mid-March, 1974, the Kepone had killed off the bacteria, and the sewage treatment plant was rendered totally ineffective. As a result, the city began pumping the Kepone-laden effluent into a nearby open field—known as Kepone Lagoon. Kepone Lagoon grew enormously, eventually holding 800,000 to 1,000,000 gallons of the contaminated sludge. Traces of Kepone later found their way into the city's industrial water pipeline, a pipeline that services a nearby federal reformatory and the U.S. Army's Fort Lee, as well as industrial users.[9]

One might think that this untidy chemical operation, with its heavy pollution and unprepossessing base of operations in a converted gas station, was being run by a fly-by-night chemical firm operating on a shoestring budget in the hopes of making a modest profit. On the face of it, that's exactly what Life Sciences Products, Inc. looked like. The company's history, however, revealed strong ties to one of the nation's largest chemical giants.

Allied Chemical was no stranger to Hopewell, Virginia. For a number of years before the birth of Life Sciences, Allied manufactured Kepone and other chemicals in an Allied plant in Hopewell. According to one Allied employee, Allied's pollution record almost rivaled that of Life Sciences, and in some respects was far worse. "There was no way in the world you could possibly duck it," recalled Ernest Raley about the Kepone dust inside Allied's Hopewell Semiworks plant. Raley worked there in 1968 and 1969. "I got it on the lips, and your lips get dry and you lick them, you know, you eat it. It had a kind of bitter, hot taste." Raley remembers seeing Kepone dust "on the ground and around the building." Conditions at the Allied Kepone plant were, according to Raley, "just about as filthy as they could be." The Allied supervisors later disagreed, saying that the Kepone area was kept "neat and clean."

Allied's handling of the Kepone outside the plant was even more disturbing. For more than two and one half years, during the early 1970s, Allied dumped Kepone into a tributary of the James River.[10] In late 1975, when Kepone was detected in James River fish, the state of Virginia closed off the river to virtually all fishing. But for years, many who ate the fish from the James and from the lower Chesapeake Bay were in all likelihood taking in a dose of Kepone. About 900,000 catfish, hundreds of thousands of pounds of shad, and 500,000 bushels of seed oysters were taken out of the river each year during the contamination period for local consumption and for sale around the nation.

In December 1975, the *Washington Post* reported that more than 100,000 pounds of James River oysters "possibly containing traces of Kepone" had been shipped to Campbell Soup plants in New Jersey and Canada during the preceding 14 months.[11] Kepone-contaminated fish were appearing in fish markets as far north as New York and Philadelphia.[12]

The early success of Kepone rested on the fact that roaches and ants hated the stuff. So did pests that attacked bananas. Kepone could kill off roaches and ants and banana pests so well that sales skyrocketed from 36,000 pounds per year in 1965 to more than 400,000 pounds in 1973. In that banner year, Allied Chemical stopped producing Kepone at its Hopewell plant. Instead, it contracted with a very small local firm across town, Life Sciences, to produce all the Kepone that Allied needed, which was, at the time, quite a lot. Production in 1974 doubled to more than 800,000 pounds of Kepone per year. Again, in 1975, production increased sharply.

Why the switch? Why did Allied transfer production from its own sizable plant to a makeshift operation run by two former Allied employees? Allied claims that it wanted to use the facilities where Kepone was being made for other purposes. But the *Wall Street Journal* reported, in December 1975, that federal investigators were "looking into the possibility that Allied ceased making Kepone because it was worried about environmental and occupational health problems."[13]

By contracting with Life Science, Allied could have its Kepone and the profits too, without the headaches involved in complying with the environmental laws. Those legal duties would be left to Life Sciences' two chief officers, Virgil A. Hundtofte and William P. Moore. Both Hundtofte and Moore were former Allied executives with chemical engineering backgrounds; both were, according to their former employer, Allied, familiar with Kepone and with the procedures necessary to produce the pesticide safely. "The principals of Life Sciences, Mr. Moore and Mr. Hundtofte," an Allied spokesman declared after the Kepone nightmare became public, "knew as much or more about Kepone production than anyone in Allied Chemical, or probably in the country."[14]

Both Moore and Hundtofte disagree. They say that they were not Kepone experts and that Allied failed to give them adequate notice of the dangers involved with the product. In the fall of 1974, for example, a Life Science supervisor, Delbert White, warned Hundtofte that "We got a problem. There are just too many people shaking." Hundtofte and Moore showed White a black book that contained information about Kepone's toxicity. As White recalls, Moore "showed me that black book. He said there was absolutely nothing out there that could hurt a human being." Moore denies that this incident occurred, but Hundtofte admits that he did become aware of "some shakiness" among Life Sciences workers in June of 1975. He wishes that at the time he had had more toxicology information about Kepone—information that was available to Allied 15 years earlier. "I have to feel that . . . at least we would have been able to consider some of the side effects," Hundtofte told a congressional hearing investigating Kepone, "that maybe he [White] would not have accepted my explanation and Bill Moore's explanation."[15]

Indeed, Hundtofte worked long hours at Life Science on a schedule that reflected a basic ignorance of Kepone's highly toxic nature. Hundtofte slept at the Kepone plant, ate his meals there, and allowed his kids to enter. At congressional hearings investigating the Kepone contamination, Hundtofte was asked whether he would have exposed himself to Kepone had he known what was available to Allied years earlier.

> SENATOR LEAHY: Tell me, Mr. Hundtofte, with what has come out about Kepone in the last week and last few months, if you knew then what you know now, would you have slept on that cot, would you have eaten your food in the plant, and would you have let your children in there, and would you have lived the way you did in regard to that plant?

> HUNDTOFTE: There is no way I could. I do not think, even not knowing anything, just knowing the effects that it has had on people that gave virtually in these cases their lives because of the incapacity that they now have, that that would have been enough to make one shun from any consideration of that. And I do, on the other hand, believe that something like that can be made safe.[16]

For years before Allied began to dump Kepone into the waters that fed the James River, and allowed Life Science to produce

Kepone in a sloppily run former gas station, information was available to Allied that should have led the company to handle the pesticide with much greater care. A 1962 Kepone experiment on quail resulted in a "heavy" death rate, and "tremors and other symptoms of poisoning implicated Kepone as the cause of death." A similar study in 1968 reported "whole body" tremors in quail, enlargement of the liver, and death. A 1964 study on chickens found "reduced production of eggs." Newly hatched chickens suffered "quivering extremities." "Kepone," reported a 1974 study, "interferes with the reproduction of birds and animals and affects various organs of the body."[17]

According to Dr. Samuel S. Epstein, author of *The Politics of Cancer,* studies contracted out by Allied years before the company dumped Kepone into the environment, found Kepone to be (1) of high acute toxicity (study date: 1949–50); (2) neurotoxic in rats (1949); (3) capable of inducing reproductive impairment in male rats (1961); and (4) hepatocarcinogenic (able to cause liver cancer) in male and female albino rats (1951).[18]

Unfortunately for the workers at the Allied and Life Sciences plants in Hopewell, and for the unknown thousands around the United States who ate Kepone-contaminated fish from the James River, there was no law strong enough to deter Allied from exposing them to this highly toxic substance. The environmental law then in place was weak, and the enforcement mechanism only a shell. Indeed, not until workers at the Life Sciences plant became chronically ill did law enforcement officials move to close the plant and act against Allied for chemical dumping that had occurred months earlier. "The compound was not discovered because it was not sought," reported the U.S. Office of Technology Assessment in December 1979. "It is unlikely that the presence of Kepone would be known today had the workers not become ill. In this case, Kepone was placed in the known environmental contaminants category as a result of illness of production workers, not chemical monitoring."[19]

On May 7, 1976, a federal grand jury indicted Allied, Life Sciences, and the city of Hopewell for hundreds of violations of federal water pollution laws. Allied and four of its employees were charged with a criminal conspiracy to defraud the U.S. government. Hundtofte and Moore were charged with 153 violations of the federal water pollution law.

Allied reacted swiftly and angrily to the largest environmental legal action ever brought by the federal government. "The scope of the criminal actions was unwarranted and unprecedented," read the company's prepared statement. "The extreme action shown by the indictments appears to reflect official frustration over the failure of regulatory agencies to coordinate their activities and to perform their duties with respect to the events which took place at the Life Sciences plant . . . "[20]

Hundtofte and Moore pleaded no contest and were fined $25,000 each and placed on five years probation. Those fines were later reduced to $10,000 each. The city was convicted and fined $10,000 and given five years probation. Life Sciences was convicted and fined $3.8 million, but at the time the company was virtually defunct.

U.S. District Court Judge Robert Merhige Jr. dismissed the conspiracy count against Allied, but if the giant chemical firm took this as a sign that the judge was soft on corporate crime, it was in for a shocking surprise. Allied pleaded no contest to 940 counts of violating federal water pollution control laws between 1971 and 1974. On October 5, 1976, Merhige imposed the maximum fine for each count, hitting Allied with a record $13.24 million fine. The fine was subsequently reduced to $5 million after Allied agreed to spend $8 million to create the Virginia Environmental Endowment, a nonprofit corporation that would "fund scientific research projects and implement remedial projects and other programs to help alleviate the problem that Kepone has created. . . ."[21]

The federal income tax laws do not allow a company to treat criminal fines as a tax-deductible cost of doing business, as Professor Christopher Stone has pointed out. However, Allied "claimed the donation as a good will expense, reducing the true after-tax costs by approximately $4 million."[22]

Before the fine was handed down, Allied attorneys conceded to Merhige that Kepone was "bad stuff" that should never have been discharged into the river. Still, Allied attorney Murray Janus told the judge that he thought a $3.8 million fine was more than enough, given Allied's reputation in Virginia as "a good corporate citizen." Allied also claimed that the company had only made "errors of judgment" in allowing the Kepone to be dumped into the river.

Merhige saw it differently. "I disagree with the defense contention that this was innocently done," the judge said, observing that Allied was concerned more with "business necessity" than with environmental concern, that the company failed to show any "true remorse" over the pollution. "It is a criminal case pure and simple and should be treated as such," he said.[23]

Merhige expressed concern for the Kepone victims, including the Life Sciences workers who suffered neurological and other illnesses, and the fishermen along the James River who lost their livelihood when the river was closed due to contamination. Allied was eventually confronted with civil lawsuits filed by Life Sciences workers, James River and Chesapeake Bay fishermen, the state of Virginia, and the company's own shareholders. Allied settled out of court with the state of Virginia for $5.6 million and with a group of 230 James River fishermen for an unspecified amount. In 1978, *Fortune* estimated that the company had paid a "staggering $20 million in fines, settlements, and legal fees."[24]

The importance of the fines and settlement figures was not their size, for $20 million amounted to less than a few days of Allied sales. It was the precedent that counted most. The relatively heavy fine levied by Merhige, and the adverse publicity that followed, undoubtedly had a deterrent effect on other corporations that were contemplating dumping their wastes into the environment. "I hope that after this sentencing every corporate officer will think 'If I don't do anything [about pollution] I will be out of a job,'" Merhige told Allied's lawyers. "The environment belongs to every citizen from the lowest to the highest. . . . I am satisfied that we, as a nation, are dedicated to clean water.

"I disagree with the defendants' position that this was done innocently. I think it was done as a business necessity to save money," he added. "I don't think we can let commercial interests rule our lives."[25]

Notes

1. *Kepone Contamination,* Hearings before the Subcommittee on Agricultural Research and General Legislation of the Committee on Agriculture and Forestry. U.S. Senate, 94th Cong., 2d Sess. Jan. 22, 23, 26, and 27, 1976, p. 148.

2. Ibid., p. 138.

3. "Life Hard for Victims of Kepone," by B. D. Cohen. *Washington Post,* p. B1, January 24, 1977.

4. "Compensation for Victims of Water Pollution," prepared for the Committee on Public Works and Transportation by the Congressional Research Service of the Library of Congress, May 1979, p. CRS 155.

5. *Kepone Contamination,* Hearings, p. 45.

6. Ibid., p. 48.

7. Ibid., p. 56.

8. *Who's Poisoning America,* ed. by Ralph Nader, Ronald Brownstein, and John Richard. Sierra Club Books, 1981, p. 95.

9. Ibid., p. 96.

10. "Kepone Indictments Cite 1096 Violations, Manufacturing Firms, Hopewell Face Charges," by Laura Kierman. *Washington Post,* May 8, 1976.

11. "Oysters in Soup May Be Tainted," by Paul G. Edwards. *Washington Post,* December 21, 1975.

12. "Kepone Discovered in Fish for Market Along East Coast," AP. *New York Times,* August 13, 1976.

13. "Chemical Firm Story Underscores Problems of Cleaning Up Plants," by Thomas Bray. *Wall Street Journal,* December 2, 1975.

14. *Who's Poisoning America,* ed. Nader, Brownstein, and Richard, p. 92.

15. Hearings, p. 275.

16. Ibid.

17. *Who's Poisoning America,* ed. Nader, Brownstein, and Richard, p. 101.

18. Ibid., p. 103.

19. "Environmental Contaminants in Food," Congress of the United States, Office of Technology Assessment, December 1979, p. 45.

20. "Kepone Indictments Cite 1096 Violations," *Washington Post,* May 8, 1976.

21. "A Slap on the Wrist for the Kepone Mob," *Business and Society Review,* Summer 1977, p. 8.

22. Ibid.

23. "Firm Is Fined $13.2 Million for Polluting," by Bill McAllister. *Washington Post,* October 10, 1976.

24. "Allied Chemical's $20 Million Ordeal With Kepone," *Fortune,* September 11, 1978; and "Firm is Fined," *Washington Post,* October 10, 1976.

25. "Allied Chemical Gets A Fine of $13 Million In Kepone Polluting," *New York Times,* October 6, 1976.

19
Lockheed

"I wish you hadn't asked that question."

> —response of Daniel J. Houghton (Lockheed
> president, 1961–67, and chairman 1967–76) to
> Senate inquiry as to whether Lockheed paid
> anything to Prince Bernhard of the Netherlands[1]

AUGUST 24, 1975, WAS the day before Senator Frank Church (D-Ida.) would convene his Senate Subcommittee on Multinational Corporations to investigate bribery abroad. It was also the day before the government's Emergency Loan Guarantee Board was to discuss whether to release an additional installment of $30 million in bailout taxpayer debt payments to the Lockheed Aircraft Corporation. The discussion would undoubtedly be colored by swirling allegations that the manufacturing giant was bribing foreign governments in an attempt to increase sales.

On that day, Robert N. Waters, vice president and treasurer and for 20 years a Lockheed employee, locked himself in his home in Valencia, California, cocked his hunting rifle, put it to his temple, pulled the trigger, and killed himself. Lockheed blamed the suicide on "personal difficulties," but a suicide note referred to business problems.[2]

Waters's suicide came just six months after Eli Black, president of United Brands, a $2 billion multinational conglomerate, smashed the tempered glass window of his 44th floor office in a New York City skyscraper, jumped through the jagged opening, and fell to his death.[3] United Brands was the world's second largest marketer of bananas, known for its brand name Chiquita. A few weeks after Black's death, the company issued a statement explaining that Eli Black had authorized a payment to an official in the government of Honduras to facilitate the reduction of the country's export tax on bananas.

The news of Black's suicide and subsequent revelation of the bribery allegations came as a shock to the business community, where Eli Black was known as a religious, morally principled man. Reports of corporate bribery abroad consumed the business world for years after Black's death, revealing that not only United Brands, and Lockheed, but many other major American corporations were engaging in paying officials of foreign governments in an effort to facilitate the operation of U.S. business broad.

As the seemingly endless flow of reports of bribery and corruption appeared in the *Wall Street Journal* and other financial periodicals, corporate public relations firms began to discourse on the immoral nature of foreigners who extorted money from decent American multinationals, and business groups explained that the payments were certainly not bribes, but gifts, or simply costs of doing business. Soon the shock value wore off, and "moral" businessmen, men of conscience, were less likely to consider such payments wrong, or illegal, or something that deserved a second thought.

Whatever the business community's perception of its own moral or legal blameworthiness in terms of bribes and their improper payment overseas, the fact remains that, in a short period during the 1970s, more than 500 major American corporations admitted to making such payments. None of these corporations drew as much attention, or created such an uproar in the United States, or created as much international political disruption as did Lockheed, one of the largest defense contractors in the United States.

Waters's suicide on the eve of Senator Frank Church's much-awaited hearings on Lockheed's corporate bribery abroad raised eyebrows on Capitol Hill. One of Church's first witnesses was Tom Jones, the president of Northrop, Lockheed's chief rival in the international airplane industry.

The Church committee wanted to know about Northrop's consultancy agreements with foreign agents and whether the money passed to these agents might be considered bribes. Jones admitted the consultancy agreements existed. In an attempt to reduce the emphasis on Northrop's activities, he mentioned that the consultancy agreements, which included bribes, were modeled on those of the company's chief rival, Lockheed.[4]

By 1975, Lockheed had grown from a small aircraft manufacturer based in Santa Barbara, California, to a multibillion-dollar, multinational corporation. Much of its growth came from overseas sales, which took off during the early 1950s when Lockheed sent salesmen across the Atlantic to persuade postwar Europe to buy its fighter planes. Fueled by the Cold War and an ingenious network of foreign agents who understood the local cultures, Lockheed began to build a foreign sales operation that would be imitated by other U.S. arms corporations seeking overseas sales. The cornerstone of Lockheed's program was neither the quality of its merchandise, nor necessarily more effective salesmanship. It was, instead, the network of agents—British fighter pilots, Australian naval officers, and other somewhat heroic and charismatic foreigners, who were hired to rub shoulders with government officials, to wine and dine them, give them compliments, gifts, and cash—all in an effort to convince them that Lockheed fighter planes were better than Northrop's or Grumman's or McDonnell Douglas's.

The first battle of the multinationals was launched in 1955, when the NATO alliance agreed, under a policy of seeking standardized arms imports wherever possible, to solicit proposals for a NATO fighter plane to defend Europe. The competition was fierce, with Northrop, Grumman, Lockheed, and Dassault (from France) seeking to convince Germany to purchase their fighters and not the others. Lockheed weighed in with its glittery Starfighter, a "missile with a man in it"—so labeled because it could reportedly climb like a rocket and travel at twice the speed of sound. But the Starfighter was an untested plane. Many had crashed during development, and although the U.S. Air Force had purchased a number of them, the planes proved unreliable and were eventually shipped off to Taiwan and Pakistan.[5]

The competition centered on Bonn, where defense minister Franz-Josef Strauss and the West German Bundestag would decide whether to buy nearly one hundred fighter planes, and, more important, from which manufacturers. Lockheed sent in a special team of 20 salesmen from California to lobby the Bundestag and to create a generally pro-Lockheed environment in Bonn. This strategy paid off when, in the fall of 1958, Strauss decided to choose the Starfighter. By the end of the year, the Bundestag voted to approve his decision. By 1960, five other countries had followed Germany's lead and decided to purchase Starfighters.

Lockheed's customer relations representative and liaison with defense minister Strauss was later to claim that Lockheed had given Strauss's party $12 million during this period, but Strauss vigorously denied this charge and a special West German board of inquiry found that there was no evidence to support allegations of bribery. Anthony Sampson notes in *The Arms Bazaar* that the role "bribes or commissions may have played in clinching the Starfighter decision will never be fully known, for when Strauss left the ministry of defence all the relevant papers were destroyed."[6]

What is known is that the purchase of the Starfighter proved an unmitigated disaster for Germany. By 1975, a total of 175 Starfighters had crashed, killing 85 German pilots. The plane became known in the German Air Force as the "flying coffin" and the "widowmaker." Some pilots heavily sedated themselves before going up in a Starfighter, and others refused to fly the plane. One was court-martialed for refusing.[7] While defense minister Von Hassel and his predecessor Strauss were to defend vigorously their purchase of the Starfighters, Von Hassel decried Lockheed's heavy-handed lobbying tactics and accused company officials of using false statistics. "Those Lockheed rogues will never get into my office again," Von Hassel exclaimed at one point. In 1970, Von Hassel's own son, a German pilot, died in a Starfighter crash.[8]

One of the many other countries to buy the Starfighter from Lockheed was the Netherlands, then under the reign of Queen Juliana. Lockheed hired Frederick Meuser, a childhood playmate of the queen, to befriend Prince Bernhard, her husband. The Dutch government's decision to choose Lockheed's Starfighter over the competition came in late 1959. Meuser immediately suggested to the Lockheed home office that the company present his friend Prince Bernhard with a Lockheed Jetstar executive plane. The company later explained that the suggestion was in no way connected to the Dutch decision to purchase the Starfighter; instead it was designed to create "a favourable atmosphere for the sale of Lockheed products in Holland."[9]

In California, Lockheed officials were nixing Meuser's airplane gift idea because of the difficulty involved in transferring an airplane without recording a commercial transaction. Instead, the company decided to give the Prince one million dollars. According to A. Carl Kotchian, president of Lockheed from 1967 to 1976, the payments were made "for a general goodwill and helpfulness on various programs that were going on in that area." The payments were "something we could give him [the prince] in the spirit of friendship and goodwill and that type of thing." Testifying before Church's subcommittee, Kotchian was pressed on his definition of the "payment" to Bernhard:

> SENATOR CHURCH: Wouldn't you call that a bribe?
>
> MR. KOTCHIAN: I think, sir, that as my understanding of a bribe is a quid pro quo for a specific item in return; and I would categorize this more of a gift. But I don't want to quibble with you, sir.
>
> SENATOR CHURCH: All right, we won't quibble on that. You gave the money because you expected a certain favorable condition.
>
> MR. KOTCHIAN: Yes sir.
>
> SENATOR CHURCH: In connection with the possible sale of Lockheed aircraft to the Dutch government?
>
> MR. KOTCHIAN: Yes, sir.[10]

In 1967, six years after Bernhard received his first million from Lockheed, the company was back offering more. This time the target was the Dutch government's plans to buy naval reconnaissance planes. Lockheed was interested in selling its Orion planes, and the French company Breguet wanted the Dutch to buy their Atlantique. With a December 27, 1967, deadline for a decision by the Dutch Ministry of Defense, the Prince was asked to intervene to postpone the deadline so that Lockheed could better prepare its lobbying effort. On December 16, three Lockheed executives met with the prince in Paris, and Bernhard told them that no decision would be made until the end of 1968.

According to journalist David Boulton, in *The Grease Machine*, "it now seems certain that it never had been the Dutch government's intention to conclude matters by December 27 and that Lockheed intelligence was faulty." Boulton adds, however, that "whether or not it was his deliberate intention to do so, Prince Bernhard left Lockheed with the firm impression that his own royal intervention was behind the invaluable postponement."[11]

Lockheed efforts were thwarted when in July 1968 the Dutch chose the French plane over Lockheed's. But a persistent Lockheed was not through. Company executives offered Bernhard half a million dollars to get the decision reversed. The prince refused the money because he felt he could not do the job. Lockheed's Kotchian was so impressed by the refusal that he immediately dispatched two emissaries to offer $100,000 in a gesture "to show his [Kotchian's] appreciation of the prince's honesty." According to Lockheed officials, the prince did not decline it, from which it was concluded that he would accept. A $100,000 cashier's check was made out in a fictitious name and cashed in a Swiss bank account.[12]

By the early seventies, the Lockheed/Bernhard relationship began to resemble a lovers' brawl. Bernhard was in need of funds. Meuser wrote to the prince, suggesting a 4 percent commission be paid for the benefit of the "World Wildlife Fund." The prince replied to the vice president of Lockheed's legal department, angrily stating that "after a hell of a lot of pushing and pulling," there now was a good chance for Lockheed to get through its sale of Orions to the Dutch government and suggested a commission that would have amounted to $4 million to $6 million. Lockheed sent an emissary to the prince explaining that that would be too much, and the prince said he meant only $1 million. Then, the prince sent a letter complaining about shabby treatment at the hands of Lockheed.

"Since 1968," he wrote, "I have in good faith spent a lot of time and effort to push things the right way in critical areas and have tried to prevent wrong decisions influenced by political considerations. I have done this based on my old friendship with Lockheed and based on past actions. So I do feel a little bitter." In an effort to calm the prince, Lockheed dispatched its legal counsel to Paris, where the prince was told that if he could produce the sale of four aircraft, he would be given a million dollars. The prince agreed, but the sale never went through and the money was never paid.[13]

More money was paid to government officials in Europe and around the world. In Italy, Lockheed paid an approximate $2 million—$1.7 million for promotional expenses and 85 percent of that "for the minister's [minister of defense] political party, past and present." In return, Italy purchased a fleet of 14 Hercules transport planes from Lockheed. The deal appeared cut-and-dried when the planes landed at an airfield in Pisa in January 1972. Four years later, however, when the Church hearings brought documentation of the payoffs, the news shook the usually skeptical Italian political world. Two defense ministers were indicted, and the scandal helped the Italian communists gain significant victories in the subsequent election. Mario Tamassi, one of the indicted ministers, was subsequently sentenced to 28 months in jail. Italian president Giovanni Leone resigned after accusations of tax evasion and kickbacks, including a $2 million Lockheed bribe.[14]

The Church committee evidence suggested that Lockheed paid $12 million to Japanese government officials to secure the sale of the Lockheed civilian jumbo Tri-Star jetliner, and that Prime Minister Tanaka was involved. A. Carl Kotchian, president of Lockheed during the scandal, later wrote a book titled *Lockheed Sales Mission*, in which he detailed the payments to the Japanese political infrastructure.

To Marubeni as regular commission $160,000 per plane, reduced by a credit	$2,900,000
To Kodama, one billion 895 million yen in several installments	$6,274,000
To Okubo for the office of Prime Minister Tanaka 500 million yen	$1,831,000
To six officials, politicians	$100,000
To the president of ANA $50,000 per plane plus $179,000 cash in 1974 for "rent" of the Tri-Star	$879,000
Total	$11,984,000[15]

The news hit Japan like a political tsunami and the resulting scandal, known in Japan as "Lockheedo," was compared with the U.S. Watergate. In July 1976, Tanaka was arrested and charged with accepting 500 million yen ($1.2 million). He was released from jail on $700,000 bail. In October 1973, after a highly publicized trial in Tokyo, Tanaka was found guilty of accepting the bribe from Lockheed and was sentenced to four years in prison and fined the equivalent of $2.2 million.[16] Sixteen other government officials in

Japan were charged with bribery, tax evasion, and foreign exchange violations in connection with Lockheedo, ten of whom have been convicted and given prison terms or suspended sentences.[17]

When, in secret session, the Church committee questioned Lockheed chairman Dan Houghton about Lockheed payments to Prince Bernhard, Houghton answered, "I wish you hadn't asked that question." The subsequent revelations of money paid to Prince Bernhard caused an uproar in the Dutch press. An official state investigation concluded that the prince,

> in the conviction that his position was unassailable and his judgment was not to be influenced, originally entered much too lightly into transactions which were bound to create the impression that he was susceptible to favors. Later he showed himself open to dishonorable requests and offers. Finally, he allowed himself to be tempted to take initiatives which were completely unacceptable and which were bound to place himself and the Netherlands' procurement policy in the eyes of others in dubious light.

The prince resigned in disgrace.

While abroad a Japanese prime minister faced trial, a Dutch prince was resigning in disgrace, two Italian defense ministers faced possible indictments, and scandals were simmering in Indonesia, the Philippines and Turkey, all as a result of Lockheed payoffs, Lockheed at home faced its own criminal trial. In June 1979, the corporation pleaded guilty to eight felony counts of covering up payoffs to Japanese officials, including $1.8 million earmarked for former prime minister Tanaka. Lockheed agreed to pay $647,000 in civil and criminal fines.[18]

The Lockheed grease machine was eventually dismantled, two top executives resigned, and a new policy against foreign payoffs was imposed. Yet, for all the international turmoil its criminal activities stirred up, Lockheed's fine was a small price to pay. Between the start of the bribery inquiry in 1975 and the guilty plea in 1979, Lockheed stock tripled in value.[19] In fact, by 1977, with the help of a bailout from U.S. taxpayers, Lockheed had pulled itself out of its financial doldrums and was doing a booming business again. More than any other corporate crime, the Lockheed scandal provides the best evidence to support the widely held notion that for some of the nations' largest corporations, crime pays.

Notes

1. *The Arms Bazaar,* by Anthony Sampson. Viking, New York, 1977, p. 277.

2. *The Grease Machine,* by David Boulton. Harper & Row, New York, 1978, p. 19.

3. *An American Company: The Tragedy of United Fruit,* by Thomas McCann, ed. by Henry Scammell. Crown Publishers, New York, 1976, p. 3.

4. *The Impact of Publicity on Corporate Offenders,* by Brent Fisse and John Braitwaithe. State University of New York Press, Albany, 1983, p. 145.

5. *The Arms Bazaar,* Sampson, p. 125.

6. Ibid., p. 131.

7. *The Grease Machine,* Boulton, p. 80.

8. *The Arms Bazaar,* Sampson, p. 130.

9. Ibid., p. 128.

10. *The Grease Machine,* Boulton, p. 96.

11. Ibid., p. 107.

12. Ibid., p. 109.

13. *The Arms Bazaar,* Sampson, p. 138.

14. *The Impact of Publicity,* Fisse and Braithwaite, p. 152.

15. *Bribes,* by John T. Noonan, Jr. Macmillan, New York, 1984, p. 671.

16. "Tanaka Guilty of Taking Bribe from Lockheed," by Urban Lehner. *Wall Street Journal,* October 12, 1983.

17. *The Impact of Publicity,* Fisse and Braithwaite, p. 152.

18. "Lockheed Pleads Guilty to Covering up Payoffs," *Journal of Commerce,* June 4, 1979.

19. *The Impact of Publicity,* Fisse and Braithwaite, p. 150.

20
Love Canal*

"Go back to Buffalo."

> —Armand Hammer, chairman of the board,
> Occidental Petroleum (owner of Hooker Chemical
> and Plastics Corporation), in Los Angeles responding
> to an attempt by Sister Joan Malone, a nun from
> western New York, to address the company's annual
> shareholders meeting in 1980 on the subject of toxic
> wastes[1]

BY 1980, THE CAMERAS, the lights, the reporters and government officials had come and gone like a rush of water over the Falls. They had come to western New York to report to the nation on how a chemical company had dumped tons of hazardous toxic wastes near a growing residential neighborhood, how those toxic wastes had escaped their containers, and how they were affecting the health of neighboring residents. Eventually, the residents were evacuated from their contaminated homes to new homes, away from the Love Canal dumpsite. When the people began to move out, the national media, following the government's lead, concluded that the crisis at Love Canal had been resolved. They took up their pencils and notepads and mikes and cameras and returned to Chicago and New York and Washington.

---

* Much of this section appeared previously in *Who's Poisoning America*, edited by Ralph Nader, Ronald Brownstein, and John Richard, Sierra Club Books, San Francisco, 1981.

For the Chambers family of Niagara Falls, New York, the crisis that is Love Canal will never end. When the TV lights were turned off, the family was still living in the Love Canal neighborhood. The government had given them $38,000 to relocate, but Brian Chambers was worried that $38,000 wasn't enough to relocate, and to get a new mortgage, and to help support his wife and children. Then there were all the reports that the chemicals that Hooker Chemical had dumped at Love Canal and that had escaped into the neighborhood—that those chemicals were adversely affecting the health of the residents.

Brian Chambers, like the vast majority of the workers in Niagara Falls, worked in the chemical industry. During the day, he would go to the giant Carborundum factory, and at night he would come home to his house and family on 98th Street, near the Love Canal dumpsite. The daily routine didn't change when the cameras left town, when the "crisis" was "officially resolved." But Brian changed.

Rose Chambers, Brian's wife, noticed it first. The changes were subtle. Brian was usually gentle and shy, but now at times he became more open, inviting people over to the house for dinner parties. At other times he would become detached and irritable. Rose Chambers became worried. "I think there might be something wrong," she told him. "Maybe you ought to talk to someone."

Brian heeded his wife's advice and called a church group that had been working in the area, counseling the Love Canal victims. The counselor Brian spoke with, Diane Shelly, remembered the call. Brian spoke with a calm voice, she said, giving no indication that something was wrong.

Three days later, Brian was dead. He was found hanging from a belt, in his workshop, in the basement of his house at Love Canal. When his wife Rose found out, she became hysterical. Brian's four-year-old child was too young to understand.

Since 1978, when the toxic chemicals at Love Canal first became news, there have been at least 22 suicides among area residents,[2] but suicide was only the most immediate and dramatic manifestation of the damage done by Love Canal. Diane Shelley, the church group counselor, contacted 560 Love Canal families. "I would say that 75 percent of them have emotional problems," she reported. "Great numbers of them will not make it without professional help. But these are blue-collar families, and they tend to solve their own problems. They don't seek outside help—that's why we have to go to them."[3]

Hooker Chemical and Plastics Corporation did not rush in to aid the victims of the company's dumping. Despite Hooker's highly publicized attempt to shift the blame for the physical and emotional damage done — shift it away from the corporation and onto the backs of local government officials, even onto the shoulders of the victims themselves — no one will deny that it was Hooker that dumped the chemicals at Love Canal.

Love Canal used to be a recreational area where residents could swim, skate, and visit with neighbors. In 1942, Hooker negotiated an agreement with the county power company, which owned the land, to dispose of company wastes in the canal. Five years later, in 1947, Hooker bought Love Canal, drained it, lined it with a clay lining, and began transporting chemical waste products to it from the company's main Niagara Falls production facility on Buffalo Avenue. The chemical refuse was transported in 55-gallon metal drums that were placed in the canal and covered with clay and dirt. Ultimately, grass and weeds grew on the top of the covered canal, creating a field that gave no indication of the deadly substances beneath the surface.

As homes and a school were built around the canal, the vacant field came to be used as a playground — on rainy days, a muddy one — by John and Joey Bulka and other neighborhood children. In the spring of 1966, while playing in the field, Joey fell into a muddy ditch and John went in to pull him out. The boys came home "covered with this oily goo," says their mother, Patricia Bulka. "I threw their clothes away and scrubbed them down good, but the smell didn't go away for two or three weeks."

Alarmed by the persistent odor, the Bulkas called the local health department and reported the unusual effects of the accident. Health Department employees arrived at the field, took samples, and told the Bulkas that "nothing was wrong." Patricia Bulka was partly relieved by this finding, but she had incurred the wrath and ridicule of her neighbors. They "were mad at us because we called the Health Department," she said. "They wouldn't talk to us for the longest time."[4]

Twelve years later, the world learned that the field Joey and John and countless other children had used as a playground was the top portion of a toxic dumping ground into which Hooker had poured 20,000 tons of more than 200 different chemical substances: oils, solvents, and other manufacturing residues. The mixture included benzene, a chemical known to cause leukemia and anemia;

chloroform, a carcinogen that affects the nervous, respiratory, and gastrointestinal systems; lindane, which causes convulsions and extra production of white blood cells; trichloroethylene, a carcinogen that also attacks the nervous system, the genes, and the liver; and methylene chloride, whose effects include chronic respiratory distress and death.[5] The list of chemicals at Love Canal goes on and on, as does the accompanying list of the acute and chronic harms they do to human beings.

Of the 200 chemicals found at the canal, one evokes more fear and anxiety among scientists and doctors than all others: trichlorophenol. The 200 tons of tricholorophenol wastes dumped at the canal contained an estimated 130 pounds of a chemical called dioxin, one of the most deadly chemicals known.[6] The dioxin compound is a contaminant created during the manufacture of certain herbicides and disinfectants, including the infamous hexachlorophene. Today, scientists warn that dioxin has many harmful effects on the human body. "Dioxin is the most poisonous small molecule known to man. It is also one of the most powerful carcinogens known," says Matthew Meselson, professor of biochemistry at Harvard. "We have not yet found any dosage at which it is safe, at which it has no observable effect . . . it is possible that dioxin is cumulative in our bodies. It is quite stable and is soluble in fat, but not in water, and will build up in body fat."[7] But during the 1940s, when Hooker was dumping the wastes into the canal, warnings about dioxin were little known. Still, some evidence did exist. Dr. Robert Mobbs, a Boston physician active in research on pesticide control, published evidence in 1948 that lindane, one of the chemicals at the canal site, was "a possible cancer-causing agent." Mobbs would later dispute Hooker's claim that the company was ignorant of this danger.

There is concrete evidence that, as early as 1958, Hooker knew that the chemicals were coming in contact with children playing atop the canal. The city of Niagara Falls had notified Hooker in 1958 that several children had been burned by wastes surfacing at the canal. Hooker sent two men to investigate and found that wastes had surfaced on both the north and south sides of the canal, and that benzene hexachloride, a carcinogen that can poison the nervous system and cause convulsions, was exposed. The investigators also learned, as a memo from a supervisor put it a few days later, "that the entire area is being used by children as a playground even though it is not officially designated for that purpose."

Hooker was more concerned about the company's financial liabilities than about the health liabilities borne by Hooker's victims. The company's policy of avoiding financial liability emerged in 1953, when Hooker sold Love Canal, with all its poisons buried underneath, to a city School Board needing the land to build schools to educate the baby boom children of the 1950s. The sale price: one dollar.

The transfer deed warned that the land had "been filled, in whole or in part, to the present ground level . . . with waste products resulting from the manufacturing of chemicals [by Hooker] . . ." and that "the [Board of Education] . . . assumes all risks and liability incident to the use thereof." Hooker gave the city no indication of the nature of the danger posed by these chemical wastes, and the school board didn't pursue the matter. Within a couple of years, an elementary school was built on the perimeter of the canal. The playground was located on top of the canal.[8]

After discussing the problems in 1958, Hooker officials decided not to take any action beyond notifying the school board of the incident. Testifying before Congress many years later, Jerome Wilkenfeld, the Hooker official who wrote the June 1958 memo, said the company did not warn residents of the dangers because "we did not feel that we could do this without incurring substantial liabilities for implying that the current owners of the property were [taking] . . . inadequate care [of] . . . the property."[9]

It has yet to be resolved whether a chemical company can absolve itself of its legal responsibility to its victims by the mere act of relinquishing ownership of land poisoned by the company. Had the chemicals stayed at the canal, liability might have been restricted to the injuries suffered by the children who played there. But during the late 1970s, the chemicals began to leak out of their containment vessels and migrate toward the homes in the area.

Residents noticed that the odors were stronger than usual, as though the fumes were coming from the basements of their houses. For Alice Warner, the assault took on an added dimension when a noxious white cloud hovered over her home, causing the paint to blacken and her eyes to burn. Things were getting worse near the school. At the baseball field adjacent to the schoolyard, large craterlike holes appeared in the outfield. The maintenance crews had to fill them in with dirt and smooth out the field. One year later, the area around third base was sucked into a large depression in the ground.

Despite these frightening occurrences, the residents of Love Canal were reluctant to seek advice or official help. As Patricia Bulka discovered, neighbors ridiculed anyone who asked questions about the air or water quality in the city. Hooker was, after all, an industrial giant in Niagara Falls, employing 3,200 people, many of them residents of Love Canal. For these working people, it was better to be quietly grateful to the company that enabled them to pay the bills than to question company or city executives.

No remedial action was taken until the chemicals actually reached the basements of the houses surrounding the canal. In the summer of 1976, Patricia Bulka discovered that a black oily substance was oozing through the drainage holes and into her basement. Alarmed, the Bulkas obtained a sump pump and began pumping the goo out of their home and into the city sewers. "The stuff coming into the basement made the air stink," complained one neighbor. He too began using a sump pump to rid his basement of the substance. Soon many of the residents whose homes bordered the canal were preoccupied with this black oily substance, and sump pumps were in great demand. The goo had risen to the surface and attracted curious reporters and then local and state health officials. Love Canal was on its way to becoming an international scandal that typified the chemical industry's dumping activities around the world.

In the spring of 1978, the state health department found that 95 percent of the homes surrounding the canal were contaminated by chemicals. In May, the federal Environmental Protection Agency (EPA) determined that the toxic vapors in the basement presented "a serious health threat."[10] What's more, women living near the former dumpsite were experiencing about 3.5 times the expected number of miscarriages, as well as a disproportionate number of birth defects and spontaneous abortions. The state found that the women who suffered miscarriages had lived at the canal an average of about 18.5 years—7 years longer than the average for women who didn't miscarry.[11] Residents, their memories jogged by the newly released health reports, began recalling medical problems they now believed were caused by the chemicals at the dumpsite. Led by Lois Gibbs, a housewife turned organizer, the citizens of Love Canal began a campaign to document their grievances and demand action.[12]

Mrs. Timothy Schroeder, a canal area resident, suffered from burning eyes and skin ailments. Her daughter, Sheri, was born with a cleft palate, a double row of bottom teeth, a deformed ear, eardrums that disintegrated, bone blockage in her left nasal passage, a hole in her heart, and slight retardation. In 1978, Sheri began to lose her hair in large clumps. Donald Donough lived at the northern end of the canal. He had five children, only one of whom was born and raised next to Love Canal. The other four were in generally good health, but the "canal child" suffered from a heart murmur.[13] One woman living in the area had three successive miscarriages before giving birth to a child. The baby was born with three ears. Her second child also was born with deformed ears.[14]

For Love Canal residents, doctors only confirmed the obvious when they suggested that the chemicals "no doubt" had affected residents' health. Indeed, the toxic effects of the dumpsite chemicals paralleled the medical complaints of neighboring residents.[15] Drowsiness and depression in children coincided with the known toxic effects of benzene, methylene chloride, and carbon tetrachloride, all dumped at the canal. Similarly, liver disorders that had been reported can be caused by several canal chemicals, including chloroform, toluene, and tetrachloroethylene.[16]

These new reports of high rates of medical problems forced Hooker to abandon its "no comment" posture and to put forth its best defense. Hooker executives claimed that the chemicals were enclosed in 55-gallon metal drums and that the drums were buried in a sealed vault at the canal site. This was considered by Hooker at the time to be a responsible waste-dumping practice. Hooker blamed the escape of the chemicals on excavations that occurred at the canal after the land was deeded over to the city. According to Hooker, in building the homes at Love Canal, the housing contractors may have scraped some of the clay off the vault, thus allowing rainwater and melting snow to fill the ditch and to raise the chemicals to the surface.[17] Hooker disowned any liability for damages or injury that might arise. Company officials further claimed that by accepting the deed on the land, the Board of Education absolved Hooker of any responsibility.

Hooker vice president John Riordan invoked this defense when questioned by reporters on NBC television's *Today Show*. Responding to questions about Hooker's dumping practices at the canal, Riordan claimed that "years ago, many companies weren't aware of the hazards of the wastes. We [Hooker] were not aware of them at the time." One of the viewers of the *Today Show* that day was Dr. Robert Mobbs, who had conducted the research into lindane 30 years ago. Mobbs was furious over Riordan's comments and charged that Hooker "damn well knew that the compounds it deposited in the canal were extremely dangerous to human beings." To support this claim, Mobbs cited his study of lindane, a chemical found at the canal site: "I presented evidence that it was a possible cancer-causing agent in 1948." Mobbs's findings were published in the December 1948 issue of the *Journal of the American Medical Association* and had been publicized further by Washington columnist Drew Pearson. "Did Hooker come looking for the evidence?" asked Mobbs. "Like hell they did! They ignored, minimized and suppressed the facts. . . . If I found it [the danger] out, why couldn't they?"[18]

By effectively denying responsibility for the Love Canal tragedy, Hooker shifted the spotlight to local, state, and federal governments. Love Canal residents spent years fighting highly publicized battles with unresponsive public officials. The Love Canal Homeowners Association even temporarily detained a federal EPA official. But no Hooker official was ever detained, nor were demonstrations regularly held at Hooker headquarters in Niagara Falls. The residents wanted money to move out of their contaminated homes, and they petitioned their government for a redress of grievances, even though it was Hooker, not the government, that had so poisoned their environment. After much footdragging and buck passing, the governments eventually accepted the demands of residents for relocation money.

Armand Hammer, the chairman of the board of Occidental Petroleum (Hooker's parent), gave an excellent demonstration of his company's policy of shifting the blame onto the government when, in 1980, a number of Love Canal residents traveled the 2,500 miles from western New York to Occidental's annual shareholders meeting in Los Angeles to present a resolution on toxic wastes. After listening to one resident describe the death of her son from a rare kidney disease, Hammer told the woman that the company "sympathized greatly with your predicament, but I would think that what you should be doing is addressing your complaint to the city of Niagara Falls." When other residents continued to speak, their floor microphones were turned off. Sister Joan Malone of Lewiston, New York, then asked Hammer, "Are you refusing to hear?" Hammer replied, "Yes I am refusing. Go back to Buffalo."[19]

Since then, hundreds of Love Canal residents have sued Hooker, and the city and state governments, asking more than $9 million to compensate them for their injuries suffered at the canal. The U.S. Justice Department also sued Hooker, seeking more than $124 million to help clean up Love Canal and three other dump sites in Niagara Falls. Some of those cleanup cases have been settled out of court. The residents' lawsuit against Hooker was settled in December 1984 when the company agreed to pay 1,300 former homeowners a total of close to $20 million.[20]

For Rose Chambers, receiving a check in the mail will not bring back her husband, and, as many other canal residents have learned, moving away from the canal does not mean moving away from the health problems it produced.

Sandra Pelfrey, for example, was born and raised near Love Canal. She remembers playing on "Canal Hill." At age 19 she married and moved to Ohio. At 21 she had her first child, Linda. Linda was born blind. At age 23 she gave birth to James. James was also born blind. Her doctor recommended that she not bear any more children. At age 25, Sandra had her kidney removed. That operation was followed by a tubal ligation.[21] For Sandra Pelfrey and her descendants, the scars will never heal.

Notes

1. "Hammer Tells Nun to Go Back to Buffalo," *Buffalo Courier Express*, May 22, 1980.

2. "Breakdown: Love Canal's Walking Wounded," by David Weinberg. *Village Voice*, September 9–15, 1981.

3. Ibid., p. 10.

4. "Ooze after Rain was Part of Life," *Niagara Falls Gazette*, August 6, 1978, p.   .

5. *State of New York, Love Canal: Public Health Time Bomb*, p. 12.

6. *The Pendulum and the Toxic Cloud*, by Thomas Whiteside. Yale University Press, 1979, p. 141.

7. Personal communication, January 1981.

8. Quitclaim deed, as read over the telephone to an associate, by a reporter from the *Niagara Falls Gazette*, November 9, 1978.

9. Memo from Jerome Wilkenfeld, assistant technical superintendant, to R.F. Schultz, works manager, "Exposed Residue at Love Canal," May 18, 1958. Cited in *Hazardous Waste Disposal*, Hearings before the Sub-

committee on Oversight and Investigations of the Committee on Interstate and Foreign Commerce, House of Representatives, 1979, p. 651.

10. *Public Health Time Bomb*, p. 12.

11. Ibid., p. 14.

12. For a detailed history of this effort, see *Love Canal: My Story*, by Lois Marie Gibbs, as told to Murray Levine. State University of New York Press, Albany, 1981.

13. "Wider Range of Illnesses Suspected," *Niagara Falls Gazette*, August 4, 1978.

14. *Hazardous Waste Disposal*, Hearings, p. 63, testimony by Dr. Beverly Paigan.

15. "Medical Complaints Coincide with Toxic Effects," *Niagara Falls Gazette*, August 17, 1978.

16. *United States of America v. Hooker Plastics and Chemical Corporation et al.*, filed December 30, 1979 (USDC for the Western District of New York) pp. 13–20.

17. *Hazardous Waster Disposal*, Hearings, 500–501, 504, testimony by Bruce Davis.

18. "Hooker Hit as Irresponsible," *Niagara Falls Gazette*, June 22, 1978.

19. *Buffalo Courier Express* (note 1, supra).

20. "$20 Million Fund in Love Canal Case," *New York Times*, January 1, 1986.

21. "Ohio Mother Blaming Canal for Kids' Defects," *Niagara Falls Gazette*, August 8, 1978.

21
Manville

"We must reserve the right to litigate against the asbestos
companies and/or the government. They have been guilty of
mass reckless homicide, and if this type of terminology seems
harsh, may I remind you, gentlemen, that mesothelioma is a
harsh cancerous disease which is terminal."

> —Constance Ruggieri, asbestos victim, testifying
> against legislation that would limit the rights of
> asbestos victims to sue asbestos companies for
> damages, before House Subcommittee on Labor
> Standards, Committee On Education and Labor,
> May 1979[1]

For FRANKLIN BROOKS, football was life. Brooks was a star player
at Georgia Tech during the 1950s, a time when the Yellow Jackets
were more than just another football team. He led his squad to
four bowl games, and at the 1965 Sugar Bowl he was voted most
valuable player. When school was out during the summer, Brooks
worked in an insulation plant where he handled asbestos boards
and other asbestos materials. The plant was dusty. No one told
him it was dangerous.

Twenty years after leaving Georgia Tech, Brooks returned as
an assistant football coach. At 42, with a wife, two children and
a full-time job, he had no time for summer employment, but the
summers he spent working in the asbestos plant now came back
to haunt him. Mesothelioma, a rare form of cancer, began to eat

away at his lungs and shorten his breath. "I can't walk fast or walk up steps," Brooks told a reporter in 1978. "If I do, I get out of breath. That's the indication that things are not as good as they were. A shortness of breath and severe chest pain."

Brooks was also well aware of what the asbestos was doing to the outside of his once well-conditioned body. "I'm down to about one-forty [140 pounds]. I wear my turtleneck to hide the loss of my muscles. I have two children . . . one youngster twenty and a daughter sixteen. And I'm not sure they realize how serious it is."[2]

Manville (previously Johns Manville) the nation's largest asbestos manufacturer, realized the serious health dangers posed by asbestos. They knew early in the game, before Brooks was chasing the pigskin at Georgia Tech and before he inhaled thousands of asbestos fibers at his summer job. A series of documents released to the public during congressional hearings in 1979 indicate that Manville and other companies within the asbestos industry covered up and failed to warn millions of Americans of the dangers associated with the fireproof, indestructible insulating fiber they called "the magic mineral."

Asbestos disease was reported for the first time in Britain in 1908, almost 30 years before Franklin Brooks was born. By 1918, the U.S. government issued its first report on asbestos, urging more investigations into the health aspects. As a result, U.S. and Canadian insurance companies decided to stop selling life insurance to those who worked with asbestos. Ten years later, in 1928, the *Journal of the American Medical Association* reported on a young woman who died of asbestosis. In 1949, Manville conducted its own study of 780 asbestos workers and found 534 workers with lung changes. The 1950s and 1960s saw a flood of reports warning of the health dangers associated with asbestos.

Despite these well-documented dangers, Manville allowed the mineral to proliferate until it became an integral part of the marketplace and of people's lives. Today millions of Americans continue to be exposed to asbestos. From schools to homes, from drum brake linings to office buildings to high school classrooms to open piles of asbestos wastes to home appliances to drinking water supplies, asbestos is almost everywhere.

Manville's attitude toward safety was perhaps best expressed in testimony given by the company's medical director, Kenneth W. Smith, under oath in 1976. When asked whether he had ever advised Manville to place warning labels on its asbestos products, Smith replied:

> The reasons why the caution labels were not implemented immediately — it was a business decision as far as I could understand. Here was a recommendation, the corporation is in business to make — to provide jobs for people and make money for stockholders and they had to take into consideration the effects of everything they did, and if the applications of a caution label identifying a product as hazardous would cut out sales, there would be serious financial implications. And the powers that be had to make some effort to judge the necessity of the label vs. the consequences of placing the label on the product.[3]

The consequences of this cost benefit analysis were not suffered by those who worked in Manville's executive office in Denver, of course. The burden fell only on those who worked with asbestos — in the shipyards where it was used as insulation on military ships, in the factories that manufactured asbestos insulation, and even in the homes of factory workers where their families inhaled the asbestos brought home on the workers' clothing.

Barbara Gurrie's father worked as an insulator in a Massachusetts shipyard. "When he came home," Gurrie recalled, "his clothing was covered with asbestos, and it, I don't know if you know what it looks like, it's a chalky substance when it accumulates and dries on clothing, and it forms like a dust-like particle when it's touched and that was my exposure to asbestos, being near my dad when he came home from work and then my mother took his work clothes and shook them over the porch to take off the excess dust before washing them."

She remembered when, as a little girl, she would run down to the bus stop to meet her father at the end of the work day and give him a big hug. "He was covered at that time with the asbestos," Gurrie remembered, "and you could see it flying around in the atmosphere."

Barbara's father had cancer, her mother had mesothelioma, and when she heard that she too had a lung problem, she was "frightened to death." "I recalled every day of my mother's illness, recalled my father's illness, and I knew what was in store for me," she said.

"I am a thirty-five-year-old mother of two children, happily married with everything to live for. It sort of put the damper on everything for me."[4]

In 1978, Barbara Gurrie and Franklin Brooks died, just months after they told their stories to a national television audience on the ABC News Closeup show, "Asbestos: The Way to A Dusty Death."

The industry's internal documents were released at the congressional hearing in 1978. The documents that became known as the "Asbestos Pentagon Papers" were reviewed in 1978 by South Carolina Judge James Price and were so persuasive that the judge ordered a new trial for a claim on behalf of a deceased asbestos insulation worker, that had previously been dismissed. In reopening the case, the judge observed that the internal documents reflected "a conscious effort by the industry in the 1930s to downplay or arguably suppress the dissemination of information to employees and the public for fear of promotion of lawsuits." Taken as a whole, the papers showed a "pattern of denial and disease and attempts at suppression of information." Judge Price took particular note of 11 compensation cases filed by asbestos workers in the early thirties and settled out of court by Manville in 1933—"all predating the time [1964] when these companies alleged they first recognized the hazards to insulators [insulation workers]."

Although the industry stuck to its line that it wasn't fully cognizant of the asbestos hazard until 1964, the Asbestos Papers clearly show that by 1932 the British had documented the occupational hazard of asbestos dust inhalation. Among the papers was a letter dated September 25, 1935, from the editor of the industry's trade journal, *Asbestos*, to Sumner Simpson, president of one of the largest asbestos firms in the United States, Raybestos-Manhattan. The editor wanted permission to publish an article about the hazards of asbestos. "Always you have requested that for certain obvious reasons we publish nothing and naturally your wishes have been respected," the editor wrote. But in an effort to persuade Simpson, who apparently had de facto editorial veto power, the editor suggested that "discussion of it [the alleged asbestos hazard] in *Asbestos* along the right lines would serve to combat the rather undesirable publicity given to it in current newspapers."[5]

Simpson was not persuaded. He wrote to his asbestos colleague Vandive Brown, secretary of Manville, and praised the magazine for "not reprinting the English articles" and added that "the less said about asbestos the better off we are. . . ." Brown wrote back saying he agreed with Simpson and suggested that if an article had to be published, it should reflect "American data rather than English."[6]

Brown's trust in the "American data" was, from his point of view, well placed. The "American data" referred to a study begun in 1929 by Anthony Lanza and sponsored by Raybestos-Manhattan, Manville, and the Metropolitan Life Insurance Company, the insurance carrier for both asbestos giants. Brown, other industry officials, and their lawyers exerted editorial control over the Lanza study. In 1934, Lanza had submitted his galleys to Brown, and Brown returned them with a note observing that Lanza had omitted a sentence that had appeared in an earlier draft, namely: "Clinically from this study, it [asbestosis] appeared to be of a type milder than silicosis."

This sentence was crucial, as Manville's New Jersey attorney, George S. Hobart, understood well. Hobart was worried about then pending legislation that would include asbestosis as a compensable disease. Manville was opposed to the legislation. "It would be helpful, for financial reasons," Hobart wrote to Brown, "to have an official report to show that there is substantial difference between asbestosis and silicosis: and by the same token it would be troublesome if an official report should appear from which the conclusion might be drawn that there is very little, if any difference, between the two diseases."[7]

Brown forwarded Hobart's suggestions to Lanza and asked that "all of the favorable aspects of the survey be included and that none of the unfavorable be unintentionally pictured in darker tones than the comments justify." Lanza certainly proved amenable to these suggestions from above and he was not inclined to use any darker tones than were necessary. Although Lanza found that 67 of the 126 workers whom he examined suffered from asbestosis, these damning numbers never found their way into his published study. Lanza also concluded that asbestosis was milder than silicosis.

It was easy for the industry, in 1935, not to print damaging information in order to cover up the hazards of asbestos. It was not easy for Charles Ay, in 1978, to breathe. Ay worked in a Long Beach, California, shipyard insulating ship boilers and pipes with asbestos. His father had worked with asbestos in the shipyards and died of asbestosis and cancer. "About 25 percent of my lung capacity is gone as a result of asbestos disease," he told a reporter in 1978. "I tire very easily going up and down stairs, and [after] any type of physical, hard physical work, I become very fatigued, very rapidly." Charles Ay has little doubt that he will follow in his father's path. "Once you get it, it is irreversible. It's a continuous thing and ultimately, I will die from it."[8]

The industry was not geared, however, to understanding the human effects of working with asbestos. It was geared to fixing health studies, and fixing just one study was not enough. A number of asbestos corporations banded together to finance asbestos dust research at the Saranac Laboratories (Trudeau Foundation). Raybestos's Simpson wrote to one of his colleagues in the industry and suggested that the corporations that paid for the research "could determine from time to time after the findings are made whether we wish any publication or not." If they decided to publish, the companies could selectively distribute the favorable studies. "It would be a good idea," wrote Simpson, "to distribute the information to the medical fraternity, providing it is of the right type and would not injure the companies." The positive studies could also be used in court against, in Simpson's words, "ambulance chasing attorneys and unscrupulous doctors."

In 1936, Simpson's ideas ripened to fruition. The asbestos industry and Saranac struck a deal whereby studies would be conducted and the asbestos companies would decide whether or not to allow publication of the scientific results. In a letter to Saranac Laboratories, Manville's Brown outlined the scope of the agreement. "It is our further understanding that the results obtained will be considered the property of those who are advancing the required funds, who will determine whether, to what extent and in what manner they shall be made public, and the manuscript of your study will be submitted to us for approval prior to publication." Saranac officials replied, agreeing that "the results of these studies shall become the property of the contributors and that the manuscripts of any reports shall be submitted for approval of the contributors before publication."[9]

The hush-hush, "keep the lid on" philosophy reflected by the "Asbestos Pentagon Papers" is, of course, not unique to the asbestos industry. "Industrial concerns are in general not particularly anxious to have the occurrence of occupational cancers among their employees or environmental cancers among the consumers of their products made a matter of public record," observed Dr. Wilhelm Hueper, a Dupont researcher, in 1943. "Such publicity might reflect unfavorably upon their business activities and oblige them to undertake extensive and expensive technical and sanitary changes in their production methods, and in the types of products manufactured."[10]

Hueper, in 1943, urged action to control industrial cancer. "Industry should devote considerably more effort than heretofore in determining the cancerous or noncancerous nature of their numerous products which may be suspected on general grounds in cancerigenic respects," he wrote. It "should make serious attempts to eliminate all potentially cancerigenic agents from further use by the development of suitable substitutes."[11] Hueper also prophetically recognized the possibility that workers or consumers would get their hands on the truth about the dangers associated with these products and sue the companies. "It is therefore not an uncommon practice that some pressure is exerted by the parties financially interested [corporations] in such matters to keep information of the occurrence of industrial cancer well under cover," Dr. Hueper observed.

Cover-up may be too kind a phrase for an action that led to disease and deaths among hundreds of asbestos workers throughout the country. Manville's practice of refusing to advise workers of early evidence of asbestosis was cruelly rationalized by the company's medical director, Kenneth Smith, in 1963.

> It must be remembered that although these men have the X-ray evidence of asbestosis, they are working today and definitely are not disabled from asbestosis. They have not been told of this diagnosis, for it is felt that as long as the man feels well, is happy at home and at work, and his physical condition remains good, nothing should be said. When he becomes disabled and sick, then the diagnosis should be made and the claim submitted *by the company*. The fibrosis of this disease is irreversible and permanent so that eventually compensation will be paid to each of these men. But as long as the man is not disabled, it is felt that he should not be told of his condition so that he can live and work in peace and the Company can benefit by his many years of experience. Should the man be told of his condition today, there is a very definite possibility that he would

become mentally and physically ill, simply through the knowledge that he has asbestosis.[12]

The industry was quick to deal with anyone who challenged the policy of concealment. As late as September 1963 the companies were still suppressing "negative" health reports. In September of that year, for example, Thomas Mancuso, a research professor of occupational health at the University of Pittsburgh's Graduate School of Public Health, issued a report to the Phillip Carey Manufacturing company that concluded that the asbestos-cancer relationship was beyond dispute and that the company should warn all concerned. "Internally within the company," Mancuso wrote, "the question had been raised as to why medical problems, particularly relating to cancer and asbestos, were not recognized before. Actually, they were recognized, but the asbestos industry chose to ignore and deny their existence."[13] The company did not warn its workers and customers. Mancuso's contract was not renewed.

The use of asbestos in molded insulations was banned in Denmark in 1972 and in the United States in 1975. Today, it is predicted that 240,000 of the million Americans who work or have worked with asbestos will die from asbestos-related cancer within the next 30 years—that's 8,000 per year or one every hour—unless a major breakthrough is made in early diagnosis and treatment. The prediction was made by Dr. Irving Selikoff, of the Mt. Sinai School of Medicine, in New York City, the premier medical expert in the field.

Selikoff's studies raise serious questions. In addition to the 1 million who work directly with asbestos, how many of the 10 million other workers, like Charles Ay and his father in the construction and shipbuilding industries, will become sick or die? How about the 1 million mechanics who repair brakes on 130 million autos throughout the country? And the hundreds of thousands of maintenance, repair, renovation, and demolition workers who work with buildings stuffed with 24.8 million tons of asbestos (through 1970)? When the buildings are demolished and the asbestos goes flying into the atmosphere, how about the neighbors or passers-by? How about consumers who use products containing asbestos—including electric french fryers, electric blankets, slow cookers, dishwashers, popcorn poppers, frying pans, and curling irons? How about residents of Boston, Philadelphia, Atlanta, San Francisco, and Seattle, where asbestos fibers have been found in the drinking water?

It wasn't as if asbestos was the only effective insulating, fire-proofing material available. Throughout the century, many alternative materials could have been substituted for asbestos. Barry Castleman, an environmental consultant and author of the comprehensive review *Asbestos: Medical and Legal Aspects*, argues that asbestos-free calcium silicate compositions, now widely used, "appear to be based essentially on technology that was available long before asbestos was banned in molded insulation in the 1970s."[14]

By early 1984, in courthouses throughout the country, more than 25,500 personal injury lawsuits were pending charging the asbestos companies with inflicting hundreds of millions of dollars worth of damages on an unwary populace—with an additional 500 lawsuits being filed every month, during that year.

Apart from all these individual claims, in 1983, school districts, cities, and states began filing "rip and replace" lawsuits seeking to force the major asbestos companies to find and cover up or remove asbestos from schools, offices, prisons, hospitals, universities, and other public buildings, or to pay for such tasks. The estimated costs of a nationwide asbestos clean-up boggle the mind. One plaintiff's lawyer estimated that to *survey* Massachusetts's 5,000 public buildings would cost $3.5 million, with an additional $190 million to clean it up. By 1984, more than 300 property lawsuits had been filed, with the number growing every week.[15]

On August 26, 1982, Manville, in a highly publicized legal maneuver, filed for bankruptcy in federal court. This move immediately froze the lawsuits in their place and forced asbestos victims to stand in line with other Manville creditors. The victims charged that Manville was illegitimately using the bankruptcy process to duck its responsibilities to those whom it injured. In a petition filed in the United States District Court for the Southern District of New York, attorneys for asbestosis victims alleged that the Manville bankruptcy petition was marred by tactics of questionable morality and legality and should be thrown out of court.

Specifically, the victims charged that Manville had lied by claiming that its former general counsel, Vandive Brown, was deceased, in order to keep key documents in which Brown acknowledged the health hazards of asbestos, from being admitted as evidence in suits against the company. In fact, Brown was later discovered alive in Scotland by an asbestos victim's attorney.

The victims also charged that Manville tried in the 1930s and

1940s to suppress studies on the health hazards of asbestos and instead created its own favorable study of asbestos; and that in 1981, a year before Manville filed for bankruptcy, the corporation carried out a corporate reorganization in order to try to insulate most of the company's operations from asbestos liability claims. Manville was also accused of avoiding its usual accountants, Coopers & Lybrand, and going instead to Price Waterhouse for an opinion that the company should establish a reserve account in order to bring an immediate default on the company's outstanding debt, thus making the company hypothetically eligible for bankruptcy.

At the time of Manville's decision to file for bankruptcy, the corporation's president, Frederick L. Pundsack, argued that such action "would be wrong" because the firm was "a viable, ongoing business enterprise" that was becoming "stronger than ever." For taking this stand, he was encouraged to retire early. He subsequently resigned, less than a week before Manville filed for bankruptcy to shield itself from the 16,500 personal injury lawsuits then on file.[16]

Michael Goldberg, a Washington, D.C.–based lawyer, is appealing Manville's reorganization plan on the ground that it seeks to discharge Manville not only from its liabilities to those who had claims against the company at the time of the filing for bankruptcy, but also from those who would develop asbestos-related health conditions in the future and who would present claims against the company after the reorganization had been completed. "Indeed, what Manville is trying to do here is exactly what A. H. Robins is trying to do in its Chapter 11 proceeding—to be discharged from its liabilities to future Dalkon Shield victims," Goldberg said.[17]

After three years of wrangling, in August 1985, Manville agreed to pay thousands of claimants $2.5 billion. The agreement called on Manville to set up a fund to which shareholders would surrender half the value of their stock, and the company would give up much of its projected earnings over the next 25 years.[18]

The certainty that industry executives long knew of the hazards of asbestos and the harms that would be done raises the serious and largely unaddressed question of how asbestos companies and their executives should be punished. When Manville filed for bankruptcy in 1982, the company acknowledged that it had been found liable for punitive damages by juries in ten separate cases, decided in 1981 and 1982, in which the punitive damages awarded averaged

$616,000 a case.[19] And the $2.5 billion settlement effectively transfers much of the company's profits to the victims.

But is compensation alone a just conclusion to what Constance Ruggieri, an asbestos victim, believed to be a case of "mass reckless homicide"? No asbestos executive was ever prosecuted for reckless homicide, although the facts call out for such a prosecution. Given the tremendous inequity of resources and the political pressure a local district attorney would face had such a prosecution been brought, need we wonder why? The failed prosecution in the Pinto case and the lack of prosecution in this one are two very powerful reasons for Congress to pass a federal homicide statute so that adequate federal resources can be marshaled to bring to justice those who threaten public health and safety.

Notes

1. Statement of Joseph and Constance Ruggieri, North Smithfield, R. I., in Hearings before the subcommittee on labor standards of the Committee on Education and Labor, House of Representatives, 96th Cong., 1st sess., May 1, 2, 8, 1979, p. 376.

2. *ABC News Close-up — Asbestos: The Way to Dusty Death,* July 14, 1978, transcript, p. 4.

3. *The Politics of Cancer,* by Samuel Epstein, M.D. Anchor Press/Doubleday, Garden City, 1979, p. 94.

4. *Asbestos: The Way to Dusty Death,* ABC, p. 22.

5. "The Lid Comes Off," by Ronald Motley. *Trial,* April 1980, p. 21.

6. Ibid., p. 22.

7. *The Politics of Cancer,* Epstein, p. 91.

8. *Asbestos: The Way to Dusty Death,* ABC, p. 19.

9. *The Politics of Cancer,* Epstein, p. 92.

10. "The Lid Comes Off," Motley, p. 21.

11. *Asbestos: Medical and Legal Aspects,* by Barry L. Castleman, with a contribution by Stephen L. Berger. Law & Business, Inc. Harcourt Brace Jovanovich, New York, 1984, p. 43.

12. *The Politics of Cancer,* Epstein, p. 93.

13. Ibid., p. 95.

14. *Asbestos: Medical and Legal Aspects,* 2d ed., by Barry L. Castleman. Law & Business, Inc., Harcourt Brace Jovanovich, New York, 1986.

15. "Second Wave Of Litigation Hits Asbestos," by Francis J. Flaherty.

National Law Journal, October 29, 1984, p. 1. See also *Asbestos: Medical and Legal Aspects,* Castleman, 1984, p. 311.

16. Statement of Peter John Robinson in response to the Court's Proposal of October 26, 1983, in *In re Johns Manville Corporation,* November 7, 1983.

17. Letter from Michael Goldberg to Joan Claybrook, December 10, 1986.

18. "Manville Offers Asbestos Victims $2.5 Billion Fund," by Stuart Diamond. *New York Times,* August 3, 1985.

19. *Outrageous Misconduct: The Asbestos Industry on Trial,* by Paul Broder. Pantheon, New York, 1985, p. 283.

22
MER/29

"I am suing the company and I intend to pursue this suit with all the vigor I have because destroying me of my sight has just put me out of business. In my type of livelihood, I must have my eyesight to see the type of products that I purchase. No payment financially would be enough to compensate me for the pain, suffering, and inconvenience that I have gone through and am still going through. So, please, Senator, keep pushing them with all the strength and guts you have. They deserve to be punished."

—letter from MER/29 drug victim to Senator Hubert Humphrey, December 27, 1963[1]

BEULAH JORDAN WAS CONCERNED. In May 1959, she was trying to do a competent professional job as a lab technician at the William S. Merrell toxicology lab in Cincinnati. Since 1957, the lab had been testing its new anticholesterol drug, MER/29, by feeding it to monkeys and observing its effects. Weight was an important indicator in testing a new drug. Any unusual gain or loss might indicate that the drug was having an adverse side effect. Every Friday, Jordan would weigh each monkey and record the weight in a laboratory notebook.

Jordan was concerned for a number of reasons. First, the lab's pet monkey, monkey 49, was sick. "Forty-niner," as the lab staff called her, had lost 2.4 kilograms during the final month of the test. The monkey was unable to jump onto the weighing pan, a simple trick all the other monkeys were able to perform. According to Jordan, number 49 "got very mean, there was a loss of weight, and it couldn't see well enough to hit the pan . . . in our opinion, this monkey was sick due to a reaction to the drug."[2] Jordan was also concerned about two other monkeys that had to be sacrificed several weeks ahead of schedule. At the end of the month, she recorded the average weights of all the monkeys on a graph. For monkey 49, the graph dipped in the last month, reflecting the loss in weight. For the two monkeys that were sacrificed early, the lines ended short of the end of the test, reflecting an early death. The graph reflected reality.

Dr. Evert Van Maanen, Merrell's director of biological sciences, was apparently not interested in Beulah Jordan's perception of reality. What mattered to Van Maanen—and to the Merrell company and to its parent, Richardson-Merrell—was MER/29's new drug application (NDA), which was then awaiting government approval. Without such approval, the company would not be allowed to market the drug, and millions of dollars in projected profits would remain projected indefinitely. The dips and short lines on Jordan's graph would raise serious questions at the Food and Drug Administration (FDA), possibly delaying a go-ahead for the drug. So when Jordan took her graph to Van Maanen she should not, perhaps, have been surprised by his reaction. But she was.

According to Jordan, Van Maanen directed her to make certain changes. He told her to extend the lines of the two monkeys that had been sacrificed so that they would be even with the lifespans of the others. He then ordered her to eliminate the dip in monkey 49's graph line. According to Jordan, Van Maanen "said he didn't like the point of this monkey dropping like this." He ordered her to bring the line "more on an even keel."[3] Jordan resented being asked to render a false report and she left Van Maanen's office after refusing to sign the charts.[4]

Jordan told her story to William King, the director of the toxicology lab. King listened to what happened there, and according to Jordan, King told her that "He [Dr. Van Maanen] is higher up. You do as he tells you and be quiet." Mrs. Jordan listened to King. She kept quiet.[5]

At the time, Merrell was eager to get FDA approval of MER/29. During the late 1950s, reports had been surfacing more and more frequently about the statistical link between cholesterol and heart disease, the number one killer of Americans, then and now. Until the mid-1950s, there existed no effective and safe cholesterol-lowering agent of universal application. Merrell believed MER/29 was the answer. Merrell touted MER/29 as "the first safe agent to inhibit body-produced cholesterol" and "the first to lower excess cholesterol levels, in both tissue and serum, irrespective of diet."[6] The message was clear: People could eat high-cholesterol foods as long as they took MER/29 regularly.

Indeed, Merrell predicted a relatively large market for MER/29, with millions of middle-aged Americans taking the drug on a daily basis for the rest of their lives. At 20 cents a pill, an estimated $4.25 billion market was projected, more than the total consumer expenditure for pharmaceuticals in 1960. The stakes were high and the rush to get MER/29 onto the market was great. No dips or shortened lines on graphs would be allowed to stand in the way.[7]

The doctored graph represented only one of many instances where Merrell failed to report honestly the results of its animal testing. In support of MER/29's NDA, Merrell submitted the results of a new 1957 rat experiment. The company stated that all the female rats had survived, when, in fact, they had all died. Data submitted on the weight and blood values of the rats were fabricated.[8]

In June 1958, the company issued a brochure, intended for clinical investigators, that noted "bizarre" changes in the lymphocytes (white blood cells) of monkeys and rats given MER/29. The brochure also noted that the MER/29-drugged rats had a higher percentage of reticulocytes (red blood cells) than did the control group of rats that were not drugged. Van Maanen was not pleased with these results either, and in a memo dated May 5, 1959, he asked his subordinate William King to "delete all material on the funny lymphocytes" from the next edition of the brochure and questioned whether the "reticulocyte change in the rat experiment needs the emphasis it has." The next edition of the brochure made no mention of the "bizarre" or "funny" occurrences. Nor did Merrell inform the FDA of these changes in the blood cells.[9]

The first brochure had, however, already been sent to clinical researchers around the country. One outside researcher, Dr. Jane Desforges, read the note about "bizarre" blood changes and asked Merrell's medical research department to send her the blood smears so that she could study the changes firsthand. The request was forwarded to Van Maanen, who discussed it with two of his associates. They refused to send the smears, reasoning that "at the moment it would not be in the interest of the company and our product to send such a smear to interested clinical hematologists." The next day, Merrell's director of medical research disagreed, arguing that "the decision not to release blood smears from our toxicological studies to our hematological consultant . . . represents a serious handicap in the MER/29 studies. . . . Dr. McMaster and I have a moral and medical obligation to use MER/29 safely. Accordingly, we are both anxious to find out more about the blood changes which have been reported in experimental animals." According to Ralph Adam Fine, in *The Great Drug Deception,* no evidence has been found indicating whether the smears were ever released.[10]

It is clear that the tests that showed "funny" and "bizarre" blood changes were misrepresented to the FDA. But even these and other polished test results that Merrell submitted as part of its NDA in July 1959 raised questions. In September 1959, Dr. Jerome Epstein, the FDA's medical officer assigned to MER/29, observed in a letter to Merrell that "data you have submitted [in the NDA] suggests a low margin of safety." In response, a Merrell official wrote to the FDA that he was "somewhat surprised by the statement that our data suggest a low margin of safety." Summarizing the tests that had been submitted, the official noted unabashedly that "body weight gains were not affected in rats or monkeys" and that there was "no untoward hematopetic [blood change] response."[11]

Monkeys, rats, and beagles. Merrell tested MER/29 on all of them and misrepresented the tests. The misrepresentations of the dog tests were perhaps the most serious. Five dogs were tested in November 1959. All were seriously harmed by MER/29. All had severely degenerated livers. Three of the five died before the end of the three-month experiment, and, most important, the two survivors developed cataracts. One researcher noted that dog 69 (one of the two survivors) "appeared to be blind."[12] A pathologist reported that he had "never seen such an involvement of the lens."[13] Merrell reported the liver changes to the FDA, but failed to report the cataracts.

Merrell also received reports from other drug companies that MER/29 affected the eyes of certain animals,[14] but failed to pass on these reports to the FDA. When Merrell's ad agency asked the company "about corneal changes recently noted in dogs," Merrell replied, "There are none."[15]

Merrell's string of deceptions did not end with animal tests. When a drug company creates a new drug, it tests the drug for safety and effectiveness not only on animals, but also on humans. The human tests are euphemistically called "clinical trials." These tests are usually conducted by independent physicians (called clinical investigators) around the country on volunteers who must give their written consent. In many instances the volunteers are prisoners, medical students, or patients affected by illnesses that the drug is designed to cure.

One such clinical investigator, Dr. Wong of Washington, D.C., wrote Merrell asking for supplies of MER/29. Wong was charged with controlling heart disease in some Pentagon generals, many of whom experienced elevated cholesterol levels "every time an interservice fight develops or a missile fails to leave the launch pad." Wong was anxious to test MER/29 so that he could "smooth out the bumps in their cholesterol curves." Merrell at first balked at Wong's request, saying that it would "hesitate to use any new drug on those valuable people." Later the company noted that "Dr. Wong claims to have other patients," including "negro hospital patients."[15]

In any event, "the objective in contacting the armed forces," according to one Merrell interoffice memo, "was to lay the groundwork for the eventual sale of the product to the various hospitals serving each branch of the armed forces when the product is released. We were not thinking here so much of honest clinical work as we were of a pre-market softening prior to the introduction of the product."[16]

In support of its NDA for MER/29, Merrell reported that clinical studies in 116 patients indicated that the drug reduced cholesterol levels and was apparently safe, despite a report received by Merrell's medical research division in the fall of 1959 that human patients tested with MER/29 had developed watering of the eyes and reddening of the skin cover of the eyes.[17] The FDA was not convinced and demanded more animal tests. In particular, the agency was concerned about the liver degeneration reported in test animals.

The company refused to take no for an answer, however, and

on March 7, 1960, Merrell representatives met with FDA officials in an attempt to convince the federal cops that MER/29 was safe. Two weeks later, the FDA told Merrell that, because of the "potential hazard of liver toxicity with the drug," and further because of the "highly theoretical value of taking such a drug as MER/29," the application would not be approved until further "long term" trials indicated that it was safe. When Merrell sent the FDA a three-page summary of human liver studies, which the company claimed "established beyond reasonable doubt that MER/29 produces no alterations in hepatic (liver) functions in man," the FDA buckled. On April 19, 1960, the agency approved Merrell's NDA for MER/29.[18]

Merrell launched MER/29 by sending packets of promotional materials to 160,000 physicians around the country via Western Union, and within months complaints could be heard. A doctor from Nebraska reported that some of his patients complained of watery eyes. "Most of the side effects you have reported," responded Dr. Robert H. McMaster, Merrell's associate director of clinical research, "have been unusual ones in that they have not been reported by other investigators. . . . Is it possible that [they] could have been coincidental with the administration of drugs other than MER/29 concurrently?"[19] By March of the next year, the same Nebraska doctor reported that the watery eyes had persisted and that now his patients were complaining of blurred vision. Other doctors reported hair loss, a dryness of the skin with scaling, and more cases of blurred vision.

In January 1961, Merck, a major drug manufacturer, informed Merrell that it tested Merrell's drug against its own anticholesterol drug and found that dogs tested with MER/29 had developed cataracts and that several rats had gone blind. Merrell responded first that such symptoms had never shown up on its own tests, and later that Merck's test results were questionable since Merck had allegedly used an impure supply of MER/29.[20]

These reports of apparent side effects posed potential problems for Merrell's salesmen around the country — known within the industry as "detail men." Rather than look inward, Merrell attempted to shift attention elsewhere. The company issued instruction sheets for its detail men titled "Simple Question Counters 90% of Side Effect Questions." The pamphlet, echoing McMaster's response to the doctor from Nebraska read, in part:

We heard eight words the other day that neatly handle one of your biggest problems. When a doctor says your drug causes a side effect, the immediate reply is: "Doctor, what other drug is the patient taking?"

Even if you know your drug can cause the side effect mentioned chances are equally good the same effect is being caused by a second drug! You let your drug take the blame when you counter with a defensive answer. Know how to anwer side effects honestly, yes, *but get the facts first.*

"Doctor, what other drugs is the patient taking? Been doing it for years? Why didn't you tell us then?"[21]

This policy of shifting attention away from the company and the company's drugs was familiar not only to Merrell salesmen in the field, but also to Merrell employees at the home office in Cincinnati. In March of 1961, for example, McMaster, the associate director of clinical research, concluded that "there can be no doubt of the association of MER/29 therapy with [hair] changes." McMaster drafted a proposed addition to the warning on the package referring to "changes in color, texture or amount" as possible side effects. This proposed change was vetoed from above as "rather frightening." Robert T. Stormont, the Merrell supervisor who vetoed the language, reasoned at the time that "none of these cases developed green, pink, or lavender hair, I hope." As a result, the package warned of only "thinning of hair."[22]

Merrell warned its salesmen not to get "panicky" at the talk of side effects and reminded them of the huge profits on the horizon. As one company newsletter put it, "MER/29 has a potential sale greater than all other Merrell products combined."[23] Merrell salesmen were urged to brush aside any talk of side effects and push ahead with the job of getting MER/29 into doctors' offices and hospitals around the country. The company urged a sales pitch that was anything but low key. One company newsletter urged Merrell salesmen to be enthusiastic:

More men have become good salesmen just through enthusiasm than by any other method. If you believe in your product—if you become excited about MER/29—and start calling on doctors—your sales start to materialize. Why? Because you are enthusiastic . . . you should be enthusiastic

about MER/29. Never before—and perhaps never again—
will you get a product like MER/29. YOU HAVE NO REASON
NOT TO BE ENTHUSIASTIC—YOU HAVE NO REASON TO GIVE A
"TONGUE IN CHEEK" DETAIL ON MER/29. YOU HAVE A PRODUCT
THAT MOST OF YOUR COMPETITORS WOULD REALLY LIKE TO HAVE.
YOU OWE IT TO YOUSELF—TO YOUR COMPANY—TO THE MILLIONS
OF PEOPLE WHO NEED MER/29, TO BE ENTHUSIASTIC!!![24]

All the pep talk in the world, however, would not make the
side effects go away. On February 1, 1961, Merrell received a call
from a doctor who reported that one of his patients, under MER/29
treatment, had undergone hair and skin changes and now had
cataracts. The reports about watery eyes and blurred vision began
to proliferate.[25] By March 1961, Merrell had received 50 reports
that patients' hair was falling out,[26] and by November 1961, the
company had received reports of five MER/29 patients who had
developed cataracts.

Nevertheless, the company persisted in reassuring the public
that MER/29 was safe. In November, Merrell ran an ad in seven
major medical magazines proclaiming that MER/29's "use in over
300,000 patients reaffirms the safety margins established in early
laboratory and clinical data."[27] A month earlier, a physician wrote
to Merrell reporting that two of his patients complained about
"black spots on their eyes." McMaster wrote to the doctor that "we
have never before heard of anything remotely resembling this."
At the time, Merrell knew of four cataract cases.[28]

In mid-October, Merrell informed the FDA that MER/29 was
producing "lens changes" in humans and asked for permission to
put out a weak warning letter to physicians. The FDA immediately
requested complete information about these reactions. As the information arrived at the FDA in Washington, "It became obvious
that the company had been withholding from us significant information about adverse toxic reactions in both animals and humans,"
reported an FDA memo. FDA staffers convened a meeting to
discuss the situation and agreed that Merrell should be forced to
pull the drug off the market.

Merrell would have none of it. Merrell executives met with
FDA officials to discuss what action the company should take. The
FDA again buckled under Merrell pressure, and both parties agreed
that Merrell would not have to pull the drug off the market but
would only be required to issue appropriate warnings to doctors

and MER/29 consumers. But Merrell and the FDA could not agree on the text of the warning, so no warning was issued. Merrell's position was that a connection between MER/29 and the cataracts "had not been established," but the FDA believed, based on its review of ophthalmological reports, that "the incidence of cataracts in MER/29 patients is extremely high."[29]

By the end of March 1962, with complaints about the drug flowing into Merrell headquarters, Robert McMaster received a call from the Mayo Clinic in Rochester, New York. A six-year old boy with severe high cholesterol was being treated with MER/29. The Mayo Clinic was calling to inform Merrell that the boy had developed cataracts. McMaster flew out to Rochester, examined the boy, and reported to Merrell that it was "hard to explain" the boy's cataracts "by anything unrelated to (MER/29)."[30]

Merrell's tissue of deceptions, lies, cover-ups, and misrepresentations began to unravel several weeks earlier. On a cold afternoon late in February 1962, in Cincinnati, Ohio, Thomas Rice, a local FDA inspector, was riding home from work. One of the members of his carpool was Carson Jordan, whose wife was Beulah Jordan, the lab technician who resented being told to falsify test results for Merrell. Carson Jordan mentioned to Rice that his wife had been asked by Merrell to falsify data.

Rice checked the story with Beulah Jordan and then informed his superiors. On April 9, 1962, three FDA officials arrived unannounced at Merrell's front gate with a certificate of inspection. During a two day investigation, they found evidence that Merrell had submitted falsified information to the FDA. Two days later, MER/29 was pulled off the market.

On December 20, 1963, a federal grand jury in Washington, D.C., handed down a 12-count indictment against Merrell, its parent company, Richardson-Merrell, and three of its employees (including King and Van Maanen), charging them with knowingly making false, fictitious, and fraudulent statements to the FDA about MER/29. The defendants pleaded "no contest"—"tantamount to a plea of guilty," according to the presiding judge.[31] The three individual defendants were sentenced to six months probation. No jail. The companies were fined a total of $80,000. Merrell's after-tax profits for MER/29 in 1960/61 were over $1 million.[32]

MER/29 was administered to approximately 400,000 persons. It has been estimated that 5,000 persons were injured by MER/29. Only a small percentage of them sought redress in the courts, but of those who did, many recovered. A jury in New York State awarded a young woman who had been taking MER/29 experimentally, $1.2 million, including $850,000 awarded specifically to punish the company (the trial judge later reduced the punitive award to $100,000).[33] Over 95 percent of the MER/29 tort cases brought against Merrell were settled between 1962 and 1967.[34]

In 1966, four years after MER/29 was withdrawn from the market, Dr. James Goddard, then head of the FDA, gave a speech to the Pharmaceutical Manufacturers Association, a drug industry association based in Washington, D.C. Goddard strongly suggested that what happened at Merrell with MER/29 was not an isolated incident. "I have been shocked," Goddard told the drug company executives, "at the materials that come to us. I have been shocked at the clear attempts to slip something by us. I am deeply disturbed at the constant, direct, personal pressure some industry representatives have placed on our people." He ended his speech with a warning:

> Gentlemen, we must keep our eyes on the patient. For—
> once you get through the medical reports and the counsel-
> ors' opinions, the advertising and the marketing data, the
> licensing and distribution agreements, the protocols and
> letters of credit, the labeling and packaging, and the reports
> by the company treasurer—once you get through all that,
> you reach the physician who will administer your product
> to a human being. At the end of the long line is a human
> life. Some of you have forgotten that basic fact.[35]

Notes

1. *The Great Drug Deception: The Shocking Story of MER/29 and the Folks Who Gave You Thalidomide,* by Ralph Adam Fine. Stein and Day, New York, 1972.

2. *Corporate Crime In the Pharmaceutical Industry,* by John Braithwaite. Routledge & Kegan Paul, London, 1984, p. 61.

3. *The Great Drug Deception,* Fine, p. 34.

4. *Corporate Crime in the Pharmaceutical Industry,* Braithwaite, p. 61.

5. *Allen D. Toole v. Richardson-Merrell, Inc.,* District Court of Appeal, State of California, Respondent's Brief, p. 10.

6. *Suffer the Children: The Story of Thalidomide,* by the Insight Team of the Sunday *Times* of London. Viking, New York, 1979, p. 65.

7. *The Great Drug Deception,* Fine, p. 16.

8. *Corporate Crime in the Pharmaceutical Industry,* Braithwaite, p. 62; United States District Court for the District of Columbia, Special Jury 1963 Grand Jury Sworn in on July 2, 1963. Grand Jury Charges, page 2.

9. *The Great Drug Deception,* Fine, p. 38.

10. Ibid., p. 42.

11. Ibid.

12. Ibid., p. 47.

13. *Corporate Crime in the Pharmaceutical Industry,* Braithwaite, p. 62.

14. Ibid.

15. *The Great Drug Deception,* Fine, p. 48.

16. *Toole vs. Richardson-Merrell, Inc.,* Respondent's Brief, p. 10.

17. *Raul Martinez-Ferrer and Nancy Martinez v. Richardson-Merrell, Inc.* Motion for an Order . . . , June 25, 1981, Superior Court for the State of California for the County of Los Angeles, p. 11.

18. *The Great Drug Deception,* Fine, p. 57.

19. "Getting Away With What You Can," by Sanford J. Ungar, in *In The Name of Profit,* ed. by Robert Heilbroner. Doubleday, Garden City, New York, 1972, p. 112.

20. Ibid., p. 113.

21. *The Great Drug Deception,* Fine, p. 70.

22. *Corporate Crime in the Pharmaceutical Industry,* Braithwaite, p. 64.

23. *The Great Drug Deception,* Fine, p. 142.

24. Ibid., p. 139.

25. Ibid., p. 68.

26. Ibid., p. 71.

27. Ibid., p. 89.

28. Ibid., p. 111.

29. "Getting Away With What You Can," Ungar, p. 116; Also, *The Great Drug Deception,* Fine, p. 118.

30. *The Great Drug Deception,* Fine, p. 119.

31. *Corporate Crime in the Pharmaceutical Industry,* Braithwaite, p. 64.

32. *The Great Drug Deception,* Fine, p. 183.

33. Ibid., p. 162.

34. "The MER/29 Story—An Instance of Successful Mass Disaster Litigation," by Paul D. Rheingold. 56 *California Law Review* 116, 137 (1968).

35. "Preclinical and Clinical Testing by the Pharmaceutical Industry, 1976," Senate subcommittee on health of the Committee on Labor and Public Welfare (1976) Part II, p. 157.

23
Minamata

"Even after death we will remember what you have done to us."

—Protesters' sign outside Chisso Corporation's headquarters, Tokyo, Japan; Summer, 1964[1]

IN THE EARLY EXTREME cases, the victims lapse into unconsciousness, involuntary movements, and often uncontrolled shouting. The brain becomes spongelike as its cells are eaten away. The nervous system begins to degenerate, to atrophy. A tingling growing numbness affects the limbs and lips. Motor functions become severely disturbed, the speech slurred, the field of vision constricted.[2]

At first, the doctors diagnosed it as everything that it wasn't: encephalitis, Japonica, alcoholism, syphilis, hereditary ataxia, infantile paralysis, cerebral palsy. Later it became known as simply the "strange disease." It affected hundreds of residents of Minamata, Japan, a small, quiet fishing village, home of the Chisso Corporation, a petrochemical company and maker of plastics. This "strange disease" was something new, unheard of, and it called for a new name. The doctors, over the objections of the local Chamber of Commerce, labeled it "Minamata Disease."[3]

The first sign that something was amiss in Minamata came in 1950, when fish were seen floating in Minamata Bay and birds began dropping out of flight into the water. Two years later, cats began committing suicide, or so the residents thought. The cats would walk out onto the pier, stagger as if drunk, whirl around in circles, convulse violently, and then jump into the ocean. Soon, there was not a cat left in all of Minamata.[4]

In April, 1956, a five-year-old girl entered Chisso's Minamata factory hospital with severe symptoms of brain damage. She could not walk, her speech was incoherent, and she was in a state of severe delirium. The doctors suspected that she had probably eaten fish from Minamata Bay, which was by then contaminated with mercury ethyl poison from the Chisso factory. She became the first reported case of "Minamata Disease."[5]

Several days later, her younger sister entered the hospital with the same symptoms. Before the disease struck them, they were "the brightest, most vibrant kids you could imagine," according to a neighbor. Now, they were in the hospital, alone, fighting an unknown disease. Soon, hundreds of others would join them.

To the people of Minamata, the sea was their livelihood, their lifeblood. To think badly of the sea, to even suggest that from the sea could come anything but good, was close to sacrilege. One villager put it this way:

> It is only the sea I can trust. When people tell me that the sea is dirty, I curse them, I want to strike them. The sea "dirty"? How dare they say the sea is dirty! It is not the sea that wrongs. The sea has done nothing wrong. The sea is my life. The sea is my religion. The sea comforts me—it has given me courage and sustenance and escape from the quarrels of shorebound men. When I thought I was dying and my hands were numb and wouldn't work—and my father was dying too—when the villagers turned against us—it was to the sea I would go to cry. The sea protected my tears. I talk crazy about the sea. No one can understand why I love the sea so much. The sea has never abandoned me. The sea is the blood in my veins.[6]

By the summer of 1956, only a few short months after the first young victims were identified, the disease had reached epidemic proportions. An uneasiness developed among neighbors who, not knowing what had invaded their town, suspected that it might be contagious. As neighbor turned against neighbor, the medical investigators turned their spotlight on Chisso.

In August 1956, a local university sponsored a research group to investigate the causes of the disease. The group found that the sickness was a heavy metal poisoning caused by eating the fish and shellfish of Minamata Bay. Other investigators released studies claiming that Chisso was pouring nearly 60 poisons into the sea.

Chisso routinely denied the allegations that its factories could be involved in any way in this human disaster, and in September 1958, the company began diverting its acetaldehyde waste water from the Bay to the Minamata River, ignoring the warning of its own company doctors. A few months later, the Minamata sickness began to appear among residents of the river area.

The most devastating indictment of the company came from Chisso's own Dr. Hajim Hosokawa. In 1959, Hosokawa began feeding cats the same chemical effluent that Chisso was pouring into the Minamata waters. Cat no. 400 fell ill with symptoms of Minamata Disease. Hosokawa took the results of his cat studies to Chisso's management—studies the doctor claimed proved Chisso's culpability. The company's reaction was swift and sure: the doctor was forbidden further access to the effluent and was taken off the experiments, and his evidence that the disease was a result of Chisso's waste-dumping activities was concealed. By the time it was made public, many more residents had fallen victim to the disease and Chisso had had the opportunity to "cut its losses" with the people already afflicted.[7]

Thanks to Hosokawa's investigation, Chisso knew that in all likelihood the company was responsible for the brain damage, and the nervous twitches, and the endless suffering of parents, and children, and fishermen. And internal company documents—released in 1985, as a result of civil litigation in Japan—reportedly show that some Chisso employees sought to dispose of mercury wastes inside the Minamata plant as early as 1957, two years before Hosokawa's investigation. One document, filed in April of 1957, is a proposal for a project to pump effluents resulting from the production of acetaldehyde into a tank where the mercurial contents could be removed.[8]

The residents of Minamata, even those not personally or physically afflicted, shared in the suffering of the community. But the possible liability did not stop there. One of the most frightening aspects of the disease was its potential to affect the unborn child. Mercury can penetrate the placenta to reach the fetus, even in apparently healthy mothers. Mothers ate fish, children were born with birth defects.

After receiving Hosokawa's findings, the company did not immediately halt the dumping of mercury-tainted waste into Minamata Bay, nor did it warn people not to eat the tainted fish. Chisso's first reaction was to offer the victims payments in consolation for their misfortune (in Japanese, *mimai*)—an offer many of the victims were in no position to refuse. Although Chisso knew about Hosokawa's findings, the affected residents did not. They only suspected that the disease was somehow contagious and that they were catching it from their neighbors. Taking advantage of the legal and scientific ignorance of their victims, Chisso negotiated one-sided contracts that limited the company's liability to the initial, minimal payment. Chisso initially accepted no legal responsibilities for the damage done and disclaimed any future monetary liability.

The company's attempt to limit its liability may have succeeded for other, lesser corporate misdeeds. In this instance, however, the people of Minamata were never allowed to forget the nature and extent of their tragedy. Every day, the deformities of their bodies, or of their children's bodies, were stark reminders of the injustice done to them. "I would ask for nothing else," said one victim of mercury poisoning, "if only I could return to my body."

Under Japanese law, Chisso's dumping of mercury wastes and other poisons into the Minamata waters was not a criminal act; the company was dumping "statutorily permissible" (noncriminal) amounts of acetaldehyde waste water into the Bay. This did not stop the more than 750 victims afflicted with the disease from demanding in a civil court that Chisso pay fair and just compensation for their injuries. On March 20, 1973, after a four-year legal struggle with the company, some of the early victims of Minamata Disease won a verdict in Kumamoto District Court. The judge ruled that "even though the quality and content of the waste water of the defendant's plant satisfied statutory limitations and administrative standards . . . the defendant cannot escape from the liability of negligence." Chisso was ordered to pay the plaintiffs $3.2 million in damages.[9]

The leaders of the fight to gain just compensation were disappointed by the verdict. The judgment covered only compensation to a handful of plaintiffs injured in 1959. It did not cover damages that occurred thereafter, nor did it allow damages for medical fees, medicines, therapeutic massages and hot baths, nursing for the bedridden, transportation to and from treatment, and an allowance to live on.

The law, exemplified by this ruling, stopped far short of any humane standard of justice. The criminal law offered no protection, and the civil law offered little compensation. The affected residents were forced to take things into their own hands and demand direct negotiations with Chisso management.

The road from Minamata to Chisso headquarters in Tokyo led past Hiroshima and Nagasaki, and two days after the Kumamoto verdict was handed down, the victims and scores of others from Minamata traversed that road to Tokyo to meet with company managers. W. Eugene Smith and Eileen Smith, in their moving photodocumentary book titled *Minamata,* report how, amidst a flock of reporters and cameramen, Chisso president Yoshiharu Tanoue entered the jampacked conference room, unfolded a slip of paper, and read a prepared statement to the affected residents. "Well," he said, "Chisso will accept all responsibilities concerning Minamata Disease . . . according to the court decision . . . and will pay with all sincerity all damages arising from the Minamata Disease." Chisso argued that, in anticipation of thousands of claims, the company would pay all damages "to the best of Chisso's ability."

This final clause angered the Minamata residents and made Chisso's offer unacceptable. It also guaranteed that the negotiations would stretch on for days. The victims were in no mood for equivocations, loopholes, or added clauses.

On the third floor of the company headquarters, face to face with Chisso executives, the affected residents began negotiating for their own economic survival and that of their children. Chisso was negotiating for the financial survival of the company. "I have come to you, Mr. President," said one resident, "to negotiate for my future. We come to ask not for luxuries but for medicine to ease our pain and for peace to die, knowing our poisoned children will be cared for." A second resident stood to address the management team assembled across the large wooden table. "Every penny spent will be spent with tears," she said. "My parents gave me life as a woman, but I have had to become like a man . . . "

With these and other personal statements describing the ravages of Minamata Disease, the patients pushed for complete and total compensation. The company held back, for fear that meeting the patients' demands would lead to bankruptcy. Hundreds of hours passed. As the emotions flowed, the response from Chisso remained the same: "We have added up the cost of your demands. We just cannot pay it." Cameras clicked. Reporters scribbled. Managers waited impatiently.

Finally, after a week of negotiation, there was a break. A newly verified patient, Kimoto Iwamoto, had had enough. He stood up, grabbed a glass ashtray, slammed it against the negotiating table, and used its shattered remains to slash his wrist. "I can't stand it anymore," he shouted. "You can see for yourself, if I don't get the indemnity money, I can't live." In the bedlam that followed, as the blood flowed, the president of Chisso was overheard saying, "Yes, yes, yes, we will pay."[10]

By early 1975, Chisso had paid out an estimated $80 million to the 785 verified victims of Minamata Disease. Yet researchers estimated that the number of people affected might eventually reach 10,000, and many cases are still pending in Japanese courts.

In September 1976, two former Chisso executives were charged with involuntary manslaughter in the deaths of six persons who ate fish contaminated by the Minamata plant's mercury wastes.[11] The two, Kiichi Yoshioka, 85, who had been president at the time, and Eiichi Nishida, 76, the former plant director, were found guilty. Their appeals are currently pending.[12]

Taking a page from American counterparts, Chisso is reportedly planning to declare bankruptcy in order to avoid paying further compensation. In 1985, Professor Takashi Yamaguchi of Tokyo's Meiji University reported that Chisso stopped investing in plant and equipment in 1959, soon after scientists identified the cause of Minamata Disease, and began establishing subsidiaries. Today, the subsidiaries far surpass the parent firm in everything from productive capacity to sales and tangible fixed assets. "They are like divisions of a single company," Yamaguchi said.

In December 1985, the major Tokyo daily, *Asahi Shimbun*, reported Professor Yamaguchi's study and added that "about 6,000 victims are angry at the long delay in official certification of their illness and fear that if Chisso goes bankrupt, they will never be indemnified for their pain and suffering."[13]

Whatever the monetary compensation, no dollar amount was enough to compensate Shinobo Sakamoto, a teenager who was born blind and suffers from convulsions. When talking about her parents, Shinobo talks to Chisso and to all corporations throughout the world: "When father and mother aren't going to be around anymore . . . when they die . . . I'm worried . . . I'm afraid. When I think I will have to do everything myself, but cannot do it by myself. Really really I want everybody to stay. . . . If Chisso could understand me, I want to say to them . . . to die to die to die . . . no to come alive again . . . no, no to die again . . . again . . . again . . . To give me back my feet, mouth . . . I want it given back . . . to be given back . . . to be like you . . . like a human being . . . like everyone else."[14]

Notes

1. *Minamata,* by Eugene Smith and Eileen M. Smith. Holt Rinehart, Winston, New York, 1975, p. 84.

2. "Minamata Disease," by Jun Ui. *Kogai,* The Newsletter from Polluted Japan, special issue, 1975, Tokyo, p. 3.

3. "Minamata Disease: A Medical Report," by Masazumi Harada, M.D. *Kogai,* special issue, 1975, p. 55.

4. Ibid.

5. *Minamata,* Smith and Smith, p. 28.

6. Ibid., p. 13.

7. "Aftermath in Minamata," by Donald R. Thurston. Reprinted in *Kogai,* special issue, 1975, p. 37.

8. "Minamata Papers Contradict Co. Claim," *Mainichi Daily News,* August 20, 1986.

9. *Minamata,* Smith and Smith, p. 129.

10. Ibid., p. 135.

11. "Two Businessmen in Japan Are Tried for Mercury Deaths," *Wall Street Journal,* September 23, 1976.

12. "Minamata Papers Contradict Co. Claim," *Mainichi Daily News,* August 20, 1986.

13. "Minamata Poisoner May Claim Bankruptcy," by Chikako Kawakatsu. *Asahi Shimbun,* December 23, 1985.

14. *Minamata,* Smith and Smith, p. 156.

24
Nestle

"Can a product which requires clean water, good sanitation, adequate family income and a literate parent to follow printed instructions be properly and safely used in areas where water is contaminated, sewage runs in the streets, poverty is severe and illiteracy is high?"

> —Senator Edward M. Kennedy (D.-Mass.), opening statement in Senate hearings on the use and promotion of artificial baby formulas in developing countries, May 23, 1978[1]

IF THE FEMALE BREAST were a corporation, it would be considered by all a natural monopoly. There would exist no effective competition, for mother's milk would have on its side all the natural advantages that could not be surmounted by men seeking a profit. In business jargon, Mother's Milk would have a "corner" on the infant food market.

Consider the advantages of human breast milk: It is always on tap from its specially designed unbreakable container. It is the most nutritious and wholesome baby food. Unsupplemented human milk is all that is required to sustain growth and good nutrition for the first six months of life for babies of well-nourished mothers. Even in poorly nourished mothers, the volume and composition of breast milk are usually surprisingly good.[2] Human breast milk contains quantities of enzymes, antibodies, and immunizing agents that protect an infant's ultrasensitive digestive tract from a wide range of diseases.

Breast-feeding has natural advantages for the mother, too. Breast feeding strengthens the psychological and emotional bond between the mother and the baby. It helps a mother get back in shape after pregnancy by stimulating contractions of the womb and thus helping it return to its normal size. It also acts as a natural contraceptive. Recent studies show that if a woman does not breast-feed her baby, she begins to ovulate about two months after the birth of her baby. By breast-feeding, the woman can postpone the time of the first ovulation by from five months to two years.[3] Finally, breast milk comes cheap to its baby consumers—it's free.

For centuries these natural advantages allowed human breast milk to retain a monopoly in the infant food market. There was no competition because there was no need for an alternative—the product satisfied the needs of billions of baby consumers and their mothers. Then came Henri Nestlé.

During the late 1800s, Nestlé, an entrepreneur, developed an infant formula as a substitute for human milk, to "save the life of a infant who could not be breast-fed." But the percentage of women throughout the world whose children could not be breast-fed was small, and Henri Nestlé could not expect to make much money selling his human milk substitute. For the vast majority of mothers in the world, there was no need for Henri Nestlé's substitute—human breast milk was perfect.

Nestle, the company named after Henri Nestlé, is the number one manufacturer of infant formula, cornering half of what is today an estimated $2 billion market. Today one of the world's largest multinational corporations, the company did not get to be that big by selling infant formula to mothers who were unable to breast-feed their babies. Instead, the company focused on a much larger market and began making their pitch to mothers who were perfectly capable of doing so. The infant formula industry did not grow by filling a need. It grew by creating a need. Millions of mothers had to be sold on the idea that breast-feeding was not a good idea—that they should feed their babies imitation breast milk instead of, or as a supplement to, the real thing. Nestle had to convince these mothers that their babies should be suckled on an artificial nipple connected to a bottle. And it did. Soon, millions of mothers, perfectly capable of breast-feeding their babies, began buying the imitation infant formula instead.

In Chile, 25 years ago, 95 percent of the one-year-olds were being breast-fed; by 1970, only 20 percent were being breast-fed at *two months*. Breast-feeding in Singapore declined 30 percent between 1951 and 1960; it declined 31 percent in the Philippines between 1958 and 1968; and 22 percent in Mexico from 1960 to 1966. Other countries around the world experienced similar declines.

This worldwide decline in breast-feeding did not occur because babies preferred formula out of a bottle to their mother's milk. Nor did it happen because the mothers of the world made informed choices. For, while the world's infant formula companies were bombarding mothers, especially third world mothers, with advertisements on radio, television, and in the print media extolling the alleged benefits of infant formula, there was little information reaching the mothers about the virtues of breast-feeding. In Sierra Leone, for example, in August 1974, Nestle broadcast 135 30-second ads for its infant formula Lactogen; in December, Unigate, another infant formula company, ran 45 30-second ads for its Cow and Gate brand, and Abbott ran 66 promoting Similac in the same month. The effects of this type of this media saturation in Sierra Leone and other parts of the third world were predictable.[4]

The World Health Organization (WHO) reported that a comprehensive study conducted between 1975 and 1977 in nine countries found the "overall exposure of mothers to industrially processed and commercially marketed infant foods was extensive. Knowledge of brand names was almost universal throughout the economically advantaged populations in all nine countries." The WHO study also found that in the Philippines, mothers from poor communities knew infant formula producers by their brand names. In Nigeria, 72 percent of the urban poor mothers knew formula products by their brand names. "The reason for the progressive decline in breast feeding," observed WHO nutrition specialist Dr. J. Kreysler, "is the massive propaganda of the milk companies which is particularly effective in poor sectors of the population. The milk companies are creating a magic belief in the white man's milk powder."[5]

In addition to using direct advertising, the infant formula companies reached mothers indirectly through doctors, nurses, and other medical professionals. Nestle did not deny this; indeed, it admitted that "the health services are recognized as the main intermediary between the manufacturers and the mothers." The companies cultivate this network of intermediaries by providing free samples of infant formula to doctors, by donating expensive equipment to needy hospitals, by sponsoring professional symposia on infant health care, by organizing conferences for pediatricians, and by befriending doctors and giving them gifts, and by paying for their expenses to and from conferences.

Dr. Leonard Barrion, chief of clinics at a hospital in the Philippines, told a Senate health subcommittee that "health professionals who otherwise know the benefits of breast-feeding often succumb to the gimmicks of milk advertisements . . . milk companies sponsor scientific meetings, research awards and material support to health or nutritional projects. They also give generous samples to pediatricians. . . . Because Filipinos have a strong trait of indebtedness for favors done, called 'utang na loob,' these health professionals feel inner constraints to advertise or prescribe milk even against their better judgment."[6]

Others report instances where companies try to catch young doctors fresh out of medical school, and influence them. "When the pediatricians graduate from college," reported Fr. Daniel Driscoll, who spent 11 years working in Venezuela, "it seems like the American Home Products company [another infant formula marketer] is very generous in providing about 20,000 boliveras worth of liquor . . . which comes to almost $5000 (US)."[7]

Fr. Driscoll also observed other companies pushing the formula on older doctors. "Whenever there are professional meetings of pediatricians and so on," Driscoll observed, "Nestle for example will fly in certain doctors, and they will always have the largest banquet. . . . So one doctor said 'I have conscience problems even eating there but I should be there as a professional, so I feel trapped.'"[8] In Malaysia, Wyeth Labs sponsored a seminar on infant feeding and infection. The seminar cost the company about $2,000, but according to one prediction, Wyeth reaped 20 times that in effective advertising "because it's so subtle, so effective."

Infant formula companies also hire "milk nurses" to visit patients in the maternity wards of hospitals, despite the fact that this practice of using nurses as salespersons is illegal in many countries. According to Dr. Cicely D. Williams, a British doctor who worked in hospitals throughout the third world, the business of these "so-called nurses is to sell milk, not look after the health of the children." Williams told how "In Africa, I wouldn't let them [the nurses] in. They came to me about it, but I said no, not as long as I'm here. Then I went to Singapore and found that Nestle had nurses, these girls dressed as nurses, dragging a good lactating breast out of the baby's mouth and pouring in baby milk [formula]."[9]

In these and other ways, infant formula companies compromised the judgment of doctors, and influenced health professionals and hospital administrators to use and recommend the use of infant formula instead of breast milk and in so doing increase sales and profits. By 1980, mothers in developing countries were paying an estimated $1 billion to Nestle, Unigate, Bristol-Myers, Abbott, Wyeth, Glaxo, and other infant formula companies for products that, in most instances, the mothers did not need.

If that were the whole of it, then the infant formula companies would hardly be distinguishable from other Western corporations that seek profits by creating a need and marketing a costly product to fulfill it, in the process displacing a product that is naturally more efficient and cheaper. In the context of the developing world, however, the marketing of infant formula through the mass media is more than just a costly hoax. Unlike mother's breast milk, infant formula does not come ready to use. It must be prepared.

Using formula requires mothers to read and understand instructions for preparation, yet in many of the developing countries where infant formula is marketed mothers can't read. Even where the mother can read her native language, in many instances she is faced with a foreign script. In Dar-es-Salaam, Tanzania, for example, where Nestle's Lactogen is widely marketed, a local doctor reported that all the instructions were in English even though most of the women were fluent only in Swahili. "I spoke with one woman the other day as she stood on the sidewalk talking to her friend, very proudly holding a can of Lactogen in her hand," reported the doctor. "She had a two-and-a-half-month-old baby. I asked her whether or not she could read and speak English. She replied 'kidogo, kidogo' (very very little) and indeed she did not understand any questions that I asked her in English."[10]

Even where a mother can read and understand printed instructions, she may not be able to carry them out adequately and safely. There must be clean water, for example, to mix with the formula. In Peru, one river was described as being used as "a laundry, as a bathroom, in some parts as a toilet and for drinking water."[9] Most formula preparations instruct the mother to boil the water used to mix with the formula. But boiling water in the third world is a luxury few can afford. Gas stoves are a rarity; even food is a scarce resource. "Now you can tell the mother to boil the water," explained one third world doctor, "but to get the fuel to boil that water, she has to go into the jungle, chop a tree trunk with a machete—which is a large knife—and carry it back on her back. No mother is going to use that hard-earned piece of wood to boil that water."[11]

Thus, third world mothers often mix the formula with unclean water, and fail to sterilize the bottle. As a result, the babies, who, if they had a choice, would undoubtedly have chosen mother's milk, drink the contaminated formula and become ill. The UN's Food and Agricultural Organization (FAO) reported in 1977 that "under the unfavorable economic and sanitary conditions found in low-income urban groups, the consequence of bottle feeding is a high prevalence of diarrhea and gastrointestinal tract infections which, coupled with frequent over-dilution of the milk, leads to increased incidence of Protein Energy Malnutrition (PEM)." The FAO report added that "bottle feeding is also associated with an earlier age of onset of malnutrition."[12]

The infant formula industry has repeatedly denied charges of substantial abuse in the marketing of its product in the third world. In 1978, Nestle asserted that "the formula products are usually purchased by people who can afford them. It is the working women and the women in the upper income groups who are most likely to use formula products."[13] But health professionals throughout the world have testified otherwise.

On May 23, 1978, health professionals from around the world came to Washington, D.C., to testify before the U.S. Senate subcommittee on health about the problems they faced with infant formula marketing. A nurse from Yemen testified that she observed a rapid rise in bottle feeding in that very poor country during the preceding ten years. "Yemen does not possess an environment compatible with safe use of the bottle," she testified. "Only 10 percent of the population has easy access to water." Fatima Patel, a registered nurse with 17 years of experience in developing countries, spoke of the problems faced by mothers in Peru.

> With both water and fuel being such a luxury, they are used sparingly. The bottle may be rinsed out in a bowl of water which has been used for many purposes; the water to mix the formula will be scooped out of the bucket with any old

utensil, hands won't be washed since soap is another luxury item. The unfinished formula will be left laying around with the nipple exposed, flies swarming and settling on it; and when needed the formula will be stuck into the crying hungry infant's mouth giving it a big dose of mortal poison.[14]

Furthermore, because infant formula is a costly item, mothers try to stretch their supply by overdiluting the product. Widespread improper dilution of the formula in the third world contributes to high malnutrition rates.

It has been estimated that 15 million children under the age of five die every year, partly from malnutrition, with an additional 10 million more paralyzed, made blind or deaf, or suffering from brain damage or stunted growth from disease. Most of this toll occurs in the third world, and the causes are numerous. But more and more specialists within the infant nutrition and health care community are focusing their attention on infant formula use as an important causal factor in the high levels of infant diarrhea, malnutrition, and mortality.

Faced with the reality of multinational corporations marketing a costly, unnecessary product in the developing world, when a cost-free, highly acceptable alternative — mother's milk — is readily available, responsible health professionals around the world have begun to speak out against infant formula abuse. In response, the companies have been forced to modify their marketing behavior. Unigate canceled advertising of its infant formula in Africa until the ad copy was approved by local pediatricians. The company later canceled all advertisements. Abbott adopted a code of marketing practices that prohibited the use of mass media to market its infant formula, and Nestle canceled all radio ads in Nigeria.

Despite these spotty reforms, marketing abuse remained widespread within the industry. In response to this pattern of corporate irresponsibility, a coalition of health, religious, labor, and citizens groups organized a worldwide boycott of Nestle products (Nestle is the largest infant formula company). In addition, many countries have imposed marketing restrictions on Nestle and other infant formula companies. Nestle claimed that it abided by these laws. But there were reports of violations, and Nestle refused to agree to abide by the World Health Organization/United Nations International Childrens Emergency Fund (WHO/UNICEF) Code of

Marketing for Infant Formula. The industry pushed instead the idea of "self-regulation" as a better method of controlling abuses. As one activist commented, "asking the industry to regulate itself is like asking Colonel Sanders to babysit your chickens."[15]

The WHO/UNICEF code was passed by 118 national governments in May 1981, with only the United States, at the instruction of President Ronald Reagan, voting against it. The WHO/UNICEF code calls upon the baby formula industry to: (1) stop giving free formula samples; (2) eliminate "milk nurses"; (3) halt direct promotion to mothers; (4) place warnings on labels; (5) end commissions to sales people to increase sales; and (6) restrict promotion to the health professions.

This code, if taken seriously by the industry, poses a sizable threat to infant formula company profits. The dilemma, which pits babies against shareholders, was crystallized when a group of nuns concerned about Abbott's marketing tactics in the third world paid a call on company executives. One observer described the meeting this way:

> They (Abbott) were being very agreeable about modifying their sales technqiues. "Use of mass media will be dropped . . . no radio, billboards . . ."
>
> Well, as we were about to leave, one of the Sisters said, "Tell me, if you stop selling to people who are too poor to use the product safely, will you still make a profit?" There was absolute silence. It must have been a full minute. Finally, one of corporate executives picked it up and said: "That is the crux of the problem."[16]

In 1983, Nestle was cited by the Infant Formula Action Coalition (INFACT), a public interest group based in Minneapolis, for disregarding key sections of the WHO code.

- In November 1983, Nestle provided bulk supplies of free infant formula to a Kuala Lumpur hospital, far in excess of the special needs of infants who have to be bottle-fed. The practice ensured that the hospital routinely bottle-fed all infants.
- In November 1983, a researcher in the Philippines found that Nestle financed nonmedical events for nursery staffs—movies, swimming, dinner parties, and special foods. The hospital used Nestle formula.

- In July 1983, Nestle distributed leaflets depicting its Nan brand infant formula in the health care facilities in Taiwan. The only English text stated they were "for medical profession only." But the entire Chinese text is directed to mothers; no effort was made to warn of possible hazards associated with bottle feeding.

In citing Nestle for violating the WHO Code, INFACT urged consumers around the world to continue the boycott against Nestle's Taster's Choice coffee, chocolate, and other Nestle products until the corporation agreed to redirect its marketing priorities. The boycott, launched in 1977, blossomed into the largest worldwide citizens' effort of its kind, mobilizing more than 100 women's, consumer, religious, and health groups in 65 countries. The company's strategy was to fight the boycott through intermediaries. "The basic strategy for dealing with the boycott," wrote one Nestle executive, in a leaked internal memo, "i.e., containment of the awareness of the activists' campaign, without being responsible for escalating awareness levels, is working . . . "

In fulfillment of this strategy, Nestle has given financial support to the Ethics and Public Policy Center, a nonprofit, tax-exempt conservative foundation in Washington, D.C., directed by Ernest W. Lefever. The *Washington Post* reported in January 1981 that Lefever met with Herman Nickel, Washington editor of *Fortune* magazine, and proposed that *Fortune* undertake a study of the infant formula issue. The result was an article highly critical of boycott organizers, labeling them "Marxists marching under the banner of Christ." The article was widely distributed by Nestle. Douglas Johnson, leader of the INFACT campaign in the United States, reacted angrily to the article, charging that Nickel "tries to pass off the data that we have collected and the human concerns of the international health agencies as an ideological attack on innocent corporations. By ideological I mean reds, Marxists. He sees a red behind every bush. So, in our view, it is a red-baiting attack and at the same time, an ideological right-wing apology for Nestle and the other infant formula manufacturers."[17]

Six years of "boycott Nestle" slogans, pickets, and press conferences around the world was enough to make even one of the largest of the multinationals cry for help. In April 1984, Nestle gave in to INFACT's demands, agreeing to abide by virtually every detail of the WHO code. The concessions by Nestle surprised boycott organizers. "If Nestle abides by the agreement," said Johnson, "it will do a lot to contribute to the lives of children. We now share with Nestle a mutual interest in seeing other infant formula companies bring their marketing practices into line with Nestle's."[18]

But two years after the boycott was ended, the problem had worsened. According to the United Nations, one million infants died in 1986 because they were bottle-fed, rather than breast-fed. Nestle had not fully implemented the policy changes it promised in 1984, and three U.S. companies—American Home Products, Bristol-Meyers, and Abbott/Ross Laboratories—maintained policies that did not conform to the UN's International Code. "During the past year," reported Carol-Linnea Salmon, associate director of action for corporate accountability at INFACT, "we have found that while some life-saving changes have been made, the corporate onslaught of baby milk promotion continues, particularly through deliveries of massive quantities of free infant formula supplies to maternity wards."[19]

Notes

1. Excerpts From Senate Hearings on Infant Formula, *The Corporate Examiner*, November 1978, p. 3a.
2. National Academy of Sciences Conference Report, August 1978, p. 3, cited in INFACT, *Policy v. Practice: The Reality of Formula Promotion*, May 1979, p. 27.
3. *The Baby Killer Scandal*, a War on Want investigation into the promotion and sale of powdered baby milks in the Third World, by Andy Chetley. War On Want, London, 1979, p. 27.
4. *Baby Killer Scandal*, Chetley, p. 58.
5. Ibid., p. 60.
6. *Policy v. Practice*, INFACT, p. 14.
7. Ibid.
8. Ibid.
9. Ibid., p. 19.
10. *Baby Killer Scandal*, Chetley, p. 48.
11. Ibid., p. 45.
12. *Policy v. Practice*, INFACT, p. 2.
13. Ibid., p. 5.
14. Ibid., p. 7.

15. "Nestle's Latest Killing in the Baby Bottle Market," by Douglas Clement. *Business and Society Review,* Summer 1978, p. 61.

16. *Baby Killer Scandal,* Chetley, p. 136.

17. "Infant-Formula Maker Battles Boycotters by Painting Them Red," by Morton Mintz. *Washington Post,* January 4, 1981, p. A2.

18. "The Taming of Nestle," by Fred Clarkson. *Multinational Monitor,* April 1984.

19. "Babies At Risk: Infant Formula Still Takes Its Toll," by Nancy Gaschott. *Multinational Monitor,* October 1986.

25
Oil

"The trouble with this country is that you can't win an election without the oil block and you can't govern with it."

—Franklin Delano Roosevelt[1]

Exxon IS THE WORLD's largest corporation. In 1980, the company rang up sales totaling $79.1 billion. That's $9 million an hour. It cleared a profit of $4.3 billion. That's $136 a second. Exxon's biggest problem in 1980 was that it had so much money that it didn't know what to do with it all.

Mobil is the world's second largest oil company. Jimmy Carter, when he was president of the United States, called Mobil "perhaps the most irresponsible company in America." Mobil's problem was the same as Exxon's—too much cash. Mobil spent its money buying other corporations. Mobil also spent lavishly on its own executives: In 1979, Mobil's top five executives took home a total of more than $10 million. That's an average of more than $2 million per executive—in one year.[2] "Quite frankly," added Frank Ikard, president of the American Petroleum Institute in 1971, "the oil industry has developed the reputation over the years of being a robber, cheating and despoiling the environment."[3]

The oil companies argue that their profit levels represent nothing but a "rightful rate of return on investment." Critics like the late senator Henry Jackson (D.-Wash.) described oil company profits as "obscene." Jackson's characterization reflects a belief deeply held by many Americans that the oil companies are ripping them off.

"Public attitudes toward the company and the industry are quite negative," admitted Exxon's president during the company's 1978 shareholders meeting.[4]

Profits are as American as apple pie. No matter how large, they are justified if they are rightfully gained in a competitive setting where market forces work to offset excesses. In America, profits become "obscene," or morally questionable, when they are gained unfairly, or illegally.

But there is no free market in oil, and that did not come about naturally. The free market was destroyed by the major oil companies. Every time it shows a glimmer of resurgence it is snuffed out by the handful of major companies that today control the supply, the marketing, and the price of oil—which, in a free market, would be vested not with the companies, but with the market itself.

The free market flickered briefly at the turn of the century, when a geologist wrote about the possibility of oil in Mesopotamia. C. S. Gulbenkian's report kicked off a wild scramble for what turned out to be the largest fields of oil in the world—in the Middle East. Until the 1920s, the American oil companies had been supplying much of the world's crude—oil that was being pumped out of the fields of Texas, Oklahoma, and Pennsylvania. But the U.S. companies were getting restless, and began searching for foreign sources of oil. Their restlessness coincided with the publication of Gulbenkian's report, and the major oil companies headed for the Middle East.

Five American oil companies (Exxon, Mobil, Gulf, Standard Oil of California, and Texaco) eventually joined with two European firms (Shell and British Petroleum [BP]) and proceeded to divvy up the oilfields among themselves. In *The Control of Oil*,[5] John Blair describes a series of joint ownership companies supplemented by supply contracts with highly restrictive provisions regarding the terms and conditions of sale of large volumes of oil. This complex arrangement enabled the seven sisters, as they came to be called, to control the supply of Middle East oil, thus keeping competitors at a safe distance, and prices artificially high.

The road to the final agreement between the American and European firms was not a smooth one. BP and Shell were in the Middle East first, and they were reluctant to let in any competitors. The American firms complained to Washington. Waving the free enterprise flag and demanding that Uncle Sam pressure the British to allow competitors into the Middle East oilfields, the oil companies argued for the adoption of an "open door" policy in the Middle East, a policy that would allow any company the freedom to obtain oil concessions.

The U.S. oil companies argued that an "open door" policy was necessary because America was running out of oil. It was not the last time they would use this argument to influence public policy. In the early 1920s, the United States Geological Survey (USGS), which based its studies on oil company data, was issuing dire warnings that "the position of the United States in regard to oil can best be described as precarious" and that "within perhaps three years, our domestic production will begin to fall off with increasing rapidity due to the exhaustion of our reserves."[6]

Soon thereafter, shortages of gasoline were reported from around the country. The price of gas in some areas nearly doubled and there were rumors that refineries were keeping gas out of the urban centers until the price went up. Was America running out of oil in 1924? Or was this a ploy by the oil companies to pressure the government into taking action in the Middle East? "There is this strange habit peculiar to the American oil industry," observed two British journalists at the time, "which one should observe in passing. Although it doubles its output roughly every 10 years, it declares every other year that its peak of production has been passed and that its oilfields are well-nigh exhausted . . . one cannot doubt that lugubrious prophecies of American oil men are in some way related to a wish for high prices."[7]

Contrived or not, the crises of 1924 sent the State Department, the Congress, and the American people into a frenzy, and the British, under intense pressure, caved in. On July 31, 1928, BP, Shell, Exxon, and Mobil, four of what would eventually become the seven sisters, cut a deal. The American companies' wish for an open door policy in the Middle East had been granted.

Within three years of that initial agreement, the open door had been "bolted, barred, and hermetically sealed," in the words of one industry observer.[8] The four sisters decided that four was enough, and that any more would cause too much competition with the inevitable free market result of lower prices to consumers and lower profits to the companies. The sisters took action to prevent competition among themselves and to prevent outsiders from intruding on their turf. To prevent competition among themselves, they drew an imaginary line that circumscribed most of the Arabian Gulf, the fertile crescent, and much of what was the Ottoman empire. They agreed not to compete with one another for oilfields within the circumscribed region. This became known as the "Red Line" agreement.

When news of the extent of the Middle East oil wealth spread around the world, other oil companies began to clamor for a piece of the action. According to one industry trade journal, what the oil industry feared most was "the entry of a powerful newcomer in the established order of world markets." Two powerful newcomers, Standard Oil of California and Texaco, were soon knocking on the door, asking that it once again be opened. Fearing that these two outside giants were capable of competing with the four sisters and disrupting world markets, i.e., sending the price of oil downward, the four opened the door, allowed Standard and Texaco into the Middle East, and formed a new agreement to replace the Red Line agreement.

The door was to be opened one more time, this time for Gulf Oil Company, and then closed again. The original Red Line agreement did not cover Kuwait, where Gulf had a strong foothold. The six sisters realized that if Gulf were allowed to market its large holdings of Kuwait oil on the world market at a price lower than the cartel price, world prices might take a nosedive. The six sisters brought Gulf into line by negotiating supply contracts with it, contracts that severely restricted the degree to which Gulf could compete with the other six. These contractual agreements were described years later in a Federal Trade Commission Report (FTC) on the International Petroleum Cartel (IPC):

> Thus the crude oil supply contracts, not only because of the large quantities of oil and the long periods of time that were specified, but also because of the unusual provisions as to price and marketing, constituted effective instruments for control of Middle East oil. As such they complement and increase the degree of joint control of Middle East oil resulting from the pattern of joint ownership. . . . The operation of these two instruments of control in effect brings the seven international oil companies, controlling practically all of the Middle East oil resources, together into a mutual community of interest.[9]

The sisters were seven and the supply of oil would remain firmly in their control for decades. Those independent oil companies that sought to gain a foothold in the Middle East were ruthlessly turned away. When, for instance, the Iranian oilfields were being developed, independents sought a role. There was a move within the U.S. government to promote a wider degree of competition for the Iranian oilfields by opening the door to independents. The State Department's petroleum attaché argued that "the U.S. government should promote the entry of new competition into the Middle East. . . . The control of Middle East resources by major international companies is subject to serious criticism by both friendly and unfriendly states. The successful participation of independent U.S. companies is a requisite to elimination of that criticism."[10] The major U.S. companies were impervious to such criticism, and in the end all the independents together were allotted a mere 5 percent of the Iranian concession. At congressional hearings on the subject in 1955, one Exxon official was asked why Exxon allowed the independents to have anything at all.

> PAGE: I don't know their reasons for it but they had a feeling, well, because people were always yacking about it we had better put some independents in there.
>
> SENATOR CHURCH: Put a few independents in?
>
> PAGE: Yes
>
> SENATOR CHURCH: Window dressing?
>
> PAGE: That's right.[11]

Despite their ironclad control of the oilfields, the seven sisters realized that controlling the supply of oil by keeping outsiders out was not enough to ensure that prices would remain artificially high. Supply was only one side of the coin. Marketing was the other, and if competition broke out on the marketing end, their efforts on the supply side would be wasted. The prices and profits would come tumbling down. The sisters saw this happen once, and they were determined to prevent it from happening again. In 1927, Shell announced a decrease in the price of kerosene in India. What followed proved, according to Blair, an important lesson in the domino-like effects of competition on prices worldwide:

> Further reductions followed, developing into a price war in India between Standard of New York and Shell. Steps were taken by each to broaden the conflict. Shell intensified competition in the United States, while Standard of New York [Exxon] intensified its advertising of ethyl fuel in England. As the competition between the two companies spread, other world markets were involved and other international marketing companies found it necessary to reduce prices to hold their respective positions. . . . Shell's action in carrying the price competition to the American market affected the operation of all American oil companies. On the other hand, the action of Standard Oil of New York [Exxon] in staying in India not withstanding low prices and in intensifying the promotion of its ethyl gasoline in England, brought sharply to the attention of Anglo Persian [BP] and Royal Dutch Shell the possibility that Standard might increase its sales in Great Britain and continental Europe and that other American interests might take similar action. The relative positions of all international companies in the principal consuming markets of the world were jeopardized.[12]

As the world price of oil began to tumble, the three major world oil companies at the time—Exxon, Shell, and BP—began getting nervous and decided to meet to discuss a remedy for this outbreak of competition. The heads of these three companies met in a Scottish castle in September 1928 and hammered out the "Achnacarry Agreement," through which the companies agreed not to engage in any effective price competition. (The agreement, for instance, provided for "preventing any surplus production in a given geographical area from upsetting the price structure in any other area."[13]) With Achnacarry, the first international oil cartel became a reality.

In the years that followed, the world's major oil companies entered into three other international agreements, each designed to keep prices artificially high by restricting competition. These agreements set quotas and prices, established conditions of sale, regulated advertising, and created central authorities to iron out differences between cartel members when they arose. Little was left to chance, and there was little chance that competition would be given another opportunity to break out as it had in India in 1928.

As they carved up the Middle East and restricted price competition throughout the world, the oil companies were aware that U.S. authorities would someday challenge their anti–free market activities. A Texaco internal memo reflected the fear that one of the proposed schemes would raise the "danger of violation of U.S. antitrust laws."[14]

On December 2, 1949, the Federal Trade Commission (FTC) ordered an investigation into the anti–free market activities of the world's major oil companies. After a three-year examination led by staff economist John M. Blair, the FTC released a scathing 400-page report, titled simply "The International Petroleum Cartel." The report revealed that the seven sisters controlled all principal oil-producing areas outside the United States, that they divided up world markets, shared pipelines and tankers, and kept prices artificially high by eliminating competition.

President Harry Truman received a copy of the report and subsequently sent a memo to his secretaries of State, Defense, Interior, and Commerce and to the FTC. It read, "I have requested the Attorney General to institute appropriate legal proceedings with respect to the operations of the International Oil Cartel. I would like for you to cooperate with him in gathering the evidence required for these proceedings."[15] In terms of the potential number of victims among consumers, this was by far the largest criminal antitrust case ever initiated by the U.S. government. For years, the international oil cartel had been keeping prices artificially high, thereby overcharging consumers untold billions of dollars. Now, in the early 1950s, Harry Truman's government was about to step in and put a stop to it all.

The Justice Department convened a special grand jury and served subpoenas on 21 oil companies, including the seven majors. Executives from the nation's largest corporations faced the possibility of going to jail. More important, the Justice Department sought to break the majors' control of the supply of oil and of prices.

As soon as Truman launched the offensive, the oil companies returned fire on two fronts, the Oval Office and the courthouse. In court, the companies objected to the subpoenas on the ground that the documents requested by the Justice Department were "sensitive" because they "involved the national security." The judge, rejecting the national security claims, ordered the companies to turn over the documents.

Truman, however, surrendered to the oil companies and their loyal representatives within the administration. His departments of State, Interior, and Defense sided with the seven sisters and urged the President not to pursue the criminal action. In a report to the chief executive the departments argued that "American oil companies are, for all practical purposes, instruments of our foreign policies toward these countries [in the Middle East]," that the companies played a significant role in the struggle for ideas with the Soviet Union, and that, therefore, "we cannot afford to leave unchallenged the assertions that these companies are engaged in a criminal conspiracy for the purpose of predatory exploitation." If Truman let the criminal action stand, other countries, the memo argued, would believe that "capitalism is synonymous with predatory exploitation."[16]

Attorney General James McGranery was cornered. Three powerful cabinet members were against his position. Nevertheless, he put forth a valiant defense of the criminal case against the oil companies:

> It is imperative that petroleum resources be freed from monopoly control by the few and be restored to free competitive private enterprise. . . . Free private enterprise can be preserved only by safeguarding it from excess of power, government and private. . . . The world petroleum cartel is an authoritarian, dominating power over a great vital world industry in private hands . . . a decision at this time to terminate the pending investigations would be regarded by the world as a confession that our abhorrence of monopoly and restrictive cartel activities does not extend to the world's most important single industry.[17]

Unfortunately, his words fell on deaf ears. The air in Washington was filled with talk of communists, not antitrust, and Truman was not persuaded by his attorney general's defense of free enterprise. Six days after hearing both sides of the issue, the President wrote to his attorney general asking that the criminal case against the major oil companies be dropped in favor of a civil antitrust suit. Truman told one Justice Department attorney that his decision to let the oil companies off the criminal hook was made "solely on the assurance of General Omar Bradley that the national security" called for it.[18]

The possibility of a civil case remained, but a new Republican administration was taking office and the oil companies always did well under the Republicans. Under Eisenhower's administration, the presumption was that "the enforcement of the antitrust laws of the United States against the western oil companies operating in the Near East may be deemed secondary to the national security interest." Pressure intensified on Justice Department attorneys to weaken the case against the oil companies. "The pressures were continuous from month to month," reported the lead attorney, Leonard J. Emmerglick, "sometimes week to week, to downgrade the importance of prosecution of the cartel case. We did not give up at the staff level, but we realized that new impediments were being thrown in our way as each of these developments took place." Another Justice Department attorney put it this way: " . . . it did not take very long when anybody was assigned to that case to realize it was heading downhill and the real relief was not going to be allowed or perhaps was impossible, and that it was drudgery."[19]

For 15 years, the drudgery continued. Then, in the spring of 1960, rumors of a sellout surfaced on Capitol Hill. The rumors were confirmed when the Justice Department announced the settlement of suits against Gulf and Jersey Standard. The consent decrees banned future agreements to fix prices, divide markets, restrict output, or exclude competitors. The decrees were riddled with loopholes, and weaker decrees were entered during the next several years against the remaining defendants. The cartel emerged largely intact, and the seven sisters continued to charge consumers around the world artificially high prices for oil.

Franklin Roosevelt believed that "the trouble with this country is that you can't win an election without the oil bloc and you can't govern with it." The International Petroleum Cartel case is just one of a number of instances in which the government has failed to enforce the law under pressure from the major oil companies, allowing the companies, in the words of economist Blair, to make "more effective their exploitation of the public interest."[20]

The government's failure in the 1950s to pursue the criminal prosecutions of the companies despite the FTC report documenting a multibillion-dollar theft is perhaps the most striking example of the meaningless nature of law not backed up by effective enforcement.[21] Similarly, in 1983, the Reagan administration closed without prosecution a six-year investigation into allegations that the major oil companies had conspired to run up the price of Persian Gulf oil in the late 1970s. Reagan's assistant attorney general for antitrust, William Webster, said that the investigation produced scant evidence of wrongdoing, and that pursuing the case any further would have international repercussions "changing the tone of Mideast relations." Citizens groups, however, objected to the decision as a continuation of the historical pattern of a hands-off policy toward the major oil companies.[22] Unless this pattern is reversed—unless the government strictly enforces the laws that protect the competitive economy and demands a return to the free market for oil—then the law as applied to the oil industry will remain meaningless and the periodic multibillion-dollar thefts will continue unabated.

Notes

1. *Fiasco,* by Jack Anderson and James Boyd. Times Books, New York, 1983, p. 27.
2. *The Seven Sisters,* by Anthony Sampson. Bantam, New York, 1975, p. 323.
3. "The Case Against the Oil Companies," by Robert Sherrill, in *Big Business Day Reader,* ed. by Mark Green and Robert Massie. Pilgrim Press, New York, 1980, p. 20.
4. *Everybody's Business, An Almanac,* ed. by Milton Moskowitz, Michael Katz, and Robert Levering. Harper & Row, San Francisco, 1980, p. 491 et. seq.
5. *The Control of Oil,* by John Blair. Vintage, New York, 1978.
6. "The Case Against the Oil Companies," Sherrill, p. 21.
7. E. H. Davenport and Sidney Russell Cooke in *The Oil Trusts and Anglo American Relations,* quoted by Sherrill in "The Case Against the Oil Companies," p. 22.
8. *The Control of Oil,* Blair, p. 34.
9. *The International Petroleum Cartel,* Staff Report of the Federal Trade Commission, 82d Cong., 2d sess., U.S. Senate Small Business Committee, p. 162.
10. *The Control of Oil,* Blair, p. 45.

11. Ibid., p. 46.
12. Ibid., p. 54.
13. *The Seven Sisters*, Sampson, p. 85.
14. *The Control of Oil*, Blair, p. 41.
15. *The Control of Oil*, Blair, p. 72.
16. *The Seven Sisters*, Sampson, p. 148.
17. Ibid., p. 149.
18. *The Control of Oil*, Blair, p. 73.
19. Ibid., p. 75.
20. Economist John Blair gives other examples where the government has made "more effective" the oil companies' exploitation of the public interest. They include: transferring valuable publicly owned reserves to the oil companies; implementing the domestic control mechanism (which artificially props up prices here in the U.S.); preventing for nearly a decade and a half the importation of low-cost foreign oil; transferring to other U.S. taxpayers the burden of making up the revenue losses stemming from the industry's preferential tax advantages; countenancing price increases of refined products not warranted by changes in either cost or demand; channeling the great bulk of federal research and development funds into technologies that will not disturb (and may actually benefit) the oil companies; restraining the development of shale oil.[25]

For additional detailed accounts of how the oil companies manipulated the energy crisis in the 1970s see: *The Oil Follies of 1970-1980: How the Petroleum Industry Stole the Show (And Much More Besides)*, by Robert Sherrill. Anchor Press, Doubleday, New York, 1983; *The Great Energy Scam*, by Fred J. Cook. MacMillan, New York, 1982; and *Fiasco*, by Jack Anderson with James Boyd. Times Books, New York, 1983.

21. *The Closed Enterprise System* by Mark Green. Grossman, New York, 1972, p. 274.
22. "Six Year Probe of Oil Firms Ended by U.S.," by Michael Isikoff. *Washington Post*, December 8, 1983.

26
Oraflex

"The people in this company [Eli Lilly] ought to be put in jail."

—Dr. Sidney Wolfe, director, Public Citizen's Health
Research Group[1]

Sʜᴇ ᴡᴀꜱ 61 ʏᴇᴀʀꜱ ᴏʟᴅ. She suffered, as did many her age, from rheumatoid arthritis. Her doctor prescribed benoxaprofen, an anti-arthritic drug manufactured by Eli Lilly under the name Oraflex in the United States and as Opren in Great Britain. Her doctor prescribed a dose of 600 mg daily, but she soon began vomiting. After several days she began vomiting blood, had abdominal pain, and was admitted to the hospital with kidney failure. Emergency dialysis brought on cardiac arrest and she died.[2]

This woman in Britain was not alone. Since Lilly began marketing benoxaprofen overseas in October 1980, at least 96 people have died after taking it.[3] Others who took Oraflex for the debilitating effects of arthritis developed jaundice, liver failure, and phototoxicity (bringing burning, itching, and redness of the skin after exposure to sunlight). In addition, some Oraflex patients suffered heartburn, stomach pain, diarrhea, hives, breathing problems, and separation of their fingernails.[4]

Little of this information was made available to arthritis sufferers, enforcement officials, or the general public until after Oraflex was put on the market in the United States, although much of it was known to Lilly *before* the company launched its $12 million high-visibility U.S. marketing campaign in the spring of 1982. "Dear Doctor," began one of Lilly's promotional letters to the medical community, dated May 5, 1982, "Eli Lilly is pleased to announce that Oraflex TM (benoxaprofen) *is now available.* Oraflex is a new, *once-a-day,* non-steroidal anti-inflammatory agent for patients with osteoarthritis or rheumatoid arthritis."[5]

A series of these "Dear Doctor" letters was followed by 6,113 press packets (including 3,240 to newspapers, 942 to television stations and 1,059 to radio stations) that Lilly distributed to major news outlets around the country on May 19, 1982, announcing the advent of Oraflex. A Washington TV station ran a story on Lilly's new drug, using film footage supplied by Lilly that showed how arthritis destroys human joints. Other TV stations showed medical films of a monocyte, which Oraflex was alleged to affect in a manner beneficial to arthritis therapy.

The Washington TV news report caught the eye of federal law enforcement officials, who immediately called the company's Washington office and obtained copies of Lilly's press kit. At the time, Arthur Yellin was an enforcement official at the Food and Drug Administration (FDA). Reviewing the press kit, he found that the materials "minimized the drug's potential for adverse reactions, as well as the adverse reactions themselves." He also found that the company was overplaying the drug's alleged benefits.

"The materials," wrote Yellin in an internal FDA memo, "also went far beyond the approved labeling for the product into the realm of theoretical benefits of the drug and laboratory effects of unproven clinical significance in a manner which represented and suggested clinical benefits." Yellin was also disturbed by Lilly's failure to make clear the serious side effects that afflicted some Oraflex users in Great Britain, where the drug had been available for two years. News broadcasts completely neglected Oraflex's "potential for phototoxicity reactions" Yellin wrote, "and none mentioned the hepatotoxicity which was the subject of a May 8 *British Medical Journal* article."

Yellin concluded that although the materials in Lilly's kit were within the letter of the law, they were "less than ethical and outside the spirit of the Food, Drug and Cosmetic Act." Yet when he called Lilly's Washington representative, he asked for only minor modifications on future press packets, to which the Lilly representative agreed.[6]

Federal enforcement officials had reason to be especially concerned about heavy-handed promotional advertisements for a mass marketed anti-arthritic drug because of the nature of arthritis and the burden it puts on elderly Americans. A progressive and painful inflammatory disease of the joints, arthritis afflicts 32 million American adults and children. It may render affected parts of the body virtually immobile and nonfunctional. There is no cure for it, but for years the big drug companies have been marketing drugs, including aspirin, to lessen the inflammation and blunt the pain. There are more than 100 varieties of arthritis, but the drugs are aimed at the two most prevalent types. Rheumatoid arthritis, the most severe type, afflicts 6.5 million Americans; the more common type, osteoarthritis, afflicts 16 million, most of them elderly.

Because arthritics suffer severe and constant pain, they are a tantalizing target for drug companies eying a $711-million-dollar anti-arthritic drug market. Seeking respite from pain, many arthritics consume large numbers of aspirin tablets every day. But not everyone can tolerate aspirin's high level of acetylsalicylic acid, which sometimes leads to stomach problems and internal bleeding. Those with severe cases of arthritis are prescribed highly dangerous steroids such as hormones and cholesterol, or potentially toxic drugs such as penicillamine.

Until recent years, those not wishing to risk taking aspirin or steroids had nowhere to turn. Enter Eli Lilly and Oraflex. Looking for a drug they could count on to safely combat their daily agony, arthritics turned on their television sets in May 1982 and saw news reports of Lilly's new "non-steroidal anti-inflammatory agent for patients with osteoarthritis or rheumatoid arthritis." Millions saw hope for relief, and Lilly was about to connect with a big market.

However, Arthur Yellin's initial phone call to Lilly had touched off a more intensive investigation within the agency. On July 27, 1982, more than two and a half months after Lilly began its promotional campaign, the FDA sent a letter to Richard Wood, chairman and president of the Eli Lilly Company in Indianapolis.

In the letter, FDA official Jerome Halperin told Wood that since Yellin's initial contact in May, enforcement officials had studied the press kit and news broadcast in greater detail and found that it was "clearly evident from these sources that the dissemination of these promotional labeling pieces has resulted in communication of false and misleading representations and suggestions to a much greater degree than we had originally anticipated when we gave our verbal communications." Halperin further explained to Wood that

> We believe that the Press Kit and related materials have resulted in the communication of false and/or misleading concepts both to the general public and to members of the health care community. This has been accomplished through careful wording, selective emphasis, inappropriate use of headlines, and minimization of adverse information about the drug. These misconceptions and false impressions of safety and/or efficacy are clearly evident in many broadcasts and printed news items which resulted from the press kit, Press Conference and disseminations of related materials. They are not obviated by the presence of a modicum of balancing information inconspicuously located in the materials.

The FDA asked the company to send out new press releases "clearly setting forth the clinically verified information about the safety and efficacy of Oraflex and its limitations as currently recognized in the approved labeling."[7]

By mid-summer 1982, new information had surfaced in Washington, information that put Lilly into even hotter water. In England, where Oraflex had been on the market for two years (as Opren), doctors were reporting the problems caused. England's two major medical journals had printed 17 articles or letters describing 12 deaths in patients ranging from 57 to 88 years of age, 8 of the deaths due to a combination of liver and kidney damage; also 23 cases of jaundice, and phototoxicity in 100 percent of 14 patients carefully studied for this adverse effect.

In June 1982, Dr. Sidney Wolfe, director of Public Citizen's Health Research Group, cited the British reports of adverse reactions and charged that "Because there is no evidence that this drug [Oraflex] is any more effective than other drugs in the family of non-steroidal anti-inflammatory drugs (NSAID's) — a family that includes the inexpensive nonprescription drug aspirin — it has no unique compensating benefits to outweigh the serious hazards associated with its use." Wolfe called on Richard Schweiker, Secretary of the U.S. Department of Health and Human Services, to "withdraw approval for marketing benoxaprofen immediately — before any more Americans are exposed to this needless risk." He added that "there can be no excuse for proceeding with marketing of a drug no better than currently available drugs when studies have clearly found it to present a unique and considerable danger."[8]

Lilly reacted harshly. Edgar G. Davis, Lilly's vice president for corporate affairs, called Wolfe's claims "sensational" and "irresponsible." Davis claimed that although Oraflex had been linked with "abnormal liver functions and other side effects in a small proportion of patients taking the medicine," it had been used by thousands in clinical trials without reports of deaths.[9]

Lilly's initial response indicated the forceful counterattack that would follow against the consumer and public health groups that were challenging Oraflex — a counterattack that can be better understood in light of what Oraflex meant to the financial health of the company, rather than to the physical health of arthritic consumers. Financial analysts on Wall Street had predicted that the marketing of Oraflex would boost earnings and push Lilly's stock price upward. "Lilly, in the presence of Oraflex, had a superb opportunity to grow faster than the industry," said David H. MacCallum, a financial analyst of the pharmaceutical industry for Paine Webber. In early 1982, MacCallum had projected that Oraflex would reach annual sales of $250 million by 1985, and as soon as Lilly began its heavy promotion of the drug in May, sales skyrocketed. In the first 21 days, 64,000 prescriptions were filled for Oraflex in the United States.[10]

The battle over whether to ban Oraflex from the U.S. market was clearly only part of a larger war shaping up between consumer and public health groups on the one side and the pharmaceutical industry on the other. Early in his first term, President Reagan had assigned his vice president, George Bush, to head a task force on regulatory relief with an eye to weakening the federal laws and the enforcement of those laws governing corporate America. Bush's support for weak law enforcement against corporate criminals was disguised in the rhetoric of a "government/business partnership." "I think we've started to see this philosophical shift," Bush told a drug industry convention in mid-June 1982, "the end or the beginning of the end of this adversary relationship. Government shouldn't be an adversary. It ought to be a partner."[11]

George Bush was not exactly a disinterested observer when it came to Lilly drugs, the drug industry, and the FDA. Before he joined the Reagan administration, George Bush was a member of the board of directors at Eli Lilly. He also held $180,000 worth of Lilly stock when he took office. By the fall of 1982, it began to look as though Bush's effort to get the government to embrace the pharmaceutical industry was succeeding. For the first six months of fiscal 1982, there was a 66.4 percent decrease in total FDA law enforcement actions compared with a similar interval before the Reagan administration took office: only 178 enforcement actions in those first six months, compared with an average of 500 enforcement actions taken during each six-month period between fiscal 1977 and fiscal 1980. "This drastic decrease in government policing of the industries FDA is supposed to regulate," commented Wolfe, "is an open invitation to drug companies and food companies to violate federal law, thus risking the health and lives of 230 million Americans."[12]

Lilly had built a record of recidivism unmatched in an industry that ranked as one of the three—along with oil/chemicals and autos—most criminogenic industries in the United States. An unpublished 1979 FDA study on the completeness of adverse reaction reports sent to the FDA showed Lilly to have the worst record of the ten drug companies studied. A total of 61.8 percent of the 324 reports of serious adverse reactions that Lilly sent to the FDA failed to include either the date the drug was started, or the date of the onset of the reaction. According to drug law experts, this information is important in order to establish the causal role of the drug in the reported adverse reactions.[13]

Lilly also was involved in marketing Darvon, a drug that had been criticized as "less effective than aspirin in killing pain [but] more common even than heroin in killing people." In 1979, a federal police force asked doctors to avoid prescribing Darvon and urged patients not to ask for it.[14]

Six weeks after the first call for a ban was made, no action had been taken. In the same six weeks, new information about the drug's adverse side effects came to light, thus strengthening the case for the ban. In Britain, where Oraflex had been on the market for 20 months (sold under the trade name Opren), reports of 45 deaths, including 19 caused by gastrointestinal hemorrhage or perforated ulcer as well as 19 deaths from liver and kidney damage, had reached the British government. In addition, a 47-year-old American woman who died had liver damage her doctor believed was caused by Oraflex.

In reiterating his call on Schweiker to take Oraflex off the U.S. market, Wolfe warned that if Schweiker did not act quickly, Wolfe would ask the courts to force him to do so. "It is time for you to quickly decide," wrote Wolfe, "whether it is more important to protect the financial health of Lilly or to spare the lives of patients, mainly the elderly, in this country. If you have not responded to our petition by the end of this month [July 1982], we will file suit in the Federal District Court to force you to follow the laws instead of the pressures of a large drug company."[15]

By the end of July, Schweiker had still not acted, and on August 2, 1982, the National Council of Senior Citizens, the American Public Health Association, and Public Citizen's Health Research Group joined together and sued Schweiker, claiming that he wasn't fulfilling his duties under law and asking that the court force him to act.

On August 4, 1982, the British government suspended sales of Oraflex. Later that day, Eli Lilly decided that rather than risk having Oraflex pulled from the U.S. market, the company would "voluntarily" do the job. "Dear Pharmacist," began the Lilly mailgram to druggists around the country, "Eli Lilly has advised the Food and Drug Administration of its intention to suspend immediately the distribution and sale of Oraflex (benoxaprofen)." But while advising pharmacists to "please set aside full and partial packages of Oraflex that you have in inventory," Lilly at the same time refused to admit that Oraflex posed an unusual danger to arthritic patients. This position was clearly stated in Lilly's August 5 mailgram:

> After careful review of all applicable scientific and clinical information, the company continues to believe that the drug is safe and effective when used as directed. During the last several weeks, the safety of Oraflex has been the subject of an unprecedented public controversy in both the United States and the United Kingdom, which culminated in the action by the United Kingdom Health ministry to suspend for 90 days the product license for the drug pending a review by the Committee on Safety of Medicines.

It is our opinion that, in this environment, rational decisions regarding the use of the drug are not possible. Because our principal concern has been and continues to be the well-being of the 31 million arthritis sufferers in the United States, we believe that the medical profession and the arthritis sufferers are best served by this action.[16]

Despite this and other similar public relations disclaimers, evidence was mounting that, in fact, Oraflex was not "safe and effective when used as directed"; and, in addition, that Lilly knew that Oraflex was a dangerous drug *before* it placed it on the market in May 1982, and even before it obtained FDA approval in April. As early as September 1981, FDA investigator Michael Hensley recommended that his agency pursue criminal prosecution of Eli Lilly because of the company's failure to report promptly to federal enforcement officials the adverse reactions that had occurred before the marketing of Oraflex and other Lilly drugs and for its failure to submit promptly postmarketing adverse reactions reports on two other Lilly drugs (Darvon and Monensin).

The top cops at FDA rejected Hensley's recommendation that Lilly be brought to justice, but the victims could no longer wait for federal enforcement agents to act. More than 100 lawsuits have been filed charging the company with negligence in the marketing of Oraflex. Depositions of Lilly executives taken in connection with these lawsuits revealed something more than mere negligence. The depositions revealed that a Lilly executive knew of 29 deaths among overseas users of the drug *before* the FDA approved it for sale on April 19, 1982. Morton Mintz reported in the *Washington Post* in July 1983 that Lilly vice president Dr. W. Ian H. Shedden testified that prior to April 19, 1982, when the FDA approved Oraflex, he had been informed of 29 deaths among the 750,000 users of the drug overseas, but did not report that to the FDA until after the FDA approval.[17]

The Shedden deposition was taken in connection with a $15 million lawsuit against Lilly brought in Atlanta by Clarence Borom. Borom's mother, Lola T. Jones, died at the age of 81 after being given Oraflex in a Georgia nursing home. At the trial, Richard D. Wood, chairman and chief executive officer of Lilly, testified that he personally decided to launch Oraflex onto the U.S. market despite seeing a report linking Oraflex to the deaths of five elderly women in Northern Ireland.[18] Borom's attorney, C. Neal Pope, in his closing argument, asked the jury to impose a $100 million punitive damage award against Lilly to "send a message" to the drug industry to behave responsibly and ethically. Pope argued that if it should be considered right to punish "one man with a pistol who goes into a 7-Eleven," it is also right for society to punish "the man in a custom tailored suit" who, making decisions based on "greed and avarice" in his "corporate tower, can kill people around the world."[19] On November 22, 1983, the jury returned a $6 million punitive damage award against Lilly.[20]

The fact that Lilly knew about the British deaths and injuries before the company marketed Oraflex in the United States in apparent violation of federal law did not intrude on George Bush's mission of getting the government off the backs of the pharmaceutical industry. What is unclear is the role if any that Bush, as a former member of Lilly's board of directors, played in this episode. In September Sidney Wolfe raised this very issue. "Every day you fail to initiate prosecution of Lilly," he told Schweiker, "adds to the concern that this is because of Vice President Bush's former directorship in that company and the fact that he held $180,000 in its stock when he took office."[21]

Finally, with public pressure mounting, the Justice Department belatedly and reluctantly moved in. On August 21, 1985, Lilly pleaded guilty to 25 misdemeanor counts of failing to notify the FDA of numerous deaths and injuries among overseas users of Oraflex. William I. Shedden, the company's chief medical officer, pleaded no contest to 15 misdemeanor counts and was fined $15,000. The company was fined $25,000.[22]

But the Justice Department prosecution raised more questions than it answered. Why, for example, did senior Justice officials overrule staff attorneys who recommended that three Lilly executives be prosecuted, not just one? Why did the Justice Department charge Lilly and Shedden only with misdemeanors even though it had evidence indicating that Lilly and its officers intentionally violated the law?

Following the announcement of the guilty pleas, Richard Wood, Lilly's chairman, told reporters that "the [Justice] Department has made no charge that Lilly . . . intentionally violated the law in its handling of the Oraflex matter" and that "the Department's decision puts to rest any speculation regarding intentional misconduct by the company or its employees."

But an 18-page report prepared by Justice Department prosecutors and attached to Lilly's guily plea reveals a number of specific occasions when Lilly knew of overseas deaths and adverse reactions and had an opportunity to report them to the FDA, but did not report them or mention them in the labeling. The report found that:

- Beginning in 1974, a Lilly employee in the United Kingdom compiled quarterly summaries of significant adverse reaction reports received by Lilly in that country.
- Lilly was kept regularly informed by telex and telephone, not only of reports of overseas adverse reactions, but also of the method and timing of sending such reports to regulatory authorities.
- In January 1982, Dr. Shedden and two other Lilly physicians in Indianapolis received a U.K. government printout that listed numerous adverse reactions associated with Oraflex use in the U.K., including 26 serious liver disorders (two of which were fatal) and 23 other fatalities.
- On February 5, 1982, information concerning foreign adverse reactions was presented at a meeting of Lilly executives in Indianapolis. A special report brought from the U.K. tabulated "serious" reactions associated with the use of Oraflex, including 27 kidney/liver reactions, 5 of which were fatal.[23]

Although Lilly's chairman saw the criminal charges as a vindication, Public Citizen's Dr. Wolfe saw it in a different light. The report showed that the company and some of its executives knew about adverse reactions and deaths, yet failed to report these to the FDA. The Justice Department's 18-page report proved to Wolfe that "the people in this company ought to be put in jail." That Lilly was charged with misdemeanors instead of felonies, that only one individual was charged, and that no one went to jail, tells us more about the politics of prosecuting corporate crime than do the damning facts of the Oraflex case.

Notes

1. "The Oraflex Fix," *Multinational Monitor*, August 15, 1985, p. 4.

2. Letter from Edgar Davis, vice-president for corporate affairs, Eli Lilly, to Richard S. Schweiker, Secretary, Dept. of Health and Human Services, July 2, 1982.

3. "First Oraflex Trial Begins; Stakes High," by Morton Mintz. *Washington Post*, November 8, 1983, p.   .

4. Letter from Eve Bargmann M.D. and Sidney Wolfe M.D. to Richard S. Schweiker, Secretary, Dept. of Health and Human Services, June 17, 1982.

5. Dear Doctor letter from Pharmaceutical Division, Eli Lilly and Company. May 5, 1982.

6. Memorandum of meeting May 21, 1982, between Arthur Yellin and a representative of the Eli Lilly Corporation.

7. Regulatory letter July 27, 1982, from Jerome A. Halperin, acting director, Office of Drugs, to Richard D. Wood, chairman of the board and president, Eli Lilly Corp.

8. Letter from Public Citizen's Health Research Group to Richard Schweiker, Secretary, Dept. of Health and Human Services, June 17, 1982.

9. "Group Seeks Ban on New Arthritis Medication," by Associated Press. *Washington Post*, June 18, 1982.

10. PCHRG letter from Wolfe to Schweiker, June 17, 1982.

11. Letter from PCHRG to John D. Dingell, Chairman of the House Committee on Energy and Commerce, August 17, 1982.

12. Ibid.

13. Letter from Wolfe to Schweiker, September 28, 1982.

14. *Everybody's Business, An Almanac.* ed. by Milton Moskowitz. Harper & Row, New York, 1980, p. 227.

15. Letter from Eve Bargmann M.D. and Sidney Wolfe M.D. to Secretary Schweiker, June 17, 1982.

16. Dear Pharmacist Mailgram from Pharmaceutical Division, Eli Lilly Company, August 5, 1982.

17. "Lilly Official Knew of Deaths Before U.S. Approved Drug," by Morton Mintz. *Washington Post*, July 22, 1983.

18. "Lilly Chairman Decided to Sell Oraflex Despite Death Reports," by Morton Mintz. *Washington Post*, November 13, 1983.

19. "Deliberation Continues Against Lilly In the $100 Million Oraflex Suit," by Morton Mintz. *Washington Post*, November 19, 1983.

20. "$6 Million Award Made in Lilly Suit," *New York Times*, November 22, 1983.

21. Letter from Wolfe to Schweiker, September 28, 1982.

22. Department of Justice Press Release, August 21, 1985.

23. *USA v. Eli Lilly. USA v. Wiliam Ian H. Shedden,* Factual Basis for the Pleas. No. 1P85 53CR Southern District of Indiana.

27
Park to Reverse

"The car ran over my left leg. I watched as the car was rolling toward the main highway with my baby in the front seat. I felt an overwhelming fear that can't be put into words."

> —Connie Bartholomew, describing her runaway
> Lincoln Continental[1]

CONNIE BARTHOLOMEW WAS one of the lucky ones. In October 1976, Bartholomew was loading groceries into her 1973 Ford Lincoln Continental. She had left the car in Park, with the engine running and the hand brake set. Suddenly, the car jumped into Reverse, triggering the parking brake to release. The open left front door knocked Bartholomew to the ground and her leg was run over by the car as it took off toward the highway with her baby son, Jordan, in the front seat.

Her baby suffered moderate injuries as the car came to a crashing halt after striking several parked cars. The baby later developed a rare crippling bone disease. Freakish as it might seem, the type of accident that crushed Bartholomew's leg was not an isolated occurrence; it had caused death or injuries to hundreds of Americans who happened to be in the way of a runaway Ford automobile. Early in the 1960s, Ford knew of a problem that allowed the transmission to slip from park to reverse, triggering a release of the parking brake. If the car happened to be running at the time the transmission slipped, it would begin running in reverse, threatening those not agile enough to get out of the way.

When Connie Bartholomew took Ford to court and demanded compensation for her injuries, Ford lawyers brought with them a simulated model of a transmission plus a steering column, transmission shift, linkage, and parking brake. Bartholomew's lawyers shrewdly used this Ford exhibit to show the jury exactly how easy it was for the Ford transmission to slip from park to reverse. Bartholomew's attorneys placed the transmission shift on a landing between park and reverse. The simulated door was then slammed shut, causing the transmission to jump dramatically into reverse and release the parking brake. Convinced by this re-enactment that the Ford transmission was defective, the jury awarded Bartholomew $50,000 to compensate for her injured leg. Later, her son Jordan would settle his case against Ford for $350,000.[2]

Despite the more than 400 mostly elderly and young Americans who have been killed and thousands more injured by runaway Fords, the Ford Motor Company has never admitted, and to this day remains unconvinced that, their automobiles are dangerously defective. And because federal police authorities have not taken seriously warnings from experts both within their own departments and from the outside, more unsuspecting Americans will be killed or injured by the 13 million defective Fords still on the highway.

The fact that most of the persons killed are elderly or young adds an especially gruesome quality to these freakish Ford transmission cases. In April 1978, Millie Lawder was just two years away from her 100th birthday when a 1970 Mercury Monterey rolled down a driveway. The open door knocked her down, fracturing her femur. Lawder died in the hospital less than three weeks later.

Brent Goheen was one year old when, in September 1977, Brent's mother was backing her 1977 Lincoln Continental down her driveway. When she saw her son start toward the car and fall down, Mrs. Goheen stopped the car and got out to help him, but the car started rolling backwards. Before she could get back into the rolling car and stop it, the left front door hit Brent, knocking him under the left front wheel, which crushed his head.

It is not even necessary for a Ford engine to be running for the automobile to become a vehicle of destruction. On May 25, 1978, five-year-old Rick Knighton was playing at the end of his driveway with his friend Jack Saunders. A 1978 Ford Mercury Zephyr that had been parked in the driveway with the *key out of the ignition* and the *emergency parking brake on* began to roll backwards and struck both Knighton and his friend. Knighton was killed when the car rolled up on his head and chest.[3]

In 1980, the Center for Auto Safety (CFAS) compiled a list of the 116 persons killed in Ford transmission accidents whose age could be verified. The Center found that 7 of the victims were 1 year old or less; 16, or 13.9 percent, were 9 years old or less; and 78, or 67.4 percent of those killed, were over 50 years old. "The victims are the old and the very young, those least able to protect themselves," Clarence Ditlow, director of the Center told a federal police panel investigating the Ford transmissions in 1980. "The defect in the Ford automatic transmissions is particularly lethal because it strikes motorists when they are most unaware — unloading groceries, opening or closing a garage door or gate, getting in or out of the car, picking up the mail or the newspaper, helping a stranded motorist, and waiting in a parked car."[4]

That a defective transmission could kill so many innocent persons should not have come as a surprise to Ford. As early as 1962, after an 18-year-old Los Angeles parking lot attendant lost his leg when a Ford slipped from park to reverse and crashed into him as he sat on his lounge chair, juries from around the country have been ruling the transmission defective and awarding sizable amounts to unsuspecting victims. A jury awarded the parking lot attendant $235,000.[5]

In addition to these early lawsuits, internal Ford Motor Company documents show that Ford was aware of the transmission problem long before consumer groups and federal authorities began pressing for a recall. On December 8, 1971, D.R. Dixon, principal engineer of Ford's Chassis Safety Engineering Department, wrote:

> The purpose of this letter is to alert you to the increasing number of customer complaint letters pertaining to the transmission control operation and recommend consideration of a design revision. The primary mode of an alleged performance problem occurs when the customer leaves the vehicle with the engine running, thinking he has moved the shift lever into "park" position, and the transmission subsequently engages in reverse. *We are now receiving approximately six letters per month of this type.* (Emphasis added.)[6]

It is also clear from a Dixon memo dated June 30, 1971, that Ford was aware of the nature of its transmission problem:

> Current Chassis shift lever detent design permits transmission lever placement on a "land" between a positive park position and reverse position with the possibility of vehicle vibration moving the lever from park to reverse in an unattended vehicle. . . . Present customer usage patterns indicate that *this condition of careless shift lever actuation is occurring frequently in the field with high accident incidence.* (Emphasis added.)[7]

In January 1972, taking heed of Dixon's warning, the Product Development Group of Ford's Chassis Division recommended a program action to "redesign column detent plate between park and reverse position to insure the trans[mission] will not jump out of park position when customers do not fully engage present park slot in detent." This design change would have eliminated an estimated 90 percent of the park to reverse failures. It could have cost Ford only three cents per vehicle. But Ford refused to adopt it.[8]

In June of 1978, Franklin Hare, a Ford engineer, was performing an electrical test on a Ford prototype with the vehicle's engine idling at high speed. Suddenly, the prototype vehicle slipped out of park and ran over Hare's ankle and took off at 25 mph toward the high speed track. A second Ford technician stopped the runaway Ford by running it down with his van.[9]

In July of 1977, with the death toll climbing, with the evidence of Ford's own knowledge and inaction growing, federal authorities launched an investigation of the defective Ford transmissions. At the time, law enforcement officials at the National Highway Traffic Safety Administration (NHTSA) had evidence of at least 31 park to reverse accidents that resulted in 14 injuries and 2 deaths. But by August 1978, the number had grown to 777 accidents, 259 injuries, and 23 deaths. While consumer groups, including the Center for Auto Safety, were urging NHTSA chief Joan Claybrook to take "immediate action to secure a defect recall," Claybrook didn't believe there was enough evidence to do so. Instead, on August 29, NHTSA issued a Consumer Advisory warning to consumers to take special precautions to lessen or prevent the chances of Fords slipping from park to reverse, including shutting off the engine, firmly engaging the transmission's park position, and setting the emergency brake.[10]

Since the warning was not sent out to each individual Ford owner, however, it is likely that many Ford owners never heard about it. And shutting off the engine didn't necessarily guarantee that if the transmission went from park to reverse, and the car was parked on a hill or a slanted driveway, that the car, rolling in reverse, wouldn't kill an innocent bystander, as in fact later happened. NHTSA's recommendation of setting the emergency brake could not have saved Connie Bartholomew's leg or her baby's collarbone, even if they had heard the warning—for, as Bartholomew's attorneys showed, the transmission popping from park to reverse often triggered the release of the parking brake.

By April 1980, the Center for Auto Safety, increasingly alarmed by the failure of the NHTSA to order a recall, released a discharge petition demanding that Claybrook reach a decision on the three-year "investigation" of the park to reverse defect on the Ford vehicles. The Center's director threatened to sue the police agency if Claybrook didn't "carry out [her] duty" within two weeks. Ditlow cited one case that had just come to the Center's attention. At the Toronto International Airport, a 1977 Ford pickup truck slipped from park to reverse and struck an airport employee, two baggage carts, and a Boeing 737 jet, causing an estimated $150,000 to $200,000 in damages.

Just four days after filing its petition, the Center learned that an 18-month-old Wisconsin child drowned when his mother's 1977 Thunderbird slipped out of park, sped down a driveway in reverse, crossed a street, and plunged into a pond roughly 30 yards away. The Center wrote to the attorney general of Wisconsin requesting that the state bring charges against Ford for "homicide by reckless conduct" in the death of the young boy. (At the time, Ford had just been cleared of reckless homicide charges in Indiana in connection with the deaths of three teenage girls in their Ford Pinto.)[11]

Still, federal enforcement officials dragged their feet, and Ditlow's two weeks passed with no federal action. Claybrook issued apologetic statements that did nothing to prevent further injuries. "[T]he unfortunate lapse of time since the opening of this investigation," read one such statement, "reflects the complexity of this case rather than any lack of interest on the part of the agency [NHTSA]."[12] At least Claybrook's statements indicated sincerity, but others within her own agency appeared to be less than sincere in their commitment to highway traffic safety. Frank Berndt, who in April 1979 was NHTSA's associate administrator for enforcement, told *Fortune* magazine that if NHTSA were "faced with a massive recall, say 15 million cars, we might try something else, rather than destroying the industry."[13]

NHTSA's failure to act in a timely fashion was costing additional lives and injuries, so on May 29, 1980, Ditlow sued the law enforcement agency to compel a recall of 26 million Ford vehicles with automatic park to reverse transmission defects. Within two weeks of the filing of this lawsuit, NHTSA notified Ford that it had made an initial determination of defect in all 1970–79 Ford vehicles equipped with automatic transmission. A recall would cover 16 million vehicles, by far the largest vehicle recall in history.

In issuing its finding of defect, NHTSA revealed over 23,000 consumer complaints, 6,000 accidents, 1,710 injuries, and 98 fatalities resulting from the park to reverse transmission defect. The report concluded that the Ford automatic transmission ". . . contained characteristics that can result in inadvertent vehicle movement." After three years of "investigating" this much-publicized problem, during which time an additional 47 people were killed by runaway Fords, federal enforcement officials had finally determined that a defect existed.[14] The next step was to get the cars off the road and to implement the three cents per car modification that had been suggested by Ford's own engineers almost a decade earlier.

Still, Ford refused to acknowledge that its car was defective. From the beginning of the controversy, Ford blamed the drivers of the cars, not the transmission. The driver was not putting the car firmly in park, and when the car was not firmly in park, of course there was a chance that it could slip back into reverse. But this defense could not explain away a very embarrassing (to Ford) statistic: Fords jump from park to reverse fourteen times more often than Chrysler cars and 12 times more often than General Motors cars.[15]

Was Ford saying that it had cornered the vast majority of careless drivers in America? "The simple fact is that Ford is factually wrong," Ditlow told a NHTSA-sponsored hearing on the transmission defect. "How else can one explain that no other manufacturer even comes close to Ford in number of accidents of automatic transmissions jumping from park to reverse?"[16]

Throughout the park to reverse controversy, Ford relied on its "the driver's the problem" defense. The company called Claybrook's finding of a defect "shocking and irresponsible" and criticized NHTSA's method of collecting complaints and its "inaccurate data and faulty analysis."[17]

Ford charged that the large number of complaints that NHTSA received was due to the fact that NHTSA and consumer groups gave widespread publicity to the defect. It was the publicity that was causing thousands of consumers to write letters of complaints about their Ford transmissions, not the defect, Ford charged. American consumers, hearing of a defect, decided that something was wrong with their Fords, too. This explanation didn't convince Ditlow, who was the expert in receiving consumer complaints about automobiles. "It has been the Center's experience," Ditlow told the NHTSA hearing on the transmission defect, "that publicity of a defect will not generate failures but can only uncover what exists."[18]

As the deadline neared for a decision on a recall, Ford officials became irritated with Ditlow's responses and charged that the Center was "picking on" the Ford Motor Company. (Ford would later charge the Center with waging a "vendetta" against the company.[19]) Ditlow found this charge amusing. "The Center is pleased to find that a $40 billion corporation that spends more in advertising every two hours than the Center's annual budget believes we can pick on it," Ditlow said, "but any credit for discovery of this defect must go to Ford Motor Co. itself."[20]

Ditlow and the attorneys representing Ford victims had the facts to prove their case and to support NHTSA's finding of defect, but Ford had on its side the agency's overseer and boss, Department of Transportation Secretary Neil Goldschmidt. Rather than order a recall for repair, as NHTSA recommended, Goldschmidt overruled the safety agency and instead decided to mail warning stickers to 20 million owners of 1966–80 Ford vehicles with the defective automatic transmissions. Ditlow, predictably angered by the secretary's action, called the sticker remedy "illegal" and "a farce" and condemned Goldschmidt's action as a "cave-in to Ford's unconscionable demands that no more than a precautionary label be applied to these vehicles."

(In 1985, Donald Peterson, who in 1981 was president of Ford and currently is chairman of the board, went to Oregon to lend a hand in Neil Goldschmidt's successful campaign for governor.)

The warning sticker that was mailed out to Ford owners, designated to be placed on the vehicle dashboard or sun visor, warned that before leaving the vehicle, the driver should: (1) verify that the shift lever is indeed in park; (2) engage the parking brake completely; and (3) turn off the engine. The sticker further warned that the vehicle might move unexpectedly if these steps are not taken. In short, it was the same warning issued by the NHTSA three years earlier, except that in this case, the warning was mailed out rather than issued in a press release.

Although this method of warning did reach more people directly concerned with the problem (i.e. Ford owners), it did little to cut the toll of death and injury. Since the sticker campaign began, an additional 150 persons have been killed by runaway Fords and more than 2,000 have been injured.[21] The sticker campaign failed for a number of reasons, among them: even where owners placed their labels on their cars and followed the instructions, the cars fail to hold or engage in park because there is a mechanical defect; Ford dealers were not putting the labels on used Fords; less than 10 percent of consumers were placing the warning labels on their cars; and Ford downplayed the seriousness of the defect.

Even Ford admitted (in a Ford Task Force engineering report) that "past history indicates that drivers tend to ignore subtle warning signals and visible aggressive warning signals."

The federal enforcement chiefs had let the company off the hook (pending litigation that challenges Goldschmidt's overturning of the NHTSA finding of defect), and no matter what the evidence, even if it was compiled by its own engineers, the company was not about to do what the law enforcement officials didn't require it to do.

This hard-line position may boomerang on Ford. Consumer dissatisfaction with the company is high. A CFAS survey found that of those who experienced transmission failures, 75 percent indicated they would not buy another Ford. "We have driven nothing but Fords since 1954," wrote Clarence P. Aday, of Lima, Ohio, to the CFAS, "but unless Ford Motor Company will admit liability and publicly proclaim the transmission is defective, and fix this 1977 wagon, I will never buy another Ford car or any Ford product."

Mounting consumer dissatisfaction had only a diffuse, unmeasurable impact on the company's treasury. More important to Ford accountants was the cost of the lawsuits that Ford victims were bringing in increasing numbers. In March 1982, Ford reported to the Securities and Exchange Commission that damages sought from pending park-to-reverse cases totaled around $1.7 billion. In one Texas case, a jury awarded a Ford victim $4.4 million, including $4 million punitive damages. The award was upheld by a Texas appeals court, which cited "interoffice memos and letters which showed that Ford was aware of the problem beginning in 1971" and made clear that "Ford did nothing to affirmatively alleviate the dangerous condition."[22]

So while Ford's defect problem continues to injure and kill Americans, it also reduces the financial stability of the nation's second largest automaker. For every case Ford wins, it loses or settles 22. The average cost of each of these settlements is around $100,000 for cases involving personal injury—and this does not include Ford's legal expenses.

Ford changed the design of its transmission beginning in its 1980 model-year cars. It would have saved the company millions of dollars had Ford listened to its own engineers and fixed the cars in 1972. Instead, Ford executives chose a short-term strategy of penny-wise, pound-foolish.

Notes

1. "Plaintiff Wins $50,000 in Ford Park to Reverse Suit," *IMPACT*, vol. V, no. 2. (November/December 1979).

2. Personal communication from Clarence Ditlow, director, Center for Auto Safety, November 16, 1986.

3. Statement of Clarence Ditlow III, director, Center for Auto Safety, before the National Highway Traffic Safety Administration, on Defects in Ford Automatic Transmissions, Washington, D.C., August 21, 1980.

4. Ibid.

5. "Running in Reverse," by Karen Brennan. *Mother Jones*, June 1980.

6. Personal communication from Ditlow, November 16, 1986.

7. Ibid.

8. Ibid.

9. "Center Urges NHTSA Investigation of Ford 'Park to Reverse' Defect be Concluded by a Recall Order," *IMPACT*, Washington, D.C., September 10, 1978. See also, "Running in Reverse," Brennan.

10. *IMPACT*, September 10, 1978.

11. "Center Petitions for Decision on Ford Park to Reverse," *IMPACT*, May 1980.

12. "Center Continues Pressuring NHTSA on Ford Park to Reverse Defect," *IMPACT*, July 8, 1979.

13. "Running in Reverse," Brennan.

14. "NHTSA Finds Ford Transmission Defective After Center Sues," *IMPACT*, vol. V, no. 5, May-June, 1980.

15. "Running in Reverse," Brennan.

16. Personal communication from Ditlow, November 16, 1986.

17. "Ford Denies US Charges on Transmissions," *Washington Star*, June 30, 1980.

18. Personal communication from Ditlow, November 16, 1986.

19. "Center for Auto Safety Faults Administration," *Washington Post*, January 1, 1982.

20. Personal communication from Ditlow, November 16, 1986.

21. Personal communication from Dan Howell, Center for Auto Safety, November 19, 1986.

22. "A Cheaper Idea—Recall Not Stonewall," Center for Auto Safety. Washington D.C., September 1, 1981, p. 6.

28
PBB

"The longer I lived on that farm the worse it became. After a time there were no worms in the soil. There were no field mice, no rats, no rabbits, no grasshoppers. As the cattle were dying, the cats and dogs were dying too. A fully grown cat would live only six weeks on that farm. Our three dogs went crazy. Our neighbors had bees that were dead in the hives. The frogs were dead in the streams. There was a five-acre swamp that used to croak at night so you could hardly sleep. Then it was silent. And it was a long time before I knew why."

—Gerald Wlotjer, a farmer from Coopersville, Michigan, describing the effects of the chemical PBB on his farm[1]

THE RATS WERE GONE and that meant something was wrong. Long ago, the farmers in Michigan stopped trying to get rid of the rats. They quickly learned that where there was grain, there were rodents, especially rats. It was accepted as part of life on the farm. Now, in the spring of 1974, the rats were gone and the farmers were perplexed. There was still grain, but no rats.

Rick Halbert, a dairy farmer from near Battle Creek, noticed the rats had disappeared from his farm. But one of Halbert's employees mentioned that he had spotted a pack of rats far away from the grain supply. Halbert went to see for himself. In a crawlspace, underneath the farmhouse kitchen, he spotted a nest of them. Halbert went over to a feed pile, grabbed a handful of feed pellets, took them back to the farmhouse, and scattered them into the crawlspace. One week later the rats were gone.

This was just one of a series of incidents that fueled Halbert's suspicion that something was wrong with the feed that he and other farmers in central Michigan had purchased for their cows, chickens, sheep, and hogs. Halbert's story is told by Joyce Eggington in *The Poisoning of Michigan*.[2] The Halberts had worked their Bradford township farm for more than a century, and for many of those years had purchased grain and feed from the Farm Bureau Services, a statewide farmers' organization. Although Rick Halbert was a member of the co-op, the organization was not what it seemed to have been in his grandfather's days. Michigan Farm Bureau, the majority owner, had become too bureaucratized and politicized, looking more to the bottom line than to the needs of the member farmers for whom it was created.

Despite these shortcomings, Halbert worked closely with the Farm Bureau staff and was a fan of the plant's best feed supplement for milking cows, Dairy Ration 402. In the spring of 1973, Halbert suggested an improvement: add magnesium oxide to 402. The soil in central Michigan was low in magnesium and the dairy cattle needed magnesium to prevent against wheat pasture fever, a potentially fatal disease. The company accepted Halbert's idea and began mixing eight pounds of magnesium oxide into every ton of feed.

The new magnesium oxide-enriched 402 proved a hit with the cows: their butterfat output was up. Halbert ordered 65 tons of the feed betweeen the end of August and the beginning of September. The first shipment was delivered September 4, 1973.

By September 20, Halbert was worried. Because of the close relationship between a dairy farmer and his cows—the farmer and his family are economically dependent on the cows' capacity to produce milk, calf, and meat—it is said that good farmers acquire a Zenlike understanding of their sensitive animals. Even the most subtle behavioral change in the animal may suggest that something is wrong. Halbert immediately recognized that the cows were losing their appetites and realized that unless the problem was quickly solved, he would be faced with decreased milk production, which could pinch his farm's slim profit margin.

At first, Halbert focused on the corn he was feeding the cows. Michigan had suffered through a poor corn crop and because of the cold weather, some of the corn had molded. Cows have ultra-sensitive digestive systems, and Halbert thought that maybe moldy corn was causing his cows to lose their appetites. But the loss of appetite was only the first in a number of symptoms that could not be explained by moldy corn alone: the cows looked mangy; they had mangy hair, thickened skin, and diarrhea; and they were emaciated. The pregnant ones were losing most of their calves to spontaneous abortions. Those calves that lived suffered birth deformities, uterine problems, loss of hair, and a heightened sensitivity to disease. On September 20, when Halbert first noticed the loss of appetite, his cows were producing 13,000 pounds of milk per day. By October 8, the production level dropped to 8,000 pounds per day.

There was little doubt in Halbert's mind that something in the feed was causing the problems. On the average farm, cows would become lackadaisical, weak, and mangy due to poor husbandry or improper care, but the Halbert farm was a modern, efficient, tightly run operation. Rick Halbert was carrying on a tradition of a century of responsible farming. The Halbert name was well-respected in farming circles in central Michigan. To prove that his farm was well managed, to save his herd from wasting away, and to cut his financial losses, Halbert was determined to find the cause and find it quickly.

He soon realized that the cows were suffering from something in the 402 feed that he had purchased from the Farm Bureau. Halbert asked the Michigan Department of Agriculture (MDA) to test a sample of the feed. MDA agreed, and fed five mice a ground up portion of 402 and fed a second group of five mice the normal grain. The first group ate the 402 cautiously, and within two weeks, all five were dead. The others ate the normal grain and lived. Halbert took the results of his test to the Michigan Farm Bureau in late December 1973. He told the people at the Farm Bureau about his problems with the cows, how the calves were dying, and the results of the MDA mice test. By this time, Halbert had lost $40,000 due to the herd's illness. If he could show that they were sick due to the feed, the liability would rest with Farm Bureau Services, the supplier. "From now on this is no longer just our problem," Halbert told FBS. "It's your problem too."

But the Farm Bureau didn't agree. They told Halbert that he was the only farmer complaining about the problem, and implied that it was Halbert's poor management of the farm that was to blame. "After perusal of all the tests, history, and clinical signs," read an internal MFS memo titled "Halbert Dairy Problem," "I am unable to conclusively indict the feed. I have a feeling that Rick's feeding and management programs have contributed to the problem."

Unknown to Halbert at the time, other Michigan farmers were experiencing similar difficulties with their cows. Many suspected the feed was the culprit, went to FBS, and were told, as Halbert was told, that their problem was unique. Many of these farmers, proud of their long histories of successful dairy farm management, took this as a personal and professional rebuke. They were reluctant to discuss the situation with neighbors. By pointing a finger at the farmers, FBS had successfully shifted responsibility away from itself.

Unlike most of the other affected farmers, Rick Halbert did not become reluctant to discuss his farming operation. Instead, by applying his chemistry background, he started an investigation of the 65 tons of 402 feed that he had purchased from the Farm Bureau. During the winter of 1973–74, Halbert spent hundreds of hours searching for an answer to the problem that was slowly destroying his livelihood. He began by sending samples of the feed to research labs around the country, asking that they search for a contaminant and report back to him. He contacted the US Department of Agriculture (USDA) Research Station at Ames, Iowa; the Michigan Department of Agriculture; Michigan State University; the Wisconsin Alumni Research Fund; the USDA's research station at Beltsville, Maryland; and the people who sold him the feed, Farm Bureau Services Inc.

Halbert believed that a toxic chemical had somehow been mixed in with the grain at the MFS mixing plant outside Battle Creek and that this contaminant was causing his cows to become ill. Since he had little idea as to the nature of the chemical, and since there were approximately 30,000 chemicals from which to choose, Halbert was effectively asking a researcher to find a needle in a haystack.

Those who agreed to test the feed produced some intriguing findings: there was virtually no magnesium oxide at all in the 402 feed, even though the Farm Bureau sold it as magnesium oxide-enriched. Researchers also found an indication of the presence of a substance similar to the toxic polychlorinated biphenyls (PCBs).

When the feed was run through a gas chromatograph, unusual peaks would appear on the resulting graph. The peaks were unusual in that those scientists who examined the graph could not identify the chemical fingerprint.

The fact that there was no magnesium oxide in the 402 was intriguing. Halbert inferred from this that workers at the Farm Bureau, while believing that they were mixing magnesium oxide into their feed, had instead mistakenly mixed in a toxic chemical. At Halbert's prodding, the Farm Bureau followed up on this idea and tracked down its supplier of magnesium oxide, the Michigan Chemical Corporation. When the Farm Bureau's Jim McKean picked up the phone and called Michigan Chemical, he was referred to the company's parent, Northwest Industries (NWI), a multi-billion-dollar giant conglomerate based in Chicago. McKean ended up speaking to someone at NWI's sales desk in Chicago. "They put me on to a sales desk," recalls McKean, "and I asked the man there where the magnesium oxide was made and how could I be sure it was pure. He gave me a whole thing about it being a food grade product, manufactured in a different warehouse from the other chemicals, and bagged separately. I had no reason to think that I was not being told the truth."

After months of searching, Halbert wondered if an answer would be found. In addition to the fact that his cows were becoming deathly ill, his children began getting sick, the farm was losing money, and Halbert found himself taking tranquilizers in order to sleep. Things looked bleak. Then, on April 7, he received a phone call from the USDA's agricultural station in Beltsville, Maryland.

Weeks before the phone call, Halbert had enlisted the help of Dr. George Fries, of the Beltsville research station, and had described to Fries what he had learned about the elusive toxic, including a description of the peaks on the graph. "I worked with a bromine which had late peaks like you are describing," Fries told Halbert. "It's a commercial fire retardant, polybrominated biphenyl (PBB)." The manufacturer of PBB, Halbert later learned, was Michigan Chemical, the same people who made the magnesium oxide as a supplement for animal feed. Somehow, Halbert theorized, there was a mix-up at the manufacturing plant, and Michigan Chemical sent out bags of PBB instead of magnesium oxide to the Farm Bureau, and the Farm Bureau then proceeded to mix in the PBB with the feed and sell it to farmers throughout Michigan.

Indeed, in the months from October 1973 through April 1974, when Halbert discovered the source of the problem, PBB was spreading to farms throughout the state of Michigan. Paul Greer, a farmer from Battle Creek, discovered that he had one of the most contaminated farms in the entire state. Like Halbert, Greer was disturbed about his animals. The cows were aborting and Greer found himself trying "to deliver dead calves." Not knowing the cause of his problems, Greer began blaming everyone around him, including his manager, his son, and himself.

Hundreds of others throughout the state suffered similar traumas. Then, on May 8, 1975, the *Wall Street Journal* ran an obscure story titled "Contamination of Some Dairy Feed is Indirectly Linked to '73 Paper Shortage." The article suggested for the first time to the farmers of Michigan that there was another cause for the problems besetting their farms: a relatively unknown chemical, a fire retardant, which had been mixed in with the feed eaten by their animals and probably had caused their illnesses. With publication of the *Wall Street Journal* story, farmers could go public with their accounts of sickly mother cows and aborted calves. The blame was publicly being shifted from the farmers to the feed and chemical companies that sold PBB-contaminated feed. If the farmers could show that PBB was the likely cause of the cows' illnesses, then they could gain some compensation from the companies, get rid of their contaminated animals, buy a new herd, and start again.[3]

At the time the PBB story appeared, little was known about the chemical or about the extent of PBB contamination throughout the state. It soon became clear to state health officials, however, that the mix-up at the Michigan Chemical plant in St. Louis, Michigan, had caused one of the greatest public health catastrophes of the century.

Few outside the chemical industry knew anything about PBBs. It was known that PBBs are very persistent. Once they get into human or animal fat, it's difficult to get them out. During pregnancy, PBBs can cross the placenta and enter the developing fetus.[4] PBB's saleable asset was that it was highly fire-resistant. Michigan Chemical marketed the compound in 1970 for manufacturers to use in plastic objects such as hair dryers, television sets, automobile fixtures, calculators, and electric typewriters. Before marketing it, the company hired an outside research firm to test it for safety. The testing firm reported that PBB "is classified as non-toxic by ingestion or dermal application, is not a primary skin irritant or corrosive material, is not an eye irritant, and is not highly toxic by inhalation or exposure." Michigan Chemical, nevertheless, sent out a warning, dated December 28, 1971, to all its customers:

> The acute [single dose] toxicity of BP-6 [the trade name for PBB] is relatively low. In common with other brominated and cholorinated hydrocarbons, however, BP-6 is oil and fat soluble. If ingested or inhaled in small quantities over a period of time, we would expect BP-6 and similar materials to accumulate in fatty tissue and in the liver, which certainly is undesirable and possibly could be dangerous.[5]

Dupont found that PBB caused liver enlargement in rats, and Dow Chemical found that PBB had "a high potential for producing chronic toxic effects." The Dow toxicologist who tested PBB recommended that in light of the experience with polychlorinated biphenyls (PCBs), "the continued development and use of this compound as a fire retardant appears very unwise." Both the Dupont and Dow reports were publicly available before the feed grain mix-up occurred at the Michigan Chemical plant. Dupont's findings were presented in 1972 at a national meeting of the Society of Toxicology.[6]

Despite these reports and warning, Michigan Chemical continued to manufacture and sell PBB as a fire-retardant. The workers at the St. Louis plant apparently never got the word that their product was unsafe. The plant manager was quoted as saying that it was so safe "you could eat the stuff." But workers complained about leaks, dust, and human contact with the chemicals used to manufacture PBB. PBB itself would spill out of ripped bags onto the warehouse floor and workers would track it around in their clothes and shoes. At one point, the men working in the PBB section wrote to the Michigan Chemical management about the poor working conditions. "We in the BP-6 dept.," read the February 21, 1974, memo, "feel we should be furnished coveralls and shower time due to the products we work in, such as HBR acid, BP-6, toluene, and biphenyl dust. These are both irritating to the skin and very destructive of clothing."

Some workers were especially concerned about high dust levels, but others accepted the plant manager's affirmative view. "We were not concerned about the product because we thought the product was safe," reported one local union member. "Most of us ate our lunches right in the area. It was quicker than using the canteen service, and if you think the chemical you are working with is harmless, why not? The toxicity of BP-6 was known at the head office in Chicago [Northwest Industries], but not by the people at the plant. When we worked with TRIS [another toxic flame retardant manufactured by Michigan Chemical] we did not know how toxic it was either."[7]

Michigan Chemical rejected the workers' request for shower time and protective clothing, but a few months later, when Northwest Industries learned that a shipping mix-up at the St. Louis plant meant that contaminants had entered the food chain, "all hell broke loose" according to one worker, and the company decided to clean up the operation.

The company's lackadaisical attitude toward worker health and safety did not bode well for workers or consumers. How the company shipped the toxic PBB to FBS instead of the feed supplement magnesium remains a mystery. It is known that the Michigan Chemical plant manufactured and sold both nontoxic products such as Nutrimaster (magnesium oxide), destined for the food chain, and toxic products such as Firemaster (PBB), which were intended for nonfood uses. Like the manufacturing section of the plant, the warehouse was not maintained neatly and precise inventories were not kept. When the company checked its inventory record, it found that 10 bags of Firemaster (PBB) were missing due to what the company called "normal bag attrition."

The bags themselves were labeled with trade names, rather than generic names, so the feed supplement bags were labeled Nutrimaster, rather than magnesium oxide, and the fire-retardant bags were labelled Firemaster, rather that PBB (or BP-6). The company should have foreseen that this would lead to possible confusion among workers on the loading dock. The print on the bags could have worn off, making it difficult for workers to distinguish the two "masters." The workers were left to assume that if a bag was in the magnesium oxide section, then the bag contained magnesium oxide. Reading the blurred labels was not easy. "You had to probably pick up two or three bags and dig down to find out whether they said magnesium oxide," reported one worker. "It was stenciled, and blurred a lot of times."[8]

Michigan Chemical did not label its Firemaster bags "poison" or "toxic." Had this been done, the workers who loaded the PBB onto the grain truck and thus started the PBB on its way into the food chain might have recognized the mistake right away. In the past the company had color-coded the magnesium oxide bags to distinguish them from the other chemicals, but due to a temporary paper shortage, there were no more color-coded bags and the company packed the magnesium into plain paper bags, bags similar to the ones used for packaging the PBB.[9] On or about May 2, 1973, between 10 and 20 50-pound bags of Michigan Chemical's Firemaster were loaded on a truck and dispatched to Farm Bureau Services' Battle Creek operation.

Believing the PBB to be feed supplement, FBS employees mixed between 500 and 1,000 pounds of the toxic chemical into tens of thousands of tons of feed and shipped that feed to farmers throughout the state of Michigan. Between the fall of 1973, when the feed was mixed, and the spring of 1975, when the disaster became publicly known, cows, sheep, chickens, and hogs ate the contaminated feed and promptly fell ill. Milk from the cows was sold to Michigan consumers from Detroit to Traverse City. The eggs, cheese, and other Michigan dairy products from the cows that ate the PBB feed became contaminated. Michigan consumers who ate these dairy products, and the contaminated beef, chickens and pork, were unknowingly allowing the toxic PBBs into their bodies.

The state of Michigan reacted slowly to the news of the contamination, but it eventually quarantined 538 of the most heavily contaminated farms. Quarantined farmers were prohibited from selling meat or dairy products, and in many instances were forced to choose between watching their cows die a slow death or killing them. Many farmers were shocked by the thought of putting a rifle to the head of an animal. "We should never have had to make that decision," reflected Garry Zuiderveen, an upstate farmer who shot many of his cows.

> It was the darkest day in my life when I shot those cows. A farmer is an immensely proud person. Anything wrong with his herd reflects on his husbandry and herdsmanship, and the sickness of those animals is a reproach to him. It hurts to see them suffer, and even when they are not get-

ting better, he still hopes that he can help them. I can still remember the pain in my gut when I would go in that barn in the morning wondering if they had made it through the night . . . and yet there was this economic necessity. It was impossible to maintain those cows and throw their milk away. I could not have made any kind of living.[10]

The final death total was staggering. Approximately 18,000 sick animals were transported to Kalkaska, an isolated town in northern Michigan, and herded into a giant pit, gunned down by riflemen, and buried.[11] Others were transported out of state, many to a burial pit in Nevada. Eventually, 29,000 cattle, 5,900 hogs, 1,400 sheep, and about 1.5 million chickens—along with 865 tons of feed, 17,900 pounds of cheese, 2,630 pounds of butter, 34,000 pounds of dry milk products, and nearly 5 million eggs were destroyed.[12]

Still, for months, the people of Michigan were eating contaminated meat, cheese, eggs, and other dairy products, and drinking contaminated milk. Many, including farmers, began getting weak and suffered from blinding headaches, digestive problems, skin eruptions, inexplicable weight loss, and changes in their sexual drive. One farmer reported that PBB toxicosis "makes you feel you are ninety years old, that you ain't worth a shit or nothing, that life ain't worth living."[13]

While the Michigan farmers suffered, Northwest Industries lived on. NWI, one of the largest conglomerates in the United States, was Michigan Chemical's parent. Michigan Chemical was rightly given a bad name by the PBB disaster, and was subsequently merged with Velsicol. Before the merger, however, the Michigan Farm Bureau, the state of Michigan, and the Michigan farmers who had lost their herds and their livelihoods sued Michigan Chemical. The company eventually settled many of these cases out of court for an estimated $40 million.

In 1977, the U.S. Attorney in Grand Rapids filed criminal charges against Velsicol and Farm Bureau Services, charging the companies with gross negligence, adulterating foodstuffs, and shipping the food across state lines. The companies were allowed by the judge to plead "no contest," over the strenuous protests of U.S. Attorney James Brady. "When it comes to the protection of the law they get all the benefits," Brady said. "When it comes to the burdens, they seem to be sheltered under the law." The judge fined each company $4,000, the maximum allowed under the statute.[14]

In November 1982, Velsicol Chemical Company settled a case brought by the Justice Department by agreeing to clean up four PBB sites in Michigan, a task projected to cost the company $38.5 million. In return, the government and the state of Michigan agreed to drop all current and future claims against Velsicol involving toxic sites in the St. Louis, Michigan area, including the state's $20 million lawsuit.[15]

The effects of the PBB poisoning will not end with the litigation. Much Michigan farmland has been permanently despoiled. More than 8 million Michiganders, roughly 90 percent of the entire population, carried PBB in their bodies. They will retain trace levels of it for the rest of their lives. A 1974 study found PBB in the breast milk of 96 percent of those women studied in downstate Michigan.

The chronic effects of PBB are unknown. What is known is that PBB's potential for toxicity is five times greater than that of its relative, PCB. Dr. Irving Selikoff, of the Mt. Sinai Hospital in New York, who studied the effects of PBB on the people in Michigan, is not optimistic about the future. "We shall not know the ultimate effects for twenty or thirty years," Selikoff reported. "In many people we have contamination without disease. The chemical is in their tissue but they feel well. They may not be well. But it may take a generation before we know."[16]

Notes

1. *The Poisoning of Michigan*, by Joyce Eggington. W. W. Norton, New York, 1980, p. 161.

2. Ibid., see pps. 31–81; see also *PBB: An American Tragedy*, by Edwin Chen. Prentice Hall, New York, 1979; see also "Michigan Dairy Farmer Who in 1974 Found PBB in Cows Now Finds his New Herd Contaminated," *Wall Street Journal*, August 1, 1978.

3. "Contamination of Some Dairy Cattle Feed is Indirectly Linked to 1973 Paper Shortage," *Wall Street Journal*, May 3, 1974.

4. *Corporate Crime*, Report of the subcommittee of the Committee on the Judiciary, House of Representatives, 96th Cong., 2nd sess., May 1980 (hereafter *Corporate Crime Report*), p. 25.

5. *The Poisoning of Michigan*, Eggington, p. 90.

6. *Who's Poisoning America*, ed. by Ralph Nader, Ronald Brownstein, and John Richard. Sierra Club Books, San Francisco, 1981, p. 74.

7. *The Poisoning of Michigan*, Eggington, p. 91.

8. Ibid., p. 118.

9. "Contamination of Some Dairy Cattle Is Directly Linked to Bag Paper Shortage," *Wall Street Journal*, May 8, 1974.

10. *The Poisoning of Michigan*, Eggington, p. 143.

11. "Nightmare On Michigan Farms," *Washington Post*, March 22, 1976.

12. *Corporate Crime Report*, p. 28.

13. *The Poisoning of Michigan*, Eggington, p. 188.

14. Ibid., p. 327.

15. "$38 Million Pact Reached for Midwest Toxic Cleanup," *New York Times*, November 19, 1982.

16. *The Poisoning of Michigan*, Eggington, p. 307.

29
PCB

"If I lived in Poughkeepsie, I'd be very concerned."

—Dr. Robert Harris, expert on drinking water, commenting on PCBs in Hudson River drinking water[1]

THE ENGINE HUMS at full power. It is running on 400 amps. When the current is cut back to 200 amps, the machine continues to hum at full power, even though it is being fed only half as much electricity. The device that allows for this phenomenal saving in energy is called a capacitator. And the chemicals that allow capacitators to work efficiently without burning up are called polychlorinated biphenyls (PCBs).

In upstate New York, along the banks of the scenic Hudson River and just south of the capital city of Albany, sit two capacitator manufacturing plants owned and operated by one of the largest corporations in the United States, General Electric. Every day since the early 1950s, the two GE plants, one at Hudson Falls and the other at Fort Edward, would turn out thousands of capacitators. Every day capacitator casings that had been drenched in PCB would be washed off with water that would be dumped into the Hudson River, a river that serves as drinking water supply, commercial fishing asset, and recreational mainstream of hundreds of thousands of New Yorkers.

No one is sure exactly how much PCB was dumped into the Hudson River from these two GE plants. A conservative estimate is an average of 30 pounds per day between 1966 and 1972. Environmentalists claim that since the facilities began operating in the mid-1950s, GE may have discharged as much as 500,000 pounds of PCB into the Hudson. The six years between 1966 and 1972, when GE dumped at least 84,000 pounds of PCB, was a time of heightened environmental awareness. Americans became educated about the fragility of nature and started to scrutinize large corporations that displayed institutional insensitivity to their natural surroundings, dumping toxic agents into the environment. GE was not oblivious to this environmental movement and GE executives should have questioned whether the incessant discharge of large amounts of a manmade, fire-resistant chemical was having an adverse effect on the fish that swam in or the humans that drank from the waters of the Hudson. It was not until 1975, almost 20 years after the dumping began, that GE moved, under orders from the government, to reduce the amount of PCB that it was releasing into the river.

Beyond mere suggestion, however, there was evidence early on that showed PCB to be a toxic substance that was widespread and would endanger the health of human and animal life. In 1964, a Swedish scientist found traces of PCB at both ends of the food chain—in plankton and in large eagles. Moreover, he found them in Sweden, a country that didn't even manufacture PCB. The closest country to Sweden that manufactured the chemical was Germany.[2]

Four years later, on the island of Kyushu, in Japan, a terrible accident happened in a rice oil factory. A machine containing PCB broke down and spilled the chemical into the rice oil. The rice oil was nevertheless marketed, and thousands of people who used it became ill with what later became known as Yusha, or rice oil, disease. The victims suffered from cloracne (a severe skin disease that covers the body with pustules), from darkening of the skin, swollen upper eyelids, nausea, impaired vision, loss of appetite, abnormal menstruation, impotence, jaundice, hearing difficulties, headaches, diarrhea, spasms, and fever. It has been estimated that as many as 15,000 persons may have been affected by the contaminated rice oil. Of the 12 babies born to the 11 pregnant women who used the contaminated rice oil, 2 were stillborn, and 9 of the 10 born alive showed signs of Yusha disease; they were nicknamed "cola babies" because of their darkened skins.[3]

As far back as the 1930s, information was available to both Monsanto and General Electric that indicated PCB's toxic effects on humans. In 1936, for example, Dr. Jack W. Jones and Herbert S. Alden published a paper in the *Archives of Dermatology and Syphilology,* reporting that a 26-year-old man who had been working on the distillation of a chlorinated biphenyl in April 1930 had developed chloracne. By October 1933, 23 of the 24 men working in that PCB plant had developed symptoms of the same disease.[4]

By 1943, a second report had surfaced, this time in *Industrial Medicine.* Dr. Leonard Greenberg reported that workers handling electrical equipment containing PCB were breaking out with chloracne. "During the past year," reported Dr. Greenberg, "the division of industrial hygiene of the New York State Department of Labor has conducted an investigation in two cable plants using chlorinated naphthalenes (a close relative of PCB) and diphenyls (the same as biphenyls). In this investigation, a large number of cases of dermatitis was found, and several deaths due to liver damage among workers in the industry." Dr. Greenberg concluded that chlorinated biphenyls "are in general highly toxic compounds and must be used with extreme care. Industrial hygienists should take every effort to see that such exposures are controlled, in so far as humanly possible."

By the 1970s, high levels of PCB began appearing in Hudson River fish. In 1970, Robert H. Boyle, a Hudson River fisherman and an editor at *Sports Illustrated* magazine, became interested in pesticide poisoning of river fish. Boyle, concerned at first with DDT residues, ordered a study of Hudson River fish. The results of this test were made public in the October 26, 1970, issue of *Sports Illustrated:* a number of fish species contained PCB.[5] The highly prized striped bass had especially high levels of PCB, averaging 11.4 parts per million (ppm) in their eggs and 4.01 ppm in their flesh. "These are grim figures," Boyle later warned Carl Parker, chief of New York State's Bureau of Fisheries, "and I certainly think the state should warn fishermen not to eat striped bass eggs." In response, Parker scoffed at the *Sports Illustrated* findings as "unproven allegations."[6]

Even before Boyle wrote his letter to Parker, the state of New York was aware that PCB was finding its way into the Hudson food chain. Beginning in 1970, Ward Stone, a wildlife pathologist with the New York Wildlife Research Laboratory, sent one hundred and two (102) memos to his superiors warning of PCB contamination in the Hudson River. "I hope the Department of Environmental Conservation [DEC] begins to take some of these toxic problems seriously," he urged in one of the memos, "because it is doubtful these problems can be put off. In fact, they have already been put off for too long." Even the force of 102 memos, however, could not prod the state enforcement apparatus into action. "It was futile," recalled Stone. "No one really cared and at times I began to wonder if I were crazy and the rest of the department were sane."

Not only did the state's DEC officials ignore Boyle's *Sports Illustrated* findings and Stone's 102 memos, but they ignored the results of DEC's own testing. From 1970 through 1975, the state conducted 99 sampling tests on Hudson River fish, more than half of which revealed PCB levels greater than the maximum allowable tolerance level (5 ppm) set by the U.S Food and Drug Administration (FDA). Still, the DEC failed to act.[7]

In addition to these findings, there were other reports that should have prodded GE, Monsanto, and the state into action but didn't. Dr. Robert Risebrough, a scientist at the University of California at Berkeley, studied PCB's effects on wildlife and in the January/February 1970 issue of *Environment* magazine called for the establishment of tolerance levels of PCB in food. "The possible PCB hazard, like so many environmental hazards," wrote Risebrough, "is one of long-term, low-level exposure and perhaps of effects from its combination with other poisons. There is also the more indirect, but no less real danger of destroying other forms of life, part of the last interconnected web of species of which man is but one part and on which he depends."[8]

Foolishly, as it turned out, people who fished in the Hudson River relied upon state and federal enforcement officials to protect them against companies that threatened this "interconnected web of species." The state did not act until August 1975. And the federal police failed to act. In fact, the federal Environmental Protection Agency (EPA), relying on a state report that the discharge from the GE facilities "complies with water quality standards," granted a permit on December 20, 1974, that allowed the company to dump 30 pounds of chlorinated hydrocarbons into the Hudson daily—with a gradual reduction to no more than 3.5 ounces by May 31, 1977.[9]

At a May 1974 hearing on federal toxic pollutant standards,

a GE official admitted that the company was releasing between 25 and 30 pounds of PCB into the Hudson every day.[10] An EPA investigation found Hudson River fish with very high levels of PCB, including one rock bass with a level of 350 ppm. "The PCB level in the rock bass is greater than the maximum level documented for fish taken from any industrial river in the United States," wrote the EPA investigators. "This represents a new record for PCB contamination of freshwater fish." The report also noted that certain areas of the Hudson were fished primarily by children. "Ingestion of these fish by the populace," the investigators warned, "would certainly lead to contamination of specific tissues in their bodies."

Despite these findings, and despite specific authority granted to the EPA to sue for an immediate restraining order against any polluting corporation that is "presenting an imminent and substantial endangerment to the health of persons," the EPA again failed to act. It didn't warn Hudson Valley residents about the PCB–laced fish. It didn't take GE to court. It did nothing. "From some of the evidence I've seen," remarked one regional EPA official, "you can eat PCB like an ice cream cone."[11]

Ogden Reid disagreed. Reid, newly appointed DEC commissioner, took seriously reports of adverse health effects of PCB and — unlike Monsanto, General Electric, federal enforcement authorities, and his predecessors at the state DEC — Reid acted swiftly upon learning of GE's dumping practices. On July 7, 1975, Reid came across a report from an alert regional EPA official in Duluth, Minnesota, warning that the Hudson River "for many miles downstream from the GE discharge could be contaminated with PCBs at levels one hundred times over the 10 ppt (parts per trillion) guideline set by the EPA in 1972 and a thousand times higher than the recommended water quality criteria [of 1 ppt]."

Reid, reportedly astounded, immediately issued an advisory, warning New Yorkers not to eat striped bass or largemouth bass taken from the Hudson, and launched his own statewide fish-sampling program to determine the nature and extent of the problem. The Reid investigation found high levels of PCB in the Hudson, including 229.3 ppm in 10 yellow perch and 559.25 ppm in 1 eel, a level 100 times the FDA standard. Reid also identified the two GE capacitor factories as the source of the pollution and immediately entered negotiations with GE representatives in an effort to encourage the company to cutback on its PCB discharges.

For GE, the carrot was not enough. Less than one month after the negotiations began, Reid had to pull out the stick, and on September 7, 1975, he ordered the company to reduce its discharges to two pounds a day by the end of the year and to stop them completely by September 30, 1976. GE immediately replied that it would be impossible to comply with Reid's order, claiming that to give a commitment to clean up in one year would represent "a breach of integrity" because "we know of no method of achieving this goal."[12]

Reid, unconvinced, ordered a hearing on the issue. "Tragically," Reid said in announcing the hearings, "we are now faced with what may be irreversible damage and serious economic loss to recreational and commercial fisheries on the Hudson River." In addition to striped bass and largemouth bass, Reid warned New Yorkers not to eat smallmouth bass, white perch, white suckers, or eels taken from the Hudson.

Unfortunately for Reid, 1975 was not a good year to enforce the law of New York against giant corporations. Governor Hugh Carey was in the middle of a campaign to attract large businesses to the Empire State, and the last thing he needed was a tough cop going after the state's largest employer. It wasn't an image Carey wanted to project into the boardrooms of the Fortune 500 companies.

Gradually, indirectly but effectively, Carey began to turn the political screws on Reid. Carey's commissioner of commerce, John S. Dyson, publicly called for an end to the hearing Reid had ordered into GE's dumping practices. Dyson argued that forcing GE to stop dumping PCB into the Hudson would result in GE's closing down its facilities, throwing 1,200 people out of work, and moving its business out of state. Dyson further argued that since PCB had never "killed specific fish or caused any demonstrable change in the environment," there was no need to force the company to end its dumping. "If zero discharge means zero jobs, and three ounces means 1,200 jobs," Dyson reasoned, "then I say we go for the three ounces."

The jobs issue was pressed by both Dyson and General Electric. Dyson delivered to the governor petitions signed by 1,068 of the more than 1,200 GE workers at the upstate plants. "New York has enough problems now without creating more unemployment," read one part of the petition. "Because of overly ambitious politicians are we to suffer needlessly?"[13]

To Judge Abraham Sofaer, however, GE, not Reid, was the problem. Sofaer, who heard the administrative case that Reid presented against the company, found that by dumping PCB into the Hudson, GE had violated state law. "GE has discharged PCBs," wrote Judge Sofaer, "in quantities that have breached applicable standards of water quality . . . injured fish, and . . . destroyed the viability of recreational fishing in various parts of the Hudson River by rendering its fish dangerous to consume." Sofaer also found that the contamination was a result of "both corporate abuse and regulatory failure; corporate abuse in that GE caused PCBs to be discharged without exercising sufficient precaution and concern; regulatory failure in that GE informed the responsible federal and state agencies of its activities and they too, exercised insufficient caution and concern."

It was now up to GE and Reid to negotiate a settlement, subject to Sofaer's approval. Buoyed by Sofaer's favorable ruling, Reid went to the governor's office to meet with Carey and GE's board chairman Reginald Jones in an attempt to settle the case. According to the *New York Times*, Jones angrily warned that he would pull all GE facilities out of New York if Reid insisted that GE's two capacitator facilities stop dumping PCB into the Hudson.[14] GE would agree to pay $2 million to settle the case, but it would settle only if Reid agreed to include a "good faith clause" in the settlement, a clause that would say that GE "acted in good faith, unintentionally and in reliance upon its [Federal pollution discharge] permit."

Reid rejected this settlement offer and told reporters that he had no intention of "caving in" to what he called "pressure from General Electric for its exoneration." "I stand ready to negotiate with General Electric but I have no intention of selling out to them," Reid said. "It would be impossible for me to suggest to the hearing officer [Sofaer] that this [GE offer] could be the basis for a settlement in the public interest."[15]

By the end of April, 1976, Reid was under fierce pressure to resign. Two months earlier, Carey had personally entered the fray, siding with GE by telling a group of waterfront union leaders, "It will do little good if we rescue our environment at the cost of our economy. . . . Anyone who doesn't agree with that principle won't be working in this government."[16]

Reid was clearly being outmaneuvered, but he did not stand alone. The victims of GE's harmful dumping quickly sided with

Reid. "You just don't make deals when it comes to public health and public welfare," proclaimed the president of the Hudson River Fishermen's Association. "GE knew for years that PCBs were a poison and now they want to be kissed and forgiven and released and exonerated. I don't know how they can ask for it."

The fishermen and Reid were no match for Carey, Jones, and GE, and on April 29, 1976, Reid announced his resignation. Before he left office, however, Reid ordered a ban on most forms of commercial fishing in the Hudson River because of PCB contamination.

With Reid's resignation, GE was off the hook. Reid's successor negotiated a settlement that required the company to pay $3 million to help clean up the Hudson, and to discontinue use of all PCB by 1977. The agreement, however, neither blamed nor exonerated GE for dumping the PCB into the Hudson. The state agreed to contribute another $3 million to help clean up the river. By 1982, all that money had been spent to *study* how to clean up the river, not to actually clean it up. Today, at least 500,000 pounds of PCB sits at the bottom of the Hudson, the fish remain contaminated, and the ban on commerical fishing of striped bass stands.[17] As of December 1986, cleanup of PCB from the Hudson had still not begun.[18]

Since 1975 more bad news has surfaced about PCB's adverse health effects. The Center for Disease Control in Atlanta found that PCB caused cancer in rats. More disturbing was a study by a University of Wisconsin Medical School pathologist who fed 16 monkeys PCB in concentrations similar to those found in Hudson River fish. The PCB affected the monkeys' reproductive abilities: seven miscarried, two could not conceive at all, and uterine growths were recorded in others. Those baby monkeys that made it into the world were undersized and had detectable levels of PCB. Within four months, half the offspring died.[19]

Hudson Valley health officials have since warned the 150,000 state residents who rely on the Hudson for its drinking water about the danger posed by PCB. Dr. Stephen Redmond, a former Dutchess County health commissioner, called Poughkeepsie's drinking water, "an environmental time bomb," and Dr. Robert Harris, a nationally known drinking water expert, brought the message home more directly: "If I lived in Poughkeepsie," he said, "I'd be very concerned."

As a result, many residents of Poughkeepsie shied away from

Hudson-supplied tap water, opting instead for local spring water despite the added time, cost, and labor involved in obtaining it. "Poughkeepsie officials have been dragging their feet for years trying to pretend that a problem doesn't exist," observed Jerry Chiumento, a Poughkeepsie resident who led a drive to make local citizens and politicians more aware of the toxics in their tap water. Every week, Chiumento filled his car with plastic bottles and drove to a public well south of the city to fill up with noncontaminated water. "I'm not going to jeopardize the health of my children while politicians squabble. That's why thousands of people in Poughkeepsie either buy bottled water or cart their water in from the outside. PCBs could be having an effect on us that even scientists don't fully understand."[20]

Notes

1. *Who's Poisoning America*, ed. by Ralph Nader, Ronald Brownstein, and John Richard. Sierra Club Books, San Francisco, 1981, p. 198.

2. "For the Hudson, Bad News and Good," by Peter Hellman. *New York Times Magazine*, Oct. 24, 1976, p. 26.

3. *Who's Poisoning America*, ed. Nader, Brownstein, and Richard, p. 181.

4. *Malignant Neglect*, by the Environmental Defense Fund and Robert H. Boyle. Vintage Books, New York, 1980, p. 61.

5. Ibid., p. 62.

6. Ibid., p. 63.

7. *Who's Poisoning America*, ed. Nader, Brownstein, and Richard, p. 183.

8. *Malignant Neglect*, EDF and Boyle, p. 64.

9. *Who's Poisoning America*, ed. Nader, Brownstein, and Richard, p. 184.

10. Ibid., p. 185.

11. *Malignant Neglect*, EDF and Boyle, p. 70.

12. "GE Ordered by State to Stop Dumping Toxic Chemical Waste Into the Hudson," by Richard Severo. *New York Times*, September 8, 1975.

13. "2 State Officials Split on Controversy over Discharge of PCBs into the Hudson," *New York Times*, January 16, 1976, p. 1.

14. "For Hudson, Bad News and Good," Hellman.

15. "$2 Million Offer by GE Reported in Pollution Case," by Richard Severo. *New York Times*, April 25, 1976.

16. *Who's Poisoning America*, ed. Nader, Brownstein, and Richard, p. 191.

17. "Toxic Pollutants Linger as Threat to the Hudson," by Elizabeth Kolbert. *New York Times*, April 28, 1986.

18. "Citing PCB, State is Widening Bass Fishing Ban," by Harold Faber. *New York Times*, April 22, 1986.

19. *Who's Poisoning America*, ed. Nader, Brownstein, and Richard, p. 178.

20. Ibid., p. 174.

30
Pinto

"Safety doesn't sell."

> —Lee Iacocca, president of the Ford Motor Co. during
> the 1970s, currently president of the Chrysler Corp.

THOSE WHO KNOW about these things will tell you that the corporate personality is rigidly molded in business school and hardened in the early years of life within the corporation, and remains virtually unchanged thereafter. Lee Iacocca, who has spent his life in the auto industry, is a case in point. Iacocca believes so strongly in the maxim "safety doesn't sell," that if you designed a safe car for him, paid all the marketing and production costs, and gave it to him on a silver platter, he most likely wouldn't allow his company to put it in the showrooms. Until December 1986, he actively opposed mandatory air bags for automobiles, despite the air bag's record as a cost-efficient life-saver. In the early 1970s he was the father of the Ford Pinto.

Despite his knee-jerk marketing bias against safety, a bias endemic to the executive suites of Detroit, even Iacocca would have a difficult time defending his thesis in certain situations. Try putting him in the same room with Richard Grimshaw. Ask him to look into Grimshaw's scarred face and say, with conviction, "safety doesn't sell."

One day in 1972, Richard Grimshaw, 13, was riding in a car on a California highway. Lee Iacocca's office was 2,500 miles away, in Dearborn, Michigan. It was the office of the president of the nation's second largest automobile manufacturer, the Ford Motor Company. Grimshaw was riding on the passenger side in a new 1972 Ford Pinto, a car that was known within the company as "Lee's car," because it was Iacocca who took a personal and professional interest in pushing the sporty little subcompact off the drawing board and into production in record time. Being Lee's car, it was made according to Lee's creed, that "safety doesn't sell."

One of those hastily produced Pintos was being driven by 52-year-old Lily Gray, with Grimshaw riding on the passenger side. Gray was driving along a California highway when the Pinto stalled suddenly and was struck from behind by a van that was traveling, according to witnesses, anywhere from 30 to 50 mph. The Pinto's gas tank crumpled, fuel leaked out, and the car caught fire. Moments later, the Pinto was engulfed in a ball of smoke. Lily Gray was burned to death. Richard Grimshaw suffered burns over 80 percent of his body. He also lost his nose, his left ear, and much of his left hand in the fire. His face was burned beyond recognition, but he survived after undergoing 60 operations. The Pinto accident left him scarred for life.

Lily Gray was not crushed to death; she was burned to death. Had the Pinto fuel tank over which she was riding not ruptured, Lily Gray would be alive today. And Richard Grimshaw could have led the life of a normal California teenager.

But to the Ford Motor Company, Lily Gray's life and Richard Grimshaw's face were just additional costs of doing business. Ford had the technology to build an automobile that could withstand rear impacts of up to 50 mph without rupturing the fuel tank. But small-sized foreign imports, especially VW's Beetle, were flooding the U.S. market, and Iacocca wanted to rush into production with Ford's answer to the Beetle. He wanted to take his small car idea and send it through planning, designing, styling, engineering, tooling, manufacturing, and finally put a Pinto in showrooms throughout America—all in a superfast 25 months. (It usually took an average of 43 months to accomplish this.) Iacocca had two other requirements: the Pinto had to weigh no more than 2,000 pounds and cost no more than $2,000.

Twenty-five months/2,000 pounds/2,000 dollars. Those were Iacocca's constraints. Any time, weight, or dollar add-ons, no matter what their benefits, safety or otherwise, were bound to be dismissed as untimely, or burdensome, or "cost ineffective."

This rigid 25-month timetable was met, and 400,000 Ford Pintos found their way onto American highways during 1971, the car's first year of production. Thanks to this timetable, a designed-in safety defect in the gas tank, a defect that would cause hundreds of deaths and injuries similar to those suffered by Lily Gray and Richard Grimshaw, would go uncorrected. The Ford Pinto was designed with its fuel tank placed between the rear bumper and the differential housing (the box that connects the rear axle to the rotary driveshaft). When the Pinto was hit from the rear, even at modest speeds of around 30 mph, the impact would smash the fuel tank into four sharp bolts that stick out from that housing. The bolts would act as a can opener, ripping through the gas tank and allowing gas to spill out. If the trailing car was going a bit faster, say at 40 mph, the doors of the Pinto would jam, trapping the passengers inside. The rear-ended Pinto thus became like a gasoline-drenched bomb ready to explode when ignited by inevitable post-crash sparks.

Ford began testing the Pinto as early as 1968. Internal company documents obtained by *Mother Jones* magazine and made public in the fall of 1977 show that Ford crash-tested the Pinto at a top-secret site more than 40 times and, according to *Mother Jones,* "every test made at over 25 mph without special structural alteration of the car has resulted in a ruptured fuel tank," and "eleven of these tests, averaging a 31-mph impact speed, came before Pintos started rolling out of the factories." In only three of the tests the Pinto gas tank did not rupture: (1) when an inexpensive plastic baffle was placed between the can-opener-like bolts on the differential housing and the gas tank; (2) when a piece of metal was placed between the bumper and the gas tank; and (3) when the inside of the gas tank was lined with a rubber bladder.[1]

Although Iacocca's 25 month/2,000 pound/2,000 dollar demands weighed against making any of three life-saving fuel tank modifications, federal law enforcement officials were at the time considering a federal rule-making procedure to require all automobiles, beginning in 1973, to withstand a rear-end collision at 30 mph (known in Washington as Federal Motor Vehicle Safety Standard no. 301 [Fuel System Integrity]). In an internal Ford memo dated April 21, 1971, Ford engineers concluded that in order to meet FMVS 301, the company would have to line the Pinto fuel tank with a flak suit or a rubber bladder. That would cost $100 million over three years. Rather than modifying the Pinto to meet the proposed standard and prevent foreseeable death and injury, Ford had a better idea: do nothing on the Pinto and instead go to Washington to fight law enforcement officials in an effort to defeat FMVS 301.

For eight years, Ford's Washington office harassed weak-kneed enforcement officials with legal memos, appendices, other paperwork, arguments, and requests for studies, and, as a result, successfully delayed implementation of the life-saving standard. From the flood of paperwork that flowed from Ford's downtown Washington office, one letter emerged that best reflects the coldblooded calculus that allowed the company to market the explosive Pintos. The letter, dated September 19, 1973, was from J. C. Eckhold, director of the Automotive Safety Office of Ford, to Dr. James B. Gregory, administrator of the National Highway Traffic Safety Administration (NHTSA), chief police officer of the auto safety beat. Ford asked that the federal police reconsider FMVS 301 because the cost to Ford of making automobile fuel tanks strong enough to withstand a 30 mph rear-end collision ouweighed the benefits of saving lives. To prove its assertion Ford attached a mathematical formula.

Using government statistics, Ford figured that the cost of a human death was $200,000, a burn injury $67,000, and an incinerated auto, $700. At 180 burn deaths, 180 serious burn injuries and 2,100 burned vehicles per year, Ford figured that FMVS 301, if implemented, would save $49.5 million per year $(180 \times \$200,000)$ + $(180 \times \$67,000)$ + $(2,100 \times \$700)$. But the costs of saving these lives and burn injuries was, according to Ford, prohibitive. Ford figured that to fix each Pinto so it wouldn't explode when rear-ended at 30 mph or less would cost the company $11 per auto and truck, or $137.5 million $(\$11 \times 11,000,000 + 11 \times 1,500,000)$.[2]

The mathematics, although convincing to corporate-trained law enforcement officials in Washington, struck Arthur Hews and Mark Robinson, Jr. as a crude attempt to justify wrongful behavior. Hews and Robinson were the attorneys representing Richard Grimshaw in his product liability lawsuit against the Ford Motor Company. In digging through documents produced by the defendant Ford in discovery, Hews and Robinson found that not only did Ford have the technology to rectify the unsafe placement of the Pinto fuel tank behind the bumper and failed to implement it, but that the company owned a patent on a much safer over-the-axle fuel tank that would withstand a rear-end collision at up to 50 mph. The over-the-axle fuel tank was, in fact, being used by Ford on its Capri automobiles.

Grimshaw's star witness at the trial of his suit against Ford was former Ford engineer Harley Copp. For 30 years head of engineering and production, Copp left in 1976 because of his strong views on auto safety. During his testimony, Copp explained to attorney Hews why Ford chose not to place the Capri over-the-axle fuel tank in the Pinto:

> Q: In your opinion, how many of the survivable, of the 700 to 2500 people who died from fire would have lived if the fuel tank had been located over the axle?
>
> A: 95 percent.
>
> Q: Why is it so safe over the axle?
>
> A: That's a good place to hide. It's one of the most rigid well-protected areas in a motor car.
>
> Q: Of your own knowledge, was this known to Ford in 1970?
>
> A: Certainly.
>
> Q: Of your own knowledge, did Ford Motor Company know in 1970 that an over-the-axle location would prevent the death of the survivable people who would otherwise have lived?
>
> A: Yes.
>
> Q: Do you know of your own knowledge why the industry and Ford Motor Company have not placed — did not place the gas tank over the axle in 1970?
>
> A: Yes.
>
> Q: Why is that?
>
> A: Cost.
>
> . . .
>
> Q: What was the cost of mounting a fuel tank over the axle to the Ford Motor Company?

A: For a fully protected tank with a metal barrier around it so it is completely between the wheel houses with metal coming up and forming an enclosure, the cost of that design was $9.95.

. . .

Q: Do you know why the Pinto did not have more crush space?

A: Because it was part of the style and an additional overhang would have cost more.[3]

After listening to Harley Copp's testimony, seeing test films that showed a Pinto bursting into flames when it was rear-ended at speeds of as low as 20 mph, and hearing other evidence that indicated that Ford knew it was producing a hazardous product before it marketed that product, the jury in Santa Ana, California deliberated for eight hours and on February 6, 1978, decided that Ford had wrongfully injured Richard Grimshaw and awarded him $2.8 million. It also found that Ford owed the family of Lily Gray $659,680.

Both of these awards represented compensatory damages only; the jury wanted Ford to compensate the victims (or their families) for their losses. The judge also instructed the jury that if it found Ford had intentionally caused the injuries or willfully disregarded the safety of Grimshaw and Gray, then the jury could award punitive damages as well, thereby punishing the manufacturer for its disregard for human life.

Disturbed by Copp's testimony and the results of five pre-1972 fuel tank tests, the jury, on that same date, voted a landmark $125 million punitive damage award, finding that Ford had willfully disregarded the safety of the Pinto occupants. "We came up with this high amount so that Ford wouldn't design cars this way again," jury foreman Andrew Quinn told the *Wall Street Journal.* Quinn said he thought the Pinto was a "lousy and unsafe product."

One jury member, C. V. Greene, a telephone company dispatcher, was especially influenced by a Ford film produced before the Pinto was put on the market, showing the car backing into a wall at 20 mph. The Pinto fuel tank was filled with a nonflammable liquid that escaped from the fuel tank upon impact with the wall. "It looked like a fireman had stuck a hose inside the car and turned it on," Greene told a reporter after the trial. "In my mind, that film beat the Ford Motor Co."[4]

The $125 million that the jury ordered Ford to pay as punishment for willfully disregarding the safety of the Pinto's occupants was not a figure plucked out of the sky. The plaintiffs had asked for $100 million in punitive damages because that was the amount Ford saved by not building the Pintos with safe tanks. On that basis, juror Greene figured that $100 million was not enough since it would only force Ford to give up what it saved by not installing safe fuel tanks. Greene suggested adding on an additional $25 million, and eight other jurors agreed. Their decision produced one of the largest punitive damage awards in California civil litigation history. "We wanted Ford to take notice," remarked foreman Quinn. "I think they've noticed."[5]

The Pinto jury's punitive damage logic went by the wayside when the judge, after hearing a Ford motion to set aside the award, decided to reduce it from $125 million to a mere $3.5 million. Nonetheless, the twelve men and women who heard the Grimshaw case had made an unprecedentedly bold statement on corporate violence that no judge could erase.

Three months after the Santa Ana jury spoke, Ford announced recall of all 1.5 million Pintos that had been travelling around the country for five years, threatening the lives of those who rode in them. The company announced the recall on June 9, 1978, but didn't inform Pinto owners directly until months later, when the parts necessary to make the fuel tank modifications were at the dealers. Thus, the public thought that Ford was finally acting responsibly by recalling the autos.

On August 10, 1978, two months after Ford announced its recall and months before the recall notice went out, three teenage girls on their way to a church volleyball game in a 1973 Pinto were struck from the rear by a van on US 33 near Elkhart, Indiana. The car exploded and all three girls were burned to death. The accident was similar in many respects to the Grimshaw accident and scores of other gruesome scenes where Pintos were being rear-ended and exploding. What was different was the location. The three girls burned to death in northern Indiana, home of Michael A. Cosentino, a Republican, no-nonsense, brash, tough, part-time prosecutor for Elkhart County, Indiana.[6]

Cosentino did what few other prosecutors had done: he brought murder charges against one of the nation's largest industrial manufacturing corporations. On September 13, 1978, an Elkhart County Grand Jury, under prodding from Cosentino, indicted Ford on three counts of reckless homicide for marketing an unsafe automobile. Cosentino went on national television and defiantly announced that he would subpoena Henry Ford II and Lee Iacocca to appear in Elkhart County Superior Court (he eventually accepted substitutes for both men).

The reckless homicide prosecution of the Ford Motor Company drew national attention. It was the first time a major American corporation would go on trial for murder. But Cosentino, working on a shoestring budget and seeking volunteer help from law students and professors, was severely outnumbered by Ford, which hired a team headed by James Neal, an experienced white-collar crime attorney, for a cool $1 million, to put forth the company's best defense.

Legal experts agreed that on the evidence available to Cosentino, much of which had also been presented to the Grimshaw jury in Santa Ana, Ford was in trouble. But Neal made two shrewd moves, both before the jury was convened, that improved his odds of getting Ford off the hook. First, Neal asked that the trial be moved from Elkhart, the county seat and place of the accident, to Winamac, a small town in neighboring Pulaski County, south of Elkhart. Even before the trial location was announced, Neal sent his people into Winamac to investigate the legal landscape.

What he found was a town with not even 10 lawyers. Two of those lawyers, Lester Wilson and Harold Staffeldt, had played dominant roles in the legal affairs of Winamac. For 20 years, they had practiced law together in the small northern Indiana town. They shared office space, they shared a secretary, they shared costs, they passed files back and forth, they discussed cases, they ate breakfast together and they ate lunch together. Wilson and Staffeldt, while not partners at law, were partners in fact. They became best of friends.

In 1969, Staffeldt was appointed judge of the circuit court for the state of Indiana, Pulaski County, the only judge in town. His two-block journey from the office building that had housed the Wilson-Staffeldt practice into the judge's chambers at the county courthouse ended the years of cooperative practice for the two.

However, it did not end their friendship. The fact that attorney Staffeldt was now Judge Staffeldt had little effect on his daily routine of breakfasts, lunches, and amiable discussions with attorney Wilson.

When the Ford Pinto case was removed from Elkhart to Winamac, Harold Staffeldt was the only judge in town. And by the time the first legal motion was made, James Neal had pulled off his second, and most important, legal maneuver: he hired Lester Wilson as local co-counsel for the defendant Ford Motor Company.

Although there is no evidence that during the trial Lester Wilson and Harold Staffeldt continued to meet for breakfast and lunch, irregularities were reported. The trial was heard from Monday through Thursday, and on Friday the judge would hear other county business. On one of these Fridays, according to persons close to the case, when Judge Staffeldt was conducting his non-Pinto business, Lester Wilson was in the courtroom, as were a couple of local criminal defendants, among others. Cosentino was informed that Wilson was overheard not only advising the judge what evidence Ford would like to introduce in the following week, but also coaching the judge on how to rule on the admissibility of such evidence. Cosentino immediately contacted Neal, and both agreed to launch an investigation of what appeared to be improper ex parte contacts between Wilson and the judge.

But when the "witnesses" to the Wilson-Staffeldt conversation were approached, no one was willing to sign an affidavit reporting the contact. The issue was dropped.

The judge's consistently pro-Ford evidentiary rulings during the trial raised serious questions in the prosecutor's mind as to the ongoing nature of the Wilson-Staffeldt friendship, and whether Wilson was coaching the judge (Staffeldt was known among Winamac lawyers as "Wilson's understudy"). At one point during the trial, certain members of the prosecution team wanted to ask the judge to step down but Cosentino overruled them.

This proved a grave misjudgment, as Judge Staffeldt consistently refused to admit crucial evidence showing that Ford was aware of the hazards of its fuel tank before it marketed the Pinto. One member of the prosecution, while admitting that the judge made irrational evidentiary rulings against both sides, said he believed the irrational rulings went 20-1 against the prosecution.

The verdict was thus preordained. The jury, precluded from

seeing key evidence that had been presented in the Grimshaw trial months earlier, found Ford not guilty of reckless homicide.

The reported $1 million that Ford had paid Neal for legal services thus proved well spent. It saved Ford from a judgment of "murder," a judgment that would have done incalculable harm to the company's image and sales. A guilty verdict would have also made it easier for other Pinto victims who were suing for compensatory and punitive damages, as Richard Grimshaw had done, to prove that Ford was at fault.

The failed Indiana prosecution did point up the need for a federal corporate homicide law that will focus national attention on the wrong-doing of the country's most powerful institution, the corporation, and apply federal resources to a national problem.

Notes

1. "Pinto Madness," by Mark Dowie. *Mother Jones*, Sept/Oct 1977.
2. *Lawsuit*, by Stuart M. Speiser. Horizon Press, New York, 1980, p. 357.
3. Ibid., p. 360.
4. "Why the Pinto Jury Felt Ford Deserved $125 Million Penalty," by Roy J. Harris, Jr. *Wall Street Journal*, February 14, 1982.
5. Ibid.
6. This section on the criminal prosecution is based on interviews with members of the prosecution team.

31
Reserve Mining

"This court cannot honor profit over human life ... "

—U.S. District Court Judge Miles W. Lord ordering
Reserve Mining Company to stop dumping
asbestoslike fibers into Lake Superior, May 11, 1974[1]

LAKE SUPERIOR IS APTLY NAMED: it is the largest, deepest, coldest, and clearest of all the Great Lakes. Lake Superior has one of the most scenic shorelines in the world. It is more an ocean than a lake, and local chambers of commerce don't miss the point—they promote it as an "inland sea." To the Native Americans who populated its shores, and to the present inhabitants of the bordering states of Minnesota, Wisconsin, and Michigan, and the province of Ontario, to the north, Lake Superior was an invaluable resource, used for transportation, fishing, recreation, and water supply.

Then came Reserve Mining Company. Reserve was formed in 1939 by a coalition of steel companies and was bought out in 1950 by two steel giants, Armco and Republic Steel. Based in northern Minnesota, the company had easy access to the Mesabi iron range and would mine and transport tons of iron-rich taconite to its processing facility on the shores of Lake Superior, in Silver Bay, Minnesota.

Reserve did not build its processing plant on the banks of Lake Superior for the scenic view. The company had another motive, less aesthetic and more functional, a motive explained by the way the company processed the raw material it mined from the Mesabi

range. To retrieve the valuable iron, Reserve crushed the hard rock
and then sent the crushed rock through a rotating drum that contained an electromagnet. The tiny iron particles would adhere to
the drum and be sent off for further processing and eventual sale,
but the bulk of the rock, of no use to Reserve, would be mixed
with water and—here's where Lake Superior came in handy—
dumped into the lake.

For more than 30 years, Reserve dumped thousands of tons
of taconite wastes into Lake Superior every day. By the mid-1950s,
the company was dumping 67,000 tons of waste rock into the lake
every day. That's a total of almost 25 million tons a year.

In 1947, when the company applied for and obtained a permit to dispose of its wastes into Lake Superior, few would have
anticipated these staggering figures. At the time, an industry spokesman argued that "it was simply a matter of economics"; that it was
cheaper to dump the wastes in the lake than pile them up at some
waste disposal site on land.[2]

Reserve also assured everyone at the permit hearings that
dumping would not affect the chemistry of the lake. The taconite
tailings would be "out of sight forever and posterity would not have
to cope with them," wrote Edward W. Davis, the father of the
taconite industry. Davis "assured Reserve that the gray, sandy tailings of magnetic taconite would in no way pollute the lake, interfere
with any domestic water supply or with navigation, and would not
adversely affect the fishing industry. It was our conclusion that
the fine tailings from all the magnetic taconite on the Mesabi could
be put into the deep water of Lake Superior and would have no
harmful effect on its usefulness or beauty."[3]

Commercial and individual fishermen, however, were skeptical.
"Herring will never live in that stuff," testified Albin Wick, a fisherman from Castle Danger, "and then we might just as well pull in
our nets." The fishermen were up against a well-funded company
presentation, and lacking organization, scientists, and lawyers, those
few who spoke out against building the processing plant on the
lake were unlikely to be taken seriously.

The economic argument, that the facility would be good for
the local economy, bringing thousands of jobs to the previously
quiet wilderness area, was the clincher, and Reserve was granted
the permit to commence dumping. Years later, a Minnesota Supreme Court justice, reflecting on what he called this "monumental
environmental error" noted that "Reserve was permitted to dump

67,000 tons of waste, amounting to thousands of truckloads, into the king of fresh water lakes each and every day." Lake Superior was, wrote the judge, "sold . . . bartered away for dollars and jobs, albeit hundreds of millions of dollars and thousands of jobs."[4]

It was not until the late 1960s that action would be started to correct this "monumental environmental error." When the environmental police moved in to put a stop to Reserve Mining's discharges into Superior, the company quickly organized to defeat the challenge. Reserve's two parent steel companies mustered all the political and economic clout they could to preserve the waste disposal habit. For ten years they succeeded in holding off the cops, giving the company that much more time to continue putting 67,000 tons of waste a day into the lake.[5]

The enforcement effort began innocuously enough in 1967, when a Department of Interior employee, Charles Stoddard, was assigned to review Reserve's federal permits. Stoddard didn't like what he found. He reported to his superiors that Reserve Mining was polluting the lake by increasing its turbidity (the concentration of suspended solids) and eutrophication (the aging of the lake). "Improvements of the lake environment cannot be expected until the taconite tailings can be disposed of elsewhere," concluded the Stoddard report. "Therefore, the Department of the Interior recommends that the permit of the U.S. Army Corps of Engineers to the Reserve Mining Company be extended conditionally for a period of three years, sufficient to investigate and construct alternate on-land waste disposal facilities. . . ."[6]

The Stoddard report was a political bombshell. Armco, Republic, Reserve Mining, and their political friends in Washington reacted accordingly. On January 1, 1969, the day after the report was mailed to federal policy makers, Steward Udall, secretary of the interior and Stoddard's boss, received a telegram from Reserve Mining president Edward M. Furness, asserting that the report contained numerous errors and requesting that the company be given an opportunity to identify the errors before the report became public. Reserve Mining also contacted John Blatnik, the congressman from northeastern Minnesota. Blatnik had built a reputation as an environmentalist and had earned the name "Mr. Water Pollution Control." When it came to controlling wastes that were being dumped into Lake Superior by one of the largest economic forces in his district, however, Blatnik became "Mr. Reserve Mining."[7]

In May of 1969, the *New York Times* reported that Blatnik was displeased with the Stoddard report. "Mr. Blatnik was depicted by a number of reliable sources this week as having played a major role in the submergence of the controversial report," the *Times* said. "Under reported pressure from congressional quarters, Mr. Udall's assistant secretary for Water Quality and Research, Max Edwards, in effect repudiated the report. . . . The report was classified as unofficial and kept out of circulation."[8] Edwards met with Reserve Mining officials in Washington and assured them that the report would not be released publicly until the company's views were heard.

Stoddard was not about to let his report be buried in the basement of the Interior building, so he told a *Minneapolis Tribune* reporter where he could find copies. On January 16, 1969, the *Tribune* printed highlights, and after 25 years of neglect, Reserve Mining's dumping was back in the news.

Just before the Nixon administration took office, Secretary Udall put the enforcement mechanism in motion. But Udall's underling, Max Edwards, was critical of the Stoddard report, saying it contained "errors in conclusion" and claiming that it was not an official Department of the Interior report, but rather an "unofficial working draft." Shortly thereafter, Edwards resigned his post at Interior and became Reserve Mining's Washington representative.

Reserve Mining joined the attack on the Stoddard report. "The facts and data gathered by state and federal scientists simply do not support the statements and conclusions that appear in the draft [Stoddard report]" asserted a Reserve Mining official. "The facts do make clear that there has been no adverse effect whatever on fish, and that as a source of drinking water, the Lake's high quality remains unchanged. The tragic result of the public release of this erroneous paper is that the public will be further alarmed and Reserve's reputation damaged—unnecessarily and unjustly." As it had done 20 years earlier, Reserve raised the economic issue in its defense. "Thousands of jobs, two communities, and a major business enterprise," the company claimed, "have been placed in jeopardy by this erroneous paper."[9]

Congressman Blatnik, "Mr. Water Pollution Control," joined with Reserve and Edwards and labeled the Stoddard report "preliminary with no official status—a report that didn't prove pollution."

The Environmental Protection Agency (EPA), born in December 1970, came under intense political pressure from Republicans and friends of the Nixon administration, including the presidents of Armco and Republic Steel, to avoid the Reserve Mining case. Reserve's lobbyists insisted that the company be allowed to continue its dumping into the lake, arguing that on-land disposal was environmentally unsound. But William Ruckelshaus, Nixon's chief environmental protection officer, stood fast. He sued Reserve Mining, charging that Reserve's emissions were crossing state lines and endangering human health, that Reserve was violating provisions of the federal Water Pollution Control Act and provisions of the Refuse Act of 1899, and that Reserve's air and water emissions constituted a public nuisance. Reserve, fresh from a victory in the Minnesota court, where it defeated a challenge from the Minnesota Pollution Control Authority, was hoping that the federal judge would see it the way the state judge saw it. He didn't.

Judge Miles W. Lord was examining startling evidence, evidence that had not been available to the state court judge. This evidence showed that the waste that Reserve was dumping into Lake Superior contained fibers that resembled cancer-causing asbestos fibers, and that these fibers were floating in the drinking water used by residents of Duluth and smaller cities in the region. Lord was at first disbelieving. He threatened not to accept the reports into evidence because the EPA itself seemed not to be taking the evidence seriously. The judge soon realized the serious implications of the findings and allowed the agency to make the bad news public. On July 15, 1973, both the EPA and local environmental protection agencies announced that the drinking water of several northshore communities was contaminated with asbestoslike fibers. "While there is not conclusive evidence to show that the present drinking water supply is unfit for human consumption," the EPA announced, "prudence dictates that an alternate source of drinking water be found."[10]

Many residents of northern Minnesota failed to take the EPA announcement seriously. Some even viewed it as a hoax, a view encouraged by Reserve Mining, which issued a statement saying that the company had no reason to believe the EPA. "It is unfortunate," said a Reserve Mining spokesman, "that this unfounded charge has been made public without testing its validity." The Mayor of Duluth agreed, saying there was not enough evidence to warrant any sense of panic,[11] and claiming that he personally had no qualms about drinking the water.[12]

Other residents of Duluth, however, were not reassured. "I push a lot of juice," said Kathleen Johnson, a Duluth mother of three. "I tell the kids, if you're going to take a shower, take it fast. I worry about the kids getting drinks that might be unfiltered and I've stopped making things like homemade soup because I can't haul that much [bottled] water."[13] A local EPA chemist, Phillip Cook, was equally skeptical about official assurances of safety. "I wouldn't let my wife shampoo the rug with it," he said. And bottled-water sales boomed. One supermarket manager reported that "the phone's been ringing all day long. And people don't care about price." Many of the 100,000 residents began filtering the water that came out of their taps, and the federal government contributed $100,000 to buy bottled water for children of low-income families.

The news of the contaminated water also adversely affected northern Minnesota's usually booming tourist trade. "We don't seem to be getting the families," reported one motel owner. "And everyone asks about the water."[14]

EPA v. Reserve Mining had become national news. It was no longer a question of whether the company's dumping practices were affecting the turbidity or eutrophication of Lake Superior, but one of public health: was Reserve Mining endangering the lives of thousands of residents in the Lake Superior region? In 139 days, beginning in August 1973, Judge Lord heard 100 witnesses and received more than 1,600 exhibits and 18,000 pages of transcript. Perhaps the most damaging testimony, from Reserve Mining's point of view, came from Dr. Irving Selikoff, the director of the Environmental Science Laboratory at Mt. Sinai Hospital in New York City. Selikoff, a specialist in asbestos-related disease, told Judge Lord that the existence of taconite fibers in the drinking water of Duluth and surrounding communities posed a distinct public health hazard to the people of the region. He also warned of the dangers posed by the asbestoslike fibers in the air of Silver Bay. "I think we ought to have a sign at the entrance of one section of the town," Selikoff testified, "[that reads] 'Please Close Your Windows Before Driving Through'. I certainly would want to close mine." (This statement led to an uproar in the local community. The next day Selikoff testified that he meant only to illustrate graphically the air pollution problem in Silver Bay and had not intended the remark to be taken literally.)[15]

After more than three months of hearing testimony from both sides, Judge Lord was convinced that the continued dumping by Reserve "substantially endangered the health of the people who procured their drinking water from the western arm of Lake Superior" and that the discharge of fibers into the air "substantially endangers the health of the people at Silver Bay and surrounding communities as far away as the eastern shore of Wisconsin." William G. Verity, chairman of the board of both Reserve and Armco, disagreed. "It is our judgment that the discharges don't constitute a health hazard," he told the judge.

Lord was not convinced. "I regard your suggestion that I change my opinion . . . as preposterous," Lord snapped at Verity, and on April 20, 1974, the judge ordered Reserve to cease all discharges into Lake Superior and into the air by one minute after midnight. The judge ruled that Reserve had violated federal law.[16]

Within two days, Reserve had persuaded the U.S. Court of Appeals to stay Lord's order. The appeals court agreed with Lord's assessment of the health risk, but disagreed with the suggested remedy. "The best that can be said," ruled the appeals court, is

> that the existence of this asbestos contaminant in air and water gives rise to a reasonable medical concern for public health. The public's exposure to asbestos fibers in air and water creates some health risk. Such a contamination should be removed. But an immediate injunction cannot be justified in striking a balance between unpredictable health effects and the clearly predictable social and economic consequences that would follow the plant closing.[17]

The case was returned to Judge Lord.

Lord was not a man of compromise. He immediately ordered Reserve Mining to deposit $100,000 with the city of Duluth to cover filtration expense. Reserve immediately appealed this order to the friendlier Court of Appeals, and the higher court once again overruled Lord, but this time it went a step further and removed Lord from the case for being biased against Reserve Mining. "Judge Lord seems to have shed the robe of the judge and to have assumed the mantle of the advocate," said the appellate opinion. "The court has become lawyer, witness and judge in the same proceeding, and abandons the greatest virtue of a fair and conscientious judge — impartiality."

The appeals court succeeded in removing Judge Lord from the case, but couldn't silence him. "I know the hearings were irregular and I knew there was a considerable risk involved," Lord admitted afterwards, "but sometimes the stakes are so high you have to take risks. You have to stand up and be counted. What we're talking about is the health of thousands of people on the north shore [of Lake Superior] and I think that justifies any risks I took by stretching normal judicial procedure."[18]

It took four more years for the judicial process, without Lord, to persuade Reserve to stop dumping 67,000 tons of waste each day into Lake Superior. In the interim, 150,000 residents were exposed to additional cancer-causing fibers in their drinking water.

Given cancer's extended latency period, the long-term effects of Reserve Mining's dumping practices must be left to speculation. In one area, the record is clear, however: Reserve Mining and its owners, Armco Steel and Republic Steel, were not fined or sanctioned for violating federal law. They were ordered to stop dumping in Lake Superior, which they did finally in 1980. Today, Reserve dumps its wastes on land. The switch from the lake onto the land came 12 years after Stoddard wrote his report warning of the danger, and four years after Judge Lord ruled that "this court cannot put profit over human life. . . ."

Lord and Stoddard were publicly rebuked for their efforts to protect the public health and bring a large corporation to justice. No Armco Steel or Republic Steel or Reserve Mining official was ever jailed or fined.

Notes

1. *The Reserve Mining Controversy, Science, Technology, and Environmental Quality,* by Robert Bartlett. Indiana University Press, Bloomington, 1980, p. 147.

2. *Who's Poisoning America,* ed. by Ralph Nader, Ronald Brownstein, and John Richard. Sierra Club Books, San Francisco, 1982, p. 210.

3. *Reserve Mining Controversy,* Bartlett, p. 21.

4. Ibid., p. 201.

5. "How Reserve Mining Made Our Largest Lake Inferior," by Tessa Namuth. *Business and Society Review,* Winter 1977–78, p. 38.

6. *Who's Poisoning America,* ed. Nader, Brownstein, and Richard, p. 214.

7. *Reserve Mining Controversy,* Bartlett, p. 59.

8. "Politics and Pollution," *New York Times,* May 11, 1969.

9. *Reserve Mining Controversy,* Bartlett, p. 60.

10. "Report Says Asbestos Fibers Found in Duluth Drinking Water," *Minneapolis Tribune,* June 16, 1973.

11. *Who's Poisoning America,* ed. Nader, Brownstein, and Richard, p. 220.

12. *Reserve Mining Controversy,* Bartlett, p. 126.

13. "Uneasy Duluth Filtering Water," by William E. Farrell. *New York Times,* February 20, 1976.

14. "Each Glass Is Another Moment of Truth," *Today's Health,* October 1973, p. 46.

15. *Reserve Mining Controversy,* Bartlett, p. 141.

16. Ibid.

17. *Who's Poisoning America,* ed. Nader, Brownstein, and Richard, p. 224.

18. "Judge Removed in Reserve Case Defends Actions," by Austin Wehrwein. *Washington Post,* January 8, 1976.

32
Selacryn

"Abnormal liver function tests and jaundice have been
reported in a few patients treated with 'Selacryn'; however,
no causal relationship has been established."

       —labeling on drug Selacryn, produced and
       marketed by Smithkline Beckman Corporation[1]

"Guilty."

       —Smithkline plea to criminal charges of falsely
       labeling Selacryn with a statement that there was
       no known cause-and-effect relationship between
       the drug and liver damage[2]

As a mother of two young children living on a farm in Lake City, Florida, Dorothy Beasley couldn't afford to allow a case of mild high blood pressure disturb her life. Following her doctor's advice, she began taking Selacryn, a new prescription drug marketed to control high blood pressure.

In January 1980, less than five months after she took her first Selacryn pill, 34-year-old Dorothy Beasley was dead. She died from massive Selacryn-induced liver damage, damage so severe that at the time of her death, only 2 percent of her liver was viable. Her autopsy report stated that "the other changes [her general physical deterioration] all followed more or less directly the devastation of the liver. This was a state from which there was no possibility of recovery."[3]

Dorothy Beasley died a senseless death, and she was not alone. According to Dr. Sidney Wolfe, director of Public Citizen's Health Research Group (HRG), Smithkline, the manufacturer of Selacryn, "illegally withheld" from the Food and Drug Administration (FDA) a series of reports showing that Selacryn was causing liver damage. The drug was eventually banned, but it was banned at least four months later than it would have been had Smithkline promptly notified the FDA of the danger. To date there have been 60 deaths, including that of Dorothy Beasley, and 513 cases of liver damage in people using the drug. According to Dr. Wolfe, the majority of these deaths and injuries were preventable.[4]

Smithkline (formerly Smith Kline & French) is an old-line pharmaceutical giant that made its mark in the industry after World War II by selling psychoactive drugs such as benzedrine, dexedrine, and thorazine. Entering the 1970s, Smithkline had been considered the senior citizen of the drug business, an unspectacular giant that wasn't going anywhere. Then, with the discovery of a new anti-ulcer drug called Tagamet, the company began a period of rapid growth and became the fastest growing maker of prescription drugs in the world. In 1978, total company sales doubled, with Tagamet alone bringing in $280 million. By 1979, Tagamet sales skyrocketed to $490 million,[5] and in 1980, hit $638 million, making it the world's largest selling prescription drug.

Encouraged by Tagamet's phenomenal sales success, Smithkline began pushing Selacryn as a possible blockbuster sequel. The high blood pressure market was ripe for the introduction of a new drug. Millions of Americans with high blood pressure were being treated with a group of drugs known as thiazides.[6] Thiazides effectively controlled high blood pressure, but at the same time often caused hyperuricemia, a condition in which enhanced levels of uric acid in the blood can lead to kidney problems. Like thiazides, Selacryn could control high blood pressure, but in addition, Selacryn was promoted as lowering uric acid levels, thereby reducing the likelihood of hyperuricemia and dangerous kidney problems.[7] If Smithkline could convince doctors that the advantage was crucial, Selacryn would have a good chance of grabbing a large chunk of the multimillion-dollar high blood pressure market.

Smithkline began testing the drug in 1976. Selacryn was shipped out to doctors around the country, including Dr. Rudolph Noble, who prescribed the drug to 62 high blood pressure patients. The drug proved effective in relieving high blood pressure, but six of Dr. Noble's patients contracted viral hepatitis, an inflammation of the liver. Similarly, Dr. Jonas Brachfield, of Willingboro, New Jersey, also tested Selacryn on 28 patients, two of whom later suffered from liver ailments. Overall, Selacryn was tested on 533 persons, 8 of whom subsequently developed liver problems.

Neither Brachfeld nor Noble was alarmed by the findings of hepatitis. To Noble, the finding of six hepatitis cases in those who used Selacryn "seemed like just a fluke." Brachfeld told a reporter that "any investigator, by himself, cannot exercise judgment" as to a drug's safety based on a small sample group.

To receive FDA marketing approval, new drugs usually are tested on 700 to 1,500 patients during clinical trials. In the case of Selacryn, the FDA made an exception, concluding that although only 533 patients had received the drug during clinical trials, no additional clinical studies were necessary to establish the drug's safety. "Some people would say 533 is too low," explained FDA's Dr. Stuart Ehrreich, "but even today, if we had a relatively simple drug like that, 533 would be a significant number of people for a test. With this experience though, maybe we'd change our minds."[8]

HRG's Wolfe thinks that the sample was too small, given Selacryn's targeted market, and that had Selacryn undergone adequate testing, the drug never would have reached the market.[9] "For a drug which was intended for long-term use by millions of people had it succeeded in displacing much of the thiazide market, adverse reaction information on just 533 subjects participating in controlled studies lasting no longer than six months appears to be inadequate," observed Wolfe. "Clinical testing on at least several thousand people would likely have uncovered the liver damage *before*, rather than after marketing."[10]

New drug applications (NDA) take an average of two years to make it through the FDA, but Selacryn zipped through in 18 months.[11] The decision to give Selacryn accelerated review status was based, in part, on a report submitted by Smithkline that surveyed patients who had used the drug. Only one case of abnormal liver function was cited. The FDA's own medical review of the drug mentioned the eight cases of liver damage, but reported that Dr. Noble's cases of hepatitis were "minimal and trivial" and characteristic "of the usual spectrum of those [side effects] commonly consequent to . . . thiazide type agents." Dr. Brachfeld's two cases of liver damage were "consistent in all respects" with other studies.[12]

On April 27, 1979, the FDA gave Smithkline the green light to sell Selacryn to American consumers, but not without a label that read in part: "ADVERSE REACTIONS . . . abnormal liver function tests, and jaundice have been reported in a few patients treated with 'Selacryn'; however, *no causal relationship has been established*" (emphasis added). Within weeks of the FDA approval, Smithkline was sending out promotional literature to doctors urging them to prescribe the tiny light blue tablets "with confidence . . . once a day . . ." as "a 'First Step' Agent for your Hypertensive (high blood pressure) Patient." The doctors responded positively to these promotions, and Selacryn began to shoot up the Smithkline sales charts.

Within days after the drug hit the market, doctors began reporting to Smithkline adverse reactions including severe abdominal pains, vomiting, painful urination, and kidney shutdowns. The kidney problems apparently resulted when doctors took the patient off thiazide, a drug that tended to increase uric acid levels, and immediately put them on Selacryn, which tended to decrease uric acid levels. The danger to kidneys posed by such a quick switch from the thiazides to Selacryn was due to an abrupt change in the patients' uric acid level. As early as August 1978, Smithkline was aware of at least 12 cases of kidney failure and other kidney abnormalities in patients who took a drug called Diflurex, the European equivalent of Selacryn. It wasn't until after Selacryn was marketed within the United States, however, and after the company learned of 11 U.S. kidney impairments that Smithkline added a warning that read: "Diuretic therapy should be interrupted for three days before starting Selacryn."

Smithkline later made this warning more forceful, but an FDA official, in a December 13, 1979, letter to the company, charged that even the new label had "not been entirely effective" in emphasizing the need for the three-day interval, and suggested that Smithkline make the warning more prominent.[13]

It was the liver, however, and not the kidney problems, that caused Selacryn's downfall. According to internal memos obtained by the *Philadelphia Inquirer*, a doctor reported on July 20, 1979, that a 68-year-old woman developed jaundice just three days after she began taking Selacryn. (Jaundice is a fatal liver condition that causes a yellowing of the eyes and skin, a darkening of the urine, clay-colored stools, and excessive destruction of red blood cells.) On August 15, 1979, a second doctor called Smithkline and reported that he had personally taken Selacryn and six weeks later developed symptoms of hepatitis. The doctor called the company a second time and reported that he had stopped taking Selacryn for a month, but he decided to test whether his initial hepatitis symptoms were drug-related. After a month without Selacryn, he started taking the drug again. Six hours after popping the first light blue Selacryn tablet, the doctor developed chills and a fever. An internal Smithkline memo notes: "This appears to have been a Selacryn-related reaction."[14]

By the end of October, 1979, Smithkline had received at least 12 reports of severe liver damage among Selacryn users. The law on reporting adverse reactions to the FDA could not have been more clear: Smithkline was required to report any unexpected side effects to the FDA "as soon as possible, and in any event within 15 working days" from the time the company was notified of the adverse reactions. Despite the law, the company did not notify the FDA about the liver damage reports until November 9 — 105 days after the company received the report of the 68-year-old Selacryn user who contracted jaundice. When the company did report the adverse reaction, it buried the information in volume three of a seven-volume, 2,500-page routine quarterly report, one of a myriad of such tomes shipped to the FDA each year from drug manufacturers around the country.

During this period, when Smithkline was failing to make timely disclosure of the adverse reaction reports to the FDA, the company was at the same time actively promoting the drug by offering free samples to doctors through a mail blitz. The accompanying ads sought to persuade doctors to switch from thiazides to Selacryn. Ads that went out to doctors in September and October, well after the company had received its first complaint about liver damage, continued to note "no causal relationship between Selacryn and abnormal liver function tests and jaundice. . . ."[15]

Reports of unexpected side effects from a new drug are usually handled expeditiously by the FDA, but the Smithkline report was not because it was buried in a massive and routine manuscript. So it was not until the end of 1979 that FDA officials came across the liver damage reports in volume three. The information "wasn't highlighted," according to one FDA spokeman.[16]

After discovering the information, the FDA called in 17 Smith-kline corporate officers and medical personnel to explain the company's behavior. At a meeting held on January 15, 1980, the company officers made another eye-opening disclosure: Smithkline reported to the FDA that an additional 40 Selacryn users had reported fever, chills, dark urine, and yellowing, all indications of hepatitis. Five of those 40 patients had died.

Within 24 hours of revealing this new information, Smithkline was forced to recall the drug from the U.S market. In a letter to doctors across the country, the company reported that "Clinical use of Selacryn has shown that the drug can cause significant hepatic injury . . ." and urged that doctors "discontinue use of Selacryn immediately."

But the recall came too late for hundreds of doctors who, prodded by company ads and free samples and relying on Smith-kline assertions of "no causal relationship" between Selacryn and liver damage, prescribed the little blue tablets for their patients. The recall came too late for those patients who, trusting their doctors, swallowed the Selacryn tablets in the hope of controlling their high blood pressure but with no idea that the drug was in some instances attacking their livers.

Of the 265,000 persons who used Selacryn during its eight-month marketing life in the United States, 60 died and 513 suffered liver damage — "the majority of which were preventable had SKF [Smithkline] not violated the drug laws," according to HRG's Wolfe. Many of these Selacryn victims, or their survivors, have brought suit against the company or are threatening to sue. As of this writing, none of the cases have gone to court, and Smithkline has settled all but 13 of some 100 cases[17] including four that totaled more than $1.8 million. Dorothy Beasley's husband and her two children settled for an estimated $350,000.

On June 12, 1984, after months of delay, the Justice Department charged Smithkline and three of its officers with 14 counts of failing to notify the FDA within 15 days of reports of adverse side effects among users of Selacryn. The complaint, which listed an additional 20 counts of mislabeling through false and misleading information on literature packaged with the drug, was the first criminal information brought against a company for failure to report adverse drug reactions.[18]

Prosecutors said they were ready to prove that on March 20, 1979, Anphar Rolland, S.A., the French pharmaceutical firm that licensed Smithkline to sell the drug in seven countries, wrote a memo reporting on 13 liver disorders in users of tichrynafen, including five "probably related to" the drug. Smithkline received the memo in May and had a full translation from the French by June 1. In addition, on June 22, 1979, at a meeting in Philadelphia, Anphar representatives told Smithkline of liver disorders in 20 Diflurex users. Two Smithkline doctors at the meeting called six of the liver disorder cases "definitely drug related," but they predicted that the hepatic problems would not occur "with any significant frequency." The doctors concluded that "it would seem judicious to closely monitor this now that 'Selacryn' is available to the general population."[19]

On December 13, 1984, Smithkline pleaded guilty to all 34 charges. The three Smithkline executives pleaded no contest to 14 counts of failing to file reports.[20] The company was fined $100,000. The three executives were placed on probation and sentenced to 200 hours of community service.

Senator Howard Metzenbaum charged that the Reagan Justice Department had "let down the American people." "Even though 36 died due to corporate irresponsibility, the department let Smithkline off the hook." Metzenbaum and other congressional critics of the Justice Department's handling of the corporate crime cases said that Smithkline and its officers should have been charged with felonies, not misdemeanors. In fact, when the FDA recommended in 1984 that the Justice Department bring criminal charges against Smithkline and its officers, it specifically urged that it bring felony charges, not misdemeanors. But the department overruled the FDA, and Smithkline was let go with a $100,000 slap on the wrist.[20] At 36 deaths, that comes to about $3,000 per death.

Notes

1. *United States of America v. Smithkline Beckman Corporation et. al.* Criminal information, p. 9.

2. "Smithkline Pleads Guilty on Drug Tied to Death," *New York Times,* December 14, 1984.

3. Letter from Sidney Wolfe, M.D., director, Public Citizen's Health Research Group, to John J.R. Shad, chairman, Securities and Exchange Commission, September 15, 1981.

4. Letter from Sidney Wolfe, M.D., to Jean Weber, May 6, 1981.

5. *Everybody's Business: An Almanac,* ed. by Milton Moskowitz, Michael Katz, and Robert Levering. Harper & Row, San Francisco, 1981, p. 243.

6. "Selacryn: A Drug's Brilliant Take-off and Tragic Fall," by Arthur Howe. *Philadelphia Inquirer,* March 8, 1981, p. 1.

7. "Selacryn: A Tale of Negligence and Concealment," TRIAL, October 1980.

8. "Drug Firm Facing Crinimal Action," by Lee Strobel. *Chicago Tribune,* August 2, 1981.

9. "Selacryn: A Drug's Brilliant Take-off . . . ," Howe.

10. "Selacryn," TRIAL.

11. "Drug Firm Facing Criminal Action," Strobel.

12. "Selacryn: A Drug's Brilliant Take-off . . .," Howe.

13. Ibid.

14. *Corporate Criminal Liability,* Hearing, Subcommittee of Crime, Committee on the Judiciary, House of Representatives, November 15, December 13, 1979, March 14, March 24, April 22, 1980, p. 267.

15. Ibid.

16. "Drug Firm Facing Criminal Action," Strobel.

17. "Smithkline Pleads Guilty to U.S. Charges It Was Slow to Report Drug's Side Effects," *Wall Street Journal,* December 13, 1984.

18. "Smithkline Faces Criminal Charges in FDA Complaint," *Philadelphia Daily News,* June 12, 1984.

19. "Smithkline Case a Study in Corporate Responsibility," Mintz, December 27, 1984, p. E1.

20. "Dispute Over Intent in Drug Case Divided FDA and Justice Dept," by Philip Shenon. *New York Times,* September 19, 1985.

33
SMON

"How could this have happened? If only we had known that the drug could have such terrible effects, we would never have prescribed it. Why didn't anybody tell us? Why weren't we warned?"

—leading Japanese doctor at Kyoto International Conference Against Drug-Induced Sufferings (KICADIS), April 14–18, 1979, Kyoto, Japan[1]

Aʟᴍᴏsᴛ ᴀʟʟ ᴏғ ᴛʜᴇᴍ had difficulty walking. Many were bedridden, and of those who could walk, half needed crutches or a walking stick. Others suffered from blindness and serious optic disorders. Ninety percent had sensory disturbances—pain, constricted blood vessels, and paralysis—centered in the lower back and limbs. Emotionally, they encountered difficulties in their daily lives. Few believed that their diseases would be cured. Many felt desperate, and some attempted to commit suicide.[2] Others developed acute epilepsylike convulsions and died.

These were the victims of one of the largest drug disasters in history. Ten thousand Japanese and hundreds of others throughout the world who consumed a drug known as clioquinol, in the hope of combating diarrhea, were stricken with a little known but devastating disease, subacute-myelo-optico-neuropathy (SMON). Like the mercury that crippled hundreds of innocent inhabitants of the fishing town of Minamata, clioquinol ruthlessly altered the lives of thousands of Japanese and again drew sharply into focus the mores of the corporations that dominate so many aspects of society in Japan.

In 1934, the giant Swiss multinational drug firm Ciba (now Ciba-Geigy) began marketing clioquinol to fight amoebic dysentery. Later the drug was widely promoted to control all types of dysentery. For more than 35 years, millions throughout the world took clioquinol to combat "holiday tummy" and "traveler's diarrhea." And in Japan Ciba-Geigy's anti-diarrheic sold big.

Ciba began marketing its clioquinol tablets worldwide under the trade name Entero-Vioform in 1934, but the company didn't enter the lucrative Japanese market until 1953. Sales skyrocketed from a meager 38.4 kilograms in 1953 to an extraordinary 8448 kg by 1962. "It would be no exaggeration," observed Kiyoshi Yamashita, an attorney and member of the Japanese Society for Hygiene, "to say that Japan was a hotbed for the development of the chinoform [clioquinol] market."[3]

Observers of the international drug industry attribute the success of Ciba's anti-diarrhea tablet in Japan to a number of factors. First, it has been noted that the Japanese are preoccupied with all sorts of digestive disorders. "The stomach (or *hara*)," explains Olle Hannson of the University of Goteborg, in Sweden, "has significance for the Japanese which far exceeds the part the heart plays for westerners." Hannson, who has investigated the SMON disaster, observed that for the Japanese:

> Hara is the center for feeling and emotions. Through concentration, the Japanese gain spirit and strength from hara. When a Japanese, as we express it, wants to look someone straight in the face and speak honestly, he or she says, "Hara o watte, hanashimasko" which means, "Let us open our stomachs and speak." The generous person—a westerner would say 'bighearted'—is, consistently in Japan, "hara go okii," of a big stomach.[4]

It is not unusual, therefore, for a Japanese to consult a doctor in the case of even the slightest of stomach disorders.

Although clioquinol was originally tested and manufactured for amoebic dysentery, within a few years, Ciba was promoting the drug to control virtually all kinds of dysentery. The Japanese took it "not only to treat diarrhea of every conceivable variety but also to prevent it," according to the authors of *Prescriptions for Death, The Drugging of the Third World*. They also note that to the Japanese, "with their traditional preoccupation with all digestive disorders, the drug was accepted as *seichozai,* a kind of 'digestive stabilizer.' It was swallowed daily by thousands of people for months or years."[5]

With the Japanese public eager to acquire medicines to combat their stomach problems, the Japanese government was not going to stand in their way. Ciba was permitted to promote clioquinol as a drug to be used for abdominal trouble in general, with no limitation as to dosage or length of treatment. According to Ciba, clioquinol was the perfect "intestinal regulator" and could be swallowed with no fear of adverse side effects.[6] And the Japanese swallowed the pitch. One SMON expert is quoted as saying that the Japanese "took it — and the physicians prescribed it — as if it were some kind of benevolent vitamin for the intestinal tract."[7]

Clioquinol turned out to be anything but benevolent. With the increase in sales of the drug came a parallel increase in the devastating disease later known as SMON. SMON at first baffled the medical and scientific establishments in Japan. Beginning in the mid-1950s, hundreds complained to doctors of tingling in the feet, tingling that eventually turned into total loss of sensation and eventually paralysis of the feet and legs. Others complained about vision disturbances, and gastrointestinal effects including diarrhea and severe abdominal pain.

As in Minamata, the medical authorities diagnosed the new affliction as everything that it wasn't: a new virus, reaction to environmental pollution, vitamin deficiencies, metabolic disturbances, multiple sclerosis, a reaction to agricultural insecticides, and a reaction to contaminated water. As the epidemic spread, the virus theory took hold, and again, the fear of contagion rippled through the populace and authorities attempted to isolate victims.

The failure to identify the cause of SMON kicked off a series of tragic events across Japan that compounded the initial damage. Hannson, the Swedish doctor who observed the episode closely, described the situation in the town of Ihara in the Okayama prefecture:

> At the Ihara City Hospital, the largest hospital in the city where the SMON patients had been concentrated, panic led to terrible consequences. A great many people who sought advice for intestinal trouble in the form of abdominal pains and/or diarrhoea were immediately suspects as having the initial symptoms of SMON and were admitted

to an isolation ward where the treatment was massive doses of oxyquinoline (clioquinol). The diarrhoea continued (that oxyquinoline can lead to loose feces was unknown to the physicians and not mentioned — despite their knowledge of it — by the drug companies). Abdominal pains increased or set in as a sign of beginning nerve damage. The admittance SMON had thereby become confirmed — the madness had been completed. A banal case of diarrhoea which in all likelihood would have subsided in a few days without any treatment was to involve a lifelong invalidity for many. The circumstances in Ihara were in no way unique. The same tragic events happened all over Japan.[8]

During the late 1960s, "epidemics" began to break out in major Japanese population centers, and the government, under public pressure to act, began a series of investigations into the mysterious illness. In 1963, Professor Tadao Tsubaki, of the Department of Neurology at the Brain Research Institute at Nigata University, in Nigata, launched an investigation of the syndrome.[9] Tsubaki began in the city of Kushiro, where he observed that the most common problem was sensory disturbances, along with muscle weakness, bladder disturbances, and visual impairment. However, none of these symptoms gave any clue to the cause of this strange disease. For years the scientists speculated and the general public continued to consume the clioquinol tablets.

It was not until 1970 that researchers identified clioquinol as the cause of SMON. During the early studies of SMON, doctors noted that the tongues of some SMON victims had turned greenish, and in 1970 it was reported that two SMON patients were excreting greenish urine. Following up on this report, two medical researchers, Yoshioka and Tamura, published a paper titled "On the nature of the green pigment found in SMON patients" (*Igaku no Ayumi*, 74, 320 [in Japanese, 1970]), in which they reported that the green pigment in the urine was in fact iron chelate, a chemical substance generated by clioquinol.[10] This was the break that researchers were looking for. Immediately studies were launched to investigate the relationship between clioquinol and SMON. Tadao Tsubaki surveyed 171 SMON patients and found that 167, or 97 percent, had a history of clioquinol administration just before complaining of the neurological symptoms.[11] He also found that

(1) neurological symptoms generally began to appear when a total dose of 10 to 50 grams had been reached; (2) the time span between the taking of clioquinol and the beginning of the neurological symptoms was 50 days at a daily dose of 600 mg and 30 days at a daily dose of 120 mg; and (3) that a larger dose tended to produce a more severe pathological picture.[12]

On August 7, 1970, Tsubaki informed the Japanese Ministry of Health and the mass media of his findings. The Swiss manufacturer, Ciba-Geigy, and the other Japanese manufacturers were not pleased. According to Silverman, Lee, and Lydecker—in *Prescription for Death: The Drugging of the Third World*—the companies released statements insisting that the drug was unquestionably safe, that it had been used on millions of patients around the world for more than 30 years without causing problems, and that clioquinol could not conceivably cause such harm because it was essentially insoluble and therefore could not be absorbed into the body.[13] But the government of Japan, faced with Tsubaki's strong evidence and mounting pressure from an increasingly fearful Japanese populace, banned the drug from the Japanese market just one month after receiving Tsubaki's report.

Although Ciba argued that its drug was "unquestionably safe," attorneys for SMON victims found evidence that raised troubling questions—evidence that had been available long before Tsubaki submitted his report to the Ministry of Health. The first warning came from the University of California team of scientists who invented the drug. From the beginning, they made clear that although clioquinol was relatively insoluble, the drug could still be absorbed into the body.

Especially revealing of Ciba's attitude toward the early warning signs of clioquinol's hazards was the company's reaction to reports that the drug caused problems in animals. In 1962, Paul Hangartner, a Swiss veterinarian, treated some diarrhea-afflicted dogs with clioquinol. The dogs developed acute epileptic convulsions and died. Hangartner reported the findings to Ciba and told the company that he thought the dogs' deaths were due to the drug. Silverman, Lee, and Lydecker report that Swedish investigators made similar observations.[14]

Rather than investigate futher the safety of clioquinol, Ciba "avoided the question, and also failed to mention that it had made similar observations in animal experiments 23 years before," reported

Hannson. When Hangartner published his dog findings in 1965, Ciba added a warning note to the Entero-Vioform (the brand name for clioquinol) package leaflet in Britain. The note read: "Note: this formulation is not suitable for the treatment of animals."[15]

Ciba apparently concluded that what was unsafe for dogs was nevertheless safe for humans. The company continued to promote the drug in Japan by telling physicians that it was safe and effective, that it had no side effects, that it was hardly absorbed into the intestines, and that any side effect was temporary, so the prescription need not be discontinued. Ciba also told Japanese physicians that clioquinol was safe for children.

But the inventors of clioquinol warned in 1944, in light of the animal studies, that the use of drugs like clioquinol to prevent amoebic dysentery "must be rigidly controlled and should not be carried out as extensively or as freely as is done in the prophylaxis of malaria with quinine." They advised that clioquinol be administered for not more than 10 to 14 days.[16]

In addition to the dog studies, other evidence was available that should have warned Ciba and should have triggered follow-up studies on the safety and effectiveness of clioquinol. In 1935, for example, two Argentinian researchers reported that some patients treated with clioquinol had developed signs of bilateral nerve damage. In 1966, Hannson and his colleague Lenart Berggen studied a three-year-old boy who had been treated with clioquinol and whose vision had been seriously affected. By revealing that clioquinol was found in the boy's urine, Hannson and Berggen did serious damage to Ciba's argument that clioquinol was hardly absorbed into the intestines.

"There's no way," the two researchers reported, "that clioquinol could have appeared in the urine unless it first had been absorbed out of the intestinal tract and into the body."[17] Berggen and Hannson warned of the possibility that clioquinol could damage the optic nerve and lead to optic atrophy and severe deterioration of vision. "This report was followed by several others in the [medical] literature and [sic] directly to Ciba," wrote Hannson in 1978, "clearly indicating the potential dangers of these drugs."[18]

These studies raised the possibility that clioquinol was not as safe as claimed by Ciba; other studies indicated that the drug was not effective in combating the "traveler's diarrhea" for which it was being promoted. A study of American students traveling in Mexico found clioquinol to be less effective than a placebo and less effective than novobiocin, another anit-diarrheic drug. Of those students who were given novobiocin, 20 percent had diarhea; 34 percent of those who took the placebos had it. A full 39 percent of those who took clioquinol were afflicted with "traveler's diarrhea."[19] (As noted above, Hannson claims that the drug companies knew that clioquinol could lead to loose feces but did not inform physicians.)

In 1960, ten years before Japan barred sales of the drug, scientists at the U.S Food and Drug Administration (FDA) were questioning the safety and efficiency of clioquinol to combat common diarrhea. Up until that time, Entero-Vioform had been available over the counter, but the FDA advised that it be placed on a prescription-only basis and prescribed to combat only amoebic dysentery, not the more common varieties. The FDA noted that chemical cousins of clioquinol could be absorbed into the intestinal tract, and concluded that Entero-Vioform might be similarly absorbed. Ciba took the advice and modified its labeling. In 1972, Ciba removed the drug from the U.S. market.[20]

All of these warning signals came and went without Ciba and the other drug companies acting to seriously investigate the potential hazard and pull the drug off the Japanese market. The result was a disaster in Japan, where 10,000 persons were afflicted with the disabling SMON, but SMON cases were also reported from Sweden, Norway, Denmark, the United Kingdom, the Netherlands, France, West Germany, Indonesia, Switzerland, Australia, India, and the United States (with only a very few), among others.

After the Japanese government banned the drug, the Japanese victims sued the drug companies and the Japanese government, claiming that the companies were to blame for damage to the victims' nervous systems. The multinational drug companies answered by first claiming that SMON was a Japanese problem because practically no cases were found outside Japan. Ciba also denied flatly that there existed a causal connection between SMON and clioquinol.

On August 3, 1978, more than seven years after the first lawsuit was filed, a Tokyo District Court found in favor of the SMON victims and against the Japanese government and the drug companies. The district court's opinion clearly and conclusively rebutted Ciba's arguments:

The cause of SMON is clioquinol. None of the proofs given in this case have substantiated that the disease is due to a virus or any substance other than clioquinol.

As to the circumstances that only in Japan has incidence of the disease been observed, the explanation is that only in this country were the drugs containing clioquinol used by large numbers of people in large doses over long periods.

In January 1956, when the defendant companies began manufacturing the clioquinol preparations in question, they were already guilty of not having taken the necessary steps to avoid possible disastrous results."[21]

As of May 1, 1981, 4,734 of the 5,309 persons who filed suit in Japan had received payments totaling 109,346,000,000 yen — the equivalent of $490 million — probably the largest drug-related settlement ever. An estimated 1,300 cases are pending in Japan; other cases await trial elsewhere.

At the conclusion of the court cases, Ciba released an extraordinary apology to the SMON victims and transmitted it through the Tokyo district court. It read:

Since the beginning of this lawsuit, the plaintiffs and their representatives have told the court of many sufferings caused by the SMON disease. It has been repeatedly stressed that only a SMON patient can truly understand his fellow patients' sufferings. We believe that we must solemnly accept their grievances. We who manufactured and sold clioquinol drugs deeply sympathize with the plaintiffs and their families in their continuing unbelievable agony; there are no words to adequately express our sorrow. In view of the fact that medical products manufactured and sold by us have been responsible for the tragedy, we extend our apologies, frankly and without reservation to the plaintiffs and their families.[22]

On March 31, 1985, Ciba suspended all worldwide sales of clioquinol.[23]

Notes

1. *Prescriptions for Death: The Drugging of the Third World,* by Milton Silverman, Philip R. Lee, and Mia Lydecker. University of California Press, Berkeley, 1982, p. 46.

2. "The Actual Condition of Drug-Induced Sufferers, Especially Those with SMON, and The Restoration of Their Original State," based on the results of a nationwide survey of SMON by Toshio Higashida, Dept. of Public Health, Kansai Medical University, Osaka, Japan, in *Drug-Induced Sufferings: Medical, Pharmaceutical and Legal Aspects,* ed. by T. Soda, International Congress Series, 513, Excerpta Medica, Amsterdam, Oxford, Princeton, 1980, p. 398.

3. "Iodochlorhydroxquin tablets and their governmental control in the Japanese market," by Kuyoshi Yamashita, attorney at law, Japanese Society for Hygiene, in *Drug-Induced Sufferings,* ed. Soda, p. 291.

4. "Is Entero-Vioform a Killer Drug?" by Olle Hannson. *New Scientist,* November 23, 1978.

5. *Prescriptions for Death,* Silverman, Lee, and Lydecker.

6. "Is Entero-Vioform a Killer Drug?" Hannson.

7. *Prescriptions for Death,* Silverman, Lee, and Lydecker, p. 45.

8. "Is Entero-Vioform a Killer Drug?" Hannson.

9. *Drug-Induced Sufferings,* ed. Soda, p. 423.

10. Ibid.

11. Ibid., p. 425.

12. "Is Entero-Vioform a Killer Drug?" Hannson.

13. *Prescriptions for Death,* Silverman, Lee, and Lydecker, p. 45.

14. Ibid., p. 57.

15. "Is Entero-Vioform a Killer Drug?" Hannson.

16. *Drug-Induced Sufferings,* ed. Soda, p. 401.

17. *Prescriptions for Death,* Silverman, Lee, and Lydecker, p. 47.

18. "Is Entero-Vioform a Killer Drug?" Hannson.

19. "The Diarrhea of Travelers. III Drug Prophylaxis in Mexico," B. H. Kean and Somerset R. Waters. *New England Journal of Medicine,* Silverman, Lee, and Lydecker.

20. *Prescriptions for Death,* Silverman, Lee, and Lydecker, p. 49.

21. "Is Entero-Vioform a Killer Drug?" Hannson.

22. *Prescriptions for Death,* Silverman, Lee, and Lydecker, p. 53.

23. Personal communication, Milton Silverman, December 17, 1986.

34
Thalidomide

"I feel like a bus driver who has run into a group of children."

—Professor Herbert Keller, co-discoverer of the drug
thalidomide, when he heard of the effects of the
drug on children[1]

T HE EFFECTS WERE LITERALLY monstrous. *Teratogenic* was the word
used to describe those babies who were born, some with no legs,
no arms—with, instead, flippers—or four or five digits emerging
from the pelvis, if there was a pelvis, or from the shoulder, if it
too hadn't been deformed (*teratogenic* means "monster making,"
or the creating of deformities).

The deformed babies had one thing in common: their mothers
had taken the drug thalidomide. Marketed during the 1950s and
early 1960s as "completely nonpoisonous . . . safe . . . astonishingly
safe . . . nontoxic . . . and fully harmless,"[2] thalidomide produced
8,000 thalidomide babies, including Alexander Flawn, born January
9, 1962, in Britain. Alex entered the world with a deformed and
shortened arm, to which was attached a hand without a thumb.
The other hand had an extra finger. His palate had a hole in it;
his face was paralyzed on one side. One ear was completely missing, the other grossly deformed. His brain was damaged, he was
deaf and mute, and he had poor vision in his left eye. For the first
18 months of his life he vomited his food across the room with
projectile-like force.

Other thalidomide babies were deformed to a greater or lesser extent, depending on the stage of development at which the mother took the drug. Many were born with shortened limbs or no limbs, with eye and ear deformities, with severe internal damage such as anal atresia, a condition where there is no external opening to the bowel, or with malformed kidneys. Some thalidomide babies were born with deformed genitals, or no genitals at all. A few, like Alex, suffered brain damage.

The story of Alex and England's other thalidomide children was brought to public attention by angry parents and a crusading newspaper, the Sunday *Times* of London, whose editors eventually produced *Suffer the Children: The Story of Thalidomide,* a book that has become the definitive work on the subject.[3]

Today, the thalidomide babies have grown up. Some have overcome their bodily disabilities and adapted extraordinarily well. Others have succumbed to the pressures placed on them by a perhaps guilt-stricken society that often forgets that the thalidomide babies did not ask for what they got—that they were born deformed, the consequence of a drug, the drug companies, and a society that succumbed to the stream of ads offering tranquility to an uneasy populace.

The facts surrounding the production and marketing of this drug by Chemie Grunenthal—and a number of other companies worldwide—indicate that the thalidomide disaster was in no sense inevitable. With an eye toward the bottom line, the company pushed thalidomide as a nontoxic tranquilizer that had none of the poisonous potential of the barbiturates then flooding the world market. Thalidomide was touted as a highly potent wonder drug that showed no sign of toxicity.

There were, however, early indications that thalidomide was worthless and produced a wide range of side effects. Before it marketed the drug, Grunenthal had information from doctors' reports that these side effects included giddiness, nausea, shivering, buzzing in the ears, constipation, a "hangover," wakefulness, and certain allergic reactions. Grunenthal knew from its own experiments that the drug could cause a "disturbance in the nervous system following too high a dosage." Nevertheless, the company claimed that thalidomide could be taken "in higher doses" than recommended without any danger.

The company also had test results suggesting an anti-hyper-thyroid effect of thalidomide—something that in the 1950s was already known to be associated with birth defects. In addition, a 1956 test completed by the American firm Smith Kline French, found thalidomide to be worthless as a sedative.[4]

Despite these warnings, and based on inadequate results from sporadic clinical trials, Grunenthal plunged recklessly into the market. The company marketed thalidomide under numerous brand names as an over-the-counter drug for a variety of purposes. The first thalidomide drug hit the German market on October 1, 1957, under the brand name Contergan. Contergan had many derivatives—one to combat the flu, another as a sedative for adults, a third, Contergan Saft, for mothers to use in sedating their infants.

Grunenthal pushed its "completely nonpoisonous, completely safe"[5] campaign in ads in 50 major medical journals, 200,000 letters to doctors around the world, and 50,000 circulars to pharmacists. Thalidomide was out of the bag, and by the end of the first year, sales had reached 90,000 packets per month. The drug found its way to all corners of the globe, including 11 European countries, 7 African, 17 Asian, and 11 in North and South America. Thanks to a wary U.S. Food and Drug Administration (FDA) officer, thalidomide was never mass marketed in the United States, but as a result of clinical trials in the U.S., many thalidomide babies were born American.

The statistics from the human population around the world confirmed the fears raised by premarketing evidence and ignored or discounted by Grunenthal. As thalidomide sales soared in 1959, the complaints grew steadily. German Dr. Gustav Smaltz complained that thalidomide was causing giddiness and a slight disturbance of balance in his older patients. Other doctors reported cold feet and hands. Then came a letter from Pharmakoler AG—a pharmaceutical company based in Basel, Switzerland—which read, in part:

> To date 20 well-known doctors have told our representatives that when they themselves or their patients took one tablet of thalidomide they found themselves still under its effects the next morning, suffering from considerable sickness, and involuntary trembling of hands. Dr. Ludwig, head of the

second medical department, Burgerhospital, Basel, told us that he gave his wife a tablet of Softenon Forte (thalidomide). He adds, "Once and never again. This is a terrible drug."[6]

Grunenthal also heard directly from customers, who complained about constipation, and from pharmacists, who suggested that thalidomide could have an effect on circulation. Dr. Ralf Voss, a well-known Dusseldorf nerve specialist, wrote asking whether Grunenthal had any knowledge of thalidomide's effects on the nervous system. Despite three reports to the company about such effects on the nervous system, Grunenthal wrote Dr. Voss, "Happily, we can tell you that such disadvantageous effects have not been brought to our notice."

Riding the wave of phenomenal worldwide thalidomide sales, Grunenthal stepped up its advertising campaign. For a 1960 promotional mailing, the company printed 250,000 leaflets that ignored all of the warnings coming in from around the globe and adhered to the original company line that thalidomide was "nontoxic," "completely harmless for infants," and "harmless even over a long period of use." Grunenthal did drop the word "completely" from the phrase "completely harmless" after doctors complained that no drug was "completely harmless." The claim that thalidomide was "harmless" indicated that the company remained willing to ignore substantial evidence to the contrary.

Most troubling were the letters received from doctors reporting peripheral neuritis, a serious illness that attacks the nervous system. Grunenthal's sales department recognized that "unfortunately we are now receiving increasingly strong reports on the side effects of thalidomide, as well as letters from doctors and pharmacists who were to put it on prescription." This was followed by the comment that "from our side, *everything must be done to avoid this* [emphasis added] since a substantial amount of our volume comes from over the counter sales."

Ralf Voss, the nerve specialist in Dusseldorf, believed that a connection existed between long-term thalidomide use and peripheral neuritis, and he "had the strong impression that Grunenthal doctors did not doubt the validity of my observations but were merely anxious to prevent as far as possible their being made public."[7]

With lies, distortions, and suppressions, Grunenthal attempted to hold off the wave of adverse publicity about its wonder drug. Through connections with a friendly editor of a German medical magazine, Grunenthal successfully delayed publication of a paper that showed a strong link between thalidomide use and peripheral neuritis.[8]

Grunenthal recognized that eventually the flood of evidence would break the company's wall of secrecy. "Sooner or later we will not be able to stop publication of the side effects of Contergan," an internal Grunenthal memo read. "We are therefore anxious to get as many positive pieces to work as possible." To attain this goal, it appears that Grunenthal went beyond the traditional norms of scientific inquiry. The company was aware of the work of a doctor in Iran who was studying the effects of thalidomide on the human population, but reported that initial approaches to the doctor by the company had not been successful. "However," wrote the head of Grunenthal's clinical research section, "since the Iranian doctor is very materialistic in his outlook, concrete results should be forthcoming soon."

While apparently trying to buy off foreign doctors, Grunenthal went on the attack at home, labeling Dr. Hubert Giggleberger, a German doctor, "troublemaker no. 1." Giggleberger had questioned the company's trustworthiness and charged Grunenthal with being "irresponsible" for not pulling the drug off the market. Grunenthal even hired a private detective to investigate certain patients and doctors who were focusing the spotlight on the company's failure to pull the drug.[9]

The negative reports piling up were so devastating that even the company's clinical research director was forced to admit that thalidomide was not "harmless." In a memo dated May 10, 1961, he wrote, "I personally maintain the view that there is no longer any doubt that, under certain circumstances that I am unable at present to understand or explain, Contergan can cause the nervous injuries described . . . I consider it simply impossible that the company should officially adopt the standpoint that these reports are exclusively a matter of unqualified polemics. . . ."

The dam was beginning to break. Dr. Heinrich Mueckter, Grunenthal's staff doctor, admitted to his colleagues during a staff meeting in July 1961, "If I were a doctor I would not prescribe Contergan any more." Since thalidomide was, from the beginning, sold over the counter, at that time no prescription was needed. But by August 1, 1961, with Grunenthal feeling the effects of the reports on side effects, thalidomide was placed on prescription in three German states. Slowly, Grunenthal began spreading the word about potential dangers of thalidomide, but the company did not come totally clean. For instance, at a meeting in Germany in September 1961, Grunenthal told its licensees from Britain, the United States, and Sweden about the risks of peripheral neuritis but failed to tell them that it already knew of 2,400 such cases in Germany alone. Similarly, in letters to licensees in developed countries, Grunenthal urged that words such as "nontoxic" be dropped, but the company continued to send out promotional literature to West Africa in which thalidomide was described as "completely harmless."[10]

In Britain, Grunenthal's distributor was a subsidiary of Distillers Ltd., the giant liquor merchant. In July 1957, Distillers Company Biochemicals Ltd. (DCBL) signed an unusually long 16-year contract with Grunenthal to market thalidomide to England. From the beginning of this agreement, DCBL accepted everything that Grunenthal said about thalidomide with absolute trust and, as one observer put it, "was prepared to turn a vacuum of knowledge about thalidomide into specific assurances of safety."

In April 1958, DCBL began marketing thalidomide under the name Distaval. Its advertisements claimed that the drug was "completely safe," that "side effects are virtually absent," and that the drug was "nontoxic." Distaval was advertised as an answer to the "mounting toll of deaths due to barbiturate poisoning."[11]

These ads were aired despite the concerns raised by DCBL's development manager, R. Grasham. Grasham thought that the phrase "no known toxicity" was "rather sweeping" and suggested it be replaced with "exceptionally low toxicity."

But DCBL saw thalidomide as a potential wonder drug that might eventually become an alternative to whiskey. If people were going to start popping thalidomide pills instead of downing Johnnie Walker, DCBL wanted to keep its share of the market. So DCBL marketed Distaval with no backup technical information on the drug except for a one-sided report provided by Grunenthal—although it was the practice of other drug companies to extensively test similar sedative-type drugs for side effects.

By March 1961, DCBL had sold nearly 64 million thalidomide

tablets. In the same year, it sent pamphlets to doctors claiming that: "Distaval can be given with complete safety to pregnant women and nursing mothers without adverse affect on mother or child. . . . "

When DCBL did its own tests on thalidomide, it tended to ignore those results that cast a shadow on the drug. For instance, two months before Distaval went on sale in Britain, the *British Medical Journal* published the results of DCBL's own clinical tests. James Murdoch, one of the men who conducted the tests for DCBL, wrote, "it would seem unjustifiable to use the drug for long-term sedative or hypnotic therapy, pending the results of more detailed study of its long term effects in a larger series of patients, notably those suffering from mild or moderately severe hyperthyroidism."[12]

Even DCBL's staff pharmacologist, when the weight of the evidence turned against thalidomide, began pushing the company to disclose all test results. The sales department, however, had the upper hand, and it instructed its sales representatives that "the possible occurrence of peripheral neuritis is a remote one and in no way detracts from the main selling point of Distaval. . . . It has a toxic effect of which you should be aware . . . but there is no need to alarm the medical profession or discuss the matter unless it is raised." Perspective was the key. As DCBL's sales executive J. Paton put it: "It is not our job to educate the medical profession how to look out for various conditions. From a sales promotion point of view, the more we write on this side effect, the more it is likely to get out of perspective."

Approximately 1,200 thalidomide babies were born in England. About 800 of those died from massive hemorrhaging at birth. The remaining 400 or so survive today, with various deformities. These thalidomide babies are relentless reminders of DCBL's sales approach.

Fortunately for the people of the United States and for the Richardson-Merrell Company (Grunenthal's U.S.–based licensee), the United States never had such experience firsthand. Richardson-Merrell pushed adamantly to get the drug approved for the U.S. market, but the FDA refused to allow thalidomide into the hands of American consumers.

Merrell's September 12, 1960, application to market thalidomide in the United States was assigned to newly arrived FDA officer Dr. Frances Kelsey. Kelsey was suspicious of the drug, even though the only side effect presented to the FDA was peripheral neuritis, the tingling of the nerves. Fifteen years earlier, Kelsey had conducted research on experimental animals and found that some substances that triggered peripheral neuritis could occasionally cause the birth of paralyzed, stunted, and deformed fetuses. So Kelsey delayed action on Merrell's application, saying it was incomplete. Merrell's assertions were deflated when news arrived from Germany of children born with phocomelia, the strange deformity whose telltale sign was seal-like flippers in place of arms and legs.[13]

In 1973, after years of litigation, threatened boycotts of Distillers products, and a massive pressure campaign administered by a group of concerned citizens representing the thalidomide children,[14] Distillers was forced to agree to pay 2 million pounds a year for ten years into a trust fund to care for the 430 British thalidomide children.[15] (In 1971, Distillers' pre-tax profits totaled 64 million pounds on assets worth 421 million pounds.)

In 1967, a public prosecutor in Achen, West Germany, drew up a bill of indictment charging Grunenthal with intent to commit bodily harm and involuntary manslaughter. After more than two years of trial, the court, with the agreement of the prosecution, dropped the criminal charges and Grunenthal agreed to pay the German thalidomide children $31 million, with the German government agreeing to contribute an additional $15 million to $27 million.[16]

Still, all the money in the world could not begin to compensate for the damage thalidomide and the drug companies inflicted. David Mason is the father of a thalidomide child and was a leader of the parents group that negotiated the settlement with Distillers. "Nobody is getting any glory out of this," Mason told reporters at the end of the settlement negotiations, "at the end of the day, my daughter Louise still has no legs."[17]

Notes

1. *Suffer the Children: The Story of Thalidomide,* by the Insight Team of the Sunday *Times* of London. Viking Press, New York, 1979, p. 110.

2. *Corporate Crime in the Pharmaceutical Industry,* by John Braithwaite. Routledge & Kegan Paul, London, 1984, p. 68.

3. The Sunday *Times'* crusading effort ran into a legal roadblock when the House of Lords upheld an injunction restraining the publication of a proposed Sunday *Times* article discussing whether the Distillers Co., the English marketer of thalidomide, had been civilly negligent in failing to test the drug or to take it off the market. The European Court of Human Rights later found the decision to be contrary to Article 10 of the European Convention. See *The Impact of Publicity on Corporate Offenders,* by Brent Fisse and John Braithwaite. State University of New York Press, Albany, 1983, p. 258.

4. *Suffer the Children, Times* of London, p. 14.

5. Ibid., p. 28.

6. Ibid., p. 31.

7. Ibid., p. 32.

8. *Corporate Crime in the Pharmaceutical Industry,* Braithwaite, p. 69.

9. *Suffer the Children, Times* of London, p. 38.

10. Ibid., p. 41.

11. Ibid., p. 46.

12. Ibid., p. 55.

13. *Pills, Profits, and Politics,* by Milton Silverman and Philip Lee. University of California Press, Berkeley, 1974, p. 95.

14. "Thalidomide Children," by Ralph Nader. *New Republic,* February 10, 1973, p. 10.

15. "Victims of Myth: The Thalidomide Affair," *Science in the Media,* AAAS, 1981, p. 82.

16. *Corporate Crime in the Pharmaceutical Industry,* Braithwaite, p. 73.

17. *Suffer the Children, Times* of London, p. 205.

35
Three Mile Island

"It is criminal negligence! These people should have been arrested for criminal negligence and there they sit. They are still operating that plant. There's only one word that keeps going through my head. What the United States government has done to its people is a terrible betrayal. That's the only word I can use and I use it over and over because that's what it boils down to. We have lost our country. We have lost our government. That constitution that our forefathers wrote—it had meaning—is lost because our Congress is bought and paid for by the oil companies and the utilities. They're bought and they're paid for."

> —Jane Lee, farmer from Etters, Pennsylvania, three and one half miles from the Three Mile Island nuclear power plant[1]

On an island in the middle of the Susquehanna River, in the center of one of the most fertile farm areas of the country, sit four gigantic cooling towers, the most identifiable parts of a nuclear power facility owned by Metropolitan Edison and operated by General Public Utilities. Less than a mile away, across the river, in the tiny town of Goldsboro, lives William Whittock, a retired civil engineer. Usually at 4 A.M. Whittock is sound asleep in his home. But on March 28, 1979, he was awakened by a roar from the nuclear reactor across the river.

"I was sleeping about four o'clock in the morning," he recalls, "and then the thing erupted. I sat up in bed and I went to the window. I could see it spurting up. The steam was escaping and rolling and going up in the air—not from the towers, but from the containment room of Unit Two. It went up as far as the towers. It was a jet of steam. It went up like a plume. It was narrow when it started, and when it went up it expanded until it was half the width of the towers as it went over the top. And roaring. That was a terrible roar. It sounded like a big jet taking off."

This was not the first time that the Three Mile Island nuclear power plant had blown off some steam. Whittock believes that the blowing off of steam was a designed-in part of the operation. "It's done that several times before," he recalls, "maybe half a dozen. I thought, well, this is just another time Old Limpy's gone off over there again!"

After rationalizing away the first blast, Whittock went back to bed, only to be awakened five minutes later by another blast. This second one lasted five minutes, then it gradually decreased. Whittock again returned to bed, this time sleeping for a couple of hours. At seven o'clock, he turned on the radio, to learn that the nuclear plant on Three Mile Island had released radioactivity into the environment.

At about nine o'clock, Whittock went outside to pick up his mail and sensed a metallic taste in his mouth. Two neighbors sensed the same taste. "Then someone came running over," he recalls, "and said there was a helicopter landing up here on the other side of the railroad. I thought it was the state police. I went up there and it was an NBC-TV crew. They asked me how to get to where they could see the towers, and I took them down on my bus. I told them I'd seen it go off, and they asked for an interview. Later on I was on national TV all over the country."[2]

William Whittock was one of the first people outside the nuclear facility to witness the effects of what the Nuclear Regulatory Commission (NRC) later called "the most severe accident in U.S. commercial nuclear power plant history."[3] Whittock and millions of his fellow central Pennsylvanians were exposed to dangerous levels of radiation released from the plant during the accident, which came within one hour of a core meltdown.

In a core meltdown, fissionable material at the heart of the nuclear facility would overheat and burn down through the containment vessel and continue to burn through the containment vessel deep into the earth. (This scenario is known within the nuclear community as "the China Syndrome" because hypothetically, the core would burn through the center of the earth all the way to China.) According to a 1975 NRC report, a core meltdown would cause upward of 3,500 immediate deaths, 45,000 cancer deaths from 10 to 40 years after the accident, 240,000 thyroid disorders, 5,100 genetic defects, and $14 billion in property damage.[4]

Before March 28, 1979, a debate raged between those who believed that the risk of a core meltdown was unacceptable to society—especially since there were other safer, less expensive methods of generating electricity—and those who argued that the odds of a core meltdown were very long (one in 100,000 chance per year of reactor operation, they said) and that this was an acceptable risk given the country's projected energy demands. Both sides agreed, however, that if the utility companies were to be allowed to operate nuclear plants in this country, there would have to be strict laws governing such operations and those laws would have to be strictly enforced. Unfortunately for the people of central Pennsylvania, enforcement of the law against the companies that manufactured and operated the Three Mile Island facility came *after* the accident.

The blast of steam that startled Whittock on that spring morning in 1978 came moments after the shutdown of the giant steam turbine in Unit Two. This initial blast of steam was not radioactive, but others that followed were, and had Brian Mehler, a TMI operator, not ordered an emergency block valve closed at 6:18 A.M., the reactor core would have continued to melt.

Due to a combination of mechanical malfunctions and human error, the TMI reactor was heating up and when the news began to seep out to Harrisburg and Middletown and Hershey, and other smaller towns in the area, people became frightened, confused, and anxious. Some became panicky. Matt and Suzanne Magda lived and worked in Harrisburg. The day after the accident, they heard that there was an uncontrolled release of radiation from the TMI plant. "When I heard that," Matt recalls, "my whole body just had a tingle through it and I got very nervous. I was trying to control myself because it had been suspicious all along and now I was sure something major was going on, that they weren't telling me the truth and that I'd better consider getting out of there."

Matt called Suzanne, a teacher at Harrisburg High School, while she was at school. Suzanne was calm, but when the students found out about the accident they became panicky, and some became hysterical. "Families were being desperately gathered together and the streets were crazy," recalls Suzanne. "There were accidents in front of the school. Hysterical parents coming to pick up their children were smashing into one another, going through stop signs and red lights, really a panic situation. When the students left, there was an incredible sense among them that they would probably not see one another again. They were leaving for Washington, New York, Ohio, Pittsburgh, some were leaving for Florida, some were going to Canada—there was a great sense of flight."

Two of Suzanne's physics students who stayed at the school retrieved Geiger counters and measured the school for radiation. A reading of 50 was normal background radiation, but the students found readings of 250 inside the building and 350 outside the building.[5]

By the time some people were sensing a metallic taste in their mouths and others were measuring the increased radiation on Geiger counters, Virginia Southard, a local community activist who was very sensitive to radiation, began feeling a prickly sensation on her skin. "I left my office that morning [the morning of the accident]," Southard recalls, "and I was getting into my car. I experienced this tingling on my skin. On my car radio they were announcing that they had already been releasing radioactive iodine, in uncontrolled amounts, for some hours. So as soon as I heard this I decided that I must leave town because I didn't want to be exposed any further." Southard, like Whittock and his neighbors, also noticed a strange metallic taste in the back of her throat. She left Harrisburg for ten days, only to return the second Sunday after the accident to a rally against what Jane Lee, a local farmer, described as Metropolitan Edison's "criminal negligence."[6]

Although the NRC didn't find that Metropolitan Edison was criminally negligent, it did find that had the utility been in compliance with the law during its operation of the plant, "the course of the accident would have been altered if not prevented entirely." An NRC investigation into the causes of the accident found "severe weaknesses" in Met Ed's "ability to maintain an effective health physics program, control maintenance activities, develop and review procedures and adhere to approved procedures and conduct [their] audit activities."[7] For endangering the lives of millions of people, the company was fined $155,000.[8]

During the accident there was total confusion, as the NRC

tried to get information from Met Ed that was necessary to bring the runaway reactor under control. "We are operating almost totally in the blind," NRC chairman Joseph Hendrie remarked at the height of the crisis."[The governor's] information is ambiguous, mine is nonexistent, and—I don't know, it's like a couple of blind men staggering around making decisions."[9]

Months after the accident it became clear that Met Ed had failed to fully inform federal, state, and local authorities and in some instances misled them. According to a congressional report on the accident, "TMI managers did not communicate information in their possession that they understood to be related to the severity of the situation." In addition, the House Interior and Insular Affairs Committee reported that "TMI managers presented state and federal officials misleading statements that conveyed the impression that the accident was substantially less severe and the situation more under control than what the managers themselves believed and what was in fact the case."

When the staff at the NRC's enforcement division found out about Met Ed's less than candid reporting, they launched their own investigation. They cited the company for failing to obtain, analyze, and report vital safety information to the commission, and recommended that the utility be fined accordingly. But the NRC's chief enforcement officer, Victor Stello, backed off. He agreed to charge the company with violating the law but refused to conclude that Met Ed had intentionally withheld information and therefore refused to impose a fine. Representative Edward Markey (D.-Mass.) called the NRC decision a "whitewash" and accused the commission of "turning a blind eye to the facts." (Markey's colleague Representative Morris Udall (D.-Ariz.) was reportedly "deeply disturbed" when he heard that Met Ed was let off the hook without a fine.)[10] In November 1984, the *Philadelphia Inquirer* reported that "a federal grand jury in Washington has begun hearing evidence on whether NRC employees might have thwarted investigation of the events surrounding the TMI accident."[11] That investigation was later dropped.

In November 1983, a federal grand jury in Harrisburg handed up an 11-count indictment charging Met Ed with falsifying safety records in the months leading up to the March 1979 accident. This included 5 counts of violating provisions of its license to operate a nuclear power plant, 5 counts of violating NRC regulations, and

1 count of violating the federal false statement statute.[12] Federal prosecutors told reporters that they were prepared to show at trial that on at least 30 occasions between October 18, 1978, and March 28, 1979, water was improperly added to the cooling system of the Unit Two reactor, and that Met Ed officials were aware as early as October 1978 that tests were showing leak rates so high that the plant might have had to be shut down.[13]

The trial promised to give both public prosecutors and the corporate defendant the opportunity to air crucial issues of corporate responsibility. Community groups eagerly anticipated thousands of pages of documentary evidence plus direct and cross-examination of corporate and government officials, and then the judgment of a jury of twelve citizens. Unfortunately, a trial was not to be.

On February 29, 1984, came a surprise announcement: federal prosecutors had cut a deal with Met Ed. The utility agreed to plead guilty to one charge of violating NRC regulations by continuing to use an "inaccurate and meaningless" test for measuring the leakage of water from the reactor's cooling system. It also agreed to plead "no contest" to two counts of violating its license and four counts of violating NRC regulations. In return, prosecutors promised not to bring additional charges against Met Ed or its subsidiaries in connection with the operation of Unit Two.

Community leaders were disappointed with the settlement. Larry Hochendoner, a commissioner of Dauphin County, charged that the settlement cheated the residents out of knowing what went on in the plant in the months before the accident. "I think they're copping a plea," Hochendoner told reporters. "I think they're finding an easy way out. I think the public interest is not being served. There's a great deal of information that has not been released."[14]

Metropolitan Edison was not the only corporate culprit in the Three Mile Island tragedy. Babcock and Willcox, the company that built the troubled TMI Unit Two reactor, was also remiss. According to the NRC, Babcock and Willcox "had on four occasions been aware of significant safety information regarding B&W nuclear reactors but failed to inform the NRC of the information as required by NRC regulations." Two B&W engineers warned their supervisors about a possible serious safety violation that occurred at an identically designed reactor in Ohio *more than one year* before the TMI Unit Two accident.[15]

Bert Dunn, one of those two B&W engineers, later told a

presidential commission on TMI that if this warning had been heeded, the accident would have been a minor event. As it turned out, only the fine that the NRC levied on Babcock and Willcox was itself a minor event: $100,000 for endangering the lives of millions of Pennsylvanians.[16]

In November 1984, TMI's former supervisor of operations James Floyd was convicted of cheating on NRC operating exams in 1979. Floyd was later fined $2,000, sentenced to two years' probation, and ordered to provide 400 hours of community service to victims of the TMI accident.[17]

After the accident, General Public Utilities pushed to restart the undamaged Unit One reactor, despite strong protests from local residents and national environmental organizations. In June 1983, NRC Commissioner Victor Gilinsky wrote his colleagues that he would not vote for restart until the top GPU management was replaced. Gilinsky condemned it as "a company management with a narrow and grudging conception of its public responsibilities, which seeks to get by with the minimum, be it in terms of plant equipment, or of staff discipline and training, or of forthrightness with public authorities."[18] Despite strong opposition from citizens groups, on May 29, 1985, the NRC voted 4-1 to allow GPU to restart the undamaged TMI reactor.[19]

During the months following the accident, some farmers noticed that their animals were getting sick or dying. Charlie Conley, a farmer from Etters, less than five miles from the TMI plant, believes that the radiation released during the accident killed off some of his cattle and affected the health of his other animals. "My sow pigs never came in heat all winter long," Conley recalls, "It [radiation] affects the breedings of animals." Conley also noticed that the trees weren't the same. "It's killed the trees around here . . . another thing I noticed toward the fall was the pear tree up here on the hill at my neighbors. The leaves were brown on that tree long before fall."[20]

Jane Lee, a neighboring farmer, noticed the effect on trees within about a ten-mile radius of the plant. "In some areas the trees were totally defoliated," she recalls. "We had two good pear trees back here on our farm that always produced very heavily but this year in July they were almost completely defoliated. The fruit remained, which was interesting. The fruit did not drop; it stayed but it was deformed. And it was not good even for canning."[21]

Louise Hardison, who lives on a small farm in Londonderry Township, across the river from TMI, also noticed peculiar changes in the animals of the area. Almost all of her 125 chickens died. "I had a lot of death in my chickens," she recalls. "They seem to get a disease and they can't breathe. They just sit around dumpy and they wheeze. You can hear them rattling all over the chicken house and they seem to be fighting for their breath and next thing you know they fall over." Hardison also noticed health problems with her goats and rabbits. A year after the accident, an entire litter of rabbits was born dead. "Last year, after TMI, I had four litters born in a row. All dead! Every baby bunny born dead. Some of them were deformed. That was strange; I never had trouble raising rabbits. Always had very good luck with rabbits."[22]

But it was threats to human health that frightened the residents the most, and those fears were not allayed by the enormous media campaign launched by the nuclear industry after the accident to convince the people of Pennsylvania that what happened at Three Mile Island had not posed serious health hazards.

In addition to the mounting physical problems, the people of central Pennsylvania suffered from severe psychological problems. "The most devastating effect that I have seen in this area," reported Dr. Michael Gluck, a general practitioner in Harrisburg, "has been severe psychological depression. In my own practice I've seen a number of patients who have come to me after the accident, telling me they cried every night; they were unable to sleep; they were afraid for their children's lives and their children's futures; they no longer had a secure home. Many of my patients have woken up screaming from night terrors and dreams about the plant." According to Gluck, patients tell him that most of their problems date back to the time of the accident.

In the aftermath of most corporate crimes, it is the victims who are the most adamant in seeking solutions to problems created by corporate wrongdoing, in seeking to prevent corporations from victimizing other citizens, and in bringing corporate wrongdoers to justice. Jane Lee, living and working within the shadows of the TMI cooling towers, is one such victim. She believes that an act of criminal negligence had been committed and that her government, by failing to prevent the accident, and by failing to adequately punish the responsible companies, betrayed her and her fellow citizens of central Pennsylvania.

As for solutions to the problems posed by nuclear power, Jane Lee is not one for half measures. "Shut them down," she says. "Amen. Shut them down before it's too late, any way you can, but shut them down. Get those plants shut down because if you don't you're going to be paying the price just like we're paying here. You're never going to have any peace of mind as long as those plants are running."[23]

Notes

1. *Voices from Three Mile Island, The People Speak Out,* by Robert Lepper. The Crossing Press, Trumansburg, N.Y., 14886, 1980, p. 51.

2. *The People of Three Mile Island,* by Robert Del Tredici. Sierra Club Books, San Francisco, 1980, p. 13.

3. Order Imposing Civil Monetary Penalties, United States Nuclear Regulatory Commission, In the Matter of Metropolitan Edison (Three Mile Island Nuclear Power Station Unit 2) Docket No. 20-320. January 23, 1980.

4. "How Safe Are Nuclear Power Plants?" *Critical Mass Energy Journal, Special Issue, Nuclear Power Primer,* March 1981, p. 3.

5. *People of TMI,* Del Tredici, p. 38.

6. Ibid., p. 59.

7. Letter from NRC to Met Ed alleging violations of law, Oct. 25, 1979.

8. Order Imposing Civil Monetary Penalties, NRC.

9. *Secret Fallout: Low-Level Radiation from Hiroshima to Three Mile Island,* by Ernest Sternglass. McGraw Hill, New York, 1981, p. 221.

10. "Cover-up at TMI?" by Richard Pollock. *Critical Mass Energy Journal,* March 1981, p. 7.

11. "In Federal Probe of Three Mile Island, Investigators Have Become a Target," *Philadelphia Inquirer,* November 25, 1984.

12. *United States of America v. Metropolitan Edison Company,* Indictment.

13. "A Glimpse at the TMI Case Developed in 4-year probe," *Philadelphia Inquirer,* March 1, 1984, p. B-4.

14. "Met Ed Pleads Guilty in Criminal Case," *Philadelphia Inquirer,* March 1, 1984.

15. "Reactor Builder Faces Big Fine Linked to Safety," by David Burnham. *New York Times,* April 11, 1980.

16. "TMI Reactor Co. Fined $100,000," *Washington Post,* May 21, 1980.

17. "TMI Restart Chronology," by Three Mile Island Alert.

18. "The TMI Accident 5th Anniversary: Industry Hasn't Learned From Its Mistakes," Union of Concerned Scientists, March 2, 1984, p. 5.

19. "NRC Backs Restart of Undamaged Unit At GPU's Three Mile Island Nuclear Site," *Wall Street Journal,* May 30, 1986.

20. *People of TMI,* Del Tredici, p. 73.

21. *Voices from TMI,* Lepper, p. 38.

22. Ibid., p. 83.

23. Ibid., p. 86.

36
Tobacco

"I was riding out to my home. I got to 110th St. and Fifth Avenue. I was sitting in the car and I looked at the corner, and there was a great big stout negro lady chewing on gum. And there was a taxicab—it was in the summertime—coming the other way. I thought, I was human and I looked, and there was a young lady sitting in the taxicab with a long cigarette holder in her mouth, and her skirts were pretty high, and she had a very good figure, I didn't know what she was smoking; maybe she was smoking a Camel.

"But right then and there it hit me; there was the colored lady that was stout and chewing, and there was the young girl that was slim and smoking a cigarette—'Reach for a Lucky Instead of a Sweet.'

"There it was, right in front of you. That campaign really went to town as everybody knows."

—George Washington Hill, father of modern corporate tobacco, explaining how the idea of his first successful radio ad was conceived[1]

IN JANUARY 1964, Hugh J. Mooney went to town, four decades after Lucky Strike's ad campaign "really went to town." He went to town to check into a hospital.

Mooney was 44 years old in 1963. He had a comfortable salary with an insurance firm, and the future seemed bright for him, his wife Eileen, and their children. Then, in May 1963, he developed a slight difficulty swallowing. The doctor diagnosed it as "a case of nerves." But when the swallowing problem persisted through the end of the year, Mooney was convinced that it was more than just nerves. He checked into a hospital and the doctor gave him the bad news. Mooney had cancer of the throat. The doctor suggested that he enter a well-known eastern hospital.

In an article titled "What the Cigarette Commercials Don't Show You," reprinted in the January 1968 issue of *Readers Digest*, Hugh Mooney vividly described his first observations:

> When I saw the three other patients in my room, I didn't want to believe my eyes. It was suppertime, and the patients were eating. It wasn't much like the television campfire scene. These men stood by their beds and carefully poured a thin pink liquid into small glass tubes. Then they held the tubes high over their heads. The fluid drained down out of the tubes through a thin, clear plastic hose which disappeared into one nostril.
>
> They had to eat this way because throat, mouth, tongue and esophagus had been cut away in surgery. I could actually see the back wall of their gullets—the entire front of the throat was laid open from just below the jaw down almost to the breast bone. Each of them had a large wad of absorbent bandage under his chin to catch the constant flow of saliva pouring out of his throat.
>
> The sight of these "tube feeders" shocked and depressed me more than anything since the day I learned I had cancer. As soon as I had changed into pajamas and robe, I rushed back to the solarium where Eileen was waiting. Shaking, I lit a cigarette and stared about me at all the other patients, some of whom would be dead in a week or so.[2]

By the end of the year, surgeons had removed Mooney's larynx, his pharynx, part of his esophagus, and in his words, "a few other random bits and pieces." He had joined the people he had described as "surgical freaks," whose appearance had so shocked him months earlier. "Eight subsequent operations were required to reconstruct the front of my neck," Mooney wrote in 1967. "Television helped pass the time. All of us there in Seven East (the cancer wing of the hospital) were, I confess, morbidly fascinated by the cigarette

commercials. After smoking approximately 19,000 packs of cigarettes, I—we all—had turned out a bit different from those hand-
some fellows and beautiful young women [in the ads]."[3]

Mooney was three years old in 1923 when George Washington
Hill took over the American Brands tobacco corporation from his
father, Percy. Considered an arrogant and vulgar man who prided
himself on manipulation, George Hill linked cigarettes and mass
media advertising and is credited—along with Albert Lasker, an
advertising pioneer—with hooking millions of people on the cigarette habit. His most famous campaign, "Reach for a Lucky Instead of a Sweet," made American Brands' Lucky Strike cigarette
the number one brand in America in 1931, and it remained one
of the country's most popular cigarettes for more than two decades.

Hill, practicing what he preached, constantly carried and smoked
his Lucky Strikes and had the spectacular habit of spitting on corporate boardroom tables. He didn't live to face the widespread
publicity given to reports of cigarettes' adverse effect on health,
but people who knew him believed that had he lived through the
fifties, he would have treated those reports with characteristic contempt. "Hill would have known what to do about this health business," one Madison Avenue executive was quoted as saying. "He
would have made cancer fashionable."[4]

George Hill was the ultimate tobacco corporation executive.
He represented what others within the industry aspired to be—a
hard driving, ruthless salesman who placed sales of tobacco above
all else. All else included, of course, the health of those who consumed his product, a product whose cancer-causing properties were
revealed as early as 1900, when an increase in cancer of the lungs
was noted by medical experts, and for the first time, a tobacco product, tobacco juice, was used to induce cancer in a test animal.*

This study represented the first trickle of what was to become a
ceaseless flood of more than 30,000 reports that would overwhelm-
ingly document the link between cigarette smoking and pulmonary
emphysema, chronic bronchitis, and other respiratory ailments,
coronary heart disease, and cancer of the lung, mouth, esophagus,

---

* There had been much suspicion, dating back to the early 1600s, of tobacco's
ill effect on health. During the early 1600s, smoking was universally condemned
as bad for the brain and lungs. And in 1761, Dr. John Hill, a well-known London physician, reported that snuff, a tobacco product, was able to produce
"swellings and excrescences."[5]

bladder, kidney, pancreas, stomach, uterus, and cervix. By 1986, cigarette smoking had been identified as the chief preventable cause of death in our society, causing in excess of 300,000 deaths each year, 135,000 of those from lung cancer. That's almost 800 deaths a day due to cigarette smoking.[6]

Much of the danger inherent in cigarette smoking was known to the tobacco barons well before their slick advertisements hooked millions of Americans on a deadly habit. In addition to the reports in 1900 linking tobacco to cancer in test animals, in 1925 a British chemist produced skin cancer on animals by painting them with condensed smoke — tar. Then, in 1938, in a report to the New York Academy of Medicine, Dr. Raymond Pearl, professor of biology at Johns Hopkins Medical School, noted the reduced life expectancies of smokers. "Smoking is associated with a definite impairment of longevity," he wrote. "This impairment is proportional to the habitual amount of tobacco usage by smoking, being great for heavy smokers and less for moderate smokers." *Time* magazine reported Pearl's findings, and commented that they would frighten tobacco manufacturers and "make tobacco users' flesh creep."[7]

Despite these reports of adverse health effects and the foreseeable carnage that would result from mass-marketing such a dangerous product, the tobacco barons decided they'd rather fight than switch.

The *Reader's Digest* kicked off an early antismoking crusade with the December 1941 publication of former heavyweight boxing champion Gene Tunney's article titled "Nicotine Knockout, or the Slow Count." However, most of the technical medical and scientific reports warning of tobacco's dangers never made it into the major metropolitan dailies or, if they did, were buried in the back pages.[8] The failure of this damning health evidence to gain widespread nationwide publicity did not give comfort to Carolina executives who recognized the damaging potential of adverse health reports to tobacco profits. The companies took the offensive with a nationwide mass marketing blitz that would have made George Washington Hill proud. The goal was to imbed in the American mind the idea that not only was cigarette smoking not harmful to health, but the converse: that, in fact, cigarettes were in some sense conducive to health.

The following lines are representative of the ad copy that saturated America to offset what the companies called the "health scare":

- "Not a cough in a carload." (Old Gold)
- "Not a single case of throat irritation due to smoking Camels." (Camel)
- "The Throat Tested Cigarette." (Phillip Morris)
- "For Digestion's sake, smoke Camels . . . stimulates the flow of digestive fluids . . . increases alkalinity." (Camel)
- "More doctors smoke Camels than any other cigarette." (Camel)[9]
- "Nose, throat, accessory organs (are) not adversely affected by smoking Chesterfields."
- "Chesterfield is Best for you."[10]

The industry's "health" campaign was complemented by campaigns to break the taboo against women's smoking ("Reach for a Lucky instead of a Sweet") and to make cigarette smoke the sedative of choice for GIs in World War II. Cigarette sales soared from 120 billion sold in 1930, to 267 billion sold in 1945, an increase of 124 percent.[11]

The 1970s were the decade of reckoning for the chemical industry, and the 1980s are proving the same for the asbestos industry, but the evidence linking lung cancer and tobacco was irrefutable by early in the 1950s. A 1953 study at what is now the Sloan-Kettering Institute found that cancer could be induced in test animals by painting their backs with "tars" from cigarette smoke. The Sloan-Kettering study led to a second article in *Readers Digest,* "Cancer by the Carton." Unlike similar studies conducted during the 1930s, this article attracted widespread publicity. The Sloan-Kettering study was followed in 1954 by an American Cancer Society study showing a much higher death rate for smokers than for nonsmokers. Articles in popular magazines about the dangers of smoking skyrocketed from an average of fewer than 5 a year between 1930 and 1950 to 35 in 1955.[12]

The publicity given to the Sloan-Kettering and ACS studies triggered a sharp fall in total and per capita cigarette consumption in 1954, but the decline was shortlived, and sales rebounded just as sharply in 1957. The rapid turnaround, coupled with a parade of reports of adverse health effects, prompted Congress to hold hearings for the first time in 1957. For the first half of the century, federal lawmaking and enforcement officials had stayed on the sidelines, but in the late 1950s antismoking forces from the health, medical, and public interest communities began to pressure federal officials to establish minimum standards of health and safety for an industry previously treated as if immune from the law.

Like their counterparts in the asbestos and chemical industries, the tobacco barons chose a course of action that had led to huge profits at the expense of millions who suffered and died from exposure to their product. Given the clout of Philip Morris, R. J. Reynolds, Brown & Williamson, American Brands, Lorillard, and Liggett & Meyers, the ensuing battle proved at best unequal. David Cohen, a lobbyist for the antismoking forces, saw the attempt to bring the tobacco industry to justice as:

> ... similar to a match between the Green Bay Packers and a high school football team. The tobacco state congressmen had powerful reasons to reverse the Federal Trade Commission action [to restrict cigarette advertising and label cigarette products with health warnings], namely their constituents' support. On the other hand, there were few if any "health" congressmen. Those members who did champion the health cause had no substantial constituent interest to back them up."[13]

The tobacco industry's control over lawmakers in Congress stemmed, in part, from the ability of tobacco state congressmen to move into positions of power. In his book *Smoking and Politics*, Lee Fritschler reports that "in the early 1960s, when the smoking and health battle lines were being drawn, tobacco interests had positioned themselves at powerful outposts." "In the Senate," he wrote, "nearly one-fourth of the committees were chaired by men from the six tobacco states. Of the twenty-one committees in the House, tobacco state congressmen chaired seven."[14]

As Robert Miles points out in *Coffin Nails and Corporate Strategies*, while the industry has "persistently bemoaned the state and municipal tax burdens borne by their cigarette brands, these payments have probably served them well by creating revenue dependencies in legislatures that could potentially do harm to the industry."[15]

Despite industry efforts to influence federal, state, and local lawmakers, the antismoking forces were armed with powerful health reports that demanded action. The most notable, the 1964 Surgeon General's Report, concluded that (1) cigarette smoking is a health hazard of sufficient importance in the United States to warrant immediate action; and (2) that cigarette smoking is causally related to lung cancer in men; the magnitude of the effect of cigarette smoking far outweighs other factors. The data for women, although less extensive, pointed in the same direction.

The Surgeon General's release of these conclusions in January 1964 "produced shock waves," according to the American Cancer Society, and "an immediate public reaction and a sharp, short-lived drop in cigarette sales." The report also gave a strong boost to law enforcement officials, who moved in to sanction the industry for aggressively marketing what it knew to be a hazardous product.

In January 1964, the police at the Federal Trade Commission announced that "smoking is a health hazard of sufficient importance in the United States to warrant remedial action," and that failure of the cigarette manufacturers to warn consumers of the danger constituted an unfair and deceptive practice. One year later, the FTC required that all cigarette packages carry a health warning, prohibited the companies from directing advertisements at young persons (under age 25), prohibited them from advertising in schools and colleges, prohibited them from using prominent athletes or "stars" in their advertising, prohibited the portrayal of strenuous activity in cigarette ads, and prohibited claims of health benefits.

Across town, at the Federal Communications Commission (FCC), police officials, at the behest of a citizens group that demanded equal access to the airwaves to counter tobacco ads, also moved into action. Communications law required that broadcasters present all sides of controversial subjects, and in 1967, FCC enforcement officials ruled that (1) cigarettes were controversial; (2) that commercials gave only the pro-cigarette view; and therefore (3) antismoking forces should be given free time to tell their side of the story.[16]

By 1969, a television viewer in America was taking in one antismoking advertisement for every 4.4 cigarette advertisements, and for the second time in less than 15 years, per capita cigarette consumption plummeted. By 1970, Congress had disregarded some of the pressure from the tobacco industry and had passed the Public Health Cigarette Smoking Act, which banished smoking advertisements from radio and TV and required a more forceful warning on cigarette labels.

Police agencies all over Washington were now following the FTC lead and taking action against the tobacco industry and its hazardous product. Police at the FAA, on the basis of evidence showing adverse health effects on nonsmokers breathing in ambient cigarette smoke, required separation of smokers and nonsmokers on airplanes, and their associates at the ICC limited smoking on interstate buses to the back of the bus. Around the country lawmakers followed up on the evidence presented in the 1972 Surgeon General's Report showing that tobacco smoke "may, depending on the length of exposure, be sufficient to be harmful to the health of the exposed person."[17] By the end of 1975, 48 states had passed 423 pieces of legislation regulating cigarette smoking and tobacco products.[18]

By June of 1974, federal enforcement officials had taken a total of 13 steps pertaining to smoking and health. In addition to those mentioned above, a number of other federal agencies (Veterans Administration, Department of Defense, Public Health Service) discontinued the anomalous practice of distributing free cigarettes to their hospitals. And federal research centers focused more intensely on the connection between cigarette smoking and disease.

All of these lawmaking and enforcement actions together failed to put a significant dent in tobacco sales, consumption, or resulting cancer deaths. It has been argued that the most forceful of these actions, the banning of cigarette commercials from the airwaves — and the parallel action of terminating the anticigarette commercials — resulted in a net victory for the industry. "Since the broadcasters could no longer advertise cigarettes," commented the American Cancer Society, "they no longer were required to carry anticigarette messages. How powerful these messages had really been was demonstrated by what happened when they were taken off the airwaves. By the end of 1971, the per capita consumption curve for cigarettes had begun to point upward again, then it continued to move up gradually through 1972, 1973, and 1974."[19]

The $225 million[20] the industry had spent in TV and radio advertising could, after the ban, be spent to consolidate its control over the print media. Thomas Whiteside, in his book *Selling Death*, found that color advertising for cigarettes in *Life* magazine almost doubled after the TV and radio ban went into effect.[21] *Time, Newsweek*, and most other popular magazines were not far behind. From 1970, the year the ban went into effect, until January of 1979, the magazine industry had taken in $800 million in tobacco advertising revenue. *Mother Jones* magazine reported in 1979 that *TV Guide* received $20 million a year in tobacco ad revenue; *Time*, $15 million; and *Playboy*, $20 million; with *Parade*, the popular

Sunday newspaper supplement, taking in 80 percent of its ad revenue from the tobacco industry.

In 1984 the industry spent $2 billion per year on advertising.[22] The payoff to the tobacco industry was made strikingly clear in 1978 when the *Columbia Journalism Review* published the results of a survey of all major magazines that accepted cigarette advertising. CJR, after flipping through seven years of these magazines, could not find one comprehensive article about the dangers of cigarette smoking.[23]

When Elizabeth Whelan, executive director of the American Council on Science and Health, was asked by *Harper's Bazaar* to write an article titled "Protect Your Man From Cancer," she complied. Whelan says she was paid in full for the piece but the article never ran because, in the words of the magazine's editor, "it focused too much on tobacco," and "the magazine is running three full-page, color ads [for tobacco] this month."[24]

In April 1982, Paul Fishman Maccabee, the music critic for the Minneapolis *Twin Cities Reader*, critiqued Brown & Williamson's sponsorship of "Kool Jazz Festivals" around the country. Pointing out that Brown & Williamson sells 55 million Kool cigarettes a year, Maccabee wrote that the adverse health effects of smoking were "definitely not sexy. Definitely un-Kool." "Strange bedfellows, cigarettes and jazz," he concluded. "Duke Ellington died of lung cancer in 1974."

As a result of writing the article, Maccabee was fired. The publisher of the small alternative weekly was fearful of losing four to five pages of ads a week, averaging about $1,750 a page. The publisher told journalist Peter Taylor that if he had to fly to Brown & Williamson's headquarters in Louisville, Kentucky and go down on bended knees to beg Kool not to take its ads out of his magazine, he would do it.[25]

Today, Americans consume a phenomenal 595 billion cigarettes a year, and almost 800 Americans die every day from cigarette-induced disease. Many Americans injured by cigarette smoking have sued the tobacco companies seeking compensation for their injuries, but to this date all have been defeated by a well-organized and funded tobacco defense litigation effort.*

* For a review of these cases see, "Cigarette Dependency and Civil Liability: A Modest Proposal," by Donald W. Garner, 53 *Southern California Law Review*, 1423 (1985).

Federal law enforcement officials have been stymied by an historically effective tobacco lobby, headed by the powerful Washington-based Tobacco Institute. Effective lawmaking and enforcement actions have been blocked—among them banning all cigarette ads, airing antismoking ads, and launching other educational efforts; strictly enforcing the law against the sale of cigarettes to minors; and eliminating billions of dollars of federal subsidies to the industry. Such ideas get nowhere in a Washington heavily influenced by the Tobacco Institute and tobacco state congressmen.

The failure of lawmakers to act effectively in the face of what Whiteside calls "manslaughter on a mass scale" is the clearest indication of the industry's impact on the lawmaking and enforcement function. Perhaps the only way to loosen the grip is to introduce corporate executives from the tobacco industry—and the lawmakers they so effectively intimidate—to cancer wards like the one described by Hugh Mooney.

Perhaps only then will Washington be willing to restrain the tobacco industry from knowingly promoting maximum access to its dangerous products.

Notes

1. From *The Story of Tobacco in America,* by Joseph C. Robert. University of North Carolina Press, Chapel Hill, 1967, in *Cigarette Country, Tobacco in American History and Politics,* by Susan Wagner. Praeger, New York, 1971, p. 57.

2. "What the Cigarette Commercials Don't Show You," *Reader's Digest,* January 1968, p. 71.

3. Ibid.

4. *Everybody's Business, An Almanac,* edited by Milton Moskowitz, Michael Katz, and Robert Levering. Harper & Row, San Francisco, 1980, p. 766.

5. *Cigarette Country: Tobacco in American History and Politics,* Wagner, p. 65.

6. *Report of the Surgeon General of the United States,* Washington, D.C., December 1986.

7. *Cigarette Country,* Wagner, p. 69.

8. Ibid.

9. Ibid., p. 72.

10. *Everybody's Business,* ed. Moskowitz, Katz, and Levering, p. 776.

11. *Cigarette Country,* Wagner, p. 74.

12. *Coffin Nails and Corporate Strategies,* by Robert H. Miles. Prentice Hall, New York, 1982, p. 39.

13. Ibid., p. 70.

14. Ibid., p. 66.

15. Ibid.

16. "The Man Behind the Ban on Cigarette Commercials," by James C. Roper. *Reader's Digest,* March 1971.

17. *Coffin Nails,* Miles, p. 45.

18. Ibid.

19. Ibid., p. 85.

20. Ibid., p. 83.

21. *Selling Death,* by Thomas Whiteside. Liveright, New York, 1971.

22. *Smoke Ring: The Politics of Tobacco,* by Peter Taylor. Pantheon Books, New York, 1984, p. 44.

23. "Why Dick Can't Stop Smoking," *Mother Jones,* January 1979, p. 40.

24. *Smoke Ring,* Taylor, p. 46.

25. Ibid.

Index